MODERN AMERICAN
PLAYS

MODERN
AMERICAN
PLAYS

Edited by

FREDERIC G. CASSIDY, 1907 -   ed.

Play Anthology Reprint Series

 BOOKS FOR LIBRARIES PRESS
FREEPORT, NEW YORK

PS
634
.C416
1970

INTERNATIONAL STANDARD BOOK NUMBER:
0-8369-8201-0

LIBRARY OF CONGRESS CATALOG CARD NUMBER:
73-111108

PRINTED IN THE UNITED STATES OF AMERICA

AUTHOR'S NOTE

The plays included in this volume have been chosen to form a representative selection from the best of contemporary American drama. The chief dramatic types are represented—the tragic, the comic, the historical, the psychological, the action, and the propaganda play. They also illustrate recent experiments in dramatic writing—verse drama, cinematic technique, expressionism, and the authors' personal versions of realism.

The criticisms given after each play are not intended to be definitive or to pronounce a rounded and final judgment on the plays or the playwrights. It is hoped they will recall the impression made by each play at the time of its first presentation, with the reasons, sometimes implicit, for that impression. It is hoped also that they will present topics for discussion in connection with the reading of the plays.

Unlike some of O'Neill's later plays, *Anna Christie* is not overgrown; it has none of the muddiness of the O'Neill who sought to interpret Freud or to scale Olympus with Euripides. It is a straightforward, honest, and moving treatment of a human situation, free of pose and excellently adapted to its medium. In it O'Neill has no concern with ideas; he treats the human heart, and this is always his safest ground.

Abe Lincoln in Illinois is less characteristic of Sherwood than some earlier plays, for one might say that much of it was written by Lincoln himself. However, it is a play which only a master dramatist could have constructed; it foreshortens and condenses without distortion; it lets the story seem to tell itself with every appearance of truth. The playwright's hand is seen, backstage, quietly arranging for Lincoln's appearance, both as a man and an idea.

Waiting for Lefty still seems to many people Odets's best

play. Certainly the clever staging, realistic dialogue and dramatic excitement are all here, though all are exaggerated through the nakedness of the "message." Odets has known inwardly what Sassoon calls "the pigmy fist held skyward and defiant," and if this play takes a political cast, this is really superficial. For the underlying human tragedy speaks through these characters as living creatures, ugly, vulgar, and raucous though they are.

Winterset has become almost a classic within the lifetime of its author. Not many dramatists today could have written successfully a tragedy on a contemporary theme, and in verse. Yet if the actual words of Bartolomeo Vanzetti, heightened by emotion, fell naturally into rhythmic phrases which can be printed as a poem, surely Anderson's use of verse in treating a cognate theme is justified. This play illustrates his artistic seriousness and his skill with stage conduct and characters.

In *Watch on the Rhine* Lillian Hellman deftly presents us with a set of believable individuals whose world of ease and safety is suddenly invaded by the forces of Hitler's Germany —we see with a shock how close the Nazi police-state came to all our lives. The play, however, is not merely topical; its fine dramatic qualities will preserve it after its timeliness has passed.

Life with Father is a classic of American humor and has been most ably adapted for the stage. The male animal, as leader of his herd, is always a fascinating subject for study. Clarence Day's "Father" is a remarkable specimen, presented with sympathy and awe.

FREDERIC G. CASSIDY

Madison, Wisconsin
September 15, 1948

CONTENTS

EUGENE O'NEILL

ANNA CHRISTIE

A Play in Four Acts

CHARACTERS

"JOHNNY-THE-PRIEST"
TWO LONGSHOREMEN
A POSTMAN
LARRY, *bartender*
CHRIS CHRISTOPHERSON, *Captain of the barge* Simeon
 Winthrop
MARTHY OWEN
ANNA CHRISTOPHERSON, *Chris's daughter*
THREE MEN OF A STEAMER'S CREW
MAT BURKE, *a stoker*
JOHNSON, *deckhand on the barge*

SCENES

ACT ONE

"Johnny-the-Priest's" saloon near the water front, New York City.

ACT TWO

The barge, *Simeon Winthrop,* at anchor in the harbor of
Provincetown, Mass. Ten days later.

ACT THREE

Cabin of the barge, at dock in Boston. A week later,

ACT FOUR

The same. Two days later.

ANNA CHRISTIE

ACT ONE

SCENE—"JOHNNY-THE-PRIEST'S" *saloon near South Street, New York City. The stage is divided into two sections, showing a small back room on the right. On the left, forward, of the barroom, a large window looking out on the street. Beyond it, the main entrance—a double swinging door. Farther back, another window. The bar runs from left to right nearly the whole length of the rear wall. In back of the bar, a small showcase displaying a few bottles of case goods, for which there is evidently little call. The remainder of the rear space in front of the large mirrors is occupied by half-barrels of cheap whisky of the "nickel-a-shot" variety, from which the liquor is drawn by means of spigots. On the right is an open doorway leading to the back room. In the back room are four round wooden tables with five chairs grouped about each. In the rear, a family entrance opening on a side street.*

It is late afternoon of a day in fall.

As the curtain rises, JOHNNY *is discovered.* "JOHNNY-THE-PRIEST" *deserves his nickname. With his pale, thin, clean-shaven face, mild blue eyes and white hair, a cassock would seem more suited to him than the apron he wears. Neither his voice nor his general manner dispel this illusion which has made him a personage of the water front. They are soft and bland. But beneath all his mildness one senses the man behind the mask—cynical, callous, hard as nails. He is lounging at ease behind the bar, a pair of spectacles on his nose, reading an evening paper.*

Two longshoremen enter from the street, wearing their working aprons, the button of the union pinned conspicuously on the caps pulled sideways on their heads at an aggressive angle.

FIRST LONGSHOREMAN [*as they range themselves at the bar*]: Gimme a shock. Number Two. [*He tosses a coin on the bar.*]
SECOND LONGSHOREMAN: Same here.

[JOHNNY *sets two glasses of barrel whisky before them.*]

FIRST LONGSHOREMAN: Here's luck!

[*The other nods. They gulp down their whisky.*]

SECOND LONGSHOREMAN [*putting money on the bar*]: Give us another.

FIRST LONGSHOREMAN: Gimme a scoop this time—lager and porter. I'm dry.

SECOND LONGSHOREMAN: Same here.

[JOHNNY *draws the lager and porter and sets the big, foaming schooners before them. They drink down half the contents and start to talk together hurriedly in low tones. The door on the left is swung open and* LARRY *enters. He is a boyish, red-cheeked, rather good-looking young fellow of twenty or so.*]

LARRY [*nodding to* JOHNNY—*cheerily*]: Hello, boss.

JOHNNY: Hello, Larry. [*With a glance at his watch.*] Just on time.

[LARRY *goes to the right behind the bar, takes off his coat, and puts on an apron.*]

FIRST LONGSHOREMAN [*abruptly*]: Let's drink up and get back to it.

[*They finish their drinks and go out left.* THE POSTMAN *enters as they leave. He exchanges nods with* JOHNNY *and throws a letter on the bar.*]

THE POSTMAN: Addressed care of you, Johnny. Know him?

JOHNNY [*picks up the letter, adjusting his spectacles.* LARRY *comes and peers over his shoulders.* JOHNNY *reads very slowly*]: Christopher Christopherson.

THE POSTMAN [*helpfully*]: Square-head name.

LARRY: Old Chris—that's who.

JOHNNY: Oh, sure. I was forgetting Chris carried a hell of a name like that. Letters come here for him sometimes before, I remember now. Long time ago, though.

THE POSTMAN: It'll get him all right then?

JOHNNY: Sure thing. He comes here whenever he's in port.

THE POSTMAN [*turning to go*]: Sailor, eh?

JOHNNY [*with a grin*]: Captain of a coal barge.

THE POSTMAN [*laughing*]: Some job! Well, s'long.

JOHNNY: S'long. I'll see he gets it. [THE POSTMAN *goes out.* JOHNNY *scrutinizes the letter.*] You got good eyes, Larry. Where's it from?

LARRY [*after a glance*]: St. Paul. That'll be in Minnesota, I'm thinkin'. Looks like a woman's writing, too, the old divil!

JOHNNY: He's got a daughter somewheres out West, I think he told me once. [*He puts the letter on the cash register.*] Come to think of it, I ain't seen old Chris in a dog's age. [*Putting his overcoat on, he comes around the end of the bar.*] Guess I'll be gettin' home. See you tomorrow.

LARRY: Good-night to ye, boss.

[*As* JOHNNY *goes toward the street door, it is pushed open and* CHRISTOPHER CHRISTOPHERSON *enters. He is a short, squat, broad-shouldered man of about fifty, with a round, weather-beaten, red face from which his light blue eyes peer short-sightedly, twinkling with a simple good humor. His large mouth, overhung by a thick, drooping, yellow mustache, is childishly self-willed and weak, of an obstinate kindliness. A thick neck is jammed like a post into the heavy trunk of his body. His arms with their big, hairy, freckled hands, and his stumpy legs terminating in large flat feet, are awkwardly short and muscular. He walks with a clumsy, rolling gait. His voice when not raised in a hollow boom, is toned down to a sly, confidential half-whisper with something vaguely plaintive in its quality. He is dressed in a wrinkled, ill-fitting dark suit of shore clothes, and wears a faded cap of gray cloth over his mop of grizzled, blond hair. Just now his face beams with a too-blissful happiness, and he has evidently been drinking. He reaches his hand out to* JOHNNY.]

CHRIS: Hello, Yohnny! Have a drink on me. Come on, Larry. Give us drink. Have one yourself. [*Putting his hand in his pocket.*] Ay gat money—plenty money....

JOHNNY [*shakes* CHRIS *by the hand*]: Speak of the devil. We was just talkin' about you.

LARRY [*coming to the end of the bar*]: Hello, Chris. Put it there.

[*They shake hands.*]

CHRIS [*beaming*]: Give us drink.

JOHNNY [*with a grin*]: You got a half-snootful now. Where'd you get it?

CHRIS [*grinning*]: Oder fallar on oder barge—Irish fallar— he gat bottle vhisky and we drank it, yust us two. Dot vhisky gat kick, by yingo! Ay yust come ashore. Give us drink, Larry. Ay vas little drunk, not much. Yust feel good. [*He laughs and commences to sing in a nasal, high-pitched quaver.*] "My Yosephine, come aboard de ship. Long time Ay vait for you.

De moon, she shi-i-i-ine. She looka yus like you.

Tchee-tchee, tchee-tchee, tchee-tchee, tchee-tchee."

[*To the accompaniment of this last he waves his hand as if he were conducting an orchestra.*]

JOHNNY [*with a laugh*]: Same old Yosie, eh Chris?

CHRIS: You don't know good song when you hear him. Italian fallar on oder barge, he learn me dat. Give us drink. [*He throws change on the bar.*]

LARRY [*with a professional air*]: What's your pleasure, gentlemen?

JOHNNY: Small beer, Larry.

CHRIS: Vhisky—Number Two.

LARRY [*as he gets their drinks*]: I'll take a cigar on you.

CHRIS [*lifting his glass*]: Skoal! [*He drinks.*]

JOHNNY: Drink hearty.

CHRIS [*immediately*]: Have oder drink.

JOHNNY: No. Some other time. Got to go home now. So you've just landed? Where are you in from this time?

CHRIS: Norfolk. Ve make slow voyage—dirty vedder—yust fog, fog, fog, all bloody time! [*There is an insistent ring from the doorbell at the family entrance in the back room.* CHRIS *gives a start—hurriedly.*] Ay go open, Larry. Ay forgat. It vas Marthy. She come with me. [*He goes into the back room.*]

LARRY [*with a chuckle*]: He's still got that same cow livin' with him, the old fool!

JOHNNY [*with a grin*]: A sport, Chris is. Well, I'll beat it home. S'long. [*He goes to the street door.*]

LARRY: So long, boss.

JOHNNY: Oh—don't forget to give him his letter.

LARRY: I won't.

[JOHNNY *goes out. In the meantime,* CHRIS *has opened the family entrance door, admitting* MARTHY. *She might be forty or fifty. Her jowly, mottled face, with its thick red nose, is streaked with interlacing purple veins. Her thick, gray hair is piled anyhow in a greasy mop on top of her round head. Her figure is flabby and fat; her breath comes in wheezy gasps; she speaks in a loud, mannish voice, punctuated by explosions of hoarse laughter. But there still twinkles in her blood-shot blue eyes a youthful lust for life which hard usage has failed to stifle, a sense of humor mocking, but good-tempered. She wears a man's cap, doublebreasted man's jacket, and a grimy, calico skirt. Her bare feet are encased in a man's brogans several sizes too large for her, which gives her a shuffling, wobbly gait.*]

MARTHY [*grumblingly*]: What yuh tryin' to do, Dutchy—keep me standin' out there all day? [*She comes forward and sits at the table in the right corner, front.*]

CHRIS [*mollifyingly*]: Ay'm sorry, Marthy. Ay talk to Yohnny. Ay forgat. What you goin' take for drink?

MARTHY [*appeased*]: Gimme a scoop of lager an' ale.

CHRIS: Ay go bring him back. [*He returns to the bar.*] Lager and ale for Marthy, Larry. Vhisky for me. [*He throws change on the bar.*]

LARRY: Right you are. [*Then remembering, he takes the letter from in back of the bar.*] Here's a letter for you—from St. Paul, Minnesota—and a lady's writin'. [*He grins.*]

CHRIS [*quickly—taking it*]: Oh, den it come from my daughter, Anna. She live dere. [*He turns the letter over in his hands uncertainly.*] Ay don't gat letter from Anna—must be a year.

LARRY [*jokingly*]: That's a fine fairy tale to be tellin'—your daughter! Sure I'll bet it's some bum.

CHRIS [*soberly*]: No. Dis come from Anna. [*Engrossed by the letter in his hand—uncertainly.*] By golly, Ay tank Ay'm too drunk for read dis letter from Anna. Ay tank Ay sat down for a minute. You bring drinks in back room, Larry. [*He goes into the room on right.*]

MARTHY [*angrily*]: Where's my lager an' ale, yuh big stiff?

CHRIS [*preoccupied*]: Larry bring him. [*He sits down opposite her.* LARRY *brings in the drinks and sets them on the table. He and* MARTHY *exchange nods of recognition.* LARRY *stands looking at* CHRIS *curiously.* MARTHY *takes a long draught of her schooner and heaves a huge sigh of satisfaction, wiping her mouth with the back of her hand.* CHRIS *stares at the letter for a moment—slowly opens it, and, squinting his eyes, commences to read laboriously, his lips moving as he spells out the words. As he reads his face lights up with an expression of mingled joy and bewilderment.*]

LARRY: Good news?

MARTHY [*her curiosity also aroused*]: What's that yuh got—a letter, fur Gawd's sake?

CHRIS [*pauses for a moment, after finishing the letter, as if to let the news sink in—then suddenly pounds his fist on the table with happy excitement*]: Py yiminy! Yust tank, Anna say she's comin' here right avay! She gat sick on yob in St. Paul, she say. It's short letter, don't tal me much more'n dat. [*Beaming.*] Py golly, dat's good news all at one time for ole fallar! [*Then turning to* MARTHY, *rather shamefacedly.*] You know, Marthy. Ay've tole you Ay don't see my Anna since she vas little gel in Sveden five year ole.

MARTHY: How old'll she be now?

CHRIS: She must be—lat me see—she must be twenty year ole, py Yo!

LARRY [*surprised*]: You've not seen her in fifteen years?

CHRIS [*suddenly growing somber—in a low tone*]: No. Ven she vas little gel, Ay vas bo'sun on vindjammer. Ay never gat home only few time dem year. Ay'm fool sailor fallar. My voman—Anna's mother—she gat tired vait all time Sveden for me ven Ay don't never come. She come dis country, bring

Anna, dey go out Minnesota, live with her cousins on farm. Den ven her mo'der die ven Ay vas on voyage, Ay tank it's better dem cousins keep Anna. Ay tank it's better Anna live on farm, den she don't know dat ole davil, sea, she don't know fa'der like me.

LARRY [*with a wink at* MARTHY]: This girl, now, 'll be marryin' a sailor herself, likely. It's in the blood.

CHRIS [*suddenly springing to his feet and smashing his fist on the table in a rage*]: No, py God! She don't do dat!

MARTHY [*grasping her schooner hastily—angrily*]: Hey, look out, yuh nut! Wanta spill my suds for me?

LARRY [*amazed*]: Oho, what's up with you? Ain't you a sailor yourself now, and always been?

CHRIS [*slowly*]: Dat's yust vhy Ay say it. [*Forcing a smile.*] Sailor vas all right fallar, but not for marry gel. No. Ay know dat. Anna's mo'der, she know it, too.

LARRY [*as* CHRIS *remains sunk in gloomy reflection*]: When is your daughter comin'? Soon?

CHRIS [*roused*]: Py yimminy, Ay forgat. [*Reads through the letter hurriedly.*] She say she come right avay, dat's all.

LARRY: She'll maybe be comin' here to look for you, I s'pose. [*He returns to the bar, whistling. Left alone with* MARTHY, *who stares at him with a twinkle of malicious humor in her eyes,* CHRIS *suddenly becomes desperately ill-at-ease. He fidgets, then gets up hurriedly.*]

CHRIS: Ay gat speak with Larry. Ay be right back. [*Mollifying.*] Ay bring you oder drink.

MARTHY [*emptying her glass*]: Sure. That's me. [*As he retreats with the glass she guffaws after him derisively.*]

CHRIS [*to* LARRY *in an alarmed whisper*]: Py yingo, Ay gat gat Marthy shore off barge before Anna come! Anna raise hell if she find dat out. Marthy raise hell, too, for go, py golly!

LARRY [*with a chuckle*]: Serve ye right, ye old divil—havin' a woman at your age!

CHRIS [*scratching his head in a quandary*]: You tal me lie for tal Marthy, Larry, so's she gat off barge quick.

LARRY: She knows your daughter's comin'. Tell her to get the hell out of it.

CHRIS: No. Ay don't like make her feel bad.

LARRY: You're an old mush! Keep your girl away from the barge, then. She'll likely want to stay ashore anyway. [*Curiously.*] What does she work at, your Anna?

CHRIS: She stay on dem cousins' farm till two year ago. Dan she gat yob nurse gel in St. Paul. [*Then shaking his head resolutely.*] But Ay don't vant for her gat yob now. Ay vant for her stay with me.

LARRY [*scornfully*]: On a coal barge! She'll not like that, I'm thinkin'.

MARTHY [*shouts from next room*]: Don't I get that bucket o' suds, Dutchy?

CHRIS [*startled—in apprehensive confusion*]: Yes, Ay come, Marthy.

LARRY [*drawing the lager and ale, hands it to* CHRIS—*laughing*]: Now you're in for it! You'd better tell her straight to get out!

CHRIS [*shaking in his boots*]: Py golly. [*He takes her drink in to* MARTHY *and sits down at the table. She sips it in silence.* LARRY *moves quietly close to the partition to listen, grinning with expectation.* CHRIS *seems on the verge of speaking, hesitates, gulps down his whisky desperately as if seeking for courage. He attempts to whistle a few bars of* "Yosephine" *with careless bravado, but the whistle peters out futilely.* MARTHY *stares at him keenly, taking in his embarrassment with a malicious twinkle of amusement in her eye.* CHRIS *clears his throat.*] Marthy——

MARTHY [*aggressively*]: Wha's that? [*Then, pretending to fly into a rage, her eyes enjoying* CHRIS' *misery.*] I'm wise to what's in back of your nut, Dutchy. Yuh want to git rid o' me, huh?—now she's comin'. Gimme the bum's rush ashore, huh? Lemme tell yuh, Dutchy, there ain't a square-head workin' on a boat man enough to git away with that. Don't start nothin' yuh can't finish!

CHRIS [*miserably*]: Ay don't start nutting, Marthy.

MARTHY [*glares at him for a second—then cannot control a burst of laughter*]: Ho-ho! Yuh're a scream, Square-head—an honest-ter-Gawd knockout! Ho-ho! [*She wheezes, panting for breath.*]

CHRIS [*with childish pique*]: Ay don't see nutting for laugh at.

MARTHY: Take a slant in the mirror and yuh'll see. Ho-ho! [*Recovering from her mirth—chuckling, scornfully.*] A square-head tryin' to kid Marthy Owen at this late day!—after me campin' with barge men the last twenty years. I'm wise to the game, up, down, and sideways. I ain't been born and dragged up on the water front for nothin'. Think I'd make trouble, huh? Not me! I'll pack up me duds an' beat it. I'm quittin' yuh, get me? I'm tellin' yuh I'm sick of stickin' with yuh, and I'm leavin' yuh flat, see? There's plenty of other guys on other barges waitin' for me. Always was, I always found. [*She claps the astonished* CHRIS *on the back.*] So cheer up, Dutchy! I'll be offen the barge before she comes. You'll be rid o' me for good—and me o' you—good riddance for both of us. Ho-ho!

CHRIS [*seriously*]: Ay don' tank dat. You vas good gel, Marthy.

MARTHY [*grinning*]: Good girl? Aw, can the bull! Well, yuh treated me square, yuhself. So it's fifty-fifty. Nobody's sore at nobody. We're still good frien's, huh? [LARRY *returns to bar.*]

CHRIS [*beaming now that he sees his troubles disappearing*]: Yes, py golly.

MARTHY: That's the talkin'! In all my time I tried never to split with a guy with no hard feelin's. But what was yuh so scared about—that I'd kick up a row? That ain't Marthy's way. [*Scornfully.*] Think I'd break my heart to lose yuh? Commit suicide, huh? Ho-ho! Gawd! The world's full o' men if that's all I'd worry about! [*Then with a grin, after emptying her glass.*] Blow me to another scoop, huh? I'll drink your kid's health for yuh.

CHRIS [*eagerly*]: Sure tang. Ay go gat him. [*He takes the two glasses into the bar.*] Oder drink. Same for both.

LARRY [*getting the drinks and putting them on the bar*]: She's not such a bad lot, that one.

CHRIS [*jovially*]: She's good gel, Ay tal you! Py golly, Ay calabrate now! Give me vhisky here at bar, too. [*He puts down money.* LARRY *serves him.*] You have drink, Larry.

LARRY [*virtuously*]: You know I never touch it.

CHRIS: You don't know what you miss. Skoal! [*He drinks— then begins to sing loudly.*] "My Yosephine, come board de ship——"

[*He picks up the drinks for* MARTHY *and himself and walks unsteadily into the back room, singing.*]

"De moon, she shi-i-i-ine. She looks yust like you.

Tchee-tchee, tchee-tchee, tchee-tchee, tchee-tchee."

MARTHY [*grinning, hands to ears*]: Gawd!

CHRIS [*sitting down*]: Ay'm good singer, yes? Ve drink, eh? Skoal! Ay calabrate! [*He drinks.*] Ay calabrate 'cause Anna's coming home. You know, Marthy, Ay never write for her to come, 'cause Ay tank Ay'm no good for her. But all time Ay hope like hell some day she vant for see me and den she come. And dat's vay it happen now, py yiminy! [*His face beaming.*] What you tank she look like, Marthy? Ay bet you she's fine, good, strong gel, pooty like hell! Living on farm made her like dat. And Ay bet you some day she marry good, steady land fallar here in East, have home all her own, have kits—and dan Ay'm ole grandfader, py golly! And Ay go visit dem every time Ay gat in port near! [*Bursting with joy.*] By yiminy crickens, Ay calabrate dat! [*Shouts.*] Bring oder drink, Larry! [*He smashes his fist on the table with a bang.*]

LARRY [*coming in from bar—irritably*]: Easy there! Don't be breakin' the table, you old goat!

CHRIS [*by way of reply, grins foolishly and begins to sing*]: "My Yosephine, come board de ship——"

MARTHY [*touching* CHRIS' *arm persuasively*]: You're soused to the ears, Dutchy. Go out and put a feed into you. It'll sober you up. [*Then as* CHRIS *shakes his head obstinately.*]

Listen, you old nut! Yuh don't know what time your kid's liable to show up. Yuh want to be sober when she comes, don't yuh?

CHRIS [*aroused—gets unsteadily to his feet*]: Py golly, yes.

LARRY: That's good sense for you. A good beef stew'll fix you. Go round the corner.

CHRIS: All right. Ay be back soon, Marthy. [CHRIS *goes through the bar and out the street door.*]

LARRY: He'll come round all right with some grub in him.

MARTHY: Sure.

[LARRY *goes back to the bar and resumes his newspaper.* MARTHY *sips what is left of her schooner reflectively. There is the ring of the family entrance bell.* LARRY *comes to the door and opens it a trifle—then, with a puzzled expression, pulls it wide.* ANNA CHRISTOPHERSON *enters. She is a tall, blond, fully-developed girl of twenty, handsome after a large, Viking-daughter fashion but now run down in health and plainly showing all the outward evidences of belonging to the world's oldest profession. Her youthful face is already hard and cynical beneath its layer of make-up. Her clothes are the tawdry finery of peasant stock turned prostitute. She comes and sinks wearily in a chair by the table, left front.*]

ANNA: Gimme a whisky—ginger ale on the side. [*Then, as* LARRY *turns to go, forcing a winning smile at him.*] And don't be stingy, baby.

LARRY [*sarcastically*]: Shall I serve it in a pail?

ANNA [*with a hard laugh*]: That suits me down to the ground. [LARRY *goes into the bar. The two women size each other up with frank stares.* LARRY *comes back with the drink which he sets before* ANNA *and returns to the bar again.* ANNA *downs her drink at a gulp. Then, after a moment, as the alcohol begins to rouse her, she turns to* MARTHY *with a friendly smile.*] Gee, I needed that bad, all right, all right!

MARTHY [*nodding her head sympathetically*]: Sure—yuh look all in. Been on a bat?

ANNA: No—traveling—day and a half on the train. Had to

sit up all night in the dirty coach, too. Gawd, I thought I'd never get here!

MARTHY [*with a start—looking at her intently*]: Where'd yuh come from, huh?

ANNA: St. Paul—out in Minnesota.

MARTHY [*staring at her in amazement—slowly*]: So— yuh're—— [*She suddenly bursts out into hoarse, ironical laughter.*] Gawd!

ANNA: All the way from Minnesota, sure. [*Flaring up.*] What you laughing at? Me?

MARTHY [*hastily*]: No, honest, kid. I was thinkin' of somethin' else.

ANNA [*mollified—with a smile*]: Well, I wouldn't blame you, at that. Guess I do look rotten—yust out of the hospital two weeks. I'm going to have another 'ski. What d'you say? Have something on me?

MARTHY: Sure I will. T'anks. [*She calls.*] Hey, Larry! Little service!

[*He comes in.*]

ANNA: Same for me.

MARTHY: Same here.

[LARRY *takes their glasses and goes out.*]

ANNA: Why don't you come sit over here, be sociable. I'm a dead stranger in this burg—and I ain't spoke a word with no one since day before yesterday.

MARTHY: Sure thing. [*She shuffles over to* ANNA'S *table and sits down opposite her.* LARRY *brings the drinks and* ANNA *pays him.*]

ANNA: Skoal! Here's how! [*She drinks.*]

MARTHY: Here's luck! [*She takes a gulp from her schooner.*]

ANNA [*taking a package of Sweet Caporal cigarettes from her bag*]: Let you smoke in here, won't they?

MARTHY [*doubtfully*]: Sure. [*Then with evident anxiety.*] On'y trow it away if yuh hear someone comin'.

ANNA [*lighting one and taking a deep inhale*]: Gee, they're fussy in this dump, ain't they? [*She puffs, staring at the table top.* MARTHY *looks her over with a new penetrating interest, taking in every detail of her face.* ANNA *suddenly becomes conscious of this appraising stare—resentfully.*] Ain't nothing wrong with me, is there? You're looking hard enough.

MARTHY [*irritated by the other's tone—scornfully*]: Ain't got to look much. I got your number the minute you stepped in the door.

ANNA [*her eyes narrowing*]: Ain't you smart! Well, I got yours, too, without no trouble. You're me forty years from now. That's you! [*She gives a hard little laugh.*]

MARTHY [*angrily*]: Is that so? Well, I'll tell you straight, kiddo, that Marthy Owen never—— [*She catches herself up short—with a grin.*] What are you and me scrappin' over? Let's cut it out, huh? Me, I don't want no hard feelin's with no one. [*Extending her hand.*] Shake and forget it, huh?

ANNA [*shakes her hand gladly*]: Only too glad to. I ain't looking for trouble. Let's have 'nother. What d'you say?

MARTHY [*shaking her head*]: Not for mine. I'm full up. And you——Had anythin' to eat lately?

ANNA: Not since this morning on the train.

MARTHY: Then yuh better go easy on it, hadn't yuh?

ANNA [*after a moment's hesitation*]: Guess you're right. I got to meet someone, too. But my nerves is on edge after that rotten trip.

MARTHY: Yuh said yuh was just outa the hospital?

ANNA: Two weeks ago. [*Leaning over to* MARTHY *confidentially.*] The joint I was in out in St. Paul got raided. That was the start. The judge give all us girls thirty days. The others didn't seem to mind being in the cooler much. Some of 'em was used to it. But me, I couldn't stand it. It got my goat right—couldn't eat or sleep or nothing. I never could stand being caged up nowheres. I got good and sick and they had to send me to the hospital. It was nice there. I was sorry to leave it, honest!

MARTHY [*after a slight pause*]: Did yuh say yuh got to meet someone here?

ANNA: Yes. Oh, not what you mean. It's my Old Man I

got to meet. Honest! It's funny, too. I ain't seen him since I was a kid—don't even know what he looks like—yust had a letter every now and then. This was always the only address he give me to write him back. He's yanitor of some building here now—used to be a sailor.

MARTHY [*astonished*]: Janitor!

ANNA: Sure. And I was thinking maybe, seeing he ain't never done a thing for me in my life, he might be willing to stake me to a room and eats till I get rested up. [*Wearily.*] Gee, I sure need that rest! I'm knocked out. [*Then resignedly.*] But I ain't expecting much from him. Give you a kick when you're down, that's what all men do. [*With sudden passion.*] Men, I hate 'em—all of 'em! And I don't expect he'll turn out no better than the rest. [*Then with sudden interest.*] Say, do you hang out around this dump much?

MARTHY: Oh, off and on.

ANNA: Then maybe you know him—my Old Man—or at least seen him?

MARTHY: It ain't old Chris, is it?

ANNA: Old Chris?

MARTHY: Chris Christopherson, his full name is.

ANNA [*excitedly*]: Yes, that's him! Anna Christopherson—that's my real name—only out there I called myself Anna Christie. So you know him, eh?

MARTHY [*evasively*]: Seen him about for years.

ANNA: Say, what's he like, tell me, honest?

MARTHY: Oh, he's short and——

ANNA [*impatiently*]: I don't care what he looks like. What kind is he?

MARTHY [*earnestly*]: Well, yuh can bet your life, kid, he's as good an old guy as ever walked on two feet. That goes!

ANNA [*pleased*]: I'm glad to hear it. Then you think he'll stake me to that rest cure I'm after?

MARTHY [*emphatically*]: Surest thing you know. [*Disgustedly.*] But where'd yuh get the idea he was a janitor?

ANNA: He wrote me he was himself.

MARTHY: Well, he was lyin'. He ain't. He's captain of a barge—five men under him.

ANNA [*disgusted in her turn*]: A barge? What kind of a barge?

MARTHY: Coal, mostly.

ANNA: A coal barge! [*With a harsh laugh.*] If that ain't a swell job to find your long lost Old Man working at! Gee, I knew something'd be bound to turn out wrong—always does with me. That puts my idea of his giving me a rest on the bum.

MARTHY: What d'yuh mean?

ANNA: I s'pose he lives on the boat, don't he?

MARTHY: Sure. What about it? Can't you live on it, too?

ANNA [*scornfully.*]: Me? On a dirty coal barge! What d'you think I am?

MARTHY [*resentfully*]: What d'yuh know about barges, huh? Bet yuh ain't never seen one. That's what comes of his bringing yuh up inland—away from the old devil sea—where yuh'd be safe—Gawd! [*The irony of it strikes her sense of humor and she laughs hoarsely.*]

ANNA [*angrily*]: His bringing me up! Is that what he tells people! I like his nerve! He let them cousins of my Old Woman's keep me on their farm and work me to death like a dog.

MARTHY: Well, he's got queer notions on some things. I've heard him say a farm was the best place for a kid.

ANNA: Sure. That's what he'd always answer back—and a lot of crazy stuff about staying away from the sea—stuff I couldn't make head or tail to. I thought he must be nutty.

MARTHY: He is on that one point. [*Casually.*] So yuh didn't fall for life on the farm, huh?

ANNA: I should say not! The old man of the family, his wife, and four sons—I had to slave for all of 'em. I was only a poor relation, and they treated me worse than they dare treat a hired girl. [*After a moment's hesitation—somberly.*] It was one of the sons—the youngest—started me—when I was sixteen. After that, I hated 'em so I'd killed 'em all if I'd stayed. So I run away—to St. Paul.

MARTHY [*who has been listening sympathetically*]: I've heard Old Chris talkin' about you bein' a nurse girl out there. Was that all a bluff yuh put up when yuh wrote him?

ANNA: Not on your life, it wasn't. It was true for two years. I didn't go wrong all at one jump. Being a nurse girl was yust what finished me. Taking care of other people's kids, always listening to their bawling and crying, caged in, when you're only a kid yourself and want to go out and see things. At last I got the chance—to get into that house. And you bet your life I took it! [*Defiantly.*] And I ain't sorry neither. [*After a pause—with bitter hatred.*] It was all men's fault—the whole business. It was men on the farm ordering and beating me—and giving me the wrong start. Then when I was a nurse, it was men again hanging around, bothering me, trying to see what they could get. [*She gives a hard laugh.*] And now it's men all the time. Gawd, I hate 'em all, every mother's son of 'em! Don't you?

MARTHY: Oh, I dunno. There's good ones and bad ones, kid. You've just had a run of bad luck with 'em, that's all. Your Old Man, now—old Chris—he's a good one.

ANNA [*sceptically*]: He'll have to show me.

MARTHY: Yuh kept right on writing him yuh was a nurse girl still, even after yuh was in the house, didn't yuh?

ANNA: Sure. [*Cynically.*] Not that I think he'd care a darn.

MARTHY: Yuh're all wrong about him, kid. [*Earnestly.*] I know Old Chris well for a long time. He's talked to me 'bout you lots o' times. He thinks the world o' you, honest he does.

ANNA: Aw, quit the kiddin'!

MARTHY: Honest! Only, he's a simple old guy, see? He's got nutty notions. But he means well, honest. Listen to me, kid——[*She is interrupted by the opening and shutting of the street door in the bar and by hearing* CHRIS' *voice.*] Ssshh!

ANNA: What's up?

CHRIS [*who has entered the bar. He seems considerably*

sobered up]: Py golly, Larry, dat grub taste good. Marthy in back?

LARRY: Sure—and another tramp with her.

[CHRIS *starts for the entrance to the back room.*]

MARTHY [*to* ANNA *in a hurried, nervous whisper*]: That's him now. He's comin' in here. Brace up!

ANNA: Who? [CHRIS *opens the door.*]

MARTHY [*as if she were greeting him for the first time*]: Why hello, Old Chris. [*Then before he can speak, she shuffles hurriedly past him into the bar, beckoning him to follow her.*] Come here. I wanna tell yuh somethin'. [*He goes out to her. She speaks hurriedly in a low voice.*] Listen! I'm goin' to beat it down to the barge—pack up me duds and blow. That's her in there—your Anna—just come—waitin' for yuh. Treat her right, see? She's been sick. Well, s'long! [*She goes into the back room—to* ANNA.] S'long kid. I gotta beat it now. See yuh later.

ANNA [*nervously*]: So long.

[MARTHY *goes quickly out of the family entrance.*]

LARRY [*looking at the stupefied Chris curiously*]: Well, what's up now?

CHRIS [*vaguely*]: Nutting—nutting. [*He stands before the door to the back room in an agony of embarrassed emotion —then he forces himself to a bold decision, pushes open the door and walks in. He stands there, casts a shy glance at* ANNA, *whose brilliant clothes, and, to him, high-toned appearance, awe him terribly. He looks about him with pitiful nervousness as if to avoid the appraising look with which she takes in his face, his clothes, etc.—his voice seeming to plead for her forbearance.*] Anna!

ANNA [*acutely embarrassed in her turn*]: Hello—father. She told me it was you. I yust got here a little while ago.

CHRIS [*goes slowly over to her chair*]: It's good—for see you —after all dem years, Anna. [*He bends down over her. After an embarrassed struggle they manage to kiss each other.*]

ANNA [*a trace of genuine feeling in her voice*]: It's good to see you, too.

CHRIS [*grasps her arms and looks into her face—then overcome by a wave of fierce tenderness*]: Anna lilla! Anna lilla! [*Takes her in his arms.*]

ANNA [*shrinks away from him, half-frightened*]: What's that—Swedish? I don't know it. [*Then as if seeking relief from the tension in a voluble chatter.*] Gee, I had an awful trip coming here. I'm all in. I had to sit up in the dirty coach all night—couldn't get no sleep, hardly—and then I had a hard job finding this place. I never been in New York before, you know, and——

CHRIS [*who has been staring down at her face admiringly, not hearing what she says—impulsively*]: You know you vas awful pooty gel, Anna? Ay bet all men see you fall in love with you, py yiminy!

ANNA [*repelled—harshly*]: Cut it! You talk same as they all do.

CHRIS [*hurt—humbly*]: Ain't no harm for your fa'der talk dat vay, Anna.

ANNA [*forcing a short laugh*]: No—course not. Only—it's funny to see you and not remember nothing. You're like—a stranger.

CHRIS [*sadly*]: Ay s'pose. Ay never come home only few times ven you vas kit in Sveden. You don't remember dat?

ANNA: No. [*Resentfully.*] But why didn't you never come home them days? Why didn't you never come out West to see me?

CHRIS [*slowly*]: Ay tank, after your mo'der die, ven Ay vas avay on voyage, it's better for you you don't never see me! [*He sinks down in the chair opposite her dejectedly—then turns to her—sadly.*] Ay don't know, Anna, vhy Ay never come home Sveden in old year. Ay vant come home end of every voyage. Ay vant see your mo'der, your two bro'der before dey vas drowned, you ven you vas born—but—Ay—don't go. Ay sign on oder ships—go South America, go Australia, go China, go every port all over world many times —but Ay never go aboard ship sail for Sveden. Ven Ay gat money for pay passage home as passenger den—— [*He bows his head guiltily.*] Ay forgat and Ay spend all money. Ven Ay tank again, it's too late. [*He sighs.*] Ay don't know why but dat's vay with most sailor fallar, Anna. Dat ole davil sea make dem crazy fools with her dirty tricks. It's so.

ANNA [*who has watched him keenly while he has been speaking—with a trace of scorn in her voice*]: Then you think the sea's to blame for everything, eh? Well, you're still workin' on it, ain't you, spite of all you used to write me about hating it. That dame was here told me you was captain of a coal barge—and you wrote me you was yanitor of a building!

CHRIS [*embarrassed but lying glibly*]: Oh, Ay vork on land long time as yanitor. Yust short time ago Ay got dis yob cause Ay vas sick, need open air.

ANNA [*sceptically*]: Sick? You? You'd never think it.

CHRIS: And, Anna, dis ain't real sailor yob. Dis ain't real boat on sea. She's yust old tub—like piece of land with house on it dat float. Yob on her ain't sea yob. No. Ay don't gat yob on sea, Anna, if Ay die first. Ay swear dat ven your mo'der die. Ay keep my word, py yingo!

ANNA [*perplexed*]: Well, I can't see no difference. [*Dismissing the subject.*] Speaking of being sick, I been there myself—yust out of the hospital two weeks ago.

CHRIS [*immediately all concern*]: You, Anna? Py golly! [*Anxiously.*] You feel better now, dough, don't you? You look little tired, dat's all!

ANNA [*wearily*]: I am. Tired to death. I need a long rest and I don't see much chance of getting it.

CHRIS: What you mean, Anna?

ANNA: Well, when I made up my mind to come to see you, I thought you was a yanitor—that you'd have a place where, maybe, if you didn't mind having me, I could visit a while and rest up—till I felt able to get back on the job again.

CHRIS [*eagerly*]: But Ay gat place, Anna—nice place. You rest all you want, py yiminy! You don't never have to vork as nurse gel no more. You stay with me, py golly!

ANNA [*surprised and pleased by his eagerness—with a smile*]: Then you're really glad to see me—honest?

CHRIS [*pressing one of her hands in both of his*]: Anna, Ay like see you like hell, Ay tal you! And don't you talk no more about gatting yob. You stay with me. Ay don't see you for long time, you don't forgat dat. [*His voice trembles.*] Ay'm gatting ole. Ay gat no one in vorld but you.

ANNA [*touched—embarrassed by this unfamiliar emotion*]: Thanks. It sounds good to hear someone—talk to me that way. Say, though—if you're so lonely—it's funny—why ain't you ever married again?

CHRIS [*shaking his head emphatically—after a pause*]: Ay love your mo'der too much for ever do dat, Anna.

ANNA [*impressed—slowly*]: I don't remember nothing about her. What was she like? Tell me.

CHRIS: Ay tal you all about everytang—and you tal me all tangs happen to you. But not here now. Dis ain't good place for young gel, anyway. Only no good sailor fallar come here for gat drunk. [*He gets to his feet quickly and picks up her bag.*] You come with me, Anna. You need lie down, gat rest.

ANNA [*half rises to her feet, then sits down again*]: Where're you going?

CHRIS: Come. Ve gat on board.

ANNA [*disappointedly*]: On board your barge, you mean? [*Dryly.*] Nix for mine! [*Then seeing his crestfallen look—forcing a smile.*] Do you think that's a good place for a young girl like me—a coal barge?

CHRIS [*dully*]: Yes, Ay tank. [*He hesitates—then continues more and more pleadingly.*] You don't know how nice it's on barge, Anna. Tug come and ve gat towed out on voyage—yust water all round, and sun, and fresh air, and good grub for make you strong, healthy gel. You see many tangs you don't see before. You gat moonlight at night, maybe; see steamer pass; see schooner make sail—see everytang dat's pooty. You need take rest like dat. You vork too hard for young gel already. You need vacation, yes!

ANNA [*who has listened to him with a growing interest—*

with an uncertain laugh]: It sounds good to hear you tell it. I'd sure like a trip on the water, all right. It's the barge idea has me stopped. Well, I'll go down with you and have a look —and maybe I'll take a chance. Gee, I'd do anything once.

CHRIS [*picks up her bag again*]: Ve go, eh?

ANNA: What's the rush? Wait a second. [*Forgetting the situation for a moment, she relapses into the familiar form and flashes one of her winning trade smiles at him.*] Gee, I'm thirsty.

CHRIS [*sets down her bag immediately—hastily*]: Ay'm sorry, Anna. What you tank you like for drink, eh?

ANNA [*promptly*]: I'll take a—— [*Then suddenly reminded —confusedly.*] I don't know. What'a they got here?

CHRIS [*with a grin*]: Ay don't think dey got much fancy drink for young gel in dis place, Anna. Yinger ale—sas-prilla, maybe.

ANNA [*forcing a laugh herself*]: Make it sas, then.

CHRIS [*coming up to her—with a wink*]: Ay tal you, Anna, ve calabrate, yes—dis one time because ve meet after many year. [*In a half whisper, embarrassedly.*] Dey gat good port wine, Anna. It's good for you, Ay tank—little bit—for give you appetite. It ain't strong, neider. One glass don't go to your head, Ay promise.

ANNA [*with a half hysterical laugh*]: All right. I'll take port.

CHRIS: Ay go gat him. [*He goes to the bar. As soon as the door closes, ANNA starts to her feet.*]

ANNA [*picking up her bag—half-aloud—stammeringly*]: Gawd, I can't stand this! I better beat it. [*Then she lets her bag drop, stumbles over to her chair again, and covering her face with her hands, begins to sob.*]

LARRY [*putting down his paper as CHRIS comes up—with a grin*]: Well, who's the blonde?

CHRIS [*proudly*]: Dat vas Anna, Larry.

LARRY [*in amazement*]: Your daughter, Anna? [*CHRIS nods. LARRY lets a long, low whistle escape him and turns away embarrassedly.*]

CHRIS: Don't you tank she vas pooty gel, Larry?

LARRY [*rising to the occasion*]: Sure! A peach!

CHRIS: You bet you! Give me drink for take back—one port vine for Anna—she calabrate dis one time with me—and small beer for me.

LARRY: [*as he gets the drinks*]: Small beer for you, eh? She's reformin' you already.

CHRIS [*pleased*]: You bet! [*He takes the drinks. As she hears him coming, ANNA hastily dries her eyes, tries to smile. CHRIS comes in and sets the drinks down on the table—stares at her for a second anxiously—patting her hand.*] You look tired, Anna. Vell, Ay make you take good long rest now. [*Picking up his beer.*] Come, you drink vine. It put new life in you. [*She lifts her glass—he grins.*] Skoal, Anna! You know dat Svedish word?

ANNA: Skoal! [*Downing her port at a gulp like a drink of whisky—her lips trembling.*] Skoal? Guess I know that word, all right!

[*The Curtain Falls*]

ACT TWO

SCENE—*Ten days later. The stern of the deeply-laden barge, Simeon Winthrop, at anchor in the outer harbor of Province-town, Mass. It is ten o'clock at night. Dense fog shrouds the barge on all sides, and she floats motionless on a calm. A lantern set up on an immense coil of thick hawser sheds a dull, filtering light on objects near it—the heavy steel bits for making fast the tow lines, etc. In the rear is the cabin, its misty windows glowing wanly with the light of a lamp inside. The chimney of the cabin stove rises a few feet above the roof. The doleful tolling of bells, on Long Point, on ships at anchor, breaks the silence at regular intervals.*

As the curtain rises, ANNA *is discovered standing near the coil of rope on which the lantern is placed. She looks healthy, trans-formed, the natural color has come back to her face. She has on a black oilskin coat, but wears no hat. She is staring out into the fog astern with an expression of awed wonder. The cabin door is pushed open and* CHRIS *appears He is dressed in yellow oil-skins—coat, pants, sou'wester—and wears high sea-boots.*

CHRIS [*the glare from the cabin still in his eyes, peers blinkingly astern*]: Anna! [*Receiving no reply, he calls again, this time with apparent apprehension.*] Anna!

ANNA [*with a start—making a gesture with her hand as if to impose silence—in a hushed whisper*]: Yes, here I am. What d'you want?

CHRIS [*walks over to her—solicitously*]: Don't you come turn in, Anna? It's late—after four bells. It ain't good for you stay out here in fog, Ay tank.

ANNA: Why not? [*With a trace of strange exultation.*] I love this fog! Honest! It's so—— [*She hesitates, groping for a word.*] Funny and still. I feel as if I was—out of things al-together.

25

CHRIS [*spitting disgustedly*]: Fog's vorst one of her dirty tricks, py yingo!

ANNA [*with a short laugh*]: Beefing about the sea again? I'm getting so's I love it, the little I've seen.

CHRIS [*glancing at her moodily*]: Dat's foolish talk, Anna. You see her more, you don't talk dat vay. [*Then seeing her irritation, he hastily adopts a more cheerful tone.*] But Ay'm glad you like it on barge. Ay'm glad it makes you feel good again. [*With a placating grin.*] You like live like dis alone with ole fa'der, eh?

ANNA: Sure I do. Everything's been so different from anything I ever come across before. And now—this fog—— Gee, I wouldn't have missed it for nothing. I never thought living on ships was so different from land. Gee, I'd yust love to work on it, honest I would, if I was a man. I don't wonder you always been a sailor.

CHRIS [*vehemently*]: Ay ain't sailor, Anna. And dis ain't real sea. You only see nice part. [*Then as she doesn't anwer, he continues hopefully.*] Vell, fog lift in morning, Ay tank.

ANNA [*the exultation again in her voice*]: I love it! I don't give a rap if it never lifts! [CHRIS *fidgets from one foot to the other worriedly.* ANNA *continues slowly, after a pause.*] It makes me feel clean—out here—'s if I'd taken a bath.

CHRIS [*after a pause*]: You better go in cabin read book. Dat put you to sleep.

ANNA: I don't want to sleep. I want to stay out here—and think about things.

CHRIS [*walks away from her toward the cabin—then comes back*]: You act funny tonight, Anna.

ANNA [*her voice rising angrily*]: Say, what're you trying to do—make things rotten? You been kind as kind can be to me and I certainly appreciate it—only don't spoil it all now. [*Then, seeing the hurt expression on her father's face, she forces a smile.*] Let's talk of something else. Come. Sit down here. [*She points to the coil of rope.*]

CHRIS [*sits down beside her with a sigh*]: It's gatting pooty late in night, Anna. Must be near five bells.

ANNA [*interestedly*]: Five bells? What time is that?

CHRIS: Half past ten.

ANNA: Funny I don't know nothing about sea talk—but those cousins was always talking crops and that stuff. Gee, wasn't I sick of it—and of them!

CHRIS: You don't like live on farm, Anna?

ANNA: I've told you a hundred times I hated it. [*Decidedly.*] I'd rather have one drop of ocean than all the farms in the world! Honest! And you wouldn't like a farm, neither. Here's where you belong. [*She makes a sweeping gesture seaward.*] But not on a coal barge. You belong on a real ship, sailing all over the world.

CHRIS [*moodily*]: Ay've done dat many year, Anna, when Ay vas damn fool.

ANNA [*disgustedly*]: Oh, rats! [*After a pause she speaks musingly.*] Was the men in our family always sailors—as far back as you know about?

CHRIS [*shortly*]: Yes. Damn fools! All men in our village on coast, Sveden, go to sea. Ain't nutting else for dem to do. My fa'der die on board ship in Indian Ocean. He's buried at sea. Ay don't never know him only little bit. Den my tree bro'der, older'n me, dey go on ships. Den Ay go, too. Den my mo'der she's left all 'lone. She die pooty quick after dat—all 'lone. Ve vas all avay on voyage when she die. [*He pauses sadly.*] Two my bro'der dey gat lost on fishing boat same like your bro'ders vas drowned. My oder bro'der, he save money, give up sea, den he die home in bed. He's only one dat old davil don't kill. [*Defiantly.*] But me, Ay bet you Ay die ashore in bed, too!

ANNA: Were all of 'em yust plain sailors?

CHRIS: Able body seaman, most of dem. [*With a certain pride.*] Dey vas all smart seaman, too—A one. [*Then after hesitating a moment—shyly.*] Ay vas bo'sun.

ANNA: Bo'sun?

CHRIS: Dat's kind of officer.

ANNA: Gee, that was fine. What does he do?

CHRIS [*after a second's hesitation, plunged into gloom*

again by his fear of her enthusiasm]: Hard vork all time. It's rotten, Ay tal you, for go to sea. [*Determined to disgust her with sea life—volubly.*] Dey're all fool fallar, dem fallar in our family. Dey all vork rotten yob on sea for nutting, don't care nutting but yust gat big pay day in pocket, gat drunk, gat robbed, ship avay again on oder voyage. Dey don't come home. Dey don't do anytang like good man do. And dat ole davil, sea, sooner, later she svallow dem up.

ANNA [*with an excited laugh*]: Good sports, I'd call 'em. [*Then hastily.*] But say—listen—did all the women of the family marry sailors?

CHRIS [*eagerly—seeing a chance to drive home his point*]: Yes—and it's bad on dem like hell vorst of all. Dey don't see deir men only once in long while. Dey set and vait all 'lone. And vhen deir boys grows up, go to sea, dey sit and vait some more. [*Vehemently.*] Any gel marry sailor, she's crazy fool! Your mo'der she tal you same tang if she vas alive. [*He relapses into an attitude of somber brooding.*]

ANNA [*after a pause—dreamily*]: Funny! I do feel sort of— nutty, tonight. I feel old.

CHRIS [*mystified*]: Ole?

ANNA: Sure—like I'd been living a long, long time—out here in the fog. [*Frowning perplexedly.*] I don't know how to tell you yust vhat I mean. It's like I'd come home after a long visit away some place. It all seems like I'd been here before lots of times—on boats—in this same fog. [*With a short laugh.*] You must think I'm off my base.

CHRIS [*gruffly*]: Anybody feel funny dat vay in fog.

ANNA [*persistently*]: But why d'you s'pose I feel so—so— like I'd found something I'd missed and been looking for— 's if this was the right place for me to fit in? And I seem to have forgot—everything that's happened—like it didn't matter no more. And I feel clean, somehow—like you feel yust after you've took a bath. And I feel happy for once—yes, honest!—happier than I ever have been anywhere before! [*As CHRIS makes no comment but a heavy sigh, she continues wonderingly*.] It's nutty for me to feel that way, don't you think?

CHRIS [*a grim foreboding in his voice*]: Ay tank Ay'm damn fool for bring you on voyage, Anna.

ANNA [*impressed by his tone*]: You talk—nutty tonight yourself. You act 's if you was scared something was going to happen.

CHRIS: Only God know dat, Anna.

ANNA [*half-mockingly*]: Then it'll be Gawd's will, like the preachers say—what does happen.

CHRIS [*starts to his feet with fierce protest*]: No! Dat ole davil, sea, she ain't God!

[*In the pause of silence that comes after his defiance a hail in a man's husky, exhausted voice comes faintly out of the fog to port.*] "Ahoy!"

[CHRIS *gives a startled exclamation.*]

ANNA [*jumping to her feet*]: What's that?

CHRIS [*who has regained his composure—sheepishly*]: Py golly, dat scare me for minute. It's only some fallar hail, Anna —loose his course in fog. Must be fisherman's power boat. His engine break down, Ay guess. [*The "ahoy" comes again through the wall of fog, sounding much nearer this time.* CHRIS *goes over to the port bulwark.*] Sound from dis side. She come in from open sea. [*He holds his hands to his mouth, megaphone-fashion, and shouts back.*] Ahoy, dere! Vhat's trouble?

THE VOICE [*this time sounding nearer but up forward toward the bow*]: Heave a rope when we come alongside. [*Then irritably.*] Where are ye, ye scut?

CHRIS: Ay hear dem rowing. Dey come up by bow, Ay tank. [*Then shouting out again.*] Dis vay!

THE VOICE: Right ye are! [*There is a muffled sound of oars in oar-locks.*]

ANNA [*half to herself—resentfully*]: Why don't that guy stay where he belongs?

CHRIS [*hurriedly*]: Ay go up bow. All hands asleep 'cepting fallar on vatch. Ay gat heave line to dat fallar. [*He picks up a coil of rope and hurries off toward the bow.* ANNA *walks back toward the extreme stern as if she wanted to remain as much isolated as possible. She turns her back on the proceedings and stares out into the fog.* THE VOICE *is heard again shouting "Ahoy" and* CHRIS *answering "Dis vay." Then there is a pause—the murmur of excited voices—then the scuffling of feet.* CHRIS *appears from around the cabin to port. He is supporting the limp form of a man dressed in dungarees, holding one of the man's arms around his neck. The deckhand,* JOHNSON, *a young blond Swede, follows him, helping along another exhausted man similar fashion.* ANNA *turns to look at them.* CHRIS *stops for a second—volubly.*] Anna! You come help, vill you? You find vhisky in cabin. Dese fallars need drink for fix dem. Dey vas near dead.

ANNA [*hurrying to him*]: Sure—but who are they? What's the trouble?

CHRIS: Sailor fallars. Deir steamer gat wrecked. Dey been five days in open boat—four fallars—only one left able stand up. Come, Anna. [*She precedes him into the cabin, holding the door open while he and* JOHNSON *carry in their burdens. The door is shut, then opened again as* JOHNSON *comes out.* CHRIS' *voice shouts after him.*] Go gat oder fallar, Yohnson.

JOHNSON: Yes, sir. [*He goes. The door is closed again.* MAT BURKE *stumbles in around the port side of the cabin. He moves slowly, feeling his way uncertainly, keeping hold of the port bulwark with his right hand to steady himself. He is stripped to the waist, has on nothing but a pair of dirty dungaree pants. He is a powerful, broad-chested six-footer, his face handsome in a hard, rough, bold, defiant way. He is about thirty, in the full power of his heavy-muscled, immense strength. His dark eyes are bloodshot and wild for sleeplessness. The muscles of his arms and shoulders are lumped in knots and bunches, the veins of his forearms stand out like blue cords. He finds his way to the coil of hawser and sits down on it facing the cabin, his back bowed, head in his hands, in an attitude of spent weariness.*]

BURKE [*talking aloud to himself*]: Row, ye divil! Row! [*Then lifting his head and looking about him.*] What's this tub? Well, we're safe anyway—with the help of God. [*He makes the sign of the cross mechanically.* JOHNSON *comes along the deck to port, supporting the fourth man, who is babbling to himself incoherently.* BURKE *glances at him disdainfully.*] Is it losing the small wits ye iver had, ye are? Deck-scrubbing scut! [*They pass him and go into the cabin, leaving the door open.* BURKE *sags forward wearily.*] I'm bate out—bate out entirely.

ANNA [*comes out of the cabin with a tumbler quarter-full of whisky in her hand. She gives a start when she sees* BURKE *so near her, the light from the open door falling full on him. Then, overcoming what is evidently a feeling of repulsion, she comes up beside him.*]: Here you are. Here's a drink for you. You need it, I guess.

BURKE [*lifting his head slowly—confusedly*]: Is it dreaming I am?

ANNA [*half smiling*]: Drink it and you'll find it ain't no dream.

BURKE: To hell with the drink—but I'll take it just the same. [*He tosses it down.*] Ahah! I'm needin' that—and 'tis fine stuff. [*Looking up at her with frank, grinning admiration.*] But 'twasn't the booze I meant when I said, was I dreaming. I thought you was some mermaid out of the sea come to torment me. [*He reaches out to feel of her arm.*] Aye, rale flesh and blood, divil a less.

ANNA [*coldly. Stepping back from him*]: Cut that.

BURKE: But tell me, isn't this a barge I'm on—or isn't it?

ANNA: Sure.

BURKE: And what is a fine handsome woman the like of you doing on this scow?

ANNA [*coldly*]: Never you mind. [*Then half-amused in spite of herself.*] Say, you're a great one, honest—starting right in kidding after what you been through.

BURKE [*delighted—proudly*]: Ah, it was nothing—aisy for a rale man with guts to him, the like of me. [*He laughs.*] All in the day's work, darlin'. [*Then, more seriously but still in a boastful tone, confidentially.*] But I won't be denying 'twas a damn narrow squeak. We'd all ought to be with Davy Jones at the bottom of the sea, be rights. And only for me, I'm telling you, and the great strength and guts is in me, we'd be being scoffed by the fishes this minute!

ANNA [*contemptuously*]: Gee, you hate yourself, don't you? [*Then turning away from him indifferently.*] Well, you'd better come in and lie down. You must want to sleep.

BURKE [*stung—rising unsteadily to his feet with chest out and head thrown back—resentfully*]: Lie down and sleep, is it? Divil a wink I'm after having for two days and nights and divil a bit I'm needing now. Let you not be thinking I'm the like of them three weak scuts come in the boat with me. I could lick the three of them sitting down with one hand tied behind me. They may be bate out, but I'm not—and I've been rowing the boat with them lying in the bottom not able to raise a hand for the last two days we was in it. [*Furiously, as he sees this is making no impression on her.*] And I can lick all hands on this tub, wan be wan, tired as I am!

ANNA [*sarcastically*]: Gee, ain't you a hard guy! [*Then, with a trace of sympathy, as she notices him swaying from weakness.*] But never mind that fight talk. I'll take your word for all you've said. Go on and sit down out here, anyway, if I can't get you to come inside. [*He sits down weakly.*] You're all in, you might as well own up to it.

BURKE [*fiercely*]: The hell I am!

ANNA [*coldly*]: Well, be stubborn then for all I care. And I must say I don't care for your language. The men I know don't pull that rough stuff when ladies are around.

BURKE [*getting unsteadily to his feet again—in a rage*]: Ladies! Ho-ho! Divil mend you! Let you not be making game of me. What would ladies be doing on this bloody hulk? [*As ANNA attempts to go to the cabin, he lurches into her path.*] Aisy, now! You're not the old Squarehead's woman, I suppose you'll be telling me next—living in his cabin with him, no less! [*Seeing the cold, hostile expression on* ANNA's *face, he suddenly changes his tone to one of boisterous joviality.*] But I do be thinking, iver since the first look my eyes took at you, that it's a fool you are to be wasting yourself—a fine, handsome girl—on a stumpy runt of a man like that old Swede. There's too many strapping great lads on the sea would give their heart's blood for one kiss of you!

ANNA [*scornfully*]: Lads like you, eh?

BURKE [*grinning*]: Ye take the words out o' my mouth. I'm the proper lad for you, if it's meself do be saying it. [*With a quick movement he puts his arms about her waist.*] Whisht, now, me daisy! Himself's in the cabin. It's wan of your kisses I'm needing to take the tiredness from me bones. Wan kiss, now! [*He presses her to him and attempts to kiss her.*]

ANNA [*struggling fiercely*]: Leggo of me, you big mutt! [*She pushes him away with all her might.* BURKE, *weak and tottering, is caught off his guard. He is thrown down backward and, in falling, hits his head a hard thump against the bulwark. He lies there still, knocked out for the moment.* ANNA *stands for a second, looking down at him frightenedly. Then she kneels down beside him and raises his head to her knee, staring into his face anxiously for some sign of life.*]

BURKE [*stirring a bit—mutteringly*]: God stiffen it! [*He opens his eyes and blinks up at her with vague wonder.*]

ANNA [*letting his head sink back on the deck, rising to her feet with a sigh of relief*]: You're coming to all right, eh? Gee, I was scared for a moment I'd killed you.

BURKE [*with difficulty rising to a sitting position—scornfully*]: Killed, is it? It'd take more than a bit of a blow to crack my thick skull. [*Then looking at her with the most intense admiration.*] But, glory be, it's a power of strength is in them two fine arms of yours. There's not a man in the world can say the same as you, that he seen Mat Burke lying at his feet and him dead to the world.

ANNA [*rather remorsefully*]: Forget it. I'm sorry it happened, see? [*Burke rises and sits on bench. Then severely.*] Only you had no right to be getting fresh with me. Listen, now, and don't go getting any more wrong notions. I'm on this barge because I'm making a trip with my father. The captain's my father. Now you know.

BURKE: The old square—the old Swede, I mean?

ANNA: Yes.

BURKE [*rising—peering at her face*]: Sure I might have known it, if I wasn't a bloody fool from birth. Where else'd you get that fine yellow hair is like a golden crown on your head.

ANNA [*with an amused laugh*]: Say, nothing stops you, does it? [*Then attempting a severe tone again.*] But don't you think you ought to be apologizing for what you said and done yust a minute ago, instead of trying to kid me with that mush?

BURKE [*indignantly*]: Mush! [*Then bending forward toward her with very intense earnestness.*] Indade and I will ask your pardon a thousand times—and on my knees, if ye like. I didn't mean a word of what I said or did. [*Resentful again for a second.*] But divil a woman in all the ports of the world has iver made a great fool of me that way before!

ANNA [*with amused sarcasm*]: I see. You mean you're a lady-killer and they all fall for you.

BURKE [*offended; passionately*]: Leave off your fooling! 'Tis that is after getting my back up at you. [*Earnestly.*] 'Tis no lie I'm telling you about the women. [*Ruefully.*] Though it's a great jackass I am to be mistaking you, even in anger, for the like of them cows on the waterfront is the only women I've met up with since I was growed to a man. [*As* ANNA *shrinks away from him at this, he hurries on pleadingly.*] I'm a hard, rough man and I'm not fit, I'm thinking, to be kissing the shoe-soles of a fine, dacent girl the like of yourself. 'Tis only the ignorance of your kind made me see you wrong. So you'll forgive me, for the love of God, and let us be friends from this out. [*Passionately.*] I'm thinking I'd rather be friends with you than have my wish for anything else in the world. [*He holds out his hand to her shyly.*]

ANNA [*looking queerly at him, perplexed and worried, but*

moved and pleased in spite of herself—takes his hand uncertainly]: Sure.

BURKE [*with boyish delight*]: God bless you! [*In his excitement he squeezes her hand tight.*]

ANNA: Ouch!

BURKE [*hastily dropping her hand—ruefully*]: Your pardon, Miss. 'Tis a clumsy ape I am. [*Then simply—glancing down his arm proudly.*] It's great power I have in my hand and arms, and I do be forgetting it at times.

ANNA [*nursing her crushed hand and glancing at his arm, not without a trace of his own admiration*]: Gee, you're some strong, all right.

BURKE [*delighted*]: It's no lie, and why shouldn't I be, with me shoveling a million tons of coal in the stokeholes of ships since I was a lad only. [*He pats the coil of hawser invitingly.*] Let you sit down, now, Miss, and I'll be telling you a bit of myself, and you'll be telling me a bit of yourself, and in an hour we'll be as old friends as if we was born in the same house. [*He pulls at her sleeve shyly.*] Sit down now, if you plaze.

ANNA [*with a half laugh*]: Well—— [*She sits down.*] But we won't talk about me, see? You tell me about yourself and about the wreck.

BURKE [*flattered*]: I'll tell you, surely. But can I be asking you one question, Miss, has my head in a puzzle?

ANNA [*guardedly*]: Well—I dunno—what is it?

BURKE: What is it you do when you're not taking a trip with the Old Man? For I'm thinking a fine girl the like of you ain't living always on this tub.

ANNA [*uneasily*]: No—of course I ain't. [*She searches his face suspiciously, afraid there may be some hidden insinuation in his words. Seeing his simple frankness, she goes on confidently.*] Well, I'll tell you. I'm a governess, see? I take care of kids for people and learn them things.

BURKE [*impressed*]: A governess, is it? You must be smart, surely.

ANNA: Let's not talk about me. Tell me about the wreck, like you promised me you would.

BURKE [*importantly*]: 'Twas this way, Miss. Two weeks out we ran into the divil's own storm, and she sprang wan hell of a leak up for'ard. The skipper was hoping to make Boston before another blow would finish her, but ten days back we met up with another storm the like of the first, only worse. Four days we was in it with green seas raking over her from bow to stern. That was a terrible time, God help us. [*Proudly.*] And if 'twasn't for me and my great strength, I'm telling you—and it's God truth—there'd been mutiny itself in the stokehole. 'Twas me held them to it, with a kick to wan and a clout to another, and they not caring a damn for the engineers any more, but fearing a clout of my right arm more than they'd fear the sea itself. [*He glances at her anxiously, eager for her approval.*]

ANNA [*concealing a smile—amused by this boyish boasting of his*]: You did some hard work, didn't you?

BURKE [*promptly*]: I did that! I'm a divil for sticking it out when them that's weak give up. But much good it did anyone! 'Twas a mad, fightin' scramble in the last seconds with each man for himself. I disremember how it come about, but there was the four of us in wan boat and when we raised high on a great wave I took a look about and divil a sight there was of ship or men on top of the sea.

ANNA [*in a subdued voice*]: Then all the others was drowned?

BURKE: They was, surely.

ANNA [*with a shudder*]: What a terrible end!

BURKE [*turns to her*]: A terrible end for the like of them swabs does live on land, maybe. But for the like of us does be roaming the seas, a good end, I'm telling you—quick and clane.

ANNA [*struck by the word*]: Yes, clean. That's yust the word for—all of it—the way it makes me feel.

BURKE: The sea, you mean? [*Interestedly.*] I'm thinking you have a bit of it in your blood, too. Your Old Man wasn't only a barge rat—begging your pardon—all his life, by the cut of him.

ANNA: No, he was bo'sun on sailing ships for years. And all the men on both sides of the family have gone to sea as far back as he remembers, he says. All the women have married sailors, too.

BURKE [*with intense satisfaction*]: Did they, now? They had spirit in them. It's only on the sea you'd find rale men with guts is fit to wed with fine, high-tempered girls [*then he adds half-boldly*] the like of yourself.

ANNA [*with a laugh*]: There you go kiddin' again. [*Then seeing his hurt expression—quickly.*] But you was going to tell me about yourself. You're Irish, of course I can tell that.

BURKE [*stoutly*]: Yes, thank God, though I've not seen a sight of it in fifteen years or more.

ANNA [*thoughtfully*]: Sailors never do go home hardly, do they? That's what my father was saying.

BURKE: He wasn't telling no lie. [*With sudden melancholy.*] It's a hard and lonesome life, the sea is. The only women you'd meet in the ports of the world who'd be willing to speak you a kind word isn't women at all. You know the kind I mane, and they're a poor, wicked lot, God forgive them. They're looking to steal the money from you only.

ANNA [*her face averted—rising to her feet—agitatedly*]: I think—I guess I'd better see what's doing inside.

BURKE [*afraid he has offended her—beseechingly*]: Don't go, I'm saying! Is it I've given you offense with the talk of the like of them? Don't heed it at all! I'm clumsy in my wits when it comes to talking proper with a girl the like of you. And why wouldn't I be? Since the day I left home for to go to sea punching coal, this is the first time I've had a word with a rale, dacent woman. So don't turn your back on me now, and we beginning to be friends.

ANNA [*turning to him again—forcing a smile*]: I'm not sore at you, honest.

BURKE [*gratefully*]: God bless you!

ANNA [*changing the subject abruptly*]: But if you honestly

think the sea's such a rotten life, why don't you get out of it?

BURKE [*surprised*]: Work on land, is it? [*She nods. He spits scornfully.*] Digging spuds in the muck from dawn to dark, I suppose? [*Vehemently.*] I wasn't made for it, Miss.

ANNA [*with a laugh*]: I thought you'd say that.

BURKE [*argumentatively*]: But there's good jobs and bad jobs at sea, like there'd be on land. I'm thinking if it's in the stokehole of a proper liner I was, I'd be able to have a little house and be home to it wan week out of four. And I'm thinking that maybe then I'd have the luck to find a fine dacent girl—the like of yourself, now—would be willing to wed with me.

ANNA [*turning away from him with a short laugh—uneasily*]: Why, sure. Why not?

BURKE [*edging up close to her—exultantly*]: Then you think a girl the like of yourself might maybe not mind the past at all but only be seeing the good herself put in me?

ANNA [*in the same tone*]: Why, sure.

BURKE [*passionately*]: She'd not be sorry for it, I'd take my oath! 'Tis no more drinking and roving about I'd be doing then, but giving my pay day into her hand and staying at home with her as meek as a lamb each night of the week I'd be in port.

ANNA [*moved in spite of herself and troubled by this half-concealed proposal—with a forced laugh*]: All you got to do is find the girl.

BURKE: I have found her!

ANNA [*half-frightenedly—trying to laugh it off*]: You have? When? I thought you was saying——

BURKE [*boldly and forcefully*]: This night. [*Hanging his head—humbly.*] If she'll be having me. [*Then raising his eyes to hers—simply.*] 'Tis you I mean.

ANNA [*is held by his eyes for a moment—then shrinks back from him with a strange, broken laugh*]: Say—are you—going crazy? Are you trying to kid me? Proposing—to me!—for Gawd's sake!—on such short acquaintance?

[CHRIS *comes out of the cabin and stands staring blinkingly astern. When he makes out* ANNA *in such intimate proximity to this strange sailor, an angry expression comes over his face.*]

BURKE [*following her—with fierce, pleading insistence*]: I'm telling you there's the will of God in it that brought me safe through the storm and fog to the wan spot in the world where you was! Think of that now, and isn't it queer——

CHRIS: Anna! [*He comes toward them, raging, his fists clenched.*] Anna, you gat in cabin, you hear!

ANNA [*all her emotions immediately transformed into resentment at his bullying tone*]: Who d'you think you're talking to—a slave?

CHRIS [*hurt—his voice breaking—pleadingly*]: You need gat rest, Anna. You gat sleep. [*She does not move. He turns on* BURKE *furiously.*] What you doing here, you sailor fallar? You ain't sick like oders. You gat in fo'c'stle. Dey give you bunk. [*Threateningly.*] You hurry, Ay tal you!

ANNA [*impulsively*]: But he is sick. Look at him. Look at him. He can hardly stand up.

BURKE [*straightening and throwing out his chest—with a bold laugh*]: Is it giving me orders ye are, me bucko? Let you look out, then! With wan hand, weak as I am, I can break ye in two and fling the pieces over the side—and your crew after you. [*Stopping abruptly.*] I was forgetting. You're her Old Man and I'd not raise a fist to you for the world. [*His knees sag, he wavers and seems about to fall.* ANNA *utters an exclamation of alarm and hurries to his side.*]

ANNA [*taking one of his arms over her shoulder*]: Come on in the cabin. You can have my bed if there ain't no other place.

BURKE [*with jubilant happiness—as they proceed toward the cabin*]: Glory be to God, is it holding my arm about your neck you are! Anna! Anna! Sure it's a sweet name is suited to you.

ANNA [*guiding him carefully*]: Sssh! Sssh!

BURKE: Whisht, is it? Indade, and I'll not. I'll be roaring

it out like a fog horn over the sea! You're the girl of the world and we'll be marrying soon and I don't care who knows it!

ANNA [*as she guides him through the cabin door*]: Ssshh! Never mind that talk. You go to sleep.

[*They go out of sight in the cabin.* CHRIS, *who has been listening to* BURKE'S *last words with open-mouthed amazement stands looking after them desperately.*]

CHRIS [*turns suddenly and shakes his fist out at the sea— with bitter hatred*]: Dat's your dirty trick, damn ole davil, you! [*Then in a frenzy of rage.*] But, py God, you don't **do** dat! Not vhile Ay'm living! No, py God, you don't!

[The Curtain Falls]

ACT THREE

SCENE—*The interior of the cabin on the barge* Simeon Winthrop (*at dock in Boston*)—*a narrow, low-ceilinged compartment
the walls of which are painted a light brown with white trim-
mings. In the rear on the left, a door leading to the sleeping
quarters. In the far left corner, a large locker-closet, painted
white, on the door of which a mirror hangs on a nail. In the rear
wall, two small square windows and a door opening out on the
deck toward the stern. In the right wall, two more windows looking out on the port deck. White curtains, clean and stiff, are at
the windows. A table with two cane-bottomed chairs stands in
the center of the cabin. A dilapidated, wicker rocker, painted
brown, is also by the table.*

*It is afternoon of a sunny day about a week later. From the
harbor and docks ontside, muffled by the closed door and windows, comes the sound of steamers' whistles and the puffing snort
of the donkey engines of some ship unloading nearby.*

As the curtain rises, CHRIS *and* ANNA *are discovered.* ANNA *is
seated in the rocking-chair by the table, with a newspaper in her
hands. She is not reading but staring straight in front of her.
She looks unhappy, troubled, frowningly concentrated on her
thoughts.* CHRIS *wanders about the room, casting quick, uneasy
side glances at her face, then stopping to peer absent-mindedly
out of the window. His attitude betrays an overwhelming, gloomy
anxiety which has him on tenterhooks. He pretends to be engaged
in setting things ship-shape, but this occupation is confined to
picking up some object, staring at it stupidly for a second, then
aimlessly putting it down again. He clears his throat and starts
to sing to himself in a low, doleful voice:* "My Yosephine, come
board de ship. Long time Ay vait for you."

ANNA [*turning on him, sarcastically*]: I'm glad someone's
feeling good. [*Wearily.*] Gee, I sure wish we was out of this
dump and back in New York.

CHRIS [*with a sigh*]: Ay'm glad vhen ve sail again, too.

[*Then, as she makes no comment, he goes on with a ponderous attempt at sarcasm.*] Ay don't see vhy you don't like Boston, dough. You have good time here, Ay tank. You go ashore all time, every day and night veek ve've been here. You go to movies, see show, gat all kinds fun—— [*His eyes hard with hatred.*] All with that damn Irish fallar!

ANNA [*with weary scorn*]: Oh, for heaven's sake, are you off on that again? Where's the harm in his taking me around? D'you want me to sit all day and night in this cabin with you —and knit? Ain't I got a right to have as good a time as I can?

CHRIS: It ain't right kind of fun—not with that fallar, no.

ANNA: I been back on board every night by eleven, ain't I? [*Then struck by some thought—looks at him with keen suspicion—with rising anger.*] Say, look here, what d'you mean by what you yust said?

CHRIS [*hastily*]: Nutting but what Ay say, Anna.

ANNA: You said "ain't right" and you said it funny. Say, listen here, you ain't trying to insinuate that there's something wrong between us, are you?

CHRIS [*horrified*]: No, Anna! No, Ay svaer to God, Ay never tank dat!

ANNA [*mollified by his very evident sincerity—sitting down again*]: Well, don't you never think it neither if you want me ever to speak to you again. [*Angrily again.*] If I ever dreamt you thought that, I'd get the hell out of this barge so quick you couldn't see me for dust.

CHRIS [*soothingly*]: Ay wouldn't never dream—— [*Then after a second's pause, reprovingly.*] You vas getting learn to svear. Dat ain't nice for young gel, you tank?

ANNA [*with a faint trace of a smile*]: Excuse me. You ain't used to such language, I know. [*Mockingly.*] That's what your taking me to sea has done for me.

CHRIS [*indignantly*]: No, it ain't me. It's dat damn sailor fallar learn you bad tangs.

ANNA: He ain't a sailor. He's a stoker.

CHRIS [*forcibly*]: Dat vas million times vorse, Ay tal you!

Dem fallars dat vork below shoveling coal vas de dirtiest, rough gang of no-good fallars in vorld!

ANNA: I'd hate to hear you say that to Mat.

CHRIS: Oh, Ay tal him same tang. You don't gat it in head Ay'm scared of him yust 'cause he vas stronger'n Ay vas. [*Menacingly.*] You don't gat for fight with fists with dem fallars. Dere's oder vay for fix him.

ANNA [*glancing at him with sudden alarm*]: What d'you mean?

CHRIS [*sullenly*]: Nutting.

ANNA: You'd better not. I wouldn't start no trouble with him if I was you. He might forget some time that you was old and my father—and then you'd be out of luck.

CHRIS [*with smoldering hatred*]: Vell, yust let him! Ay'm ole bird maybe, but Ay bet Ay show him trick or two.

ANNA [*suddenly changing her tone—persuasively*]: Aw come on, be good. What's eating you, anyway? Don't you want no one to be nice to me except yourself?

CHRIS [*placated—coming to her—eagerly*]: Yes, Ay do, Anna —only not fallar on sea. But Ay like for you marry steady fallar got good yob on land. You have little home in country all your own——

ANNA [*rising to her feet—brusquely*]: Oh, cut it out! [*Scornfully.*] Little home in the country! I wish you could have seen the little home in the country where you had me in jail till I was sixteen! [*With rising irritation.*] Some day you're going to get me so mad with that talk, I'm going to turn loose on you and tell you—a lot of things that'll open your eyes.

CHRIS [*alarmed*]: Ay don't vant——

ANNA: I know you don't; but you keep on talking yust the same.

CHRIS: Ay don't talk no more den, Anna.

ANNA: Then promise me you'll cut out saying nasty things about Mat Burke every chance you get.

CHRIS [*evasive and suspicious*]: Vhy? You like dat fallar— very much, Anna?

ANNA: Yes, I certainly do! He's a regular man, no matter

what faults he's got. One of his fingers is worth all the hundreds of men I met out there—inland.

CHRIS [*his face darkening*]: Maybe you tank you love him, den?

ANNA [*defiantly*]: What of it if I do?

CHRIS [*scowling and forcing out the words*]: Maybe—you tank you—marry him?

ANNA [*shaking her head*]: No! [CHRIS' *face lights up with relief.* ANNA *continues slowly, a trace of sadness in her voice.*] If I'd met him four years ago—or even two years ago—I'd have jumped at the chance, I tell you that straight. And I would now—only he's such a simple guy—a big kid—and I ain't got the heart to fool him. [*She breaks off suddenly.*] But don't never say again he ain't good enough for me. It's me ain't good enough for him.

CHRIS [*snorts scornfully*]: Py yimmy, you go crazy, Ay tank!

ANNA [*with a mournful laugh*]: Well, I been thinking I was myself the last few days. [*She goes and takes a shawl from a hook near the door and throws it over her shoulders.*] Guess I'll take a walk down to the end of the dock for a minute and see what's doing. I love to watch the ships passing. Mat'll be along before long, I guess. Tell him where I am, will you?

CHRIS [*despondently*]: All right, Ay tal him.

[ANNA *goes out the doorway in rear.* CHRIS *follows her out and stands on the deck outside for a moment looking after her. Then he comes back inside and shuts the door. He stands looking out of the window—mutters—"Dirty ole davil, you." Then he goes to the table, sets the cloth straight mechanically, picks up the newspaper* ANNA *has let fall to the floor and sits down in the rocking-chair. He stares at the paper for a while, then puts it on table, holds his head in his hands and sighs drearily. The noise of a man's heavy footsteps comes from the deck outside and there is a loud knock on the door.* CHRIS *starts, makes a move as if to get up and go to the door, then thinks better of it and sits still. The knock is repeated—then as no answer comes, the door is flung open and* MAT BURKE *appears.* CHRIS *scowls at the intruder and his hand instinctively goes back to the sheath knife on his hip.* BURKE *is dressed up—wears a cheap blue suit, a striped cotton shirt with a black tie, and black shoes newly shined. His face is beaming with good humor.*]

BURKE [*as he sees* CHRIS—*in a jovial tone of mockery*]: Well, God bless who's here! [*He bends down and squeezes his huge form through the narrow doorway.*] And how is the world treating you this afternoon, Anna's father?

CHRIS [*sullenly*]: Pooty goot—if it ain't for some fallars.

BURKE [*with a grin*]: Meaning me, do you? [*He laughs.*] Well, if you ain't the funny old crank of a man! [*Then soberly.*] Where's herself? [CHRIS *sits dumb, scowling, his eyes averted.* BURKE *is irritated by this silence.*] Where's Anna, I'm after asking you?

CHRIS [*hesitating—then grouchily*]: She go down end of dock.

BURKE: I'll be going down to her, then. But first I'm thinking I'll take this chance when we're alone to have a word with you. [*He sits down opposite* CHRIS *at the table and leans over toward him.*] And that word is soon said. I'm marrying your Anna before this day is out, and you might as well make up your mind to it whether you like it or no.

CHRIS [*glaring at him with hatred and forcing a scornful laugh*]: Ho-ho! Dat's easy for say!

BURKE: You mean I won't? [*Scornfully.*] Is it the like of yourself will stop me, are you thinking?

CHRIS: Yes, Ay stop it, if it comes to vorst.

BURKE [*with a scornful pity*]: God help you!

CHRIS: But ain't no need for me do dat. Anna——

BURKE [*smiling confidently*]: Is it Anna you think will prevent me?

CHRIS: Yes.

BURKE: And I'm telling you she'll not. She knows I'm loving her, and she loves me the same, and I know it.

CHRIS: Ho-ho! She only have fun. She make big fool of you, dat's all!

BURKE [*unshaken—pleasantly*]: That's a lie in your throat, divil mend you!

CHRIS: No, it ain't lie. She tal me yust before she go out she never marry fallar like you.

BURKE: I'll not believe it. 'Tis a great old liar you are, and a divil to be making a power of trouble if you had your way. But 'tis not trouble I'm looking for, and me sitting down here. [*Earnestly.*] Let us be talking it out now as man to man. You're her father, and wouldn't it be a shame for us to be at each other's throats like a pair of dogs, and I married with Anna? So out with the truth, man alive. What is it you're holding against me at all?

CHRIS [*a bit placated, in spite of himself, by* BURKE's *evident sincerity—but puzzled and suspicious*]: Vell—Ay don't vant for Anna get married. Listen, you fallar. Ay'm a ole man. Ay don't see Anna for fifteen years. She vas all Ay gat in vorld. And now ven she come on first trip—you tank Ay vant her leave me 'lone again?

BURKE [*heartily*]: Let you not be thinking I have no heart at all for the way you'd be feeling.

CHRIS [*astonished and encouraged—trying to plead persuasively*]: Den you do right tang, eh? You ship avay again, leave Anna alone. [*Cajolingly.*] Big fallar like you dat's on sea, he don't need vife. He gat new gel in every port, you know dat.

BURKE [*angrily for a second*]: God stiffen you! [*Then controlling himself—calmly.*] I'll not be giving you the lie on that. But divil take you, there's a time comes to every man, on sea or land, that isn't a born fool, when he's sick of the lot of them cows, and wearing his heart out to meet up with a fine dacent girl, and have a home to call his own and be rearing up children in it. 'Tis small use you're asking me to leave Anna. She's the wan woman of the world for me, and I can't live without her now, I'm thinking.

CHRIS: You forget all about her in one veek out of port, Ay bet you!

BURKE: You don't know the like I am. Death itself wouldn't

make me forget her. So let you not be making talk to me about leaving her. I'll not, and be damned to you! It won't be so bad for you as you'd make out at all. She'll be living here in the States, and her married to me. And you'd be seeing her often so—a sight more often than ever you saw her the fifteen years she was growing up in the West. It's quare you'd be the one to be making great trouble about her leaving you when you never laid eyes on her once in all them years.

CHRIS [*guiltily*]: Ay taught it vas better Anna stay away, grow up inland vhere she don't ever know ole davil, sea.

BURKE [*scornfully*]: Is it blaming the sea for your troubles ye are again, God help you? Well, Anna knows it now. 'Twas in her blood, anyway.

CHRIS: And Ay don't vant she ever know no-good fallar on sea——

BURKE: She knows one now.

CHRIS [*banging the table with his fist—furiously*]: Dat's yust it! Dat's yust what you are—no-good sailor fallar! You tank Ay lat her life be made sorry by you like her mo'der's vas by me! No, Ay svear! She don't marry you if Ay gat kill you first!

BURKE [*looks at him a moment, in astonishment—then laughing uproariously*]: Ho-ho! Glory be to God, it's bold talk you have for a stumpy runt of a man!

CHRIS [*threateningly*]: Vell—you see!

BURKE [*with grinning defiance*]: I'll see, surely! I'll see myself and Anna married this day, I'm telling you. [*Then with contemptuous exasperation.*] It's quare fool's blather you have about the sea done this and the sea done that. You'd ought to be 'shamed to be saying the like, and you an old sailor yourself. I'm after hearing a lot of it from you and a lot more that Anna's told me you do be saying to her, and I'm thinking it's a poor weak thing you are, and not a man at all!

CHRIS [*darkly*]: You see if Ay'm man—maybe quicker'n you tank.

BURKE [*contemptuously*]: Yerra, don't be boasting. I'm

thinking 'tis out of your wits you've got with fright of the sea. You'd be wishing Anna married to a farmer, she told me. That'd be a swate match, surely! Would you have a fine girl the like of Anna lying down at nights with a muddy scut stinking of pigs and dung? Or would you have her tied for life to the like of them skinny, shriveled swabs does be working in cities?

CHRIS: Dat's lie, you fool!

BURKE: 'Tis not. 'Tis your own mad notions I'm after telling. But you know the truth in your heart, if great fear of the sea has made you a liar and coward itself. [*Pounding the table.*] The sea's the only life for a man with guts in him isn't afraid of his own shadow! 'Tis only on the sea he's free, and him roving the face of the world, seeing all things, and not giving a damn for saving up money, or stealing from his friends, or any of the black tricks that a landlubber'd waste his life on. 'Twas yourself knew it once, and you a bo'sun for years.

CHRIS [*sputtering with rage*]: You vas crazy fool, Ay tal you!

BURKE: You've swallowed the anchor. The sea gives you a clout once, knocked you down, and you're not man enough to get up for another, but lie there for the rest of your life howling bloody murder. [*Proudly.*] Isn't it myself the sea has nearly drowned, and me battered and bate till I was that close to hell I could hear the flames roaring, and never a groan out of me till the sea gave up and it seeing the great strength and guts of a man was in me?

CHRIS [*scornfully*]: Yes, you vas hell of fallar, hear you tal it!

BURKE [*angrily*]: You'll be calling me a liar once too often, me old bucko! Wasn't the whole story of it and my picture itself in the newspapers of Boston a week back? [*Looking* CHRIS *up and down belittlingly.*] Sure I'd like to see you in the best of your youth do the like of what I done in the storm and after. 'Tis a mad lunatic, screeching with fear, you'd be this minute!

CHRIS: Ho-ho! You vas young fool! In ole years when Ay vas on windyammer, Ay vas through hundred storms vorse'n dat! Ships vas ships den—and men dat sail on dem vas real men. And now what you gat on steamers? You gat fallars on deck don't know ship from mudscow. [*With a meaning glance at* BURKE.] And below deck you gat fallars yust know how for shovel coal—might yust as vell work on coal vagon ashore!

BURKE [*stung—angrily*]: Is it casting insults at the men in the stokehole ye are, ye old ape? God stiffen you! Wan of them is worth any ten stock-fish-swilling Square-heads ever shipped on a windbag!

CHRIS [*his face working with rage, his hand going back to the sheath-knife on his hip*]: Irish swine, you!

BURKE [*tauntingly*]: Don't ye like the Irish, ye old baboon? 'Tis that you're needing in your family, I'm telling you—an Irishman and a man of the stokehole—to put guts in it so that you'll not be having grandchildren would be fearful cowards and jackasses the like of yourself!

CHRIS [*half rising from his chair—in a voice choked with rage*]: You look out!

BURKE [*watching him intently—a mocking smile on his lips*]: And it's that you'll be having, no matter what you'll do to prevent; for Anna and me'll be married this day, and no old fool the like of you will stop us when I've made up my mind.

CHRIS [*with a hoarse cry*]: You don't! [*He throws himself at* BURKE, *knife in hand, knocking his chair over backwards.* BURKE *springs to his feet quickly in time to meet the attack. He laughs with the pure love of battle. The old Swede is like a child in his hands.* BURKE *does not strike or mistreat him in any way, but simply twists his right hand behind his back and forces the knife from his fingers. He throws the knife into a far corner of the room—tauntingly.*]

BURKE: Old men is getting childish shouldn't play with knifes. [*Holding the struggling* CHRIS *at arm's length—with a sudden rush of anger, drawing back his fist.*] I've half a mind to hit you a great clout will put sense in your square head. Kape off me now, I'm warning you! [*He gives* CHRIS *a push with the flat of his hand which sends the old Swede staggering back against the cabin wall, where he remains standing, panting heavily, his eyes fixed on* BURKE *with hatred, as if he were only collecting his strength to rush at him again.*]

BURKE [*warningly*]: Now don't be coming at me again, I'm saying, or I'll flatten you on the floor with a blow, if 'tis Anna's father you are itself! I've not patience left for you. [*Then with an amused laugh.*] Well, 'tis a bold old man you are just the same, and I'd never think it was in you to come tackling me alone.

[*A shadow crosses the cabin windows. Both men start.* ANNA *appears in the doorway.*]

ANNA [*with pleased surprise as she sees* BURKE.] Hello, Mat. Are you here already? I was down—— [*She stops, looking from one to the other, sensing immediately that something has happened.*] What's up? [*Then noticing the overturned chair —in alarm.*] How'd that chair get knocked over? [*Turning on* BURKE *reproachfully.*] You ain't been fighting with him, Mat —after you promised?

BURKE [*his old self again*]: I've not laid a hand on him, Anna. [*He goes and picks up the chair, then turning on the still questioning* ANNA—*with a reassuring smile.*] Let you not be worried at all. 'Twas only a bit of an argument we was having to pass the time till you'd come.

ANNA: It must have been some argument when you got to throwing chairs. [*She turns on* CHRIS.] Why don't you say something? What was it about?

CHRIS [*relaxing at last—avoiding her eyes—sheepishly*]: Ve vas talking about ships and fallars on sea.

ANNA [*with a relieved smile*]: Oh—the old stuff, eh?

BURKE [*suddenly seeming to come to a bold decision—with a defiant grin at* CHRIS]: He's not after telling you the whole of it. He was arguing about you mostly.

ANNA [*with a frown*]: About me?

BURKE: And we'll be finishing it out right here and now in your presence if you're willing. [*He sits down at the left of table.*]

ANNA [*uncertainly—looking from him to her father*]: Sure. Tell me what it's all about.

CHRIS [*advancing toward the table—protesting to* BURKE]: No! You don't do dat, you! You tal him you don't vant for hear him talk, Anna.

ANNA: But I do. I want this cleared up.

CHRIS [*miserably afraid now*]: Vell, not now, anyvay. You vas going ashore, yes? You ain't got time——

ANNA [*firmly*]: Yes, right here and now. [*She turns to* BURKE.] You tell me, Mat, since he don't want to.

BURKE [*draws a deep breath—then plunges in boldly*]: The whole of it's in a few words only. So's he'd make no mistake, and him hating the sight of me. I told him in his teeth I loved you. [*Passionately.*] And that's God truth, Anna, and well you know it!

CHRIS [*scornfully—forcing a laugh.*]: Ho-ho! He tal same tang to gel every port he go!

ANNA [*shrinking from her father with repulsion—resentfully*]: Shut up, can't you? [*Then to* BURKE—*feelingly.*] I know it's true, Mat. I don't mind what he says.

BURKE [*humbly grateful*]: God bless you!

ANNA: And then what?

BURKE: And then—— [*Hesitatingly.*] And then I said—— [*He looks at her pleadingly.*] I said I was sure—I told him I thought you have a bit of love for me, too. [*Passionately.*] Say you do, Anna! Let you not destroy me entirely, for the love of God! [*He grasps both her hands in his two.*]

ANNA [*deeply moved and troubled—forcing a trembling laugh*]: So you told him that, Mat? No wonder he was mad. [*Forcing out the words.*] Well, maybe it's true, Mat. Maybe I do. I been thinking and thinking—I didn't want to, Mat, I'll own up to that—I tried to cut it out—but—— [*She laughs helplessly.*] I guess I can't help it anyhow. So I guess I do,

Mat. [*Then with a sudden joyous defiance.*] Sure I do! What's the use of kidding myself different? Sure I love you, Mat!

CHRIS [*with a cry of pain*]: Anna! [*He sits crushed.*]

BURKE [*with a great depth of sincerity in his humble gratitude*]: God be praised!

ANNA [*assertively*]: And I ain't never loved a man in my life before, you can always believe that—no matter what happens.

BURKE [*goes over to her and puts his arms around her*]: Sure I do be believing ivery word you iver said or iver will say. And 'tis you and me will be having a grand, beautiful life together to the end of our days! [*He tries to kiss her. At first she turns away her head—then, overcome by a fierce impulse of passionate love, she takes his head in both her hands and holds his face close to hers, staring into his eyes. Then she kisses him full on the lips.*]

ANNA [*pushing him away from her—forcing a broken laugh*]: Good-by. [*She walks to the doorway in rear—stands with her back toward them, looking out. Her shoulders quiver once or twice as if she were fighting back her sobs.*]

BURKE [*too in the seventh heaven of bliss to get any correct interpretation of her word—with a laugh*]: Good-by, is it? The divil you say! I'll be coming back at you in a second for more of the same! [*To* CHRIS, *who has quickened to instant attention at his daughter's good-by, and has looked back at her with a stirring of foolish hope in his eyes.*] Now, me old bucko, what'll you be saying? You heard the words from her own lips. Confess I've bate you. Own up like a man when you're bate fair and square. And here's my hand to you—— [*Holds out his hand.*] And let you take it and we'll shake and forget what's over and done, and be friends from this out.

CHRIS [*with implacable hatred*]: Ay don't shake hands with you fallar—not vhile Ay live!

BURKE [*offended*]: The back of my hand to you then, if that suits you better. [*Growling.*] 'Tis a rotten bad loser you are, divil mend you!

CHRIS: Ay don't lose. [*Trying to be scornful and self-convincing.*] Anna say she like you little bit but you don't hear her say she marry you, Ay bet. [*At the sound of her name* ANNA *has turned round to them. Her face is composed and calm again, but it is the dead calm of despair.*]

BURKE [*scornfully*]: No, and I wasn't hearing her say the sun is shining either.

CHRIS [*doggedly*]: Dat's all right. She don't say it, yust same.

ANNA [*quietly—coming forward to them*]: No, I didn't say it, Mat.

CHRIS [*eagerly*]: Dere! You hear!

BURKE [*misunderstang her—with a grin*]: You're waiting till you do be asked, you mane? Well, I'm asking you now. And we'll be married this day, with the help of God!

ANNA [*gently*]: You heard what I said, Mat—after I kissed you?

BURKE [*alarmed by something in her manner*]: No—I disremember.

ANNA: I said good-by. [*Her voice trembling.*] That kiss was for good-by, Mat.

BURKE [*terrified*]: What d'you mane?

ANNA: I can't marry you, Mat—and we've said good-by. That's all.

CHRIS [*unable to hold back his exultation*]: Ay know it! Ay know dat vas so!

BURKE [*jumping to his feet—unable to believe his ears*]: Anna! Is it making game of me you'd be? 'Tis a quare time to joke with me, and don't be doing it, for the love of God.

ANNA [*looking him in the eyes—steadily*]: D'you think I'd kid you? No, I'm not joking, Mat. I mean what I said.

BURKE: Ye don't! Ye can't! 'Tis mad you are, I'm telling you!

ANNA [*fixedly*]: No, I'm not.

BURKE [*desperately*]: But what's come over you so sudden? You was saying you loved me——

ANNA: I'll say that as often as you want me to. It's true.

BURKE [*bewilderedly*]: Then why—what, in the divil's name—— Oh, God help me, I can't make head or tail to it at all!

ANNA: Because it's the best way out I can figure, Mat. [*Her voice catching.*] I been thinking it over and thinking it over day and night all week. Don't think it ain't hard on me, too, Mat.

BURKE: For the love of God, tell me then, what is it that's preventing you wedding me when the two of us have love? [*Suddenly getting an idea and pointing at* CHRIS—*exasperatedly.*] Is it giving heed to the like of that old fool ye are, and him hating me and filling your ears full of bloody lies against me?

CHRIS [*getting to his feet—raging triumphantly before* ANNA *has a chance to get in a word*]: Yes, Anna believe me, not you! She know her old fa'der don't lie like you.

ANNA [*turning on her father angrily*]: You sit down, d'you hear? Where do you come in butting in and making things worse? You're like a devil, you are! [*Harshly.*] Good Lord, and I was beginning to like you, beginning to forget all I've got held up against you!

CHRIS [*crushed feebly*]: You ain't got nutting for hold against me, Anna.

ANNA: Ain't I yust! Well, lemme tell you—— [*She glances at* BURKE *and stops abruptly.*] Say, Mat, I'm s'prised at you. You didn't think anything he'd said——

BURKE [*glumly*]: Sure, what else would it be?

ANNA: Think I've ever paid any attention to all his crazy bull? Gee, you must take me for a five-year-old kid.

BURKE [*puzzled and beginning to be irritated at her too*]: I don't know how to take you, with your saying this one minute and that the next.

ANNA: Well, he has nothing to do with it.

BURKE: Then what is it has? Tell me, and don't keep me waiting and sweating blood.

ANNA [*resolutely*]: I can't tell you—and I won't. I got a good reason—and that's all you need to know. I can't marry you, that's all there is to it. [*Distractedly.*] So, for Gawd's sake, let's talk of something else.

BURKE: I'll not! [*Then fearfully.*] Is it married to someone else you are—in the West maybe?

ANNA [*vehemently*]: I should say not.

BURKE [*regaining his courage*]: To the divil with all other reasons then. They don't matter with me at all. [*He gets to his feet confidently, assuming a masterful tone.*] I'm thinking you're the like of them women can't make up their mind till they're drove to it. Well, then, I'll make up your mind for you bloody quick. [*He takes her by the arms, grinning to soften his serious bullying*]. We've had enough of talk! Let you be going into your room now and be dressing in your best and we'll be going ashore.

CHRIS [*aroused—angrily*]: No, py God, she don't do that! [*Takes hold of her arm.*]

ANNA [*who has listened to* BURKE *in astonishment. She draws away from him, instinctively repelled by his tone, but not exactly sure if he is serious or not—a trace of resentment in her voice*]: Say, where do you get that stuff?

BURKE [*imperiously*]: Never mind, now! Let you go get dressed, I'm saying. [*Then turning to* CHRIS.] We'll be seeing who'll win in the end—me or you.

CHRIS [*to* ANNA—*also in an authoritative tone*]: You stay right here, Anna, you hear! [ANNA *stands looking from one to the other of them as if she thought they had both gone crazy. Then the expression of her face freezes into the hardened sneer of her experience.*]

BURKE [*violently*]: She'll not! She'll do what I say! You've had your hold on her long enough. It's my turn now.

ANNA [*with a hard laugh*]: Your turn? Say, what am I, anyway?

BURKE: 'Tis not what you are, 'tis what you're going to be this day—and that's wedded to me before night comes. Hurry up now with your dressing.

CHRIS [*commandingly*]: You don't do one tang he say, Anna! [ANNA *laughs mockingly.*]

BURKE: She will, so!

CHRIS: Ay tal you she don't! Ay'm her fa'der.

BURKE: She will in spite of you. She's taking my orders from this out, not yours.

ANNA [*laughing again*]: Orders is good!

BURKE [*turning to her impatiently*]: Hurry up now, and shake a leg. We've no time to be wasting. [*Irritated as she doesn't move.*] Do you hear what I'm telling you?

CHRIS: You stay dere, Anna!

ANNA [*at the end of her patience—blazing out at them passionately*]: You can go to hell, both of you! [*There is something in her tone that makes them forget their quarrel and turn to her in a stunned amazement.* ANNA *laughs wildly.*] You're just like all the rest of them—you two! Gawd, you'd think I was a piece of furniture! I'll show you! Sit down now! [*As they hesitate—furiously.*] Sit down and let me talk for a minute. You're all wrong, see? Listen to me! I'm going to tell you something—and then I'm going to beat it. [*To* BURKE—*with a harsh laugh.*] I'm going to tell you a funny story, so pay attention. [*Pointing to* CHRIS.] I've been meaning to turn it loose on him every time he'd get my goat with his bull about keeping me safe inland. I wasn't going to tell you, but you've forced me into it. What's the dif? It's all wrong anyway, and you might as well get cured that way as any other. [*With hard mocking.*] Only don't forget what you said a minute ago about it not mattering to you what other reason I got so long as I wasn't married to no one else.

BURKE [*manfully*]: That's my word, and I'll stick to it!

ANNA [*laughing bitterly*]: What a chance! You make me laugh, honest! Want to bet you will? Wait 'n see! [*She stands at the table rear, looking from one to the other of the two men with her hard, mocking smile. Then she begins, fighting to control her emotion and speak calmly.*] First thing is, I want to tell you two guys something. You was going on 's if one of you had got to own me. But nobody owns me, see?— 'cepting myself. I'll do what I please and no man, I don't give a hoot who he is, can tell me what to do! I ain't asking either

of you for a living. I can make it myself—one way or other.
I'm my own boss. So put that in your pipe and smoke it! You
and your orders!

BURKE [*protestingly*]: I wasn't meaning it that way at all
and well you know it. You've no call to be raising this rumpus with me. [*Pointing to* CHRIS.] 'Tis him you've a right——

ANNA: I'm coming to him. But you—you did mean it that
way, too. You sounded—yust like all the rest. [*Hysterically.*]
But, damn it, shut up! Let me talk for a change!

BURKE: 'Tis quare, rough talk, that—for a dacent girl the
like of you!

ANNA [*with a hard laugh*]: Decent? Who told you I was?
[CHRIS *is sitting with bowed shoulders, his head in his hands.
She leans over him in exasperation and shakes him violently
by the shoulder.*] Don't go to sleep, Old Man! Listen here,
I'm talking to you now!

CHRIS [*straightening up and looking about as if he were
seeking a way to escape—with frightened foreboding in his
voice*]: Ay don't vant for hear it. You vas going out of head,
Ay tank, Anna.

ANNA [*violently*]: Well, living with you is enough to drive
anyone off their nut. Your bunk about the farm being so fine!
Didn't I write you year after year how rotten it was and
what a dirty slave them cousins made of me? What'd you
care? Nothing! Not even enough to come out and see me!
That crazy bull about wanting to keep me away from the sea
don't go down with me! You yust didn't want to be bothered
with me! You're like all the rest of 'em!

CHRIS [*feebly*]: Anna! It ain't so——

ANNA [*not heeding his interruption—revengefully*]: But
one thing I never wrote you. It was one of them cousins that
you think is such nice people—the youngest son—Paul—that
started me wrong. [*Loudly.*] It wasn't none of my fault. I
hated him worse'n hell and he knew it. But he was big and
strong—[*pointing to* BURKE]—like you!

BURKE [*half springing to his feet—his fists clenched*]: God
blarst it! [*He sinks slowly back in his chair again, the*

knuckles showing white on his clenched hands, his face tense with the effort to suppress his grief and rage.]

CHRIS [*in a cry of horrified pain*]: Anna!

ANNA [*to him—seeming not to have heard their interruptions*]: That was why I run away from the farm. That was what made me get a yob as nurse girl in St. Paul. [*With a hard, mocking laugh.*] And you think that was a nice yob for a girl, too, don't you? [*Sarcastically.*] With all of them nice inland fellers yust looking for a chance to marry me, I s'pose. Marry me? What a chance! They wasn't looking for marrying. [*As* BURKE *lets a groan of fury escape him—desperately.*] I'm owning up to everything fair and square. I was caged in, I tell you—yust like in yail—taking care of other people's kids—listening to 'em bawling and crying day and night—when I wanted to be out—and I was lonesome—lonesome as hell! [*With a sudden weariness in her voice.*] So I give up finally. What was the use? [*She stops and looks at the two men. Both are motionless and silent.* CHRIS *seems in a stupor of despair, his house of cards fallen about him.* BURKE's *face is livid with the rage that is eating him up, but he is too stunned and bewildered yet to find a vent for it. The condemnation she feels in their silence goads* ANNA *into a harsh, strident defiance.*] You don't say nothing—either of you—but I know what you're thinking. You're like all the rest! [*To* CHRIS—*furiously.*] And who's to blame for it, me or you? If you'd even acted like a man—if you'd even had been a regular father and had me with you—maybe things would be different!

CHRIS [*in agony*]: Don't talk dat vay, Anna! Ay go crazy! Ay won't listen! [*Puts his hands over his ears.*]

ANNA [*infuriated by his action—stridently*]: You will too listen! [*She leans over and pulls his hands from his ears—with hysterical rage.*] You—keeping me safe inland—I wasn't no nurse girl the last two years—I lied when I wrote you—I was in a house, that's what!—yes, that kind of a house—the kind sailors like you and Mat goes to in port—and your nice inland men, too—and all men, God damn 'em! I hate 'em!

Hate 'em! [*She breaks into hysterical sobbing, throwing her-self into the chair and hiding her face in her hands on the table. The two men have sprung to their feet.*]

CHRIS [*whimpering like a child*]: Anna! Anna! It's a lie! It's a lie! [*He stands wringing his hands together and begins to weep.*]

BURKE [*his whole great body tense like a spring—dully and gropingly*]: So that's what's in it!

ANNA [*raising her head at the sound of his voice—with ex-treme mocking bitterness*]: I s'pose you remember your promise, Mat? No other reason was to count with you so long as I wasn't married already. So I s'pose you want me to get dressed and go ashore, don't you? [*She laughs.*] Yes, you do!

BURKE [*on the verge of his outbreak—stammering*]: God stiffen you!

ANNA [*trying to keep up her hard, bitter tone, but gradually letting a note of pitiful pleading creep in*]: I s'pose if I tried to tell you I wasn't—that—no more you'd believe me, wouldn't you? Yes, you would! And if I told you that yust getting out in this barge, and being on the sea had changed me and made me feel different about things, 's if all I'd been through wasn't me and didn't count and was yust like it never hap-pened—you'd laugh, wouldn't you? And you'd die laughing sure if I said that meeting you that funny way that night in the fog, and afterwards seeing that you was straight goods stuck on me, had got me to thinking for the first time, and I sized you up as a different kind of man—a sea man as differ-ent from the ones on land as water is from mud—and that was why I got stuck on you, too. I wanted to marry you and fool you, but I couldn't. Don't you see how I've changed? I couldn't marry you with you believing a lie—and I was shamed to tell you the truth—till the both of you forced my hand, and I seen you was the same as all the rest. And now, give me a bawling out and beat it, like I can tell you're going to. [*She stops, looking at* BURKE. *He is silent, his face averted, his features beginning to work with fury. She pleads passionately.*] Will you believe it if I tell you that loving you has made me—clean? It's the straight goods, honest! [*Then as he doesn't reply—bitterly.*] Like hell you will! You're like all the rest!

BURKE [*blazing out—turning on her in a perfect frenzy of rage—his voice trembling with passion*]: The rest, is it? God's curse on you! Clane, is it? You slut, you, I'll be killing you now! [*He picks up the chair on which he has been sitting and, swinging it high over his shoulder, springs toward her. CHRIS rushes forward with a cry of alarm, trying to ward off the blow from his daughter. ANNA looks up into BURKE's eyes with a fearlessness of despair. BURKE checks himself, the chair held in the air.*]

CHRIS [*wildly*]: Stop, you crazy fool! You vant for murder her!

ANNA [*pushing her father away brusquely, her eyes still holding BURKE's*]: Keep out of this, you! [*To BURKE—dully.*] Well, ain't you got the nerve to do it? Go ahead! I'll be thankful to you, honest. I'm sick of the whole game.

BURKE [*throwing the chair away into a corner of the room —helplessly*]: I can't do it, God help me, and your two eyes looking at me. [*Furiously.*] Though I do be thinking I'd have a good right to smash your skull like a rotten egg. Was there iver a woman in the world had the rottenness in her that you have, and was there iver a man the like of me was made the fool of the world, and me thinking thoughts about you, and having great love for you, and dreaming dreams of the fine life we'd have when we'd be wedded! [*His voice high pitched in a lamentation that is like a keen.*] Yerra, God help me! I'm destroyed entirely and my heart is broken in bits! I'm asking God Himself, was it for this He'd have me roaming the earth since I was a lad only, to come to black shame in the end, where I'd be giving a power of love to a woman is the same as others you'd meet in any hooker-shanty in port, with red gowns on them and paint on their grinning mugs, would be sleeping with any man for a dollar or two!

ANNA [*in a scream*]: Don't, Mat! For Gawd's sake! [*Then

raging and pounding on the table with her hands.] Get out of here! Leave me alone! Get out of here!

BURKE [*his anger rushing back on him*]: I'll be going, surely! And I'll be drinking sloos of whisky will wash that black kiss of yours off my lips; and I'll be getting dead rotten drunk so I'll not remember if 'twas iver born you was at all; and I'll be shipping away on some boat will take me to the other end of the world where I'll never see your face again! [*He turns toward the door.*]

CHRIS [*who has been standing in a stupor—suddenly grasping* BURKE *by the arm—stupidly*]: No, you don't go. Ay tank maybe it's better Anna marry you now.

BURKE [*shaking* CHRIS *off—furiously*]: Lave go of me, ye old ape! Marry her, it is? I'd see her roasting in hell first! I'm shipping away out of this, I'm telling you! [*Pointing to* ANNA—*passionately.*] And my curse on you and the curse of Almighty God and all the Saints! You've destroyed me this day and may you lie awake in the long nights, tormented with thoughts of Mat Burke and the great wrong you've done him!

ANNA [*in anguish*]: Mat! [*But he turns without another word and strides out of the doorway.* ANNA *looks after him wildly, starts to run after him, then hides her face in her outstretched arms, sobbing.* CHRIS *stands in a stupor, staring at the floor.*]

CHRIS [*after a pause, dully*]: Ay tank Ay go ashore, too.

ANNA [*looking up, wildly*]: Not after him! Let him go! Don't you dare——

CHRIS [*somberly*]: Ay go for gat drink.

ANNA [*with a harsh laugh*]: So I'm driving you to drink, too, eh? I s'pose you want to get drunk so's you can forget—like him?

CHRIS [*bursting out angrily*]: Yes, Ay vant! You tank Ay like hear dem tangs. [*Breaking down—weeping.*] Ay tank you vasn't dat kind of gel, Anna.

ANNA [*mockingly*]: And I s'pose you want me to beat it, don't you? You don't want me here disgracing you, I s'pose?

CHRIS: No, you stay here! [*Goes over and pats her on the shoulder, the tears running down his face.*] Ain't your fault, Anna, Ay know dat. [*She looks up at him, softened. He bursts into rage.*] It's dat ole davil, sea, do this to me! [*He shakes his fist at the door.*] It's her dirty tricks! It vas all right on barge with yust you and me. Den she brings dat Irish fallar in fog, she make you like him, she make you fight with me all time! If dat Irish fallar don't never come, you don't never tal me dem tangs, Ay don't never know, and everytang's all right. [*He shakes his fist again.*] Dirty ole davil!

ANNA [*with spent weariness*]: Oh, what's the use? Go on ashore and get drunk.

CHRIS [*goes into room on left and gets his cap. He goes to the door, silent and stupid—then turns*]: You vait here, Anna?

ANNA [*dully*]: Maybe—and maybe not. Maybe I'll get drunk, too. Maybe I'll—— But what the hell do you care what I do? Go on and beat it.

[CHRIS *turns stupidly and goes out.* ANNA *sits at the table, staring straight in front of her.*]

[The Curtain Falls]

ACT FOUR

SCENE—*Same as Act Three, about nine o'clock of a foggy night two days later. The whistles of steamers in the harbor can be heard. The cabin is lighted by a small lamp on the table. A suit case stands in the middle of the floor.* ANNA *is sitting in the rocking-chair. She wears a hat, is all dressed up as in Act One. Her face is pale, looks terribly tired and worn, as if the two days just past had been ones of suffering and sleepless nights. She stares before her despondently, her chin in her hands. There is a timid knock on the door in rear.* ANNA *jumps to her feet with a startled exclamation and looks toward the door with an expression of mingled hope and fear.*

ANNA [*faintly*]: Come in. [*Then summoning her courage —more resolutely.*] Come in.

[*The door is opened and* CHRIS *appears in the doorway. He is in a very bleary, bedraggled condition, suffering from the after-effects of his drunk. A tin pail full of foaming beer is in his hand. He comes forward, his eyes avoiding* ANNA's. *He mutters stupidly.*] It's foggy.

ANNA [*looking him over with contempt*]: So you come back at last, did you? You're a fine looking sight! [*Then jeeringly.*] I thought you'd beaten it for good on account of the disgrace I'd brought on you.

CHRIS [*wincing—faintly*]: Don't say dat, Anna, please! [*He sits in a chair by the table, setting down the can of beer, holding his head in his hands.*]

ANNA [*looks at him with a certain sympathy*]: What's the trouble? Feeling sick?

CHRIS [*dully*]: Inside my head feel sick.

ANNA: Well, what d'you expect after being soused for two days? [*Resentfully.*] It serves you right. A fine thing—you leaving me alone on this barge all that time!

63

CHRIS [*humbly*]: Ay'm sorry, Anna.

ANNA [*scornfully*]: Sorry!

CHRIS: But Ay'm not sick inside head vay you mean. Ay'm sick from tank too much about you, about me.

ANNA: And how about me? D'you suppose I ain't been thinking, too?

CHRIS: Ay'm sorry, Anna. [*He sees her bag and gives a start.*] You pack your bag, Anna? You vas going——?

ANNA [*forcibly*]: Yes, I was going right back to what you think.

CHRIS: Anna!

ANNA: I went ashore to get a train for New York. I'd been waiting and waiting till I was sick of it. Then I changed my mind and decided not to go today. But I'm going first thing tomorrow, so it'll all be the same in the end.

CHRIS [*raising his head—pleadingly*]: No, you never do dat, Anna!

ANNA [*with a sneer*]: Why not, I'd like to know?

CHRIS: You don't never gat to do—dat vay—no more, Ay tal you. Ay fix dat up all right.

ANNA [*suspiciously*]: Fix what up?

CHRIS [*not seeming to have heard her question—sadly*]: You vas vaiting, you say? You vasn't vaiting for me, Ay bet.

ANNA [*callously*]: You'd win.

CHRIS: For dat Irish fallar?

ANNA [*defiantly*]: Yes—if you want to know! [*Then with a forlorn laugh.*] If he did come back it'd only be 'cause he wanted to beat me up or kill me, I suppose. But even if he did, I'd rather have him come than not show up at all. I wouldn't care what he did.

CHRIS: Ay guess it's true you vas in love with him all right.

ANNA: You guess!

CHRIS [*turning to her earnestly*]: And Ay'm sorry for you like hell he don't come, Anna!

ANNA [*softened*]: Seems to me you've changed your tune a lot.

CHRIS: Ay've been tanking, and Ay guess it vas all my fault

—all bad tangs dat happen to you. [*Pleadingly.*] You try for not hate me, Anna. Ay'm crazy old fool, dat's all.

ANNA: Who said I hated you?

CHRIS: Ay'm sorry for everytang Ay do wrong for you, Anna. Ay vant for you be happy all rest of your life for make up! It make you happy marry dat Irish fallar, Ay vant it, too.

ANNA [*dully*]: Well, there ain't no chance. But I'm glad you think different about it, anyway.

CHRIS [*supplicatingly*]: And you tank—maybe—you forgive me sometime?

ANNA [*with a wan smile*]: I'll forgive you right now.

CHRIS [*seizing her hand and kissing it—brokenly*]: Anna lilla! Anna lilla!

ANNA [*touched but a bit embarrassed*]: Don't bawl about it. There ain't nothing to forgive, anyway. It ain't your fault, and it ain't mine, and it ain't his neither. We're all poor nuts, and things happen, and we yust get mixed in wrong, that's all.

CHRIS [*eagerly*]: You say right tang, Anna, py golly! It ain't nobody's fault! [*Shaking his fist.*] It's dat ole davil sea!

ANNA [*with an exasperated laugh*]: Gee, won't you ever can that stuff? [CHRIS *relapses into injured silence. After a pause* ANNA *continues curiously.*] You said a minute ago you'd fixed something up—about me. What was it?

CHRIS [*after a hesitating pause*]: Ay'm shipping avay on sea again, Anna.

ANNA [*astounded*]: You're—what?

CHRIS: Ay sign on steamer sail tomorrow. Ay gat my ole yob—bo'sun. [ANNA *stares at him. As he goes on, a bitter smile comes over her face.*] Ay tank dat's best tang for you. Ay only bring you bad luck, Ay tank. Ay make your mo'der's life sorry. Ay don't vant make yours dat way, but Ay do yust same. Dat ole davil, sea, she make me Yonah man ain't no good for nobody. And Ay tank now it ain't no use fight with sea. No man dat live going to beat her, py yingo!

ANNA [*with a laugh of helpless bitterness*]: So that's how you've fixed me, is it?

CHRIS: Yes, Ay tank if dat ole davil gat me back she leave you alone den.

ANNA [*bitterly*]: But, for Gawd's sake, don't you see you're doing the same thing, you've always done? Don't you see——? [*But she sees the look of obsessed stubbornness on her father's face and gives it up helplessly.*] But what's the use of talking? You ain't right, that's what. I'll never blame you for nothing no more. But how you could figure out that was fixing me——!

CHRIS: Dat ain't all. Ay gat dem fallars in steamship office to pay you all money coming to me every month vhile Ay'm avay.

ANNA [*with a hard laugh*]: Thanks. But I guess I won't be hard up for no small change.

CHRIS [*hurt—humbly*]: It ain't much, Ay know, but it's plenty for keep you so you never gat go back——

ANNA [*shortly*]: Shut up, will you? We'll talk about it later, see?

CHRIS [*after a pause—ingratiatingly*]: You like Ay go ashore look for dat Irish fallar, Anna?

ANNA [*angrily*]: Not much! Think I want to drag him back?

CHRIS [*after a pause—uncomfortably*]: Py golly, dat booze don't go vell. Give me fever, Ay tank. Ay feel hot like hell. [*He takes off his coat and lets it drop on the floor. There is a loud thud.*]

ANNA [*with a start*]: What you got in your pocket, for Pete's sake—a ton of lead? [*She reaches down, takes the coat and pulls out a revolver—looks from it to him in amazement.*] A gun? What were you doing with this?

CHRIS [*sheepishly*]: Ay forget. Ain't nothing. Ain't loaded, anyvay.

ANNA [*breaking it open to make sure—than closing it again —looking at him suspiciously*]: That ain't telling me why you got it?

CHRIS: Ay'm ole fool. Ay got it when Ay go ashore first. Ay tank den it's all fault of dat Irish fallar.

ANNA [*with a shudder*]: Say, you're crazier than I thought. I never dreamt you'd go that far.

CHRIS [*quickly*]: Ay don't. Ay gat better sense right avay. Ay don't never buy bullets even. It ain't his fault, Ay know.

ANNA [*still suspicious of him*]: Well, I'll take care of this for a while, loaded or not. [*She puts it in the drawer of table and closes the drawer.*]

CHRIS [*placatingly*]: Throw it overboard if you vant. Ay don't care. [*Then after a pause.*] Py golly, Ay tank Ay go lie down. Ay feel sick. [ANNA *takes a magazine from the table.* CHRIS *hesitates by her chair.*] Ve talk again before Ay go, yes?

ANNA [*dully*]: Where's this ship going to?

CHRIS: Cape Town. Dat's in South Africa. She's British steamer called Londonderry. [*He stands hesitatingly—finally blurts out.*] Anna—you forgive me sure?

ANNA [*wearily*]: Sure I do. You ain't to blame. You're yust—what you are—like me.

CHRIS [*pleadingly*]: Den—you lat me kiss you again once?

ANNA [*raising her face—forcing a wan smile*]: Sure. No hard feelings.

CHRIS [*kisses her brokenly*]: Anna lilla! Ay—— [*He fights for words to express himself, but finds none—miserably—with a sob.*] Ay can't say it. Good-night, Anna.

ANNA: Good-night. [*He picks up the can of beer and goes slowly into the room on left, his shoulders bowed, his head sunk forward dejectedly. He closes the door after him.* ANNA *turns over the pages of the magazine, trying desperately to banish her thoughts by looking at the pictures. This fails to distract her, and flinging the magazine back on the table, she springs to her feet and walks about the cabin distractedly, clenching and unclenching her hands. She speaks aloud to herself in a tense, trembling voice.*] Gawd, I can't stand this much longer! What am I waiting for anyway?—like a damn fool! [*She laughs helplessly, then checks herself abruptly, as she hears the sound of heavy footsteps on the deck outside. She appears to recognize these and her face lights up with joy. She gasps.*] Mat! [*A strange terror seems suddenly to seize*

*her. She rushes to the table, takes the revolver out of drawer
and crouches down in the corner, left, behind the cupboard.
A moment later the door is flung open and* MAT BURKE
*appears in the doorway. He is in bad shape—his clothes torn
and dirty, covered with sawdust as if he had been grovelling
or sleeping on barroom floors. There is a red bruise on his
forehead over one of his eyes, another over one cheekbone,
his knuckles are skinned and raw—plain evidence of the
fighting he has been through on his "bat." His eyes are blood-
shot and heavy-lidded, his face has a bloated look. But beyond
these appearances—the results of heavy drinking—there is an
expression in his eyes of wild mental turmoil, of impotent
animal rage baffled by its own abject misery.*]

BURKE [*peers blinkingly about the cabin—hoarsely*]: Let
you not be hiding from me, whoever's here—though 'tis well
you know I'd have a right to come back and murder you. [*He
stops to listen. Hearing no sound, he closes the door behind
him and comes forward to the table. He throws himself into
the rocking-chair—despondently.*] There's no one here, I'm
thinking, and 'tis a great fool I am to be coming. [*With a sort
of dumb, uncomprehending anguish.*] Yerra, Mat Burke, 'tis
a great jackass you've become and what's got into you at all,
at all? She's gone out of this long ago, I'm telling you, and
you'll never see her face again. [ANNA *stands up, hesitating,
struggling between joy and fear.* BURKE's *eyes fall on* ANNA's
bag. He leans over to examine it.] What's this? [*Joyfully.*] It's
hers. She's not gone! But where is she? Ashore? [*Darkly.*]
What would she be doing ashore on this rotten night? [*His
face suddenly convulsed with grief and rage.*] 'Tis that, is it?
Oh, God's curse on her! [*Raging.*] I'll wait till she comes and
choke her dirty life out.

[ANNA *starts, her face grows hard. She steps into the room,
the revolver in her right hand by her side.*]

ANNA [*in a cold, hard tone*]: What are you doing here?

BURKE [*wheeling about with a terrified gasp*]: Glory be to
God! [*They remain motionless and silent for a moment, holding each other's eyes.*]

ANNA [*in the same hard voice*]: Well, can't you talk?

BURKE [*trying to fall into an easy, careless tone*]: You've a year's growth scared out of me, coming at me so sudden and me thinking I was alone.

ANNA: You've got your nerve butting in here without knocking or nothing. What d'you want?

BURKE [*airily*]: Oh, nothing much. I was wanting to have a last word with you, that's all. [*He moves a step toward her.*]

ANNA [*sharply—raising the revolver in her hand*]: Careful now! Don't try getting too close. I heard what you said you'd do to me.

BURKE [*noticing the revolver for the first time*]: Is it murdering me you'd be now, God forgive you? [*Then with a contemptuous laugh.*] Or is it thinking I'd be frightened by that old tin whistle? [*He walks straight for her.*]

ANNA [*wildly*]: Look out, I tell you!

BURKE [*who has come so close that the revolver is almost touching his chest*]: Let you shoot, then! [*Then with sudden wild grief.*] Let you shoot, I'm saying, and be done with it! Let you end me with a shot and I'll be thanking you, for it's a rotten dog's life I've lived the past two days since I've known what you are, till I'm after wishing I was never born at all!

ANNA [*overcome—letting the revolver drop to the floor, as if her fingers had no strength to hold it—hysterically*]: What d'you want coming here? Why don't you beat it? Go on! [*She passes him and sinks down in the rocking-chair.*]

BURKE [*following her—mournfully*]: 'Tis right you'd be asking why did I come. [*Then angrily.*] 'Tis because 'tis a great weak fool of the world I am, and me tormented with the wickedness you'd told of yourself, and drinking oceans of booze that'd make me forget. Forget? Divil a word I'd forget, and your face grinning always in front of my eyes, awake or asleep, till I do be thinking a madhouse is the proper place for me.

ANNA [*glancing at his hands and face—scornfully*]: You

look like you ought to be put away some place. Wonder you wasn't pulled in. You been scrapping, too, ain't you?

BURKE: I have—with every scut would take off his coat to me! [*Fiercely.*] And each time I'd be hitting one a clout in the mug, it wasn't his face I'd be seeing at all, but yours, and me wanting to drive you a blow would knock you out of this world where I wouldn't be seeing or thinking more of you.

ANNA [*her lips trembling pitifully*]: Thanks!

BURKE [*walking up and down—distractedly*]: That's right, make game of me! Oh, I'm a great coward surely, to be coming back to speak with you at all. You've a right to laugh at me.

ANNA: I ain't laughing at you, Mat.

BURKE [*unheeding*]: You to be what you are, and me to be Mat Burke, and me to be drove back to look at you again! 'Tis black shame is on me!

ANNA [*resentfully*]: Then get out. No one's holding you!

BURKE [*bewilderedly*]: And me to listen to that talk from a woman like you and be frightened to close her mouth with a slap! Oh, God help me, I'm a yellow coward for all men to spit at! [*Then furiously.*] But I'll not be getting out of this till I've had me word. [*Raising his fist threateningly.*] And let you look out how you drive me! [*Letting his fist fall helplessly.*] Don't be angry now! I'm raving like a real lunatic, I'm thinking, and the sorrow you put on me has my brains drownded in grief. [*Suddenly bending down to her and grasping her arm intensely.*] Tell me it's a lie, I'm saying! That's what I'm after coming to hear you say.

ANNA [*dully*]: A lie? What?

BURKE [*with passionate entreaty*]: All the badness you told me two days back. Sure it must be a lie! You was only making game of me, wasn't you? Tell me 'twas a lie, Anna, and I'll be saying prayers of thanks on my two knees to the Almighty God!

ANNA [*terribly shaken—faintly*]: I can't, Mat. [*As he turns away—imploringly.*] Oh, Mat, won't you see that no matter what I was I ain't that any more? Why, listen! I packed up my bag this afternoon and went ashore. I'd been waiting here all alone for two days, thinking maybe you'd come back—thinking maybe you'd think over all I'd said—and maybe—oh, I don't know what I was hoping! But I was afraid to even go out of the cabin for a second, honest—afraid you might come and not find me here. Then I gave up hope when you didn't show up and I went to the railroad station. I was going to New York. I was going back——

BURKE [*hoarsely*]: God's curse on you!

ANNA: Listen, Mat. You hadn't come, and I'd gave up hope. But—in the station—I couldn't go. I'd bought my ticket and everything. [*She takes the ticket from her dress and tries to hold it before his eyes.*] But I got to thinking about you—and I couldn't take the train—I couldn't! So I come back here—to wait some more. Oh, Mat, don't you see I've changed? Can't you forgive what's dead and gone—and forget it?

BURKE [*turning on her—overcome by rage again*]: Forget, is it? I'll not forget till my dying day, I'm telling you, and me tormented with thoughts. [*In a frenzy.*] Oh, I'm wishing I had wan of them fornenst me this minute and I'd beat him with my fists till he'd be a bloody corpse! I'm wishing the whole lot of them will roast in hell till the Judgment Day—and yourself along with them, for you're as bad as they are.

ANNA [*shuddering*]: Mat! [*Then after a pause—in a voice of dead, stony calm.*] Well, you've had your say. Now you better beat it.

BURKE [*starts slowly for the door—hesitates—then after a pause*]: And what'll you be doing?

ANNA: What difference does it make to you?

BURKE: I'm asking you!

ANNA [*in the same tone*]: My bag's packed and I got my ticket. I'll go to New York tomorrow.

BURKE [*helplessly*]: You mean—you'll be doing the same again?

ANNA [*stonily*]: Yes.

BURKE [*in anguish*]: You'll not! Don't torment me with

that talk! 'Tis a she-devil you are sent to drive me mad entirely!

ANNA [*her voice breaking*]: Oh, for Gawd's sake, Mat, leave me alone! Go away! Don't you see I'm licked? Why d'you want to keep on kicking me?

BURKE [*indignantly*]: And don't you deserve the worst I'd say, God forgive you?

ANNA: All right. Maybe I do. But don't rub it in. Why ain't you done what you said you was going to? Why ain't you got that ship was going to take you to the other side of the earth where you'd never see me again?

BURKE: I have.

ANNA [*startled*]: What—then you're going—honest?

BURKE: I signed on today at noon, drunk as I was—and she's sailing tomorrow.

ANNA: And where's she going to?

BURKE: Cape Town.

ANNA [*the memory of having heard that name a little while before coming to her—with a start, confusedly*]: Cape Town? Where's that? Far away?

BURKE: 'Tis at the end of Africa. That's far for you.

ANNA [*forcing a laugh*]: You're keeping your word all right, ain't you? [*After a slight pause—curiously.*] What's the boat's name?

BURKE: The Londonderry.

ANNA [*it suddenly comes to her that this is the same ship her father is sailing on*]: The Londonderry! It's the same— Oh, this is too much! [*With wild, ironical laughter.*] Ha-ha-ha!

BURKE: What's up with you now?

ANNA: Ha-ha-ha! It's funny, funny! I'll die laughing!

BURKE [*irritated*]: Laughing at what?

ANNA: It's a secret. You'll know soon enough. It's funny. [*Controlling herself—after a pause—cynically.*] What kind of a place is this Cape Town? Plenty of dames there, I suppose?

BURKE: To hell with them! That I may never see another woman to my dying hour!

ANNA: That's what you say now, but I'll bet by the time you get there you'll have forgot all about me and start in talking the same old bull you talked to me to the first one you meet.

BURKE [*offended*]: I'll not, then! God mend you, is it making me out to be the like of yourself you are, and you taking up with this one and that all the years of your life?

ANNA [*angrily assertive*]: Yes, that's yust what I do mean! You been doing the same thing all your life, picking up a new girl in every port. How're you any better than I was?

BURKE [*thoroughly exasperated*]: Is it no shame you have at all? I'm a fool to be wasting talk on you and you hardened in badness. I'll go out of this and lave you alone forever. [*He starts for the door—then stops to turn on her furiously.*] And I suppose 'tis the same lies you told them all before that you told to me?

ANNA [*indignantly*]: That's a lie! I never lied!

BURKE [*miserably*]: You'd be saying that, anyway.

ANNA [*forcibly, with growing intensity*]: Are you trying to accuse me—of being in love—really in love—with them?

BURKE: I'm thinking you were, surely.

ANNA [*furiously, as if this were the last insult—advancing on him threateningly*]: You mutt, you! I've stood enough from you. Don't you dare. [*With scornful bitterness.*] Love 'em! Oh, my Gawd! You damn thick-head! Love 'em? [*Savagely.*] I hated 'em, I tell you! Hated 'em, hated 'em, hated 'em! And may Gawd strike me dead this minute and my mother, too, if she was alive, if I ain't telling you the honest truth!

BURKE: [*immensely pleased by her vehemence—a light beginning to break over his face—but still uncertain, torn between doubt and the desire to believe—helplessly*]: If I could only be believing you now!

ANNA [*distractedly*]: Oh, what's the use? What's the use of me talking? What's the use of anything? [*Pleadingly.*] Oh, Mat, you mustn't think that for a second! You mustn't! Think all the other bad about me you want to, and I won't kick, 'cause you've a right to. But don't think that! [*On the point of tears.*] I couldn't bear it! It'd be yust too much to know you was going away where I'd never see you again—thinking that about me!

BURKE [*after an inward struggle—tensely—forcing out the words with difficulty*]: If I was believing—that you'd never had love for any other man in the world but me—I could be forgetting the rest, maybe.

ANNA [*with a cry of joy*]: Mat!

BURKE [*slowly*]: If 'tis truth you're after telling, I'd have a right, maybe, to believe you'd changed—and that I'd changed you myself till the thing you'd been all your life wouldn't be you any more at all.

ANNA [*hanging on his words—breathlessly*]: Oh, Mat! That's what I been trying to tell you all along!

BURKE [*simply*]: For I've a power of strength in me to lead men the way I want, and women, too, maybe, and I'm thinking I'd change you to a new woman entirely, so I'd never know, or you either, what kind of woman you'd been in the past at all.

ANNA: Yes, you could, Mat! I know you could!

BURKE: And I'm thinking 'twasn't your fault, maybe, but having that old ape for a father that left you to grow up alone, made you what you was. And if I could be believing 'tis only me you——

ANNA [*distractedly*]: You got to believe it, Mat! What can I do? I'll do anything, anything you want to prove I'm not lying!

BURKE [*suddenly seems to have a solution. He feels in the pocket of his coat and grasps something—solemnly*]: Would you be willing to swear an oath, now—a terrible, fearful oath would send your soul to the divils in hell if you was lying?

ANNA [*eagerly*]: Sure, I'll swear, Mat—on anything!

BURKE [*takes a small, cheap old crucifix from his pocket and holds it up for her to see*]: Will you swear on this?

ANNA [*reaching out for it*]: Yes. Sure I will. Give it to me.

BURKE [*holding it away*]: 'Tis a cross was given me by my mother, God rest her soul. [*He makes the sign of the cross mechanically.*] I was a lad only, and she told me to keep it by me if I'd be waking or sleeping and never lose it, and it'd bring me luck. She died soon after. But I'm after keeping it with me from that day to this, and I'm telling you there's great power in it, and 'tis great bad luck it's saved me from and me roaming the seas, and I having it tied round my neck when my last ship sunk, and it bringing me safe to land when the others went to their death. [*Very earnestly.*] And I'm warning you now, if you'd swear an oath on this, 'tis my old woman herself will be looking down from Hivin above, and praying Almighty God and the Saints to put a great curse on you if she'd hear you swearing a lie!

ANNA [*awed by his manner—superstitiously*]: I wouldn't have the nerve—honest—if it was a lie. But it's the truth and I ain't scared to swear. Give it to me.

BURKE [*handing it to her—almost frightenedly, as if he feared for her safety*]: Be careful what you'd swear, I'm saying.

ANNA [*holding the cross gingerly*]: Well—what do you want me to swear? You say it.

BURKE: Swear I'm the only man in the world ivir you felt love for.

ANNA [*looking into his eyes steadily*]: I swear it.

BURKE: And that you'll be forgetting from this day all the badness you've done and never do the like of it again.

ANNA [*forcibly*]: I swear it! I swear it by God!

BURKE: And may the blackest curse of God strike you if you're lying. Say it now!

ANNA: And may the blackest curse of God strike me if I'm lying!

BURKE [*with a stupendous sigh*]: Oh, glory be to God, I'm after believing you now! [*He takes the cross from her hand, his face beaming with joy, and puts it back in his pocket. He puts his arm about her waist and is about to kiss her when he stops, appalled by some terrible doubt.*]

ANNA [*alarmed*]: What's the matter with you?

BURKE [*with sudden fierce questioning*]: Is it Catholic ye are?

ANNA [*confused*]: No. Why?

BURKE [*filled with a sort of bewildered foreboding*]: Oh, God, help me! [*With a dark glance of suspicion at her.*] There's some divil's trickery in it, to be swearing an oath on a Catholic cross and you wan of the others.

ANNA [*distractedly*]: Oh, Mat, don't you believe me?

BURKE [*miserably*]: If it isn't a Catholic you are——

ANNA: I ain't nothing. What's the difference? Didn't you hear me swear?

BURKE [*passionately*]: Oh, I'd a right to stay away from you—but I couldn't! I was loving you in spite of it all and wanting to be with you, God forgive me, no matter what you are. I'd go mad if I'd not have you! I'd be killing the world—— [*He seizes her in his arms and kisses her fiercely.*]

ANNA [*with a gasp of joy*]: Mat!

BURKE [*suddenly holding her away from him and staring into her eyes as if to probe into her soul—slowly*]: If your oath is no proper oath at all, I'll have to be taking your naked word for it and have you anyway, I'm thinking—I'm needing you that bad!

ANNA [*hurt—reproachfully*]: Mat! I swore, didn't I?

BURKE [*defiantly, as if challenging fate*]: Oath or no oath, 'tis no matter. We'll be wedded in the morning, with the help of God. [*Still more defiantly.*] We'll be happy now, the two of us, in spite of the divil! [*He crushes her to him and kisses her again. The door on the left is pushed open and* CHRIS *appears in the doorway. He stands blinking at them. At first the old expression of hatred of* BURKE *comes into his eyes instinctively. Then a look of resignation and relief takes its place. His face lights up with a sudden happy thought. He turns back into the bedroom—reappears immediately with the tin can of beer in his hand—grinning.*]

CHRIS: Ve have a drink on this, py golly! [*They break away from each other with startled exclamations.*]

BURKE [*explosively*]: God stiffen it! [*He takes a step toward* CHRIS *threateningly.*]

ANNA [*happily—to her father*]: That's the way to talk! [*With a laugh.*] And say, it's about time for you and Mat to kiss and make up. You're going to be shipmates on the Londonderry, did you know it?

BURKE [*astounded*]: Shipmates—— Has himself——

CHRIS [*equally astounded*]: Ay vas bo'sun on her.

BURKE: The divil! [*Then angrily.*] You'd be going back to sea and leaving her alone, would you?

ANNA [*quickly*]: It's all right, Mat. That's where he belongs, and I want him to go. You got to go, too; we'll need the money. [*With a laugh, as she gets the glasses.*] And as for me being alone, that runs in the family, and I'll get used to it. [*Pouring out their glasses.*] I'll get a little house somewhere and I'll make a regular place for you two to come back to,— wait and see. And now you drink up and be friends.

BURKE [*happily—but still a bit resentful against the old man*]: Sure! [*Clinking his glass against* CHRIS'.] Here's luck to you! [*He drinks.*]

CHRIS [*subdued—his face melancholy*]: Skoal. [*He drinks.*]

BURKE [*to* ANNA, *with a wink*]: You'll not be lonesome long. I'll see to that, with the help of God. 'Tis himself here will be having a grandchild to ride on his foot, I'm telling you!

ANNA [*turning away in embarrassment*]: Quit the kidding now. [*She picks up her bag and goes into the room on left. As soon as she is gone* BURKE *relapses into an attitude of gloomy thought.* CHRIS *stares at his beer absent-mindedly. Finally* BURKE *turns on him.*]

BURKE: Is it any religion at all you have, you and your Anna?

CHRIS [*surprised*]: Vhy yes. Ve vas Lutheran in ole country.

BURKE [*horrified*]: Luthers, is it? [*Then with a grim resignation, slowly, aloud to himself.*] Well, I'm damned then surely. Yerra, what's the difference? 'Tis the will of God, anyway.

CHRIS [*moodily preoccupied with his own thoughts—speaks with somber premonition as* ANNA *re-enters from the left*]: It's funny. It's queer, yes—you and me shipping on same boat dat vay. It ain't right. Ay don't know—it's dat funny vay ole davil sea do her vorst dirty tricks, yes. It's so. [*He gets up and goes back and, opening the door, stares out into the darkness.*]

BURKE [*nodding his head in gloomy acquiescence—with a great sigh*]: I'm fearing maybe you have the right of it for once, divil take you.

ANNA [*forcing a laugh*]: Gee, Mat, you ain't agreeing with him, are you? [*She comes forward and puts her arm about his shoulder—with a determined gayety.*] Aw say, what's the matter? Cut out the gloom. We're all fixed now, ain't we, me and you? [*Pours out more beer into his glass and fills one for herself—slaps him on the back.*] Come on! Here's to the sea, no matter what! Be a game sport and drink to that! Come on! [*She gulps down her glass.* BURKE *banishes his superstitious premonitions with a defiant jerk of his head, grins up at her, and drinks to her toast.*]

CHRIS [*looking out into the night—lost in his somber preoccupation—shakes his head and mutters*]: Fog, fog, fog, all bloody time. You can't see vhere you vas going, no. Only dat ole davil, sea—she knows!

[*The two stare at him. From the harbor comes the muffled, mournful wail of steamers' whistles.*]

[*The Curtain Falls*]

EUGENE O'NEILL

The foremost figure in American drama, O'Neill was the first American to win the Nobel Prize for Literature (1936). He has also won the Pulitzer Prize three times (for *Beyond the Horizon, Anna Christie,* and *Strange Interlude*), and his plays have been presented on every continent for over twenty-five years. His themes and treatment have repeatedly caused sensations in the theater, but his real power lies in his ability to put on the stage genuine human beings who stir our pity or terror.

Born on October 16, 1888, in a hotel on Broadway, O'Neill had a younger life crammed with adventure, hand-to-mouth living, and uncertainty about what he was to do with himself. His father, the popular actor, James O'Neill, sent him to Betts Academy and to Princeton University, but the son did not comfortably tolerate the academic life and was dropped from Princeton in 1906.

For the next six years he knocked about the world working only enough to keep alive—prospecting for gold in Honduras, shipping as a common sailor, living as a bum in the dives of Buenos Aires, making a trip to Africa in a cattle boat. Experiences stored up in these years have often appeared later in his plays.

In 1912, he spent five months in a tuberculosis sanitarium at Wallingford, Connecticut. Digesting his experiences and reading the plays of August Strindberg, he came to realize the possibilities of playwriting. During the next two years he wrote eleven one-act plays. In 1914-15 he attended George Pierce Baker's "Workshop 47" at Harvard, where he appears to have felt somewhat like the ugly duckling, shy and uncomfortable among proper ducks.

By 1916, he had gone to Provincetown, Massachusetts, where he joined the Wharf Theater group of young experimenters led by George Cram Cook who were dissatisfied with the commercial theater. Here was produced his one-act play, *Bound East for Cardiff.* The interest it created led to the establishment of the Provincetown Players in New York.

In 1920, appeared his first Broadway production, *Beyond the*

Horizon, and from then until 1925 many others followed at the Provincetown Playhouse and the Greenwich Village Theater.

O'Neill's originality and fertility are shown in his experimentation with unconventional stage techniques in *The Emperor Jones* and *The Hairy Ape,* his uses of masks in *The Great God Brown* and *Lazarus Laughed,* his revival of "asides" in *Strange Interlude,* his daring treatment of daring subjects in *All God's Chillun Got Wings* and *Desire under the Elms,* and the unusual length of *Strange Interlude, Mourning Becomes Electra,* and *The Iceman Cometh.* Though the quality of his plays is often uneven and the treatment sometimes pretentious and false, his successes have been far more numerous and greater than his failures. It has been truly said that with him the American theater came of age.

After living on Cape Cod, in France, California, and elsewhere, O'Neill has returned to New York where he continues to write.

A list of his full-length plays and the dates of their first production:

Beyond the Horizon, February 2, 1920.
The Emperor Jones, November 3, 1920.
Diff'rent, February 4, 1921.
Gold, June 1, 1921.
Anna Christie, November 2, 1921.
The Straw, November 10, 1921.
The First Man, March 4, 1922.
The Hairy Ape, March 9, 1922.
Welded, March 17, 1924.
All God's Chillun Got Wings, May 15, 1924.
Desire under the Elms, November 11, 1924.
The Fountain, December 10, 1925.
The Great God Brown, January 23, 1926.
Marco Millions, January 9, 1928.
Strange Interlude, January 30, 1928.
Lazarus Laughed, April 9, 1928.
The Dynamo, February 11, 1929.
Mourning Becomes Electra, October 26, 1931.
Ah, Wilderness, October 2, 1933.
Days without End, January 8, 1934.
The Iceman Cometh, October 9, 1946.
A Moon for the Misbegotten, February 20, 1947.

CRITICAL COMMENTS

ANNA CHRISTIE

Eugene O'Neill's vision of the world is not an ordinary one. It is this that lifts him above most of our dramatists, whose intuitions concerning the universe, as indicated in their works, are usually those of a prosperous restaurateur. O'Neill sometimes has so much to convey that his vehicle of expression creaks and groans under the load. Each of his plays has the supreme merit of arousing our interest in the next one, since we always anticipate a greater mastery of his medium, a fresher recreation of structure, a more dynamic unity of matter and form. In "Anna Christie," for instance, he seems to have come into closer contact with his problem, to have attained a greater intensity of vision. Yet we are apt to be sidetracked by the purely picturesque, the tang and color of his dialogue, his power to saturate us in the heavy atmosphere of that waterfront saloon and grimy coal barge in which the action is placed. Old Chris, Anna his daughter, Mat Burke, might seem to be mere portraits painted from the life. But, considered more deeply, these figures of the sea and of the underworld, dirty and drunken, and generally disreputable as they are, are placed before us because in them Eugene O'Neill finds embodied the fundamental realities of his world. Unflinchingly men and women must face the bitter realities of this mysterious universe in which we seem to find ourselves more or less aliens. Useless, he seems to imply, is the effort to patch together makeshift shelters in any futile attempt to shut out the ruthless universe; useless, even cowardly, not to measure one's strength against these stern eternal realities. Morally and physically men befoul themselves in their eternal whining for another world, in creating for themselves the illusion of happiness to be found "somewhere else."

For Eugene O'Neill the sea is usually the constant symbol of these eternal realities, the inhuman powers of nature against which men and women must measure their puny strength. Yet in facing unafraid this reality, this very act brings out into full expression all of their latent qualities of courage, honesty, and strength. The ending, happy or unhappy, has really nothing to do with the case, provided in the conflict people shed their pettiness, dishonesty, and fatuity. . . .

If there is any particular weakness in the play, it is to be found in the author's dependence upon "exposition." The great danger of expository first acts is not that the audience may learn too little, but that it may be told too much. It seems to me that in "Anna Christie" the impact of Anna's relentless confession in the third act would have been tenfold more overwhelming if she had refrained, in that first act, from telling the detailed story of her downfall and degradation at first meeting with an apparently chance passer-by. To have suggested this past would have sharpened our interest; to expose it completely seems to me to have loosened rather than to have tightened the screws of Mr. O'Neill's dramatic mechanism. . . .

[Robert Allerton Parker, "An American Dramatist Developing," in *The Independent and Weekly Review*, 107 (Dec. 3, 1921), p. 236. Reprinted by permission.]

ANNA CHRISTIE

Yes, let us be emphatic: *Anna Christie* is the best play in London.

Only three characters, but they are admirably characteristic, sharply differentiated, each a complete whole filling a part as clear and vital as the people of Ibsen. They are an old Swedish bos'n, his daughter, and an Irish stoker and another. The charm of the thing lies in this real chunk of heterogeneous America as seen and re-created by an Irishman who has a natural dramatic sense. Each character is necessary and complete. There are no frills, no concessions, no sentimentalities. The play is Art. . . .

The drama is symbolic. Nothing, that is, happens theatrically; and though the tragedy is real and the scene of it haunting, like Greek drama, the natural comedy of life plays it away, as it were, dissolves it into charming facets of fun and triviality, and neither predominates. That is a great feat. The balance of the play is remarkable, and to the end one hardly knows whether to regard it as delightful comedy or aching tragedy.

[S. O., in *The English Review*, 36 (May 1923), pp. 469-70. Reprinted by permission.]

ROBERT E. SHERWOOD

———

ABE LINCOLN IN ILLINOIS

CHARACTERS

MENTOR GRAHAM	MARY TODD
ABE LINCOLN	THE EDWARDS' MAID
ANN RUTLEDGE	JIMMY GALE
BEN MATTLING	AGGIE GALE
JUDGE BOWLING GREEN	GOBEY
NINIAN EDWARDS	STEPHEN A. DOUGLAS
JOSHUA SPEED	WILLIE LINCOLN
TRUM COGDAL	TAD LINCOLN
JACK ARMSTRONG	ROBERT LINCOLN
BAB	THE LINCOLNS' MAID
FEARGUS	CRIMMIN
JASP	BARRICK
SETH GALE	STURVESON
NANCY GREEN	JED
WILLIAM HERNDON	KAVANAGH
ELIZABETH EDWARDS	MAJOR

SOLDIERS, RAILROAD MEN,
TOWNSPEOPLE

ACT ONE

In and about New Salem, Illinois, in the 1830's.

Scene *1* *Mentor Graham's cabin near New Salem, Illinois.*
Scene *2* *The Rutledge Tavern, New Salem.*
Scene *3* *Bowling Green's house near New Salem.*

Act Two

In and about Springfield, Illinois, in the 1840's.

Act Three

In Springfield, 1858–61.

ABE LINCOLN IN ILLINOIS

ACT ONE

SCENE I

MENTOR GRAHAM'S *cabin near New Salem, Illinois. Late at night.*

There is one rude table, piled with books and papers. Over it hangs an oil lamp, the only source of light.

[*At one side of the table sits* MENTOR GRAHAM, *a sharp but patient school teacher.*

Across from him is ABE LINCOLN—*young, gaunt, tired but intent, dressed in the ragged clothes of a backwoodsman. He speaks with the drawl of southern Indiana—an accent which is more Kentuckian than Middle-Western.*

MENTOR *is leaning on the table.* ABE'S *chair is tilted back, so that his face is out of the light.* MENTOR *turns a page in a grammar book.*]

MENTOR: The Moods. [MENTOR *closes the book and looks at* ABE.] Every one of us has many moods. You yourself have more than your share of them, Abe. They express the various aspects of your character. So it is with the English language—and you must try to consider this language as if it were a living person, who may be awkward and stumbling. or pompous and pretentious, or simple and direct. Name me the five moods.

ABE: The Indicative, Imperative, Potential, Subjunctive, and Infinitive.

MENTOR: And what do they signify?

ABE: The Indicative Mood is the easy one. It just indicates a thing—like "He loves," "He is loved"—or, when you put it in the form of a question, "Does he love?" or "Is he loved?"

The Imperative Mood is used for commanding, like "Get out and be damned to you."

MENTOR [*smiling*]: Is that the best example you can think of?

ABE: Well—you can put it in the Bible way—"Go thou in peace." But it's still imperative.

MENTOR: The mood derives its name from the implication of command. But you can use it in a very different sense— in the form of the humblest supplication.

ABE: Like "Give us this day our daily bread and forgive us our trespasses."

MENTOR: [*reaching for a newspaper in mess on the table*]: I want you to read this—it's a speech delivered by Mr. Webster before the United States Senate. A fine document, and a perfect usage of the Imperative Mood in its hortatory sense. Here it is. Read this—down here. [*He leans back to listen.*]

ABE [*takes paper, leans forward into the lights and reads*]: "Sir," the Senator continued, in the rich deep tones of the historic church bells of his native Boston, "Sir—I have not allowed myself to look beyond the Union, to see what might be hidden in the dark recess behind. While the Union lasts..." [ABE *has been reading in a monotone, without inflection.*]

MENTOR [*testily*]: Don't read it off as if it were an inventory of Denton Offut's groceries. Imagine that *you're* making the speech before the Senate, with the fate of your country at stake. Put your own life into it!

ABE: I couldn't use words as long as Dan'l Webster.

MENTOR: That's what you're here for—to learn! Go ahead.

ABE: [*reading slowly, gravely*]: "While the Union lasts, we have high prospects spread out before us, for us and our children. Beyond that, I seek not to penetrate the veil. God grant that in my day, at least, the curtain may not rise."

MENTOR: Notice the use of verbs from here on.

ABE [*reads*]: "When my eyes shall be turned to behold for the last time the sun in heaven, may I not see him shining on the broken and dishonored fragments of a once glorious Union; on States dissevered, discordant, belligerent; on a land rent with civil feuds, or drenched, it may be, in fraternal blood! Let their last feeble glance rather behold the glorious ensign of the republic, now known and honored throughout the earth, not a single star of it obscured, bearing for its motto no such miserable interrogatory..." [*He stumbles over the pronunciation.*]

MENTOR: Interrogatory.

ABE [*continuing*]: "...interrogatory as 'What is all this worth?' Nor, those other words of delusion and folly, 'Liberty first and Union afterwards'; but everywhere, spread all over in characters of living light, that other sentiment, dear to every true American heart—Liberty and Union..."

MENTOR: Emphasize the *"and."*

ABE: "Liberty *and* Union, now and forever, one and inseparable!" [*He puts the paper back on the table.*] He must have had 'em up on their feet cheering with *that,* all right.

MENTOR: Some cheered, and some spat, depending on which section they came from.

ABE: What was he talking about?

MENTOR: It was in the debate over the right of any state to secede from the Union. Hayne had pleaded South Carolina's cause—pleaded it ably. He said that just as we have liberty as individuals—so have we liberty as states—to go as we please. Which means, if we don't like the Union, as expressed by the will of its majority, then we can leave it, and set up a new nation, or many nations—so that this continent might be as divided as Europe. But Webster answered him all right. He proved that without Union, we'd have precious little liberty left. Now—go on with the Potential Mood.

ABE: That signifies possibility—usually of an unpleasant nature. Like, "If I ever get out of debt, I will probably get right back in again."

MENTOR [*smiles*]: Why did you select that example, Abe?

ABE: Well—it just happens to be the thought that's always heaviest on my mind.

MENTOR: Is the store in trouble again?

ABE [*calmly*]: Yes. Berry's drunk all the whiskey we ought to have sold, and we're going to have to shut up any day now. I guess I'm my father's own son. Give me a steady job, and I'll fail at it.

MENTOR: You haven't been a failure here, Abe. There isn't a manjack in this community that isn't fond of you and anxious to help you get ahead.

ABE [*with some bitterness*]: I know—just like you, Mentor, sitting up late nights, to give me learning, out of the goodness of your heart. And now, Josh Speed and Judge Green and some of the others I owe money to want to get me the job of post-master, thinking that maybe I can handle *that,* since there's only one mail comes in a week. I've got friends, all right—the best friends. But they can't change my luck, or maybe it's just my nature.

MENTOR: What you want to do is get out of New Salem. This poor little forgotten town will never give any one any opportunity.

ABE: Yes—I've thought about moving, think about it all the time. My family have always been movers, shifting about, never knowing what they were looking for, and whatever it was, never finding it. My old father ambled from Virginia, to one place after another in Kentucky, where I was born, and then into Indiana, and then here in Illinois. About all I can remember of when I was a boy was hitching up, and then unhitching, and then hitching up again.

MENTOR: Then get up and go, Abe. Make a new place for yourself in a new world.

ABE: As a matter of fact, Seth Gale and me have been talking a lot about moving—out to Kansas or Nebraska territory. But—wherever I go—it'll be the same story—more friends, more debts.

MENTOR: Well, Abe—just bear in mind that there are always two professions open to people who fail at everything else: there's school-teaching, and there's politics.

ABE: Then I'll choose school-teaching. You go into politics, and you may get elected.

MENTOR: Yes—there's always that possibility.

ABE: And if you get elected, you've got to go to the city. I don't want none of that.

MENTOR: What did I say about two negatives?

ABE: I meant, any of that.

MENTOR: What's your objection to cities, Abe? Have you ever seen one?

ABE: Sure. I've been down river twice to New Orleans. And, do you know, every minute of the time I was there, I was scared?

MENTOR: Scared of what, Abe?

ABE: Well—it sounds kind of foolish—I was scared of people.

MENTOR: [*laughs*]: Did you imagine they'd rob you of all your gold and jewels?

ABE [*serious*]: No. I was scared they'd kill me.

MENTOR [*also serious*]: Why? Why should they want to kill you?

ABE: I don't know.

MENTOR [*after a moment*]: You think a lot about death, don't you?

ABE: I've had to, because it has always seemed to be so close to me—always—as far back as I can remember. When I was no higher than this table, we buried my mother. The milksick got her, poor creature. I helped Paw make the coffin—whittled the pegs for it with my own jackknife. We buried her in a timber clearing beside my grandmother, old Betsy Sparrow. I used to go there often and look at the place— used to watch the deer running over her grave with their little feet. I never could kill a deer after that. One time I catched hell from Paw because when he was taking aim I knocked his gun up. And I always compare the looks of those deer with the looks of men—like the men in New Orleans—that you could see had murder in their hearts.

MENTOR [*after a moment*]: You're a hopeless mess of incon-
sistency, Abe Lincoln.

ABE: How do you mean, Mentor?

MENTOR: I've never seen any one who is so friendly and
at the same time so misanthropic.

ABE: What's that?

MENTOR: A misanthrope is one who distrusts men and
avoids their society.

ABE: Well—maybe that's how I am. Oh—I like people, well
enough—when you consider 'em one by one. But they seem
to look different when they're put into crowds, or mobs, or
armies. But I came here to listen to you, and then I do all the
talking.

MENTOR: Go right on, Abe. I'll correct you when you say
things like "catched hell."

ABE: [*grins*]: I know. Whenever I get talking about Paw,
I sort of fall back into his language. But—you've got your own
school to teach tomorrow. I'll get along. [*He stands up.*]

MENTOR: Wait a minute. . . . [*He is fishing about among
the papers. He takes out a copy of an English magazine.*]
There's just one more thing I want to show you. It's a poem.
[*He finds the place in the magazine.*] Here it is. You read it,
Abe. [*He hands* ABE *the magazine.*]

[ABE *seats himself on the edge of the table, and holds the
magazine under the light.*]

ABE [*reads*]: " 'On Death,' written at the age of nineteen
by the late John Keats: 'Can death be sleep, when life is but
a dream,
And scenes of bliss pass as a phantom by?
The transient [*He hesitates on that word.*] pleasures as a
    vision seem,
And yet we think the greatest pain's to die.
[*He moves closer to the light.*]
How strange it is that man on earth should roam,
And lead a life of woe, but not forsake
His rugged path—nor dare he view alone
His future doom—which is but to awake.' " [*He looks at*

Mentor.] That sure is good, Mentor. It's *fine*. [*He is reading it again, to himself, when the lights fade.*]

Scene 2

The Rutledge Tavern, New Salem. Noon on the Fourth of July.

It is a large room, with log walls, but with curtains on the windows and pictures on the walls to give it an air of dressiness. The pictures include likenesses of all the Presidents from Washington to Jackson, and there is also a picture (evidently used for campaign purposes) of Henry Clay.

At the left is a door leading to the kitchen. At the back, toward the right, is the main entrance, which is open. The sun is shining brightly.

The furniture of the room consists of two tables, two benches, and various chairs and stools.

[Ben Mattling *is seated on a bench at the rear of the room. He is an ancient, paunchy, watery-eyed veteran of the Revolution, and he wears a cocked hat and the tattered but absurd semblance of a Colonial uniform.* Judge Bowling Green *and* Ninian Edwards *come in, followed by* Joshua Speed. Bowling *is elderly, fat, gentle.* Ninian *is young, tall, handsome, prosperous.* Josh *is quiet, mild, solid, thoughtful, well-dressed.*]

Bowling [*as they come in*]: This is the Rutledge Tavern, Mr. Edwards. It's not precisely a gilded palace of refreshment.

Ninian: Make no apologies, Judge Green. As long as the whiskey is wet.

[Josh *has crossed to the door at the left. He calls off:*]

Josh: Miss Rutledge.

Ann. [*appearing at the door*]: Yes, Mr. Speed?

Josh: Have you seen Abe Lincoln?

Ann: No. He's probably down at the foot races. [*She goes back into the kitchen.* Josh *turns to* Bowling.]

Josh: I'll find Abe and bring him here.

Ninian: Remember, Josh, we've got to be back in Springfield before sundown.

[JOSH *has gone out.*]

BOWLING: [*to* MATTLING]: Ah, good day, Uncle Ben. Have a seat, Mr. Edwards.

[*They cross to the table at the right.*]

BEN: Good day to you, Bowling.

[ANN *comes in from the kitchen.*]

ANN: Hello, Judge Green.

BOWLING: Good morning, Ann. We'd be grateful for a bottle of your father's best whiskey.

ANN: Yes, Judge. [*She starts to go off.*]

BEN [*stopping her*]: And git me another mug of that Barbadoes rum.

ANN: I'm sorry, Mr. Mattling, but I've given you one already and you know my father said you weren't to have any more till you paid for ...

BEN: Yes, wench—I know what your father said. But if a veteran of the Revolutionary War is to be denied so much as credit, then this country has forgot its gratitude to them that made it.

BOWLING: Bring him the rum, Ann. I'll be happy to pay for it.

[TRUM COGDAL *comes in. He is elderly, pernicketty.*]

BEN: [*reluctantly*]: I have to say thank you, Judge.

TRUM: Ann, bring me a pot of Sebago tea.

ANN: Mr. Cogdal. [*She goes out at the left.* TRUM *sits down at the table.*]

BOWLING: Don't say a word, Ben.

TRUM: Well, Mr. Edwards—what's your impression of our great and enterprising metropolis?

NINIAN: Distinctly favorable, Mr. Cogdal. I could not fail to be impressed by the beauty of your location, here on this hilltop, in the midst of the prairie land.

TRUM: Well, we're on the highroad to the West—and when we get the rag, tag, and bobtail cleaned out of here, we'll grow. Yes, sir—we'll grow!

NINIAN [*politely*]: I'm sure of it.

[ANN *has returned with the whiskey, rum and tea.*]

BOWLING: Thank you, Ann.

ANN: Has the mud-wagon come in yet?

TRUM: No. I been waiting for it.

BOWLING: Not by any chance expecting a letter, are you, Ann?

ANN: Oh, no—who'd be writing to *me*, I'd like to know?

BOWLING: Well—you never can tell what might happen on the Fourth of July. [*He and* NINIAN *lift their glasses.*] But I beg to wish you all happiness, my dear. And let me tell you that Mr. Edwards here is a married man, so you can keep those lively eyes to yourself.

ANN [*giggles*]: Oh, Judge Green—you're just joking me! [*She goes to the kitchen.*]

NINIAN: A mighty pretty girl.

TRUM: Comes of good stock, too.

NINIAN: With the scarcity of females in these parts, it's a wonder some one hasn't snapped her up.

BOWLING: Some one has. The poor girl promised herself to a man who called himself McNiel—it turned out his real name's McNamar. Made some money out here and then left town, saying he'd return soon. She's still waiting for him. But your time is short, Mr. Edwards; so if you tell us just what it is you want in New Salem, we'll do our utmost to . . .

NINIAN: I'm sure you gentlemen know what I want.

TRUM: Naturally, you want votes. Well you've got mine. Anything to frustrate that tyrant, Andy Jackson. [*He shakes a finger at the picture of* ANDREW JACKSON.]

NINIAN: I assure you that I yield to none in my admiration for the character of our venerable president, but when he goes to the extent of ruining our banking structure, destroying faith in our currency and even driving sovereign states to the point of secession—then, gentlemen, it is time to call a halt.

BOWLING: We got two more years of him—if the old man lives that long. You can't make headway against his popularity.

NINIAN: But we can start now to drive out his minions here

in the government of the state of Illinois. We have a great battle cry: "End the reign of Andrew Jackson."

[JACK ARMSTRONG *and three others of the Clary's Grove boys have come in during this speech. The others are named* BAB, FEARGUS *and* JASP. *They are the town bullies—boisterous, good-natured but tough.*]

JACK: [*going to the door at the left*]: Miss Rutledge!

ANN [*appearing in the doorway*]: What do you want, Jack Armstrong?

JACK: Your humble pardon, Miss Rutledge, and we will trouble you for a keg of liquor.

BAB: And we'll be glad to have it quick, because we're powerful dry.

ANN: You get out of here—you get out of here right now—you low *scum!*

JACK: I believe I said a keg of liquor. Did you hear me say it, boys?

FEARGUS: That's how it sounded to me, Jack.

JASP: Come along with it, Annie——

ANN: If my father were here, he'd take a gun to you, just as he would to a pack of prairie wolves.

JACK: If your Paw was here, he'd be scareder than you. 'Cause he knows we're the wildcats of Clary's Grove, worse'n any old wolves, and we're a-howlin', and a-spittin' for drink. So get the whiskey, Miss Annie, and save your poor old Paw a lot of expenses for damages to his property.

[ANN *goes.*]

TRUM [*in an undertone to* NINIAN]: That's the rag, tag, and bobtail I was . . .

JACK: And what are you mumblin' about, old measely-weasely Trum Cogdal—with your cup of tea on the Fourth of July?

BAB: He's a cotton-mouthed traitor and I think we'd better whip him for it.

FEARGUS: [*at the same time*]: Squeeze that air tea outen him, Jack.

JASP [*shouting*]: Come on you, Annie, with that liquor!

JACK: And you, too, old fat-pot Judge Bowling Green that sends honest men to prison—and who's the stranger? Looks kind of damn elegant for New Salem.

BOWLING: This is Mr. Ninian Edwards of Springfield, Jack—and for the Lord's sake, shut up, and sit down, and behave yourselves.

JACK: Ninian Edwards, eh! The Governor's son, I presume. Well—well!

NINIAN: [*amiably*]: You've placed me.

JACK: No wonder you've got a New Orleans suit of clothes and a gold fob and a silver-headed cane. I reckon you can buy the best of everything with that steamin' old pirate land-grabber for a Paw. I guess them fancy pockets of yourn are pretty well stuffed with the money your Paw stole from us taxpayers—eh, Mr. Edwards?

BAB: Let's take it offen him, Jack.

FEARGUS: Let's give him a lickin', Jack.

JACK: [*still to* NINIAN]: What you come here for anyway? Lookin' for a fight? Because if that's what you're a-cravin', I'm your man—wrasslin', clawin', bitin', and tearin'.

ANN [*coming in*]: Jack Armstrong, here's your liquor! Drink it and go away. [ANN *carries four mugs.*]

JASP: He told you to bring a keg!

JACK [*contemplating the mugs*]: One little noggin apiece? Why—that ain't enough to fill a hollow tooth! Get the keg, Annie.

FEARGUS: Perhaps she can't tote it. I'll get it, Jack. [*He goes out into the kitchen.*]

ANN: [*desperate*]: Aren't there any of you men can do anything to protect decent people from these ruffians?

NINIAN: I'll be glad to do whatever I ... [*He starts to rise.*]

BOWLING [*restraining him*]: I'd be rather careful, Mr. Edwards.

JACK: That's right, Mr. Edwards. You be careful. Listen to the old Squire. He's got a round pot but a level head. He's seen the Clary's Grove boys in action, and he can tell you you might get that silver-headed cane rammed down your gullet.

Hey, Bab—you tell him what we did to Hank Spears and Gus Hocheimer. Just tell him!

BAB: Jack nailed the two of 'em up in a barr'l and sent 'em rollin' down Salem hill and it jumped the bank and fotched up in the river and when we opened up the barr'l they wasn't inclined to move much.

JACK: Of course, it'd take a bigger barr'l to hold you and your friend here, Squire, but I'd do it for you and I'd do it for any by God rapscallions and sons of thieves that come here a-preachin' treachery and disunion and pisenin' the name of Old Hickory, the people's friend.

[FEARGUS *returns with the keg.*]

BEN: Kill him, boys! You're the only *real* Americans we got left!

NINIAN [*rising*]: If you gentlemen will step outside, I'll be glad to accommodate you with the fight you seem to be spoiling for.

TRUM: You're committing suicide, Mr. Edwards.

JACK: Oh, no—he ain't. We ain't killers—we're just bone crushers. After a few months, you'll be as good as new, which ain't saying much. You bring that keg, Feargus.

[*They are about to go when* ABE *appears in the door. He now is slightly more respectably dressed, wearing a battered claw-hammer coat and pants that have been "foxed" with buckskin. He carries the mail. Behind him is* JOSH SPEED.]

ABE: The mud-wagon's in! Hello, Jack. Hello, boys. Ain't you fellers drunk yet? Hello, Miss Ann. Got a letter for you. [*There is a marked shyness in his attitude toward* ANN.]

ANN: Thank you, Abe. [*She snatches the letter and runs out with it.*]

BEN: Abe, there's goin' to be a fight!

NINIAN [*to* JACK]: Well—come on, if you're coming.

JACK: All right, boys.

ABE: Fight? Who—and why?

JACK: This is the son of Ninian Edwards, Abe. Come from Springfield lookin' for a little crotch hoist and I'm aimin' to oblige.

[ABE *looks* NINIAN *over*.]

BOWLING: Put a stop to it, Abe. It'd be next door to murder.

JACK: You shut your trap, Pot Green. Murder's too good for any goose-livered enemy of Andy Jackson. Come on, boys!

ABE: Wait a minute, boys. Jack, have you forgotten what day it is?

JACK: No, I ain't! But I reckon the Fourth is as good a day as any to whip a politician!

ABE [*amiably*]: Well, if you've just got to fight, Jack, you shouldn't give preference to strangers. Being postmaster of this thriving town, I can rate as a politician, myself, so you'd better try a fall with me—[*He thrusts* JACK *aside and turns to* NINIAN.] And as for you, sir, I haven't the pleasure of your acquaintance; but my name's Lincoln, and I'd like to shake hands with a brave man.

NINIAN [*shaking hands with* ABE]: I'm greatly pleased to know you, Mr. Lincoln.

ABE: You should be. Because I come here just in time to save you quite some embarrassment, not to mention injury. Oh, got a couple of letters for you, Bowling. And here's your *Cincinnati Journal,* Trum.

JACK: Look here, Abe—you're steppin' into something that ain't none of your business. This is a private matter of patriotic honor . . .

ABE: Everything in this town is my business, Jack. It's the only kind of business I've got. And besides—I saw Hannah down by the grove and she says to tell you to come on to the picnic and that means *now* or she'll give the cake away to the Straders children and you and the boys'll go hungry. So get moving.

FEARGUS [*to* JACK]: Are you goin' to let Abe talk you out of it?

ABE: Sure he is. [*He turns to* TRUM.] Say, Trum—if you ain't using that *Journal* for a while, would you let me have a read?

TRUM: By all means, Abe. Here you are. [*He tosses the paper to* ABE.]

ABE: Thanks. [*He turns again to* JACK.] You'd better hurry, Jack, or *you'll* get a beating from Hannah. [*He starts to take the wrapper off, as he goes over to a chair at the left.* JACK *looks at* ABE *for a moment, then laughs.*]

JACK [*to* NINIAN]: All right! Abe Lincoln's saved your hide. I'll consent to callin' off the fight just because he's a friend of mine.

ABE [*as he sits*]: And also because I'm the only one around here you can't lick.

JACK: But I just want to tell you, Mr. Ninian Edwards, Junior, that the next time you come around here a-spreadin' pisen and . . .

ABE: Go on, Jack. Hannah's waiting.

JACK [*walking over to* ABE]: I'm going, Abe. But I warn you—you'd better stop this foolishness of readin'—readin'—readin', mornin', noon, and night, or you'll be gettin' soft and you won't be the same fightin' man you are now—and it would break my heart to see you licked by anybody, includin' me! [*He laughs, slaps* ABE *on the back, then turns to go.*] Glad to have met you, Mr. Edwards. [*He goes out, followed by* BAB *and* JASP. FEARGUS *picks up the keg and starts after them.*]

NINIAN [*to* JACK]: It's been a pleasure.

ABE: Where'd you get that keg, Feargus?

FEARGUS [*nervously*]: Jack told me to take it outen Mis' Rutledge's kitchen and I . . .

ABE: Well—put it down. . . . If you see Seth Gale, tell him I've got a letter for him.

FEARGUS: I'll tell him, Abe. [FEARGUS *puts down the keg and goes.* JOSH SPEED *laughs and comes up to the table.*]

JOSH: Congratulations, Ninian. I shouldn't have enjoyed taking you home to Mrs. Edwards after those boys had done with you.

NINIAN [*grinning*]: I was aware of the certain consequences,

Josh. [*He turns to* ABE.] I'm deeply in your debt, Mr. Lincoln.

ABE: Never mind any thanks, Mr. Edwards. Jack Armstrong talks big but he means well.

NINIAN: Won't you join us in a drink?

ABE: No, thank you. [*He's reading the paper.* BOWLING *fills the glasses.*]

BOWLING: *I'm* going to have another! I don't mind telling you, I'm still trembling. [*He hands a glass to* NINIAN, *then drinks himself.*]

TRUM: You see, Mr. Edwards. It's that very kind of lawlessness that's holding our town back.

NINIAN: You'll find the same element in the capital of our nation, and everywhere else, these days. [*He sits down and drinks.*]

ABE: Say, Bowling! It says here that there was a riot in Lyons, France. [*He reads.*] "A mob of men, deprived of employment when textile factories installed the new sewing machines, re-enacted scenes of the Reign of Terror in the streets of this prosperous industrial center. The mobs were suppressed only when the military forces of His French Majesty took a firm hand. The rioters carried banners inscribed with the incendiary words, 'We will live working or die fighting!' " [ABE *looks at the group at the right.*] That's Revolution!

BOWLING: Maybe, but it's a long way off from New Salem.

JOSH: Put the paper down, Abe. We want to talk to you.

ABE: Me? What about? [*He looks curiously at* JOSH, BOWLING, *and* NINIAN.]

JOSH: I brought Mr. Edwards here for the sole purpose of meeting you—and with his permission, I shall tell you why.

NINIAN: Go right ahead, Josh.

[*All are looking intently at* ABE.]

JOSH: Abe—how would you like to run for the State Assembly?

ABE: When?

JOSH: Now—for the election in the fall.

ABE: Why?

NINIAN: Mr. Lincoln, I've known you for only a few minutes, but that's long enough to make me agree with Josh Speed that you're precisely the type of man we want. The whole Whig organization will support your candidacy.

ABE: This was all your idea, Josh?

JOSH [*smiling*]: Oh, no, Abe—you're the people's choice!

TRUM: What do you think of it, Bowling?

BOWLING [*heartily*]: I think it's as fine a notion as I ever heard. Why, Abe—I can hear you making speeches, right and left, taking your stand on all the issues—secession, Texas, the National Bank crisis, abolitionism—it'll be more fun than we ever had in our lives!

ABE [*rising*]: Isn't anybody going to ask what *I* think?

JOSH [*laughs*]: All right, Abe—*I'll* ask you.

ABE [*after a moment's pause*]: It's a comical notion, all right—and I don't know if I can give you an answer to it offhand. But my first, hasty impression is that I don't think much of it.

BOWLING: Don't overlook the fact that, if elected, your salary would be three whole dollars a day.

ABE: That's fine money. No doubt of that. And I see what you have in mind, Bowling. I owe you a considerable sum of money; and if I stayed in the legislature for, say, twenty years I'd be able to pay off—let me see—two dollars and a half a day.... [*He is figuring it up on his fingers.*]

BOWLING: I'm not thinking about the debts, Abe.

ABE: I know you ain't, Bowling. But I've got to. And so should you, Mr. Edwards. The Whig party is the party of sound money and God save the National Bank, ain't it?

NINIAN: Why, yes—among other things. . . .

ABE: Well, then—how would it look if you put forward a candidate who has demonstrated no earning power but who has run up the impressive total of fifteen hundred dollars of debts?

BOWLING [*to* NINIAN]: I can tell you something about those debts. Abe started a grocery store in partnership with an unfortunate young man named Berry. Their stock included whiskey, and Berry started tapping the keg until he had consumed all the liquid assets. So the store went bankrupt—and Abe voluntarily assumed all the obligations. That may help to explain to you. Mr. Edwards, why we think pretty highly of him around here.

NINIAN: It's a sentiment with which I concur most heartily.

ABE: I thank you one and all for your kind tributes, but don't overdo them, or I'll begin to think that three dollars a day ain't enough!

JOSH: What's the one thing that you want most, Abe? You want to learn. This will give you your chance to get at a good library, to associate with the finest lawyers in the State.

ABE: I've got a copy of Blackstone already. Found it in an old junk barrel. And how can I tell that the finest lawyers would welcome association with *me*?

NINIAN: You needn't worry about that. I saw how you dealt with those ruffians. You quite obviously know how to handle men.

ABE: I can handle the Clary's Grove boys because I can outwrassle them—but I can't go around Sangamon County throwing *all* the voters.

BOWLING [*laughing*]: I'll take a chance on that, Abe.

ABE [*to* NINIAN]: Besides—how do you know that my political views would agree with yours? How do you know I wouldn't say the wrong thing?

NINIAN: What *are* your political leanings, Mr. Lincoln?

ABE: They're all toward staying out. . . . What sort of leanings did you want?

NINIAN: We have a need for good conservative men to counteract all the radical firebrands that have swept over this country in the wake of Andrew Jackson. We've got to get this country back to first principles!

ABE: Well—I'm conservative, all right. If I got into the legislature you'd never catch me starting any movements for reform or progress. I'm pretty certain I wouldn't even have the nerve to open my mouth.

JOSH [*laughs*]: I told you, Ninian—he's just the type of candidate you're looking for.

[NINIAN *laughs too, and rises.*]

NINIAN [*crossing toward* ABE]: The fact is, Mr. Lincoln, we want to spike the rumor that ours is the party of the more privileged classes. That is why we seek men of the plain people for candidates. As postmaster, you're in an excellent position to establish contacts. While delivering letters, you can also deliver speeches and campaign literature, with which our headquarters will keep you supplied.

ABE: Would you supply me with a suit of store clothes? A candidate mustn't look *too* plain.

NINIAN [*smiling*]: I think even that could be arranged, eh, Judge?

BOWLING: I think so.

NINIAN [*pompously*]: So—think it over, Mr. Lincoln, and realize that this is opportunity unlimited in scope. Just consider what it means to be starting up the ladder in a nation which is now expanding southward, across the vast area of Texas; and westward, to the Empire of the Californias on the Pacific Ocean. We're becoming a continent, Mr. Lincoln— and all that we need is men! [*He looks at his watch.*] And now, gentlemen, if you will excuse me—I must put in an appearance at the torch-light procession in Springfield this evening, so I shall have to be moving on. Good-by, Mr. Lincoln. This meeting has been a happy one for me.

ABE [*shaking hands*]: Good-by, Mr. Edwards. Good luck in the campaign.

NINIAN: And the same to you.

[*All at the right have risen and are starting to go, except* BEN MATTLING, *who is still sitting at the back, drinking.*]

ABE: Here's your paper, Trum.

TRUM: Go ahead and finish it, Abe. I won't be looking at it yet awhile.

ABE: Thanks, Trum. I'll leave it at your house.

[TRUM *and* NINIAN *have gone.*]

BOWLING: I'll see you later, Abe. Tell Ann I'll be back to pay for the liquor.

ABE: I'll tell her, Bowling.

[BOWLING *goes.* JOSH *is looking at* ABE, *who, after a moment, turns to him.*]

ABE: I'm surprised at you, Josh. I thought you were my friend.

JOSH: I know, Abe. But Ninian Edwards asked me is there anybody in that God-forsaken town of New Salem that stands a chance of getting votes, and the only one I could think of was you. I can see you're embarrassed by this—and you're annoyed. But—whether you like it or not—you've got to grow; and here's your chance to get a little scrap of importance.

ABE: Am I the kind that wants importance?

JOSH: You'll deny it, Abe—but you've got a funny kind of vanity—which is the same as saying you've got some pride— and it's badly in need of nourishment. So, if you'll agree to this—I don't think you'll be sorry for it or feel that I've betrayed you.

ABE [*grins*]: Oh—I won't hold it against you, Josh. [*He walks away and looks out the door.*] But that Mr. Ninian Edwards—he's rich and he's prominent and he's got a high-class education. Politics to him is just a kind of game. And maybe I'd like it if I could play it *his* way. [*He turns to* JOSH.] But when you get to reading Blackstone, not to mention the Bible, you can't help feeling maybe there's some serious responsibility in the giving of laws—and maybe there's something more important in the business of government than just getting the Whig Party back into power.

[SETH GALE *comes in. He is a young, husky frontiersman, with flashes of the sun of Western empire in his eyes.*]

SETH: Hey, Abe—Feargus said you've got a letter for me.

ABE [*fishing in his mail pouch*]: Yes.

SETH: Hello, Mr. Speed.

JOSH: How are you, Mr. Gale?

ABE: Here you are, Seth. [*He hands him a letter.* SETH *takes it to the right, sits down and starts to read.*]

JOSH: I've got to get home to Springfield, Abe, but I'll be down again in a week or so.

ABE: I'll be here, Josh.

[JOSH *goes.* ABE *sits down again at the right, picks up his paper, but doesn't read it.* BEN *stands up and comes down a bit unsteadily.*]

BEN [*angrily*]: Are you going to do it, Abe? Are you goin' to let them make you into a *candidate?*

ABE: I ain't had time to think about it yet.

BEN: Well—I tell you to stop thinkin' before it's too late. Don't let 'em get you. Don't let 'em put you in a store suit that's the uniform of degradation in this miserable country. You're an honest man, Abe Lincoln. You're a good-for-nothin', debt-ridden loafer—but you're an honest man. And you have no place in that den of thieves that's called gov'-ment. They'll corrupt you as they've corrupted the whole damn United States. Look at Washington, look at Jefferson, and John Adams—[*He points grandly to the pictures.*]—where are they today? Dead! And everything they stood for and fought for and *won*—that's dead too. [ANN *comes in to collect the mugs from the table at the left.* ABE *looks at her.*] Why—we'd be better off if we was all black niggers held in the bonds of slavery. *They* get fed—*they* get looked after when they're old and sick. [ANN *goes*]. But *you* don't care—you ain't listen-in' to me, neither ... [*He starts slowly toward the door.*]

ABE: Of course I'm listening, Ben.

BEN: No, you ain't. *I* know. You're goin' to the assembly and join the wolves who're feedin' off the carcass of Liberty. [*He goes out.*]

ABE: You needn't worry. I'm not going.

[ANN *comes in. She crosses to the right to pick up the glasses. She seems extremely subdued.* ABE *looks at her, curiously.*]

ABE: Bowling Green said to tell you he'd be back later, to pay you what he owes.

ANN [*curtly*]: That's all right. [ANN *puts the glasses and bottle on a tray and picks it up.* ABE *jumps to his feet.*]

ABE: Here, Ann. Let me take that.

ANN [*irritably*]: No—leave it alone! I can carry it! [*She starts across to the left.*]

ABE: Excuse me, Ann....

ANN: [*stopping*]: Well?

ABE: Would you come back after you're finished with that? I—I'd like to talk to you.

[SETH *has finished the letter. Its contents seem to have depressed him.*]

ANN: All right. I'll talk to you—if you want. [*She goes out. SETH crosses toward ABE, who, during the subsequent dialogue, is continually looking toward the kitchen.*]

SETH: Abe ... Abe—I got a letter from my folks back in Maryland. It means—I guess I've got to give up the dream we had of moving out into Nebraska territory.

ABE: What's happened, Seth?

SETH [*despondently*]: Well—for one thing, the old man's took sick, and he's pretty feeble.

ABE: I'm sorry to hear that.

SETH: So am I. They've sent for me to come back and work the farm. Measly little thirty-six acres—sandy soil. I tell you, Abe, it's a bitter disappointment to me, when I had my heart all set on going out into the West. And the worst of it is—I'm letting *you* down on it, too.

ABE [*with a glance toward the kitchen*]: Don't think about that, Seth. Maybe I won't be able to move for a while myself. And when your father gets to feeling better, you'll come back ...

SETH: He won't get to feeling better. Not at his age. I'll be stuck there, just like he was. I'll be pushed in and cramped all the rest of my life, till the malaria gets me, too.... Well—there's no use crying about it. If I've got to go back East, I've got to go. [ANN *comes back.*] I'll tell you good-by, Abe, before I leave. [*He goes.* ABE *turns and looks at* ANN, *and she at him.*]

ANN: Well—what is it, Abe?

ABE [*rising*]: I just thought—you might like to talk to me.

ANN [*sharply*]: What about?

ABE: That letter you got from New York State.

ANN: What do *you* know about that letter?

ABE: I'm the postmaster. I know more than I ought to about people's private affairs. I couldn't help seeing that that was the handwriting of Mr. McNiel. And I couldn't help seeing, from the look on your face, that the bad news you've been afraid of has come.

[ANN *looks at him with surprise. He is a lot more observant than she had thought.*]

ANN: Whatever the letter said, it's no concern of yours, Abe.

ABE: I know that, Ann. But—it appears to me that you've been crying—and it makes me sad to think that something could have hurt you. The thing is—I think quite a lot of you—always have—ever since I first came here, and met you. I wouldn't mention it, only when you're distressed about something it's a comfort sometimes to find a pair of ears to pour your troubles into—and the Lord knows my ears are big enough to hold a lot.

[*Her attitude of hostility softens and she rewards him with a tender smile.*]

ANN: You're a Christian gentleman, Abe Lincoln. [*She sits down.*]

ABE: No, I ain't. I'm a plain, common sucker with a shirt-tail so short I can't sit on it.

ANN [*laughs*]: Well—sit down, anyway, Abe—here, by me.

ABE: Why—it'd be a pleasure. [*He crosses and sits near her.*]

ANN: You can always say something to make a person laugh, can't you?

ABE: Well—I don't even have to *say* anything. A person just has to *look* at me.

ANN: You're right about that letter, Abe. It's the first I've heard from him in months—and now he says he's delayed by family troubles and doesn't know when he'll be able to get to New Salem again. By which he probably means—never.

ABE: I wouldn't say that, Ann.

ANN: I would. [*She looks at him.*] I reckon you think I'm a silly fool for ever having promised myself to Mr. McNiel.

ABE: I think no such thing. I liked him myself, and still do, and whatever reasons he had for changing his name I'm sure were honorable. He's a smart man, and a handsome one—and I—I wouldn't blame any girl for—loving him.

ANN [*too emphatically*]: I guess I don't love him, Abe. I guess I couldn't love anybody that was as—as faithless as that.

ABE [*trying to appear unconcerned*]: Well, then. There's nothing to fret about. Now—poor Seth Gale—he got some *really* bad news. His father's sick and he has to give up his dream which was to go and settle out West.

ANN [*looks at him*]: I don't believe you know much about females, Abe.

ABE: Probably I don't—although I certainly spend enough time thinking about 'em.

ANN: You're a big man, and you can lick anybody, and you can't understand the feelings of somebody who is weak. But—I'm a female, and I can't help thinking what they'll be saying about me—all the old gossips, all over town. They'll make it out that he deserted me; I'm a rejected woman. They'll give me their sympathy to my face, but they'll snigger at me behind my back. [*She rises and crosses toward the right.*]

ABE: Yes—that's just about what they would do. But—would you let *them* disturb you?

ANN [*rising*]: I told you—it's just weakness—it's just vanity. It's something you couldn't understand, Abe. [*She has crossed to the window and is staring out.* ABE *twists in his chair to look at her.*]

ABE: Maybe I can understand it, Ann. I've got a kind of vanity myself. Josh Speed said so, and he's right. . . . It's—it's nothing but vanity that's kept me from declaring my inclinations toward you. [*She turns, amazed, and looks at him.*] You see, I don't like to be sniggered at, either. I know what I am—and I know what I look like—and I know that I've got nothing to offer any girl that I'd be in love with.

ANN: Are you saying that you're in love with me, Abe?

ABE [*with deep earnestness*]: Yes—I am saying that. [*He stands up, facing her. She looks intently into his eyes.*] I've been loving you—a long time—with all my heart. You see, Ann—you're a particularly fine girl. You've got sense, and you've got bravery—those are two things that I admire particularly. And you're powerful good to look at, too. So—it's only natural I should have a great regard for you. But—I don't mean to worry you about it, Ann. I only mentioned it because—if you would do me the honor of keeping company with me for a while, it might shut the old gossips' mouths. They'd figure you'd chucked McNiel for—for someone else. Even me.

ANN [*going to him*]: I thought I knew you pretty well, Abe. But I didn't.

ABE [*worried*]: Why do you say that? Do you consider I was too forward, in speaking out as I did?

ANN [*gravely*]: No, Abe. . . . I've always thought a lot of you—the way I thought you were. But—the idea of love between you and me—I can't say how I feel about that, because now you're like some other person, that I'm meeting for the first time.

ABE [*quietly*]: I'm not expecting you to feel anything for me. I'd never dream of expecting such a thing.

ANN: I know that, Abe. You'd be willing to give everything you have and never expect anything in return. Maybe you're different in that way from any man I've ever heard of. And I can tell you this much—now, and truthfully—if I ever do love you, I'll be happy about it—and lucky, to be loving a good, decent man. . . . If you just give me time—to think about it. . . .

ABE [*unable to believe his eyes and ears*]: You mean—if you took time—you might get in your heart something like the feeling I have for you?

ANN [*with great tenderness*]: I don't know, Abe. [*She clutches his lapel.*] But I do know that you're a man who could fill any one's heart—yes, fill it and warm it and make it glad to be living.

[ABE *covers her hand with his.*]

ABE: Ann—I've always tried hard to believe what the orators tell us—that this is a land of equal opportunity for all. But I've never been able to credit it, any more than I could agree that God made all men in his own image. But—if I could win you, Ann—I'd be willing to disbelieve everything I've ever seen with my own eyes, and have faith in everything wonderful that I've ever read in poetry books. [*Both are silent for a moment. Then* ANN *turns away.*] But—I'm not asking you to say anything now. And I won't ask you until the day comes when I know I've got a right to. [*He turns and walks quickly toward the door, picking up his mail pouch.*]

ANN: Abe! Where are you going?

ABE: I'm going to find Bowling Green and tell him a good joke. [*He grins. He is standing in the doorway.*]

ANN: A *joke?* What about?

ABE: I'm going to tell him that I'm a candidate for the assembly of the State of Illinois. [*He goes.*]

[*The lights fade.*]

SCENE 3

Bowling Green's house near New Salem. It is a small room, but the walls are lined with books and family pictures. In the center is a table with a lamp on it. Another light—a candle in a glass globe—is on a bureau at the right. There are comfortable chairs on either side of the table, and a sofa at the left.

At the back, toward the left, is the front door. A rifle is leaning against the wall by the door. There is another door in the right wall. Toward the right, at the back, is a ladder fixed against the wall leading up through an opening to the attic.

It is late in the evening, a year or so after Scene 2. A storm is raging outside.

[BOWLING *is reading aloud from a sort of pamphlet. His comfortable wife,* NANCY, *is listening and sewing.*]

BOWLING: "And how much more interesting did the spectacle become when, starting into full life and animation, as a simultaneous call for 'Pickwick' burst from his followers, that illustrious man slowly mounted into the Windsor chair, on which he had been previously seated, and addressed the club himself had founded." [BOWLING *chuckles.* NANCY *laughs.*]

NANCY: He sounds precisely like *you,* Bowling.

[*There is a knock at the door.*]

NANCY [*nervous*]: That's not Abe's knock. Who can it be?

BOWLING [*rising*]: We don't know yet, my dear.

NANCY: It's a strange hour for any one to be calling. You'd better have that gun ready.

[BOWLING *unbolts and opens the door. It is* JOSH SPEED.]

BOWLING: Why—Josh Speed!

JOSH: Good evening, Bowling.

BOWLING: We haven't seen you in a coon's age.

NANCY: Good evening, Mr. Speed.

JOSH: Good evening, Mrs. Green. And I beg you to forgive me for this untimely intrusion.

NANCY: We're delighted to see you. Take your wrap off.

JOSH: Thank you. I've just come down from Springfield. I heard Abe Lincoln was in town and I was told I might find him here.

BOWLING: He's been sleeping here, up in the attic.

NANCY: But he's out at the Rutledge Farm, tending poor little Ann.

JOSH: Miss Rutledge? What's the matter with her?

NANCY: She's been taken with the brain sickness. It's the most shocking thing. People have been dying from it right and left.

BOWLING: But Ann's young. She'll pull through, all right. Sit down, Josh.

JOSH: Thank you. [*He sits.* BOWLING *places the pamphlet on the top of the bookcase and stands there, filling his pipe.*]

NANCY: I suppose you know that Abe came rushing down from Vandalia the moment he heard she was taken. He's deeply in love with her.

BOWLING: Now, Nancy—don't exaggerate.

[JOSH *is listening to all this, intently.*]

JOSH: So Abe is in love. I wondered what has been the matter with him lately.

NANCY: Why, it's written all over his poor, homely face.

JOSH: The last time I saw him, he seemed pretty moody. But when I asked him what was wrong, he said it was his liver.

BOWLING [*laughing*]: That sounds more likely. Has he been getting on well in the Assembly?

JOSH: No. He has just been sitting there—drawing his three dollars a day—and taking no apparent interest in the proceedings. Do you fancy that Miss Rutledge cares anything for him?

NANCY: Indeed she does! She broke her promise to that Mr. McNiel because of her feelings for Abe!

JOSH: Has he any notion of marrying her?

NANCY: It's the only notion of his life right now. And the sooner they are married, the better for both of them.

BOWLING [*seating himself*]: Better for her, perhaps—but the worse for him.

NANCY [*finishing her sewing*]: And why? The Rutledges are fine people, superior in every way to those riff-raff Hankses and Lincolns that are Abe's family!

BOWLING: I think you feel as I do, Josh. Abe has his own way to go and—sweet and pretty as Ann undoubtedly is— she'd only be a hindrance to him.

JOSH: I guess it wouldn't matter much if she could give him a little of the happiness he's never had.

NANCY [*rising*]: That's just it! I think as much of Abe as you do, Bowling. But we can't deny that he's a poor man, and he's failed in trade, and he's been in the legislature for a year without accomplishing a blessed thing ... [*She goes to the bookcase to put her sewing-basket away.*]

BOWLING: He could go to Springfield and set up a law practice and make a good thing of it. Ninian Edwards would help him to get started. And he'd soon forget little Ann. He has just happened to fasten on her his own romantic ideal of what's beautiful and unattainable. Let him ever attain her, and she'd break his heart.

NANCY [*seating herself*]: Do you agree with Bowling on that, Mr. Speed?

JOSH [*sadly*]: I can't say, Mrs. Green. I've abandoned the attempt to predict anything about Abe Lincoln. The first time I ever saw him was when he was piloting that steamboat, the *Talisman*. You remember how she ran into trouble at the dam. I had a valuable load of goods aboard for my father's store, and I was sure that steamboat, goods, and all were a total loss. But Abe got her through. It was a great piece of work. I thought, "Here is a reliable man." So I cultivated his acquaintance, believing, in my conceit, that I could help him to fame and fortune. I soon learned differently. I found out that he has plenty of strength and courage in his body—but in his mind he's a hopeless hypochondriac. He can split rails, push a plough, crack jokes, all day—and then sit up all night reading "Hamlet" and brooding over his own fancied resemblance to that melancholy prince. Maybe he's a great philosopher—maybe he's a great fool. I don't know what he is.

BOWLING [*laughs*]: Well—if only Ann had sense enough to see all the things *you* saw, Josh, she'd be so terrified of him she'd run all the way back to York State and find McNiel. At least, *he's* not complicated.

NANCY [*with deeper emotion*]: You're talking about Abe Lincoln as if he were some problem that you found in a book, and it's interesting to try to figure it out. Well—maybe he is a problem—but he's also a man, and a miserable one. And what do you do for his misery? You laugh at his comical jokes and you vote for him on election day and give him board and lodging when he needs it. But all that doesn't give a scrap of satisfaction to Abe's soul—and never will. Because the one thing he needs is a woman with the will to face life for him.

BOWLING: You think he's afraid to face it himself?

NANCY: He is! He listens too much to the whispers that he heard in the forest where he grew up, and where he always goes now when he wants to be alone. They're the whispers of the women behind him—his dead mother—and *her* mother, who was no better than she should be. He's got that awful fear on him, of not knowing what the whispers mean, or where they're directing him. And none of your back-slapping will knock that fear out of him. Only a woman can free him —a woman who loves him truly, and believes in him. . . .

[*There is a knock on the door.*]

BOWLING: That's Abe now. [*He gets up and opens it.*]

[ABE *is there, bareheaded, wet by the storm. He now wears a fairly respectable dark suit of clothes. He looks older and grimmer.*]

BOWLING: Why, hello, Abe! We've been sitting up waiting for you. Come on in out of the wet!

[ABE *comes in.* BOWLING *shuts the door behind him.*]

NANCY: We were reading "The Posthumous Papers of the Pickwick Club" when Mr. Speed came in.

ABE. Hello, Josh. Glad to see you.

JOSH: Hello, Abe.

[ABE *turns to* NANCY.]

ABE: Nancy . . .

NANCY: Yes, Abe?

ABE: She's dead.

BOWLING: Ann? She's dead?

ABE: Yes. Tonight the fever suddenly got worse. They couldn't seem to do anything for it.

[NANCY *gives* BOWLING *a swift look, then goes quickly to* ABE *and takes his hand.*]

NANCY: Oh, Abe—I'm so sorry. She was such a dear little girl. Every one who knew her will join in mourning for her.

ABE: I know they will. But it won't do any good. She's dead.

BOWLING: Sit down, Abe, and rest yourself.

ABE: No—I'm not fit company for anybody. I'd better be going. [*He turns toward the door.*]

JOSH [*stopping him*]: No, you don't, Abe. You'll stay right here.

BOWLING: You better do what Josh tells you.

NANCY: Come here, Abe. Please sit down. [ABE *looks from one to the other, then obediently goes to a chair and sits.*] Your bed is ready for you upstairs when you want it.

ABE [*dully*]: You're the best friends I've got in the world, and it seems a pretty poor way to reward you for all that you've given me, to come here now, and inflict you with a corpse.

BOWLING: This is your home, Abe. This is where you're loved.

ABE: Yes, that's right. And I love you, Bowling and Nancy. But I loved her more than everything else that I've ever known.

NANCY: I know you did, Abe. I know it.

ABE: I used to think it was better to be alone. I was always most contented when I was alone. I had queer notions that if you got too close to people, you could see the truth about them, that behind the surface they're all insane, and they could see the same in you. And then—when I saw her, I knew there could be beauty and purity in people—like the purity you sometimes see in the sky at night. When I took hold of her hand and held it, all fear, all doubt, went out of me. I believed in God. I'd have been glad to work for her until I die, to get for her everything out of life that she wanted. If she thought I could do it, then I could. That was my belief. . . . And then I had to stand there, as helpless as a twig in a whirlpool; I had to stand there and watch her die. And her father and mother were there, too, praying to God for her soul. "The Lord giveth, and the Lord taketh away, blessed be the name of the Lord!" That's what they kept on saying. But I couldn't pray with them. I couldn't give any devotion to one who has the power of death, and uses it. [*He has stood up, and is speaking with more passion.*] I'm making a poor exhibition of myself—and I'm sorry—but—I can't stand it. I can't live with myself any longer. I've got to die and be with her again, or I'll go crazy! [*He goes to the door and opens it. The storm continues.*] I can't bear to think of her out there alone!

[NANCY *looks at* BOWLING *with frantic appeal. He goes to* ABE, *who is standing in the doorway, looking out.*]

BOWLING [*with great tenderness*]: Abe ... I want you to go upstairs and see if you can't get some sleep.... Please, Abe— as a special favor to Nancy and me.

ABE [*after a moment*]: All right, Bowling. [*He turns and goes to the ladder.*]

NANCY: Here's a light for you, dear Abe. [*She hands him the candle.*]

ABE: Thank you, Nancy.... Good night. [*He goes up the ladder into the attic.*]

[*They all look up after him.*]

NANCY [*tearful*]: Poor, lonely soul.

[BOWLING *cautions her to be quiet.*]

JOSH: Keep him here with you, Mrs. Green. Don't let him out of your sight.

BOWLING: We won't, Josh.

JOSH: Good night. [*He picks up his hat and cloak and goes.*]

BOWLING: Good night, Josh. [*He closes and bolts the door, then comes down to the table and picks up the lamp.*]

[NANCY *looks up once more, then goes out at the right.* BOWLING *follows her out, carrying the lamp with him. He closes the door behind him, so that the only light on the stage is the beam from the attic.*]

[*Curtain*]

ACT TWO

Law office of Stuart and Lincoln on the second floor of the Court House in Springfield, Illinois. A sunny summer's afternoon, some five years after the preceding scene.

The room is small, with two windows and one door, upstage, which leads to the hall and staircase.

At the right is a table and chair, at the left an old desk, littered with papers. At the back is a ramshackle bed, with a buffalo robe thrown over it. Below the windows are some rough shelves, sagging with law books. There is an old wood stove.

On the wall above the desk is hung an American flag, with 26 stars. Between the windows is an election poster, for Harrison and Tyler, with a list of Electors, the last of whom is Ab'm Lincoln, of Sangamon.

[BILLY HERNDON is working at the table. He is young, slight, serious-minded, smouldering. He looks up as ABE comes in. ABE wears a battered plug hat, a light alpaca coat, and carries an ancient, threadbare carpet-bag. He is evidently not in a talkative mood. His boots are caked in mud. He is only thirty-one years old, but his youth was buried with Ann Rutledge.

He leaves the office door open, and lettered on it we see the number 4, and the firm's name—Stuart & Lincoln, Attorneys & Counsellors at Law.]

BILLY: How de do, Mr. Lincoln? Glad to see you back.

ABE: Good day, Billy. [*He sets down the carpet-bag, takes off his hat and puts it on his desk.*]

BILLY: How was it on the circuit, Mr. Lincoln?

ABE: About as usual.

BILLY: Have you been keeping in good health?

ABE: Not particularly. But Doc Henry dosed me enough to keep me going. [*He sits down at the desk and starts looking at letters and papers that have accumulated during his ab-*

*sence. He takes little interest in them, pigeonholing some
letters unopened.*]

BILLY: Did you have occasion to make any political
speeches?

ABE: Oh—they got me up on the stump a couple of times.
Ran into Stephen Douglas—he was out campaigning, of
course—and we had some argument in public.

BILLY [*greatly interested*]: That's good! What issues did
you and Mr. Douglas discuss?

ABE: Now—don't get excited, Billy. We weren't taking it
serious. There was no blood shed. . . . What's the news here?

BILLY: Judge Stuart wrote that he arrived safely in Washington and the campaign there is getting almost as hot as
the weather. Mrs. Fraim stopped in to say she couldn't possibly pay your fee for a while.

ABE: I should hope not. I ought to be paying her, seeing as
I defended her poor husband and he hanged.

[BILLY *hands him a letter and watches him intently while
he reads it.*]

BILLY: That was left here by hand, and I promised to call
it especially to your attention. It's from the Elijah P. Lovejoy
League of Freemen. They want you to speak at an Abolitionist rally next Thursday evening. It'll be a very important
affair.

ABE [*reflectively*]: It's funny, Billy—I was thinking about
Lovejoy the other day—trying to figure what it is in a man
that makes him glad to be a martyr. I was on the boat coming
from Quincy to Alton, and there was a gentleman on board
with twelve Negroes. He was shipping them down to Vicks-
burg for sale—had 'em chained six and six together. Each of
them had a small iron clevis around his wrist, and this was
chained to the main chain, so that those Negroes were strung
together precisely like fish on a troutline. I gathered they were
being separated forever from their homes—mothers, fathers,
wives, children—whatever families the poor creatures had
got—going to be whipped into perpetual slavery, and no
questions asked. It was quite a shocking sight.

BILLY [*excited*]: Then you will give a speech at the Love-joy rally?

ABE [*wearily*]: I doubt it. That Freemen's League is a pack of hell-roaring fanatics. Talk reason to them and they scorn you for being a mealy-mouth. Let 'em make their own noise. [ABE *has opened a letter. He starts to read it.* BILLY *looks at him with resentful disappointment, but he knows too well that any argument would be futile. He resumes his work. After a moment,* BOWLING GREEN *comes in, followed by* JOSH SPEED.]

BOWLING: Are we interrupting the majesty of the Law?

ABE [*heartily*]: Bowling! [*He jumps up and grasps* BOWL-ING's *hand.*] How are you, Bowling?

BOWLING: Tolerably well, Abe—and glad to see you.

ABE: This is Billy Herndon—Squire Green, of New Salem. Hello, Josh.

JOSH: Hello, Abe.

BILLY [*shaking hands with* BOWLING]: I'm proud to know you, sir. Mr. Lincoln speaks of you constantly.

BOWLING: Thank you, Mr. Herndon. Are you a lawyer, too?

BILLY [*seriously*]: I hope to be, sir. I'm serving here as a clerk in Judge Stuart's absence.

BOWLING: So now you're teaching others, Abe?

ABE: Just providing a bad example.

BOWLING: I can believe it. Look at the mess on that desk. Shameful!

ABE: Give me another year of law practice and I'll need a warehouse for the overflow. . . . But—sit yourself down, Bowling, and tell me what brings you to Springfield.

[BOWLING *sits.* JOSH *has sat on the couch, smoking his pipe.* BILLY *is again at the table.*]

BOWLING: I've been up to Lake Michigan—fishing—came in today on the steam-cars—scared me out of a year's growth. But how are you doing, Abe? Josh says you're still broke, but you're a great social success.

ABE: True—on both counts. I'm greatly in demand at all the more elegant functions. You remember Ninian Edwards?

BOWLING: Of course.

ABE: Well, sir—I'm a guest at his mansion regularly. He's got a house so big you could race horses in the parlor. And his wife is one of the Todd family from Kentucky. Very high-grade people. They spell their name with two D's—which is pretty impressive when you consider that one was enough for God.

JOSH: Tell Bowling whom you met over in Rochester.

ABE: The President of the United States!

BOWLING: You don't tell me so!

ABE: Do you see that hand? [*He holds out his right hand, palm upward.*]

BOWLING: Yes—I see it.

ABE: It has shaken the hand of Martin Van Buren!

BOWLING [*laughing*]: Was the President properly respectful to you, Abe?

ABE: Indeed he was! He said to me, "We've been hearing great things of you in Washington." I found out later he'd said the same thing to every other cross-roads politician he'd met. [*He laughs.*] But Billy Herndon there is pretty disgusted with me for associating with the wrong kind of people. Billy's a firebrand—a real, radical abolitionist—and he can't stand anybody who keeps his mouth shut and abides by the Constitution. If he had his way, the whole Union would be set on fire and we'd all be burned to a crisp. Eh, Billy?

BILLY [*grimly*]: Yes, Mr. Lincoln. And if you'll permit me to say so, I think you'd be of more use to your fellow-men if you allowed some of the same incendiary impulses to come out in you.

ABE: You see, Bowling? He wants me to get down into the blood-soaked arena and grapple with all the lions of injustice and oppression.

BOWLING: Mr. Herndon—my profound compliments.

BILLY [*rising and taking his hat*]: Thank you, sir. [*He shakes hands with* BOWLING, *then turns to* ABE.] I have the writ prepared in the Willcox case. I'll take it down to the Clerk of Court to be attested.

ABE: All right, Billy.

BILLY [*to* BOWLING]: Squire Green—Mr. Lincoln regards you and Mr. Speed as the best friends he has on earth, and I should like to beg you, in his presence, for God's sake drag him out of this stagnant pool in which he's rapidly drowning himself. Good day, sir—good day, Mr. Speed.

JOSH: Good day, Billy.

[BILLY *has gone.*]

BOWLING: That's a bright young man, Abe. Seems to have a good grasp of things.

ABE [*looking after* BILLY]: He's going downstairs to the Clerk's office, but he took his hat. Which means that before he comes back to work, he'll have paid a little visit to the Chenery House saloon.

BOWLING: Does the boy drink?

ABE: Yes. He's got great fires in him, but he's putting 'em out fast. . . . Now—tell me about New Salem. [*He leans against the wall near the window.*]

BOWLING: Practically nothing of it left.

ABE: How's that blessed wife of yours?

BOWLING: Nancy's busier than ever, and more than ever concerned about your innermost thoughts and yearnings. In fact, she instructed me expressly to ask what on earth is the matter with you?

ABE [*laughs*]: You can tell her there's nothing the matter. I've been able to pay off my debts to the extent of some seven cents on the dollar, and I'm sound of skin and skeleton.

BOWLING: But why don't we hear more from you and of you?

ABE: Josh can tell you. I've been busy.

BOWLING: What at?

ABE: I'm a candidate.

JOSH [*pointing to the poster*]: Haven't you noticed his name? It's here—at the bottom of the list of Electors on the Whig ticket.

ABE: Yes, sir—if old Tippecanoe wins next fall, I'll be a member of the Electoral College.

BOWLING: The Electoral College! And is that the best you can do?

ABE: Yes—in the limited time at my disposal. I had a letter from Seth Gale—remember—he used to live in New Salem and was always aiming to move West. He's settled down in Maryland now and has a wife and a son. He says that back East they're powerful worried about the annexation of Texas.

BOWLING: They have reason to be. It would probably mean extending slavery through all the territories, from Kansas and Nebraska right out to Oregon and California. That would give the South absolute rule of the country—and God help the rest of us in the free states.

JOSH: It's an ugly situation, all right. It's got the seeds in it of nothing more nor less than civil war.

ABE: Well, if so, it'll be the abolitionists' own fault. They know where this trouble might lead, and yet they go right on agitating. They ought to be locked up for disturbing the peace, all of them.

BOWLING: I thought you were opposed to slavery, Abe. Have you changed your mind about it?

ABE [*ambles over to the couch and sprawls on it*]: No. I am opposed to slavery. But I'm even more opposed to going to war. And, on top of that, I know what you're getting at, both of you. [*He speaks to them with the utmost good nature.*] You're following Billy Herndon's lead—troubling your kind hearts with concerns about me and when am I going to amount to something. Is that it?

BOWLING: Oh, no, Abe. Far be it from me to interfere in your life.

JOSH: Or me, either. If we happen to feel that, so far, you've been a big disappointment to us, we'll surely keep it to ourselves.

ABE [*laughs*]: I'm afraid you'll have to do what I've had to do—which is, learn to accept me for what I am. I'm no fighting man. I found that out when I went through the Black

Hawk War, and was terrified that I might have to fire a shot at an Indian. Fortunately, the Indians felt the same way, so I never saw one of them. Now, I know plenty of men who like to fight; they're willing to kill, and not scared of being killed. All right. Let them attend to the battles that have to be fought.

BOWLING: Peaceable men have sometimes been of service to their country.

ABE: They may have been peaceable when they started, but they didn't remain so long after they'd become mixed in the great brawl of politics. [*He sits up.*] Suppose I ran for Congress and got elected. I'd be right in the thick of that ugly situation you were speaking of. One day I might have to cast my vote on the terrible issue of war or peace. It might be war with Mexico over Texas; or war with England over Oregon; or even war with our own people across the Ohio River. What attitude would I take in deciding which way to vote? "The Liberal attitude," of course. And what is the Liberal attitude? To go to war, for a tract of land, or a moral principle? Or to avoid war at all costs? No, sir. The place for me is in the Electoral College, where all I have to do is vote for the President whom everybody else elected four months previous.

BOWLING: Well, Abe—you were always an artful dodger—and maybe you'll be able to go on to the end of your days avoiding the clutch of your own conscience.

[NINIAN EDWARDS *comes in. He is a little stouter and more prosperous*].

ABE-JOSH: Hello, Ninian.

NINIAN: Hello. I saw Billy Herndon at the Chenery House and he said you were back from the circuit. [*He sees* BOWLING.] Why—it's my good friend Squire Green. How de do?—and welcome to Springfield. [*He shakes hands with* BOWLING.]

BOWLING: Thank you, Mr. Edwards.

NINIAN: I just called in, Abe, to tell you you must dine with us. And, Squire, Mrs. Edwards would be honored to receive you, if your engagements will permit—and you, too, Josh.

JOSH: Delighted!

NINIAN: We're proudly exhibiting my sister-in-law, Miss Mary Todd, who has just come from Kentucky to grace our home. She's a very gay young lady—speaks French like a native, recites poetry at the drop of a hat, and knows the names and habits of all the flowers. I've asked Steve Douglas and some of the other eligibles to meet her, so you boys had better get in early.

BOWLING: My compliments to Mrs. Edwards, but my own poor wife awaits me impatiently, I hope.

NINIAN: I appreciate your motives, Squire, and applaud them. You'll be along presently, Abe?

ABE: I wouldn't be surprised.

NINIAN: Good. You'll meet a delightful young lady. And I'd better warn you she's going to survey the whole field of matrimonial prospects and select the one who promises the most. So you'd better be on your guard, Abe, unless you're prepared to lose your standing as a free man.

ABE: I thank you for the warning, Ninian.

NINIAN: Good day to you, Squire. See you later, Josh. [*He goes out.*]

ABE: There, Bowling—you see how things are with me. Hardly a day goes by but what I'm invited to meet some eager young female who has all the graces, including an ability to speak the language of diplomacy.

BOWLING: I'm sorry, Abe, that I shan't be able to hear you carrying on a flirtation in French.

[ABE *looks at him, curiously.*]

ABE: I'm not pretending with you, Bowling—or you, Josh. I couldn't fool you any better than I can fool myself. I know what you're thinking about me, and I think so, too. Only I'm not so merciful in considering my own shortcomings, or so ready to forgive them, as you are. But—you talk about civil war—there seems to be one going on inside me all the time.

Both sides are right and both are wrong and equal in strength.
I'd like to be able to rise superior to the struggle—but—it
says in the Bible that a house divided against itself cannot
stand, so I reckon there's not much hope. One of these days,
I'll just split asunder, and part company with myself—and
it'll be a good riddance from both points of view. However
—come on. [*He takes his hat.*] You've got to get back to
Nancy, and Josh and I have got to make a good impression
upon Miss Mary Todd, of Kentucky. [*He waves them to the
door. As they go out, the light fades.*]

SCENE 5

*Parlor of the Edwards house in Springfield. An evening in
November, some six months after the preceding scene.*

*There is a fireplace at the right, a heavily curtained bay win-
dow at the left, a door at the back leading into the front hall.*

*At the right, by the fireplace, are a small couch and an easy
chair. There is another couch at the left, and a table and chairs
at the back. There are family portraits on the walls. It is all
moderately elegant.*

[NINIAN *is standing before the fire, in conversation with* ELIZA-
BETH, *his wife. She is high-bred, ladylike—excessively so. She is,
at the moment, in a state of some agitation.*]

ELIZABETH: I cannot believe it! It is an outrageous reflection on my sister's good sense.

NINIAN: I'm not so sure of that. Mary has known Abe for
several months, and she has had plenty of chance to observe
him closely.

ELIZABETH: She has been entertained by him, as we all
have. But she has been far more attentive to Edwin Webb
and Stephen Douglas and many others who are distinctly
eligible.

NINIAN: Isn't it remotely possible that she sees more in
Abe than you do?

ELIZABETH: Nonsense! Mr. Lincoln's chief virtues is that

he hides no part of his simple soul from any one. He's a most amiable creature, to be sure; but as the husband of a high-bred, high-spirited young lady...

NINIAN: Quite so, Elizabeth. Mary *is* high-spirited! That is just why she set her cap for him.

[ELIZABETH *looks at him sharply, then laughs.*]

ELIZABETH: You're making fun of me, Ninian. You're deliberately provoking me into becoming excited about nothing.

NINIAN: No, Elizabeth—I am merely trying to prepare you for a rude shock. You think Abe Lincoln would be overjoyed to capture an elegant, cultivated girl, daughter of the President of the Bank of Kentucky, descendant of a long line of English gentlemen. Well, you are mistaken...

[MARY TODD *comes in. She is twenty-two—short, pretty, remarkably sharp. She stops short in the doorway, and her suspecting eyes dart from* ELIZABETH *to* NINIAN.]

MARY: What were you two talking about?

NINIAN: I was telling your sister about the new song the boys are singing:

"What is the great commotion, motion,
　Our country through?
　It is the ball a-rolling on
　For Tippecanoe and Tyler, too—for Tippecanoe..."

MARY [*with a rather grim smile*]: I compliment you for thinking quickly, Ninian. But you were talking about *me!* [*She looks at* ELIZABETH, *who quails a little before her sister's determination.*] Weren't you?

ELIZABETH: Yes, Mary, we were.

MARY: And quite seriously, I gather.

NINIAN: I'm afraid that our dear Elizabeth has become unduly alarmed...

ELIZABETH [*snapping at him*]: Let me say what I have to say! [*She turns to* MARY.] Mary—you must tell me the truth. Are you—have you ever given one moment's serious thought to the possibility of marriage with Abraham Lincoln? [MARY *looks at each of them, her eyes flashing.*] I promise you, Mary, that to me such a notion is too far beyond the bounds of credibility to be . . .

MARY: But Ninian has raised the horrid subject, hasn't he? He has brought the evil scandal out into the open, and we must face it, fearlessly. Let us do so at once, by all means. I shall answer you, Elizabeth: I have given more than one moment's thought to the possibility you mentioned—and I have decided that I shall be Mrs. Lincoln. [*She seats herself on the couch.* NINIAN *is about to say, "I told you so," but thinks better of it.* ELIZABETH *can only gasp and gape.*] I have examined, carefully, the qualifications of all the young gentlemen, and some of the old ones, in this neighborhood. Those of Mr. Lincoln seem to me superior to all others, and he is my choice.

ELIZABETH: Do you expect me to congratulate you upon this amazing selection?

MARY: No! I ask for no congratulations, nor condolences, either.

ELIZABETH [*turning away*]: Then I shall offer none.

NINIAN: Forgive me for prying, Mary—but have you as yet communicated your decision to the gentleman himself?

MARY [*with a slight smile at* NINIAN]: Not yet. But he is coming to call this evening, and he will ask humbly for my hand in marriage; and, after I have displayed the proper amount of surprise and confusion, I shall murmur, timidly, "Yes!"

ELIZABETH [*pitiful*]: You make a brave jest of it, Mary. But as for me, I am deeply and painfully shocked. I don't know what to say to you. But I urge you, I beg you, as your elder sister, responsible to our father and our dead mother for your welfare . . .

MARY [*with a certain tenderness*]: I can assure you, Elizabeth—it is useless to beg or command. I have made up my mind.

NINIAN: I admire your courage, Mary, but I should like . . .

ELIZABETH: I think, Ninian, that this is a matter for discussion solely between my sister and myself!

MARY: No! I want to hear what Ninian has to say. [*To* NINIAN.] What is it?

NINIAN: I only wondered if I might ask you another question.

MARY [*calmly*]: You may.

NINIAN: Understand, my dear—I'm not quarreling with you. My affection for Abe is eternal—but—I'm curious to know—what is it about him that makes you choose him for a husband?

MARY [*betraying her first sign of uncertainty*]: I should like to give you a plain, simple answer, Ninian. But I cannot.

ELIZABETH [*jumping at this*]: Of course you cannot! You're rushing blindly into this. You have no conception of what it will mean to your future.

MARY: You're wrong about that, Elizabeth. This is not the result of wild, tempestuous infatuation. I have not been swept off my feet. Mr. Lincoln is a Westerner, but that is his only point of resemblance to Young Lochinvar. I simply feel that of all the men I've ever known, he is the one whose life and destiny I want most to share.

ELIZABETH: Haven't you sense enough to know you could never be happy with him? His breeding—his background—his manner—his whole point of view . . . ?

MARY [*gravely*]: I could not be content with a "happy" marriage in the accepted sense of the word. I have no craving for comfort and security.

ELIZABETH: And have you a craving for the kind of life you would lead? A miserable cabin, without a servant, without a stitch of clothing that is fit for exhibition in decent society?

MARY [*raising her voice*]: I have not yet tried poverty, so I cannot say how I should take to it. But I might well prefer it to anything I have previously known—so long as there is forever before me the chance for high adventure—so long as I can know that I am always going forward, with my husband, along a road that leads across the horizon. [*This last is said with a sort of mad intensity.*]

ELIZABETH: And how far do you think you will go with any one like Abe Lincoln, who is lazy and shiftless and prefers to stop constantly along the way to tell jokes?

MARY [*rising; furious*]: He will *not* stop, if I am strong enough to make him go on! And I am strong! I know what *you* expect of me. You want me to do precisely as you have done—and marry a man like Ninian—and I know many, that are *just* like him! But with all due respect to my dear brother-in-law—I don't want that—and I won't have it! Never! You live in a house with a fence around it—presumably to prevent the common herd from gaining access to your sacred precincts—but really to prevent you, yourselves, from escaping from your own narrow lives. In Abraham Lincoln I see a man who has split rails for other men's fences, but who will never build one around himself!

ELIZABETH: What are you *saying*, Mary? You are talking with a degree of irresponsibility that is not far from sheer madness . . .

MARY [*scornfully*]: I imagine it does seem like insanity to you! You married a man who was settled and established in the world, with a comfortable inheritance, and no problems to face. And you've never made a move to change your condition, or improve it. You consider it couldn't be improved. To you, all this represents perfection. But it doesn't to me! I want the chance to *shape* a new life, for myself, and for my husband. Is that irresponsibility?

[*A* MAID *appears.*]

MAID: Mr. Lincoln, ma'am.

ELIZABETH: He's here.

MARY [*firmly*]: I shall see him!

MAID: Will you step in, Mr. Lincoln?

[ABE *comes in, wearing a new suit, his hair nearly neat.*]

ABE: Good evening, Mrs. Edwards. Good evening, Miss Todd. Ninian, good evening.

ELIZABETH: Good evening.

MARY: Good evening, Mr. Lincoln. [*She sits on the couch at the left.*]

NINIAN: Glad to see you, Abe.

[ABE *sees that there is electricity in the atmosphere of this parlor. He tries hard to be affably casual.*]

ABE: I'm afraid I'm a little late in arriving, but I ran into an old friend of mine, wife of Jack Armstrong, the champion rowdy of New Salem. I believe you have some recollection of him, Ninian.

NINIAN [*smiling*]: I most certainly have. What's he been up to now?

ABE [*stands in front of the fireplace*]: Oh, he's all right, but Hannah, his wife, is in fearful trouble because her son Duff is up for murder and she wants me to defend him. I went over to the jail to interview the boy and he looks pretty tolerably guilty to me. But I used to give him lessons in the game of marbles while his mother fixed my pants for me. [*He turns to* ELIZABETH.] That means, she sewed buckskin around the legs of my pants so I wouldn't tear 'em to shreds going through underbrush when I was surveying. Well—in view of old times, I felt I had to take the case and do what I can to obstruct the orderly processes of justice.

NINIAN [*laughs, with some relief*]: And the boy will be acquitted. I tell you, Abe—this country would be law-abiding and peaceful if it weren't for you lawyers. But—if you will excuse Elizabeth and me, we must hear the children's prayers and see them safely abed.

ABE: Why—I'd be glad to hear their prayers, too.

NINIAN: Oh, no! You'd only keep them up till all hours with your stories. Come along, Elizabeth.

[ELIZABETH *doesn't want to go, but doesn't know what to do to prevent it.*]

ABE [*to* ELIZABETH]: Kiss them good night, for me.

NINIAN: We'd better not tell them you're in the house, or they'll be furious.

ELIZABETH [*making one last attempt*]: Mary! Won't you come with us and say good night to the children?

NINIAN: No, my dear. Leave Mary here—to keep Abe entertained. [*He guides* ELIZABETH *out, following her.*]

MARY [*with a little laugh*]: I don't blame Ninian for keeping you away from those children. They all adore you.

ABE: Well—I always seemed to get along well with children. Probably it's because they never want to take me seriously.

MARY: You understand them—that's the important thing ... But—do sit down, Mr. Lincoln. [*She indicates that he is to sit next to her.*]

ABE: Thank you—I will. [*He starts to cross to the couch to sit beside* MARY. *She looks at him with melting eyes. The lights fade.*]

SCENE 6

Again the Law Office. It is afternoon of New Year's Day, a few weeks after the preceding scene.

[ABE *is sitting, slumped in his chair, staring at his desk. He has his hat and overcoat on. A muffler is hanging about his neck, untied.*

JOSH SPEED *is half-sitting on the table at the right. He is reading a long letter, with most serious attention. At length he finishes it, refolds it very carefully, stares at the floor.*]

ABE: Have you finished it, Josh?

JOSH: Yes.

ABE: Well—do you think it's all right?

JOSH: No, Abe—I don't. [ABE *turns slowly and looks at him.*] I think the sending of this letter would be a most grave mistake—and that is putting it mildly and charitably.

ABE: Have I stated the case too crudely?

[ABE *is evidently in a serious state of distress, although he is making a tremendous effort to disguise it by speaking in what he intends to be a coldly impersonal tone. He is struggling mightily to hold himself back from the brink of nervous collapse.*]

JOSH: No—I have no quarrel with your choice of words. None whatever. If anything, the phraseology is too correct. But your method of doing it, Abe! It's brutal, it's heartless, it's so unworthy of you that I—I'm at a loss to understand how you ever thought you could do it this way.

ABE: I've done the same thing before with a woman to whom I seemed to have become attached. She approved of my action.

JOSH: This is a different woman. [*He walks over to the window, then turns again toward* ABE.] You cannot seem to accept the fact that women are human beings, too, as variable as we are. You act on the assumption that they're all the same one—and that one is a completely unearthly being of your own conception. This letter isn't written to Mary Todd —it's written to yourself. Every line of it is intended to provide salve for your own conscience.

ABE [*rising; coldly*]: Do I understand that you will not deliver it for me?

JOSH: No, Abe—I shall not.

ABE [*angrily*]: Then some one else will!

JOSH [*scornfully*]: Yes. You could give it to the minister, to hand to the bride when he arrives for the ceremony. But— I hope, Abe, you won't send it till you're feeling a little calmer in your mind. . . .

ABE [*vehemently, turning to* JOSH]: How can I ever be calm in my mind until this thing is settled, and out of the way, once and for all? Have you got eyes in your head, Josh? Can't you see that I'm desperate?

JOSH: I can see that plainly, Abe. I think your situation is more desperate even than you imagine, and I believe you should have the benefit of some really intelligent medical advice.

ABE [*seating himself at* BILLY's *table*]: The trouble with me isn't anything that a doctor can cure.

JOSH: There's a good man named Dr. Drake, who makes a specialty of treating people who get into a state of mind like yours, Abe . . .

ABE [*utterly miserable*]: So that's how you've figured it! I've done what I've threatened to do many times before: I've gone crazy. Well—you know me better than most men, Josh—

and perhaps you're not far off right. I just feel that I've got to the end of my rope, and I must let go, and drop—and where I'll land, I don't know, and whether I'll survive the fall, I don't know that either. . . . But—this I *do* know: I've got to get out of this thing—I can't go through with it—I've got to have my release!

[JOSH *has turned to the window. Suddenly he turns back, toward* ABE.]

JOSH: Ninian Edwards is coming up. Why not show this letter to him and ask for his opinion. . . .

ABE [*interrupting, with desperation*]: No, no! Don't say a word of any of this to him! Put that letter in your pocket. I can't bear to discuss this business with him, now.

[JOSH *puts the letter in his pocket and crosses to the couch.*]

JOSH: Hello, Ninian.

NINIAN [*heartily, from off*]: Hello, Josh! Happy New Year! [NINIAN *comes in. He wears a handsome, fur-trimmed great-coat, and carries two silver-headed canes, one of them in a baize bag, which he lays down on the table at the right.*]

NINIAN: And Happy New Year, Abe—in fact, the happiest of your whole life!

ABE: Thank you, Ninian. And Happy New Year to you.

NINIAN [*opening his coat*]: That didn't sound much as if you meant it. [*He goes to the stove to warm his hands.*] However, you can be forgiven, Abe. I suppose you're inclined to be just a wee bit nervous. [*He chuckles and winks at* JOSH.] God—but it's cold in here! Don't you ever light this stove?

ABE: The fire's all laid. Go ahead and light it, if you want.

NINIAN [*striking a match*]: You certainly are in one of your less amiable moods today. [*He lights the stove.*]

JOSH: Abe's been feeling a little under the weather.

NINIAN: So it seems. He looks to me as if he'd been to a funeral.

ABE: That's where I have been.

NINIAN [*disbelieving*]: What? A funeral on your wedding day?

JOSH: They buried Abe's oldest friend, Bowling Green, this morning.

NINIAN [*shocked*]: Oh—I'm mighty sorry to hear that, Abe. And—I hope you'll forgive me for—not having known about it.

ABE: Of course, Ninian.

NINIAN: But I'm glad you were there, Abe, at the funeral. It must have been a great comfort to his family.

ABE: I wasn't any comfort to any one. They asked me to deliver an oration, a eulogy of the deceased—and I tried—and I couldn't say a thing. Why do they expect you to strew a lot of flowery phrases over anything so horrible as a dead body? Do they think that Bowling Green's soul needs quotations to give it peace? All that mattered to me was that he was a good, just man—and I loved him—and he's dead.

NINIAN: Why didn't you say that, Abe?

ABE [*rising*]: I told you—they wanted an oration.

NINIAN: Well, Abe—I think Bowling himself would be the first to ask you to put your sadness aside in the prospect of your own happiness, and Mary's—and I'm only sorry that our old friend didn't live to see you two fine people married. [*He is making a gallant attempt to assume a more cheerily nuptial tone.*] I've made all the arrangements with the Reverend Dresser, and Elizabeth is preparing a bang-up dinner—so you can be sure the whole affair will be carried off handsomely *and* painlessly. [BILLY HERNDON *comes in. He carries a bottle in his coat pocket, and is already more than a little drunk and sullen, but abnormally articulate.*] Ah, Billy—Happy New Year!

BILLY: The same to you, Mr. Edwards. [*He puts the bottle down on the table and takes his coat off.*]

NINIAN: I brought you a wedding present, Abe. Thought you'd like to make a brave show when you first walk out with your bride. It came from the same place in Louisville where I bought mine. [*He picks up one of the canes and hands it proudly to* ABE, *who takes it and inspects it gravely.*]

ABE: It's very fine, Ninian. And I thank you. [*He takes the cane over to his desk and seats himself.*]

NINIAN: Well—I'll frankly confess that in getting it for you, I was influenced somewhat by consideration for Mary and her desire for keeping up appearances. And in that connection—I know you'll forgive me, Josh, and you, too, Billy, if I say something of a somewhat personal nature.

BILLY [*truculent*]: If you want me to leave you, I shall be glad to. . . .

NINIAN: No, please, Billy—I merely want to speak a word or two as another of Abe's friends; it's my last chance before the ceremony. Of course, the fact that the bride is my sister-in-law gives me a little added responsibility in wishing to promote the success of this marriage. [*He crosses to* ABE.] And a success it will be, Abe . . . if only you will bear in mind one thing: you must keep a tight rein on her ambition. My wife tells me that even as a child, she had delusions of grandeur—she predicted to one and all that the man she would marry would be President of the United States. [*He turns to* JOSH.] You know how it is—every boy in the country plans some day to be President, and every little girl plans to marry him. [*Again to* ABE:] But Mary is one who hasn't entirely lost those youthful delusions. So I urge you to beware. Don't let her talk you into any gallant crusades or wild goose chases. Let her learn to be satisfied with the estate to which God hath brought her. With which, I shall conclude my pre-nuptial sermon. [*He buttons his coat.*] I shall see you all at the house at five o'clock, and I want you to make sure that Abe is looking his prettiest.

JOSH: Good-by, Ninian.

[NINIAN *goes out.* ABE *turns again to the desk and stares at nothing.* BILLY *takes the bottle and a cup from his desk and pours himself a stiff drink. He raises the cup toward* ABE.]

BILLY [*huskily*]: Mr. Lincoln, I beg leave to drink to your health and happiness . . . and to that of the lady who will become your wife. [ABE *makes no response.* BILLY *drinks it down, then puts the cup back on the table.*] You don't want to accept my toast because you think it wasn't sincere. And I'll admit I've made it plain that I've regretted the step you've taken. I thought that in this marriage, you were lowering yourself—you were trading your honor for some exalted family connections. . . . I wish to apologize for so thinking. . . .

ABE: No apologies required, Billy.

BILLY: I doubt that Miss Todd and I will ever get along well together. But I'm now convinced that our aims are the same—particularly since I've heard the warnings delivered by her brother-in-law. [*A note of scorn colors his allusion to* NINIAN.] If she really is ambitious for you—if she will never stop driving you, goading you—then I say, God bless her, and give her strength! [*He has said all this with* ABE's *back to him.* BILLY *pours himself another drink, nearly emptying the large bottle.* ABE *turns and looks at him.*]

ABE: Have you had all of that bottle today?

BILLY: This bottle? Yes—I have.

JOSH: And why not? It's New Year's Day!

BILLY [*looking at* JOSH]: Thank you, Mr. Speed. Thank you for the defense. And I hope you will permit me to propose one more toast. [*He takes a step toward* ABE.] To the President of the United States, and Mrs. Lincoln! [*He drinks.*]

ABE [*grimly*]: I think we can do without any more toasts, Billy.

BILLY: Very well! That's the last one—until after the wedding. And then, no doubt, the Edwards will serve us with the costliest champagne. And, in case you're apprehensive, I shall be on my best behavior in that distinguished gathering!

ABE: There is not going to be a wedding. [BILLY *stares at him, and then looks at* JOSH, *and then again at* ABE.] I have a letter that I want you to deliver to Miss Todd.

BILLY: What letter? What is it?

ABE: Give it to him, Josh. [JOSH *takes the letter out of his pocket, and puts it in the stove.* ABE *jumps up.*] You have no right to do that!

JOSH: I know I haven't! But it's done. [ABE *is staring at* JOSH.] And don't look at me as if you were planning to break my neck. Of course you could do it, Abe—but you won't. [JOSH *turns to* BILLY.] In that letter, Mr. Lincoln asked Miss Todd for his release. He told her that he had made a mistake in his previous protestations of affection for her, and so he couldn't go through with a marriage which could only lead to endless pain and misery for them both.

ABE [*deeply distressed*]: If that isn't the truth, what is?

JOSH: I'm not disputing the truth of it. I'm only asking you to tell her so, to her face, in the manner of a man.

ABE: It would be a more cruel way. It would hurt her more deeply. For I couldn't help blurting it *all* out—all the terrible things I didn't say in that letter. [*He is speaking with passion.*] I'd have to tell her that I have hatred for her infernal ambition—that I don't want to be ridden and driven, upward and onward through life, with her whip lashing me, and her spurs digging into me! If her poor soul craves importance in life, then let her marry Stephen Douglas. He's ambitious, too. . . . I want only to be left alone! [*He sits down again and leans on the table.*]

JOSH [*bitterly*]: Very well, then—tell her all that! It will be more gracious to admit that you're afraid of her, instead of letting her down flat with the statement that your ardor, such as it was, has cooled.

[BILLY *has been seething with a desire to get into this conversation. Now, with a momentary silence, he plunges.*]

BILLY: May I say something?

ABE: I doubt that you're in much of a condition to contribute. . . .

JOSH: What is it, Billy?

BILLY [*hotly*]: It's just this. Mr. Lincoln, you're not abandoning Miss Mary Todd. No! You're only using her as a living sacrifice, offering her up, in the hope that you will thus gain forgiveness of the gods for your failure to do your great duty!

ABE [*smouldering*]: Yes! My own great duty. Every one

feels called upon to remind me of it, but no one can tell me what it is.

BILLY [*almost tearful*]: I can tell you! I can tell you what is the duty of every man who calls himself an American! It is to perpetuate those truths which were once held to be self-evident: that all men are created equal—that they are endowed with certain inalienable rights—that among these are the right to life, liberty, and the pursuit of happiness.

ABE [*angrily*]: And are those rights denied to *me?*

BILLY: Could you ever enjoy them while your mind is full of the awful knowledge that two million of your fellow beings in this country are slaves? Can you take any satisfaction from looking at that flag above your desk, when you know that ten of its stars represent states which are willing to destroy the Union—rather than yield their property rights in the flesh and blood of those slaves? And what of all the States of the future? All the territories of the West—clear out to the Pacific Ocean? Will they be the homes of free men? Are you answering *that* question to your own satisfaction? That is your flag, Mr. Lincoln, and you're proud of it. But what are you doing to save it from being ripped into shreds?

[ABE *jumps to his feet, towers over* BILLY *and speaks with temper restrained, but with great passion.*]

ABE: I'm minding my own business—that's what I'm doing! And there'd be no threat to the Union if others would do the same. And as to slavery—I'm sick and tired of this righteous talk about it. When you know more about law, you'll know that those property rights you mentioned are guaranteed by the Constitution. And if the Union can't stand on the Constitution, then let it fall!

BILLY: The hell with the Constitution! This is a matter of the rights of living men to freedom—and those come before the Constitution! When the Law denies those rights, the the Law is wrong, and it must be changed, if not by moral protest, then by force! There's no course of action that isn't justified in the defense of freedom! And don't dare to tell me that any one in the world knows that better than you do,

Mr. Lincoln. You, who honor the memory of Elijah Lovejoy and every other man who ever died for that very ideal!

ABE [*turning away from him*]: Yes—I honor them—and envy them—because they could believe that their ideals are worth dying for. [*He turns to* JOSH *and speaks with infinite weariness.*] All right, Josh—I'll go up now and talk to Mary— and then I'm going away....

JOSH: Where, Abe?

ABE [*dully*]: I don't know. [*He goes out and closes the door after him. After a moment,* BILLY *rushes to the door, opens it, and shouts after* ABE.]

BILLY: You're quitting, Mr. Lincoln! As surely as there's a God in Heaven, He knows that you're running away from your obligation to Him, and to your fellow-men, and your own immortal soul!

JOSH [*drawing* BILLY *away from the door*]: Billy—Billy— leave him alone. He's a sick man.

BILLY [*sitting down at the table*]: What can we do for him, Mr. Speed? What can we do? [BILLY *is now actually in tears.*]

JOSH: I don't know, Billy. [*He goes to the window and looks out.*] He'll be in such a state of emotional upheaval, he'll want to go away by himself, for a long time. Just as he did after the death of poor little Ann Rutledge. He'll go out and wander on the prairies, trying to grope his way back into the wilderness from which he came. There's nothing we can do for him, Billy. He'll have to do it for himself.

BILLY [*fervently*]: May God be with him!

[*The lights fade.*]

SCENE 7

On the prairie near New Salem. It is a clear, cool, moonlit eve-ning, nearly two years after the preceding scene.

In the foreground is a campfire. Around it are packing cases, blanket rolls and one ancient trunk. In the background is a

*covered wagon, standing at an angle, so that the opening at the
back of it is visible to the audience.*

[SETH GALE *is standing by the fire, holding his seven-year-old
son,* JIMMY, *in his arms. The boy is wrapped up in a blanket.*]

JIMMY: I don't want to be near the fire, Paw. I'm burning
up. Won't you take the blanket offen me, Paw?

SETH: No, son. You're better off if you keep yourself
covered.

JIMMY: I want some water, Paw. Can't I have some water?

SETH: Yes! Keep quiet, Jimmy! Gobey's getting the water
for you now. [*He looks off to the right, and sees* JACK ARM-
STRONG *coming.*] Hello, Jack. I was afraid you'd got lost.

JACK [*coming in*]: I couldn't get lost anywhere's around
New Salem. How's the boy?

SETH [*with a cautionary look at* JACK]: He—he's a little bit
thirsty. Did you find Abe?

JACK: Yes—it took me some time because he'd wandered off
—went out to the old cemetery across the river to visit Ann
Rutledge's grave.

SETH: Is he coming here?

JACK: He said he'd better go get Doc Chandler who lives
on the Winchester Road. He'll be along in a while. [*He
comes up to* JIMMY.] How you feelin', Jimmy?

JIMMY: I'm burning . . .

[AGGIE *appears, sees* JACK.]

AGGIE: Oh—I'm glad you're back, Mr. Armstrong.

JACK: There'll be a doctor here soon, Mrs. Gale.

AGGIE: Thank God for that! Bring him into the wagon,
Seth. I got a nice, soft bed all ready for him.

SETH: You hear that, Jimmy? Your ma's fixed a place
where you can rest comfortable.

[AGGIE *retreats into the wagon.*]

JIMMY: When'll Gobey come back? I'm thirsty. When'll he
bring the water?

SETH: Right away, son. You can trust Gobey to get your
water. [*He hands* JIMMY *into the wagon.*]

JACK: He's worse, ain't he?

SETH [*in a despairing tone*]: Yes. The fever's been raging something fierce since you left. It'll sure be a relief when Abe gets here. He can always do something to put confidence in you.

JACK: How long since you've seen Abe, Seth?

SETH: Haven't laid eyes on him since I left here—eight—nine years ago. We've corresponded some.

JACK: Well—you may be surprised when you see him. He's changed plenty since he went to Springfield. He climbed up pretty high in the world, but he appears to have slipped down lately. He ain't much like his old comical self.

SETH: Well, I guess we all got to change. [*He starts up, hearing* GOBEY *return.*] Aggie! [GOBEY, *a Negro, comes in from the left, carrying a bucket of water.* AGGIE *appears from the wagon.*] Here's Gobey with the water.

GOBEY: Yes, Miss Aggie. Here you are. [*He hands it up.*]

AGGIE: Thanks, Gobey. [*She goes back into the wagon.*]

GOBEY: How's Jimmy now, Mr. Seth?

SETH: About the same.

GOBEY [*shaking his head*]: I'll get some more water for the cooking. [*He picks up a kettle and a pot and goes.*]

SETH [*to* JACK]: It was a bad thing to have happen, all right—the boy getting sick—when we were on an expedition like this. No doctor—no way of caring for him.

JACK: How long you been on the road, Seth?

SETH: More than three months. Had a terrible time in the Pennsylvania Mountains, fearful rains and every stream flooded. I can tell you, there was more than one occasion when I wanted to turn back and give up the whole idea. But —when you get started—you just can't turn . . . [*He is looking off right.*] Say! Is that Abe coming now?

JACK [*rising*]: Yep. That's him.

SETH [*delighted*]: My God, look at him! Store clothes and a plug hat! Hello—Abe!

ABE: Hello, Seth. [*He comes on and shakes hands, warmly.*] I'm awful glad to see you again, Seth.

SETH: And me, too, Abe.

ABE: It did my heart good when I heard you were on your way West. Where's your boy?

SETH: He's in there—in the wagon. . . .

[AGGIE *has appeared from the wagon.*]

AGGIE: Is that the doctor?

SETH: No, Aggie—this is the man I was telling you about I wanted so much to see. This is Mr. Abe Lincoln—my wife, Mrs. Gale.

ABE: Pleased to meet you, Mrs. Gale.

AGGIE: Pleased to meet you, Mr. Lincoln.

ABE: Doc Chandler wasn't home. They said he was expected over at the Boger farm at midnight. I'll go there then and fetch him.

SETH: It'll be a friendly act, Abe.

AGGIE: We'll be in your debt, Mr. Lincoln.

ABE: In the meantime, Mrs. Gale, I'd like to do whatever I can. . . .

SETH: There's nothing to do, Abe. The boy's got the swamp fever, and we're just trying to keep him quiet.

AGGIE [*desperately*]: There's just one thing I would wish—is—is there any kind of a preacher around this God-forsaken place?

SETH [*worried*]: Preacher?

ABE: Do you know of any, Jack?

JACK: No. There ain't a preacher within twenty miles of New Salem now.

AGGIE: Well—I only thought if there was, we might get him here to say a prayer for Jimmy. [*She goes back into the wagon.* SETH *looks after her with great alarm.*]

SETH: She wants a preacher. That looks as if she'd given up, don't it?

JACK: It'd probably just comfort her.

ABE: Is your boy very sick, Seth?

SETH: Yes—he is.

JACK: Why don't *you* speak a prayer, Abe? You could always think of somethin' to say.

ABE: I'm afraid I'm not much of a hand at praying. I couldn't think of a blessed thing that would be of any comfort.

SETH: Never mind. It's just a—a religious idea of Aggie's. Sit down, Abe.

ABE [*looking at the wagon*]: So you've got your dream at last, Seth. You're doing what you and I used to talk about—you're moving.

SETH: Yes, Abe. We got crowded out of Maryland. The city grew up right over our farm. So—we're headed for a place where there's more room. I wrote you—about four months back—to tell you we were starting out, and I'd like to meet up with you here. I thought it was just possible you might consider joining in this trip.

ABE: It took a long time for your letter to catch up with me, Seth. I've just been drifting—down around Indiana and Kentucky where I used to live. [*He sits down on a box.*] Do you aim to settle in Nebraska?

SETH: No, we're not going to stop there. We're going right across the continent—all the way to Oregon.

ABE [*deeply impressed*]: Oregon?

JACK: Sure. That's where they're all headin' for now.

SETH: We're making first for a place called Westport Landing—that's in Kansas right on the frontier—where they outfit the wagon trains for the far West. You join up there with a lot of others who are like-minded, so you've got company when you're crossing the plains and the mountains.

ABE: It's staggering—to think of the distance you're going. And you'll be taking the frontier along with you.

SETH: It may seem like a fool-hardy thing to do—but we heard too many tales of the black earth out there, and the balance of rainfall and sunshine.

JACK: Why don't you go with them, Abe? That country out west is gettin' settled fast. Why—last week alone, I counted more than two hundred wagons went past here—people from all over—Pennsylvania, Connecticut, Vermont—all full of jubilation at the notion of gettin' land. By God, I'm goin' too, soon as I can get me a wagon. They'll need men like me to fight the Indians for 'em—and they'll need men with brains, like you, Abe, to tell 'em how to keep the peace.

ABE [*looking off*]: It's a temptation to go, I can't deny that.

JACK: Then what's stoppin' you from doin' it? You said yourself you've just been driftin'.

ABE: Maybe that's it—maybe I've been drifting too long. ... [*He changes the subject.*] Is it just the three of you, Seth?

SETH: That's all. The three of us and Gobey the nigger.

ABE: Is he your slave?

SETH: Gobey? Hell, no! He's a free man! My father freed his father twenty years ago. But we've had to be mighty careful about Gobey. You see, where we come from, folks are pretty uncertain how they feel about the slave question, and lots of good free niggers get snaked over the line into Virginia and then sold down river before you know it. And when you try to go to court and assert their legal rights, you're beaten at every turn by the damned, dirty shyster lawyers. That's why we've been keeping well up in free territory on this trip.

ABE: Do you think it will be free in Oregon?

SETH: Of course it will! It's got to...

ABE [*bitterly*]: Oh no, it hasn't, Seth. Not with the politicians in Washington selling out the whole West piece by piece to the slave traders.

SETH [*vehemently*]: That territory has got to be free! If this country ain't strong enough to protect its citizens from slavery, then we'll cut loose from it and join with Canada. Or, better yet, we'll make a *new* country out there in the far west.

ABE [*gravely*]: A new country?

SETH: Why not?

ABE: I was just thinking—old Mentor Graham once said to me that some day the United States might be divided up into many hostile countries like Europe.

SETH: Well—let it be! Understand—I love this country and I'd fight for it. And I guess George Washington and the rest of them loved England and fought for it when they were young—but they didn't hesitate to cut loose when the government failed to play fair and square with 'em. . . .

JACK: By God, if Andy Jackson was back in the White House, he'd run out them traitors with a horsewhip!

ABE: It'd be a bad day for us Americans, Seth, if we lost you, and your wife, and your son.

SETH [*breaking*]: My son!—Oh!—I've been talking big—but it's empty talk. If he dies—there won't be enough spirit left in us to push on any further. What's the use of working for a future when you know there won't be anybody growing up to enjoy it. Excuse me, Abe—but I'm feeling pretty scared.

ABE [*suddenly rises*]: You mustn't be scared, Seth. I know I'm a poor one to be telling you that—because I've been scared all my life. But—seeing you now—and thinking of the big thing you've set out to do—well, it's made me feel pretty small. It's made me feel that I've got to do something, too, to keep you and your kind in the United States of America. You mustn't quit, Seth! Don't let anything beat you—don't you ever give up!

[AGGIE *comes out of the wagon. She is very frightened.*]

AGGIE: Seth!

SETH: What is it, Aggie?

AGGIE: He's worse, Seth! He's moaning in his sleep, and he's gasping for breath. . . . [*She is crying.* SETH *takes her in his arms.*]

SETH: Never mind, honey. Never mind. When the doctor gets here, he'll fix him up in no time. It's all right, honey. He'll get well.

ABE: If you wish me to, Mrs. Gale—I'll try to speak a prayer.

[*They look at him.*]

JACK: That's the way to talk, Abe!

SETH: We'd be grateful for anything you might say, Abe.

[ABE *takes his hat off. As he starts speaking,* GOBEY *comes in from the left and stops reverently to listen.*]

ABE: Oh God, the father of all living, I ask you to look with gentle mercy upon this little boy who is here, lying sick in this covered wagon. His people are travelling far, to seek a new home in the wilderness, to do your work, God, to make this earth a good place for your children to live in. They can see clearly where they're going, and they're not afraid to face all the perils that lie along the way. I humbly beg you not to take their child from them. Grant him the freedom of life. Do not condemn him to the imprisonment of death. Do not deny him his birthright. Let him know the sight of great plains and high mountains, of green valleys and wide rivers. For this little boy is an American, and these things belong to him, and he to them. Spare him, that he too may strive for the ideal for which his fathers have labored, so faithfully and for so long. Spare him and give him his father's strength—give us all strength, O God, to do the work that is before us. I ask you this favor, in the name of *your* son, Jesus Christ, who died upon the Cross to set men free. Amen.

GOBEY [*with fervor*]: Amen!

SETH-AGGIE [*murmuring*]: Amen!

[ABE *puts his hat on.*]

ABE: It's getting near midnight. I'll go over to the Boger farm and get the doctor. [*He goes out.*]

SETH: Thank you, Abe.

AGGIE: Thank you—thank you, Mr. Lincoln.

GOBEY: God bless you, Mr. Lincoln!

[*The lights fade quickly.*]

SCENE 8

Again the parlor of the Edwards house. A few days after preceding scene.

[MARY *is seated, reading a book. After a moment, the* MAID *enters.*]

MAID: Miss Mary—Mr. Lincoln is here.

MARY: Mr. Lincoln! [*She sits still a moment in an effort to control her emotions, then sharply closes the book and rises.*]

MAID: Will you see him, Miss Mary?

MARY: Yes—in one moment. [*The* MAID *goes off.* MARY *turns, drops her book on the sofa, then moves over toward the right, struggling desperately to compose herself. At the fireplace, she stops and turns to face* ABE *as he enters.*] I'm glad to see you again, Mr. Lincoln. [*There is considerable constraint between them. He is grimly determined to come to the point with the fewest possible words; she is making a gallant, well-bred attempt to observe the social amenities.*]

ABE: Thank you, Mary. You may well wonder why I have thrust myself on your mercy in this manner.

MARY [*quickly*]: I'm sure you're always welcome in Ninian's house.

ABE: After my behavior at our last meeting here, I have not been welcome company for myself.

MARY: You've been through a severe illness. Joshua Speed has kept us informed of it. We've been greatly concerned.

ABE: It is most kind of you.

MARY: But you're restored to health now—you'll return to your work, and no doubt you'll be running for the assembly again—or perhaps you have larger plans?

ABE: I have no plans, Mary. [*He seems to brace himself.*] But I wish to tell you that I am sorry for the things that I said on that unhappy occasion which was to have been our wedding day.

MARY: You need not say anything about that, Mr. Lincoln. Whatever happened then, it was my own fault.

ABE [*disturbed by this unforeseen avowal*]: *Your* fault! It was my miserable cowardice . . .

MARY: I was blinded by my own self-confidence! I—I loved you. [*For a moment her firm voice falters, but she immediately masters that tendency toward weakness.*] And I believed I could make you love me. I believed we might achieve a real communion of spirit, and the fire of my determination would burn in you. You would become a man and a leader of men! But you didn't wish that. [*She turns away.*] I knew you had strength—but I did not know you would use it, all of it, to resist your own magnificent destiny.

ABE [*deliberately*]: It is true, Mary—you once had faith in me which I was far from deserving. But the time has come, at last, when I wish to strive to deserve it. [MARY *looks at him sharply.*] When I behaved in that shameful manner toward you, I did so because I thought that our ways were separate and could never be otherwise. I've come to the conclusion that I was wrong. I believe that our destinies are together, for better or for worse, and I again presume to ask you to be my wife. I fully realise, Mary, that taking me back now would involve humiliation for you.

MARY [*flaring*]: I am not afraid of humiliation, if I know it will be wiped out by ultimate triumph! But there can be no triumph unless you yourself are sure. What was it that brought you to this change of heart and mind?

ABE: On the prairie, I met an old friend of mine who was moving West, with his wife and child, in a covered wagon. He asked me to go with him, and I was strongly tempted to do so. [*There is great sadness in his tone—but he seems to collect himself, and turns to her again, speaking with a sort of resignation.*] But then I knew that was not my direction. The way I must go is the way you have always wanted me to go.

MARY: And you will promise that never again will you falter, or turn to run away?

ABE: I promise, Mary—if you will have me—I shall devote myself for the rest of my days to trying—to do what is right —as God gives me power to see what is right.

[*She looks at him, trying to search him. She would like to torment him, for a while, with artful indecision. But she cannot do it.*]

MARY: Very well, then—I shall be your wife. I shall fight by your side—till death do us part. [*She runs to him and clutches him.*] Abe! I love you—oh, I love you! Whatever becomes of the two of us, I'll die loving you! [*She is sobbing wildly on his shoulder.*]

[*Awkwardly, he lifts his hands and takes hold of her in a loose embrace. He is staring down at the carpet, over her shoulder.*]

[*Curtain*]

ACT THREE

Scene 9

A speakers' platform in an Illinois town. It is a summer evening in the year 1858.

A light shines down on the speaker at the front of the platform.

[At the back of the platform are three chairs. At the right sits Judge Stephen A. Douglas—*at the left,* Abe, *who has his plug hat on and makes occasional notes on a piece of paper on his knee. The chair in the middle is for* Ninian, *acting as Moderator, who is now at the front of the platform.]*

Ninian: We have now heard the leading arguments from the two candidates for the high office of United States Senator from Illinois—Judge Stephen A. Douglas and Mr. Abraham Lincoln. A series of debates between these two eminent citizens of Illinois has focused upon our state the attention of the entire nation, for here are being discussed the vital issues which now affect the lives of all Americans and the whole future history of our beloved country. According to the usual custom of debate, each of the candidates will now speak in rebuttal. . . . Judge Douglas.

*[*Ninian *retires and sits, as* Douglas *comes forward. He is a brief but magnetic man, confident of his powers.]*

Douglas: My fellow citizens: My good friend, Mr. Lincoln, has addressed you with his usual artless sincerity, his pure, homely charm, his perennial native humor. He has even devoted a generously large portion of his address to most amiable remarks upon my fine qualities as a man, if not as a statesman. For which I express deepest gratitude. But—at the same time—I most earnestly beg you not to be deceived by his seeming innocence, his carefully cultivated spirit of good will. For in each of his little homilies lurk concealed weapons. Like Brutus, in Shakespeare's immortal tragedy, Mr. Lincoln is an honorable man. But, also like Brutus, he is an adept at the art of inserting daggers between an opponent's ribs, just when said opponent least expects it. Behold me, gentlemen—I am covered with scars. And yet— somehow or other—I am still upright. Perhaps because I am supported by that sturdy prop called "Truth." Truth—which, crushed to earth by the assassin's blades, doth rise again! Mr. Lincoln makes you laugh with his pungent anecdotes. Then he draws tears from your eyes with his dramatic pictures of the plight of the black slave labor in the South. Always, he guides you skilfully to the threshold of truth, but then, as you are about to cross it, diverts your attention elsewhere. For one thing he never, by any mischance, makes reference to the condition of labor here in the North! Oh, no! Perhaps New England is so far beyond the bounds of his parochial ken that he does not know that tens of thousands of working men and women in the textile industry are now on STRIKE! And why are they on strike? Because from early morning to dark of night—fourteen hours a day—those "free" citizens must toil at shattering looms in soulless factories and never see the sun; and then, when their fearful day's work at last comes to its exhausted end, these ill-clad and undernourished laborers must trudge home to their foul abodes in tenements that are not fit habitations for rats! What kind of Liberty is this? And if Mr. Lincoln has not heard of conditions in Massachusetts—how has it escaped his attention that here in our own great state no wheels are now turning on that mighty railroad, the Illinois Central? Because its oppressed workers are also on STRIKE! Because they too demand a living wage! So it is throughout the North. Hungry men, marching through the streets in ragged order, promoting riots, because they are not paid enough to keep the flesh upon the bones of their babies! What kind of Liberty is *this?* And what kind of equality? Mr. Lincoln harps constantly on this subject of equality. He repeats over and over the argument used by Lovejoy and other abolitionists: to wit, that the Declaration of Independence having declared all men free and equal, by divine law, thus Negro equality is an inalienable right. Contrary to this absurd assumption stands the verdict of the Supreme Court, as it was clearly stated by Chief Justice Taney in the case of Dred Scott. The Negroes are established by this decision as an inferior race of beings, subjugated by the dominant race, enslaved and, therefore, *property*—like all other property! But Mr. Lincoln is inclined to dispute the constitutional authority of the Supreme Court. He has implied, if he did not say so outright, that the Dred Scott decision was a prejudiced one, which must be overruled by the voice of the people. Mr. Lincoln is a lawyer, and I presume, therefore, that he knows that when he seeks to destroy public confidence in the integrity, the inviolability of the Supreme Court, he is preaching *revolution!* He is attempting to stir up odium and rebellion in this country against the constituted authorities; he is stimulating the passions of men to resort to violence and to mobs, instead of to the law. He is setting brother against brother! There can be but one consequence of such inflammatory persuasion—and that is *Civil War!* He asks me to state my opinion of the Dred Scott decision, and I answer him unequivocally by saying, "I take the decisions of the Supreme Court as the law of the land, and I intend to obey them as such!" Nor will I be swayed from that position by all the rantings of all the fanatics who preach "racial equality," who ask us to vote, and eat, and sleep, and marry with Negroes! And I say further— Let each State mind its own business and leave its neighbors alone. If we will stand by that principle, then Mr. Lincoln will find that this great republic can exist forever divided into free and slave states. We can go on as we have done, increasing in wealth, in population, in power, until we shall be the admiration and the terror of the world! [*He glares at the audience, then turns, mopping his brow, and resumes his seat.*]

NINIAN [*rising*]: Mr. Lincoln.

[ABE *glances at his notes, takes his hat off, puts the notes in it, then rises slowly and comes forward. He speaks quietly, reasonably. His words come from an emotion so profound that it needs no advertisement.*]

ABE: Judge Douglas has paid tribute to my skill with the dagger. I thank him for that, but I must also admit that he can do more with that weapon than I can. He can keep ten daggers flashing in the air at one time. Fortunately, he's so good at it that none of the knives ever falls and hurts anybody. The Judge can condone slavery in the South and protest hotly against its extension to the North. He can crowd loyalty to the Union and defense of states' sovereignty into the same breath. Which reminds me—and I hope the Judge will allow me one more homely little anecdote, because I'd like to tell about a woman down in Kentucky. She came out of her cabin one day and found her husband grappling with a ferocious bear. It was a fight to the death, and the bear was winning. The struggling husband called to his wife, "For heaven's sake, *help* me!" The wife asked what could *she* do? Said the husband, "You could at least *say* something encouraging." But the wife didn't want to seem to be taking sides in this combat, so she just hollered, "Go it, husband— go it, bear!" Now, you heard the Judge make allusion to those who advocate voting and eating and marrying and sleeping with Negroes. Whether he meant me specifically, I do not know. If he did, I can say that just because I do not want a colored woman for a slave, I don't necessarily want her for a wife. I need not have her for either. I can just leave her alone. In some respects, she certainly is not my equal, any more than I am the Judge's equal, in some respects; but in her natural right to eat the bread she earns with her own hands without asking leave of some one else, she is my equal, and the equal of all others. And as to sleeping with Negroes —the Judge may be interested to know that the slave states have produced more than four hundred thousand mulattoes— and I don't think many of them are the children of abolitionists. That word "abolitionists" brings to mind New England, which also has been mentioned. I assure Judge

Douglas that I have been there, and I have seen those cheer-
less brick prisons called factories, and the workers trudging
silently home through the darkness. In those factories, cotton
that was picked by black slaves is woven into cloth by white
people who are separated from slavery by no more than fifty
cents a day. As an American, I cannot be proud that such
conditions exist. But—as an American—I can ask: would any
of those striking workers in the North elect to change places
with the slaves in the South? Will they not rather say, "The
remedy is in *our* hands!" And, still as an American, I can
say—thank God we live under a system by which men have
the *right* to strike! I am not preaching rebellion. I don't have
to. This country, with its institutions, belongs to the people
who inhabit it. Whenever they shall grow weary of the existing government, they can exercise their constitutional right
of amending it, or their revolutionary right to dismember or
overthrow it. If the founding fathers gave us anything, they
gave us that. And I am not preaching disrespect for the
Supreme Court. I am only saying that the decisions of mortal
men are often influenced by unjudicial bias—and the Supreme Court is composed of mortal men, most of whom, it
so happens, come from the privileged class in the South.
There is an old saying that judges are just as honest as other
men, and not more so; and in case some of you are wondering
who said that, it was Thomas Jefferson. [*He has half turned
to* DOUGLAS.] The purpose of the Dred Scott decision is to
make property, and nothing but property, of the Negro in
all states of the Union. It is the old issue of property rights
versus human rights—an issue that will continue in this
country when these poor tongues of Judge Douglas and myself shall long have been silent. It is the eternal struggle
between two principles. The one is the common right of
humanity, and the other the divine right of kings. It is the
same spirit that says, "You toil and work and earn bread, and
I'll eat it." Whether those words come from the mouth of a
king who bestrides his people and lives by the fruit of their
labor, or from one race of men who seek to enslave another

race, it is the same tyrannical principle. As a nation, we began by declaring, "All men are created equal." There was no mention of any exceptions to the rule in the Declaration of Independence. But we now practically read it, "All men are created equal except Negroes." If we accept this doctrine of race or class discrimination, what is to stop us from decreeing in the future that "All men are created equal except Negroes, foreigners, Catholics, Jews, or—just poor people?" That is the conclusion toward which the advocates of slavery are driving us. Many good citizens, North and South, agree with the Judge that we should accept that conclusion—don't stir up trouble—"Let each State mind its own business." That's the safer course, for the time being. But—I advise you to watch out! When you have enslaved any of your fellow beings, dehumanized him, denied him all claim to the dignity of manhood, placed him among the beasts, among the damned, are you quite sure that the demon you have thus created will not turn and rend *you?* When you begin qualifying freedom, watch out for the consequences to *you!* And I am not preaching civil war. All I am trying to do—now, and as long as I live—is to state and restate the fundamental virtues of our democracy, which have made us great, and which can make us greater. I believe most seriously that the perpetuation of those virtues is now endangered, not only by the honest proponents of slavery, but even more by those who echo Judge Douglas in shouting, "Leave it alone!" This is the complacent policy of indifference to evil, and that policy I cannot but hate. I hate it because of the monstrous injustice of slavery itself. I hate it because it deprives our republic of its just influence in the world; enables the enemies of free institutions everywhere to taunt us as hypocrites; causes the real friends of freedom to doubt our sincerity; and especially because it forces so many good men among ourselves into an open war with the very fundamentals of civil liberty, denying the good faith of the Declaration of Independence, and insisting that there is no right principle of action but *self-interest.* . . . In his final words tonight, the

Judge said that we may be "the terror of the world." I don't think we want to be that. I think we would prefer to be the encouragement of the world, the proof that man is at last worthy to be free. But—we shall provide no such encouragement, unless we can establish our ability as a nation to live and grow. And we shall surely do neither if these states fail to remain *united*. There can be no distinction in the definitions of liberty as between one section and another, one race and another, one class and another. "A house divided against itself cannot stand." This government can not endure permanently, half slave and half free! [*He turns and goes back to his seat.*]

[*The lights fade.*]

SCENE 10

Parlor of the Edwards home, now being used by the Lincolns. Afternoon of a day in the early Spring of 1860.

[ABE *is sitting on the couch at the right, with his seven-year-old son,* TAD, *on his lap. Sitting beside them is another son,* WILLIE, *aged nine. The eldest son,* ROBERT, *a young Harvard student of seventeen, is sitting by the window, importantly smoking a pipe and listening to the story* ABE *has been telling the children.* JOSHUA SPEED *is sitting at the left.*]

ABE: You must remember, Tad, the roads weren't much good then—mostly nothing more than trails—and it was hard to find my way in the darkness. . . . .

WILLIE: Were you scared?

ABE: Yes—I was scared.

WILLIE: Of Indians?

ABE: No—there weren't any of them left around here. I was afraid I'd get lost, and the boy would die, and it would be all my fault. But, finally, I found the doctor. He was very tired, and wanted to go to bed, and he grumbled a lot, but I made him come along with me then and there.

WILLIE: Was the boy dead?

ABE: No, Willie. He wasn't dead. But he was pretty sick. The doctor gave him a lot of medicine.

TAD: Did it taste bad, Pa?

ABE: I presume it did. But it worked. I never saw those nice people again, but I've heard from them every so often. That little boy was your age, Tad, but now he's a grown man with a son almost as big as you are. He lives on a great big farm, in a valley with a river that runs right down from the tops of the snow mountains. . . .

[MARY *comes in*.]

MARY: Robert! You are smoking in my parlor!

ROBERT [*wearily*]: Yes, Mother. [*He rises.*]

MARY: I have told you that I shall not tolerate tobacco smoke in my parlor or, indeed, in any part of my house, and I mean to . . .

ABE: Come, come, Mary—you must be respectful to a Harvard man. Take it out to the woodshed, Bob.

ROBERT: Yes, Father.

MARY: And this will not happen again!

ROBERT: No, Mother. [*He goes out.*]

ABE: I was telling the boys a story about some pioneers I knew once.

MARY: It's time for you children to make ready for your supper.

[*The* CHILDREN *promptly get up to go.*]

WILLIE: But what happened after that, Pa?

ABE: Nothing. Everybody lived happily ever after. Now run along.

[WILLIE *and* TAD *run out.*]

JOSH: What time *is* it, Mary?

MARY: It's nearly half past four. [*She is shaking the smoke out of the curtains.*]

JOSH: Half past four, Abe. Those men will be here any minute.

ABE [*rising*]: Good Lord!

MARY: [*turning sharply to* ABE]: What men?

ABE: Some men from the East. One of them's a political

leader named Crimmin—and there's a Mr. Sturveson—he's a manufacturer—and ...

MARY [*impressed*]: Henry D. Sturveson?

ABE: That's the one—and also the Reverend Dr. Barrick from Boston.

MARY [*sharply*]: What are they coming here for?

ABE: I don't precisely know—but I suspect that it's to see if I'm fit to be a candidate for President of the United States. [MARY *is, for the moment, speechless.*] I suppose they want to find out if we still live in a log cabin and keep pigs under the bed....

MARY [*in a fury*]: And you didn't *tell* me!

ABE: I'm sorry, Mary—the matter just slipped my ...

MARY: You forgot to tell me that we're having the most important guests who ever crossed the threshold of my house.

ABE: They're not guests. They're only here on business.

MARY [*bitterly*]: Yes! Rather important business, it seems to me. They want to see us as we *are*—crude, sloppy, vulgar Western barbarians, living in a house that reeks of foul tobacco smoke.

ABE: We can explain about having a son at Harvard.

MARY: If I'd only known! If you had only given me a little time to prepare for them. Why didn't you put on your best suit? And those filthy old boots!

ABE: Well, Mary, I clean forgot....

MARY: I declare, Abraham Lincoln, I believe you would have treated me with much more consideration if I had been your slave, instead of your wife! You have never, for one moment, stopped to think that perhaps I have some interests, some concerns, in the life we lead together....

ABE: I'll try to clean up my boots a little, Mary. [*He goes out, glad to escape from this painful scene.* MARY *looks after him. Her lip is quivering. She wants to avoid tears.*]

MARY [*seating herself; bitterly*]: You've seen it all, Joshua Speed. Every bit of it—courtship, if you could call it that, change of heart, change back again, and marriage, eighteen years of it. And you probably think just as all the others do

—that I'm a bitter, nagging woman, and I've tried to kill his spirit, and drag him down to my level. . . .

[JOSH *rises and goes over to her.*]

JOSH [*quietly*]: No, Mary. I think no such thing. Remember, I know Abe, too.

MARY: There never could have been another man such as he is! I've read about many that have gone up in the world, and all of them seemed to have to fight to assert themselves every inch of the way, against the opposition of their enemies and the lack of understanding in their own friends. But he's never had any of that. He's never had an enemy, and every one of his friends has always been completely confident in him. Even before I met him, I was told that he had a glorious future, and after I'd known him a day, I was sure of it myself. But he didn't believe it—or, if he did, secretly, he was so afraid of the prospect that he did all in his power to avoid it. He had some poem in his mind, about a life of woe, along a rugged path, that leads to some future doom, and it has been an obsession with him. All these years, I've tried and tried to stir him out of it, but all my efforts have been like so many puny waves, dashing against the Rock of Ages. And now, opportunity, the greatest opportunity, is coming here, to him, right into his own house. And what can I do about it? He *must* take it! He *must* see that this is what he was meant for! But I can't persuade him of it! I'm tired —I'm tired to death! [*The tears now come.*] I thought I could help to shape him, as I knew he should be, and I've succeeded in nothing—but in breaking myself. . . . [*She sobs bitterly.*]

[JOSH *sits down beside her and pats her hand.*]

JOSH [*tenderly*]: I know, Mary. But—there's no reason in heaven and earth for you to reproach yourself. Whatever becomes of Abe Lincoln is in the hands of a God who controls the destinies of all of us, including lunatics, and saints.

[ABE *comes back.*]

ABE [*looking down at his boots*]: I think they look all right now, Mary. [*He looks at* MARY, *who is now trying hard to control her emotion.*]

MARY: You can receive the gentlemen in here. I'll try to prepare some refreshment for them in the dining-room. [*She goes out. ABE looks after her, miserably. There are a few moments of silence. At length, ABE speaks, in an offhand manner.*]

ABE: I presume these men are pretty influential.

JOSH: They'll have quite a say in the delegations of three states that may swing the nomination away from Seward.

ABE: Suppose, by some miracle, or fluke, they did nominate me; do you think I'd stand a chance of winning the election?

JOSH: An excellent chance, in my opinion. There'll be four candidates in the field, bumping each other, and opening up the track for a dark horse.

ABE: But the dark horse might run in the wrong direction.

JOSH: Yes—you can always do that, Abe. I know *I* wouldn't care to bet two cents on you.

ABE [*grinning*]: It seems funny to be comparing it to a horse-race, with an old, spavined hack like me. But I've had some mighty energetic jockeys—Mentor Graham, Bowling Green, Bill Herndon, you, and Mary—most of all, Mary.

JOSH [*looking at ABE*]: They don't count now, Abe. You threw 'em all, long ago. When you finally found yourself running against poor little Douglas, you got the bit between your teeth and went like greased lightning. You'd do the same thing to him again, if you could only decide to get started, which you probably won't ... [*The doorbell jangles. JOSH gets up.*]

ABE: I expect that's them now.

JOSH: I'll go see if I can help Mary. [*He starts for the door but turns and looks at ABE, and speaks quietly.*] I'd just like to remind you, Abe—there are pretty nearly thirty million people in this country; most of 'em are common people, like you. They're in serious trouble, and they need somebody who understands 'em, as you do. So—when these gentlemen come in—try to be a *little* bit polite to them. [*ABE grins. JOSH looks off.*] However—you won't listen to any advice from me.

[JOSH *goes. The door is opened by a* MAID *and* STURVESON, BARRICK, *and* CRIMMIN *come in.* STURVESON *is elderly, wealthy, and bland.* BARRICK *is a soft Episcopalian dignitary.* CRIMMIN *is a shrewd, humorous fixer.*]

ABE: Come right in, gentlemen. Glad to see you again, Mr. Crimmin.

[*They shake hands.*]

CRIMMIN: How de do, Mr. Lincoln? This is Dr. Barrick of Boston, and Mr. Sturveson, of Philadelphia.

DR. BARRICK: Mr. Lincoln.

STURVESON: I'm honored, Mr. Lincoln.

LINCOLN: Thank you, sir. Pray sit down, gentlemen.

STURVESON: Thank you.

[*They sit.*]

CRIMMIN: Will Mrs. Lincoln seriouly object if I light a seegar?

LINCOLN: Go right ahead! I regret that Mrs. Lincoln is not here to receive you, but she will join us presently. [*He sits down.*]

BARRICK [*with great benignity*]: I am particularly anxious to meet Mrs. Lincoln, for I believe, with Mr. Longfellow, that "as unto the bow the cord is, so unto the man is woman."

STURVESON [*very graciously*]: And we are here dealing with a bow that is stout indeed. [ABE *bows slightly in acknowledgment of the compliment.*] And one with a reputation for shooting straight. So you'll forgive us, Mr. Lincoln, for coming directly to the point.

ABE: Yes, sir. I understand that you wish to inspect the prairie politician in his native lair, and here I am.

STURVESON: It is no secret that we are desperately in need of a candidate—one who is sound, conservative, safe—and clever enough to skate over the thin ice of the forthcoming campaign. Your friends—and there's an increasingly large number of them throughout the country—believe that you are the man.

ABE: Well, Mr. Sturveson, I can tell you that when first I was considered for political office—that was in New Salem, twenty-five year ago—I assured my sponsors of my conservatism. I have subsequently proved it, by never progressing anywhere.

BARRICK [*smiling*]: Then you agree that you are the man we want?

ABE: I'm afraid I can't go quite that far in self-esteem, Dr. Barrick, especially when you have available a statesman and gentleman as eminent as Mr. Seward, who, I believe, is both ready and willing.

STURVESON: That's as may be. But please understand that this is not an inquisition. We merely wish to know you better, to gain a clearer idea of your theories on economics, religion, and national affairs, in general. To begin with—in one of your memorable debates with Senator Douglas, your opponent indulged in some of his usual demagoguery about industrial conditions in the North, and you replied shrewdly that whereas the slaves in the South . . .

ABE: Yes, I remember the occasion. I replied that I was thankful that laborers in free states have the right to strike. But that wasn't shrewdness, Mr. Sturveson. It was just the truth.

STURVESON: It has gained for you substantial support from the laboring classes, which is all to the good. But it has also caused a certain amount of alarm among business men, like myself.

ABE: I cannot enlarge on the subject. It seems obvious to me that this nation was founded on the supposition that men have the right to protest, violently if need be, against authority that is unjust or oppressive. [*He turns to* BARRICK.] The Boston Tea Party was a kind of strike. So was the Revolution itself. [*Again to* STURVESON.] So was Nicholas Biddle's attempt to organize the banks against the Jackson administration.

STURVESON: Which is all perfectly true—but—the days of anarchy are over. We face an unprecedented era of industrial expansion—mass production of every conceivable kind of goods—railroads and telegraph lines across the continent—

all promoted and developed by private enterprise. In this great work, we must have a free hand, and a firm one, Mr. Lincoln. To put it bluntly, would you, if elected, place the interests of labor above those of capital?

ABE: I cannot answer that, bluntly, or any other way; because I cannot tell what I should do, if elected.

STURVESON: But you must have inclinations toward one side or the other. . . .

ABE: I think you know, Mr. Sturveson, that I am opposed to slavery.

BARRICK: And we of New England applaud your sentiments! We deplore the inhumanity of our Southern friends in . . .

ABE [*to* BARRICK]: There are more forms of slavery than that which is inflicted upon the Negroes in the South. I am opposed to all of them. [*He turns again to* STURVESON.] I believe in our democratic system—the just and generous system which opens the way to all—gives hope to all, and consequent energy and improvement of condition to all, including employer and employee alike.

BARRICK: We support your purpose, Mr. Lincoln, in steadfastly proclaiming the rights of men to resist unjust authority. But I am most anxious to know whether you admit One Authority to whom devotion is unquestioned?

ABE: I presume you refer to the Almighty?

BARRICK: I do.

ABE: I think there has never been any doubt of my submission to His will.

BARRICK: I'm afraid there is a great deal of doubt as to your devotion to His church.

ABE: I realize that, Doctor. They say I'm an atheist, because I've always refused to become a church member.

BARRICK: What have been the grounds of your refusal?

ABE: I have found no churches suitable for my own form of worship. I could not give assent without mental reservations to the long, complicated statements of Christian doctrine which characterize their Articles of Belief and Confessions of Faith. But I can promise you, Dr. Barrick—I shall gladly join any church at any time if its sole qualification for membership is obedience to the Saviour's statement of Law and Gospel: "Thou shalt love the Lord thy God with all thy heart and with all thy soul and with all thy mind, and thou shalt love thy neighbor as thyself.". . . But—I beg you gentlemen to excuse me for a moment. I believe Mrs. Lincoln is preparing a slight collation, and I must see if I can help with it. . . .

CRIMMIN: Certainly, Mr. Lincoln. [ABE *goes, closing the door behind him.* CRIMMIN *looks at the door, then turns to the others.*] Well?

BARRICK: The man is unquestionably an infidel. An idealist—in his curious, primitive way—but an infidel!

STURVESON: And a radical!

CRIMMIN: A radical? Forgive me, gentlemen, if I enjoy a quiet laugh at that.

STURVESON: Go ahead and enjoy yourself, Crimmin—but I did not like the way he evaded my direct question. I tell you, he's as unscrupulous a demagogue as Douglas. He's a rabble rouser!

CRIMMIN: Of course he is! As a dealer in humbug, he puts Barnum himself to shame.

STURVESON: Quite possibly—but he is not safe!

CRIMMIN: Not safe, eh? And what do you mean by that?

STURVESON: Just what I say. A man who devotes himself so whole-heartedly to currying favor with the mob develops the mob mentality. He becomes a preacher of discontent, of mass unrest. . . .

CRIMMIN: And what about Seward? If we put him up, he'll start right in demanding liberation of the slaves—and then there *will* be discontent and unrest! I ask you to believe me when I tell you that this Lincoln *is* safe—in economics and theology and everything else. After all—what is the essential qualification that we demand of the candidate of our party? It is simply this: that he be able to get himself elected! And there is the man who can do that. [*He points offstage.*]

STURVESON [*smiling*]: I should like to believe you!

BARRICK: So say we all of us!

CRIMMIN: Then just keep faith in the èternal stupidity of the voters, which is what *he* will appeal to. In that uncouth rail splitter you may observe one of the smoothest, slickest politicans that ever hoodwinked a yokel mob! You complain that he evaded your questions. Of course he did, and did it perfectly! Ask him about the labor problem, and he replies, "I believe in democracy." Ask his views on religion, and he says, "Love thy neighbor as thyself." Now—you know you couldn't argue with that, either of you. I tell you, gentlemen, he's a vote-getter if I ever saw one. His very name is right— Abraham Lincoln! Honest Old Abe! He'll play the game with us now, and he'll go right on playing it when we get him into the White House. He'll do just what we tell him. . . .

DR. BARRICK [*cautioning him*]: Careful, Mr. Crimmin. . . .

[ABE *returns.*]

ABE: If you gentlemen will step into the dining-room, Mrs. Lincoln would be pleased to serve you with a cup of tea.

BARRICK: Thank you.

STURVESON: This is most gracious. [*He and* BARRICK *move off toward the door.*]

ABE: Or perhaps something stronger for those who prefer it.

[STURVESON *and* BARRICK *go.* CRIMMIN *is looking for a place to throw his cigar.*]

ABE [*heartily*]: Bring your seegar with you, Mr. Crimmin!

CRIMMIN: Thank you—thank you. [*He smiles at* ABE, *gives him a slap on the arm, and goes out,* ABE *following. The lights fade.*]

SCENE 11

Lincoln campaign headquarters in the Illinois State House. The evening of Election Day, November 6th, 1860.

It is a large room with a tall window opening out on to a wide balcony. There are doors upper right and upper left. At the left is a table littered with newspapers and clippings. There are many chairs about, and a liberal supply of spittoons. At the back is a huge chart of the thirty-three states, with their electoral votes, and a space opposite each side for the posting of bulletins. A short ladder gives access to Alabama and Arkansas at the top of the list.

On the wall at the left is an American flag. At the right is a map of the United States, on which each state is marked with a red, white, or blue flag.

[ABE *is sitting at the table, with his back to the audience, reading newspaper clippings. He wears his hat and has spectacles on.* MRS. LINCOLN *is sitting at the right of the table, her eyes darting nervously from* ABE, *to the chart, to the map. She wears her bonnet, tippet and muff.*

ROBERT LINCOLN *is standing near her, studying the map.* NINIAN EDWARDS *is sitting at the left of the table and* JOSH SPEED *is standing near the chart. They are both smoking cigars and watching the chart.*

The door at the left is open, and through it the clatter of telegraph instruments can be heard. The window is partly open, and we can hear band music from the square below, and frequent cheers from the assembled mob, who are watching the election returns flashed from a magic lantern on the State House balcony.

Every now and then, a telegraph operator named JED *comes in from the left and tacks a new bulletin up on the chart. Another man named* PHIL *is out on the balcony taking bulletins from* JED.]

ROBERT: What do those little flags mean, stuck into the map?

JOSH: Red means the state is sure for us. White means doubtful. Blue means hopeless.

[ABE *tosses the clipping he has been reading on the table and picks up another.* JED *comes in and goes up to pin bulletins opposite Illinois, Maryland, and New York.*]

NINIAN [*rising to look*]: Lincoln and Douglas neck and neck in Illinois.

[JOSH *and* ROBERT *crowd around the chart.*]

JOSH: Maryland is going all for Breckenridge and Bell. Abe—you're nowhere in Maryland.

MARY [*with intense anxiety*]: What of New York?

JED [*crossing to the window*]: Say, Phil—when you're not getting bulletins, keep that window closed. We can't hear ourselves think.

PHIL: All right. Only have to open 'er up again. [*He closes the window.*]

MARY: What does it say about New York?

[JED *goes.*]

NINIAN: Douglas a hundred and seventeen thousand—Lincoln a hundred and six thousand.

MARY [*desperately, to* ABE]: He's winning from you in New York, Abe!

JOSH: Not yet, Mary. These returns so far are mostly from the city, where Douglas is bound to run the strongest.

ABE [*interested in a clipping*]: I see the New York *Herald* says I've got the soul of a Uriah Heep encased in the body of a baboon. [*He puts the clipping aside and starts to read another.*]

NINIAN [*who has resumed his seat*]: You'd better change that flag on Rhode Island from red to white, Bob. It looks doubtful to me.

[ROBERT, *glad of something to do, changes the flag as directed.*]

MARY: What does it look like in Pennsylvania, Ninian?

NINIAN: There's nothing to worry about there, Mary. It's safe for Abe. In fact, you needn't worry at all.

MARY [*very tense*]: Yes. You've been saying that over and over again all evening. There's no need to worry. But how can we help worrying when every new bulletin shows Douglas ahead?

JOSH: But every one of them shows Abe gaining.

NINIAN [*mollifying*]: Just give them time to count all the votes in New York and then you'll be on your way to the White House.

MARY: Oh, why don't they hurry with it? Why don't those returns come in?

ABE [*preoccupied*]: They'll come in, soon enough.

[BILLY HERNDON *comes in from the right. He has been doing a lot of drinking but has hold of himself.*]

BILLY: That mob down there is sickening! They cheer every bulletin that's flashed on the wall, whether the news is good or bad. And they cheer every picture of every candidate, including George Washington, with the same, fine, ignorant enthusiasm.

JOSH: That's logical. They can't tell 'em apart.

BILLY [*to* ABE]: There are a whole lot of reporters down there. They want to know what will be your first official action after you're elected.

NINIAN: What do you want us to tell 'em, Abe?

ABE [*still reading*]: Tell 'em I'm thinking of growing a beard.

JOSH: A beard?

NINIAN [*amused*]: Whatever put that idea into your mind?

ABE [*picking up another clipping*]: I had a letter the other day from some little girl. She said I ought to have whiskers, to give me more dignity. And I'll need it—if elected.

[JED *arrives with new bulletins.* BILLY, NINIAN, JOSH *and* ROBERT *huddle around* JED, *watching him post the bulletins.*]

MARY: What do they say now?

[JED *goes to the window and gives some bulletins to* PHIL.]

MARY: Is there anything new from New York?

NINIAN: Connecticut—Abe far in the lead. That's eleven safe electoral votes anyway. Missouri—Douglas thirty-five thousand—Bell thirty-three—Breckenridge sixteen—Lincoln, eight. . . .

[*Cheers from the crowd outside until* PHIL *closes the window.* JED *returns to the office at the left.*]

MARY: What are they cheering for?

BILLY: They don't know!

ABE [*with another clipping*]: The Chicago *Times* says, "Lincoln breaks down! Lincoln's heart fails him! His tongue fails him! His legs fail him! He fails all over! The people refuse to support him! They laugh at him! Douglas is champion of the people! Douglas skins the living dog!" [*He tosses the clipping aside.* MARY *stands up.*]

MARY [*her voice is trembling*]: I can't stand it any longer!

ABE: Yes, my dear—I think you'd better go home. I'll be back before long.

MARY [*hysterical*]: I won't go home! You only want to be rid of me. That's what you've wanted ever since the day we were married—and before that. Anything to get me out of your sight, because you hate me! [*Turning to* JOSH, NINIAN, *and* BILLY.] And it's the same with all of you—all of his friends—you hate me—you wish I'd never come into his life.

JOSH: No, Mary.

[ABE *has stood up, quickly, at the first storm signal. He himself is in a fearful state of nervous tension—in no mood to treat* MARY *with patient indulgence. He looks sharply at* NINIAN *and at the others.*]

ABE: Will you please step out for a moment?

NINIAN: Certainly, Abe. [*He and the others go into the telegraph office.* JOSH *gestures to* ROBERT *to go with them.* ROBERT *casts a black look at his mother and goes....* ABE *turns on* MARY *with strange savagery.*]

ABE: Damn you! Damn you for taking every opportunity you can to make a public fool of me—and yourself! It's bad enough, God knows, when you act like that in the privacy of our own home. But here—in front of people! You're not to do that again. Do you hear me? You're never to do that again!

[MARY *is so aghast at this outburst that her hysterical temper vanishes, giving way to blank terror.*]

MARY [*in a faint, strained voice*]: Abe! You cursed at me. Do you realize what you did? You cursed at me.

[ABE *has the impulse to curse at her again, but with considerable effort, he controls it.*]

ABE [*in a strained voice*]: I lost my temper, Mary. And I'm sorry for it. But I still think you should go home rather than endure the strain of this—this Death Watch.

[*She stares at him, uncomprehendingly, then turns and goes to the door.*]

MARY [*at the door*]: This is the night I dreamed about, when I was a child, when I was an excited young girl, and all the gay young gentlemen of Springfield were courting me, and I fell in love with the least likely of them. This is the night when I'm waiting to hear that my husband has become President of the United States. And even if he does—it's ruined, for me. It's too late. . . .

[*She opens the door and goes out.* ABE *looks after her, anguished, then turns quickly, crosses to the door at the left and opens it.*]

ABE [*calling off*]: Bob! [ROBERT *comes in.*] Go with your mother.

ROBERT: Do I have to?

ABE: Yes! Hurry! Keep right with her till I get home.

[ROBERT *has gone.* ABE *turns to the window.* PHIL *opens it.*]

PHIL: Do you think you're going to make it, Mr. Lincoln?

ABE: Oh—there's nothing to worry about.

CROWD OUTSIDE [*singing*]:

Old Abe Lincoln came out of the wilderness
     Out of the wilderness
     Out of the wilderness
Old Abe Lincoln came out of the wilderness
     Down in Illinois!

[NINIAN, JOSH, BILLY, *and* JED *come in, the latter to post new bulletins. After* JED *has communicated these,* PHIL *again closes the window.* JED *goes.*]

NINIAN: It looks like seventy-four electoral votes sure for you. Twenty-seven more probable. New York's will give you the election.

[ABE *walks around the room.* JOSH *has been looking at* ABE.]

JOSH: Abe, could I get you a cup of coffee?

ABE: No, thanks, Josh.

NINIAN: Getting nervous, Abe?

ABE: No. I'm just thinking what a blow it would be to Mrs. Lincoln if I should lose.

NINIAN: And what about me? I have ten thousand dollars bet on you.

BILLY [*scornfully*]: I'm afraid that the loss to the nation would be somewhat more serious than that.

JOSH: How would you feel, Abe?

ABE [*sitting on the chair near the window*]: I guess I'd feel the greatest sense of relief of my life.

[JED *comes in with a news despatch.*]

JED: Here's a news despatch. [*He hands it over and goes.*]

NINIAN [*reads*]: "Shortly after nine o'clock this evening, Mr. August Belmont stated that Stephen A. Douglas has piled up a majority of fifty thousand votes in New York City and carried the state."

BILLY: Mr. Belmont be damned!

[CRIMMIN *comes in, smoking a cigar, looking contented.*]

CRIMMIN: Good evening, Mr. Lincoln. Good evening, gentlemen—and how are you feeling *now?*

[*They all greet him.*]

NINIAN: Look at this, Crimmin. [*He hands the despatch to* CRIMMIN.]

CRIMMIN [*smiles*]: Well—Belmont is going to fight to the last ditch, which is just what he's lying in now. I've been in Chicago and the outlook there is cloudless. In fact, Mr. Lincoln, I came down tonight to protect you from the office-seekers. They're lining up downstairs already. On the way in I counted four Ministers to Great Britain and eleven Secretaries of State.

[JED *has come in with more bulletins to put on the chart and then goes to the window to give* PHIL *the bulletins.*]

BILLY [*at the chart*]: There's a bulletin from New York! Douglas a hundred and eighty-three thousand—Lincoln a hundred and eighty-*one* thousand!

[JED *goes.*]

JOSH: Look out, Abe! You're catching up!

CRIMMIN: The next bulletin from New York will show

you winning. Mark my words, Mr. Lincoln, this election is all wrapped up tightly in a neat bundle, ready for delivery on your doorstep tonight. We've fought the good fight, and we've won!

ABE [*pacing up and down the room*]: Yes—we've fought the good fight—in the dirtiest campaign in the history of corrupt politics. And if I have won, then I must cheerfully pay my political debts. All those who helped to nominate and elect me must be paid off. I have been gambled all around, bought and sold a hundred times. And now I must fill all the dishonest pledges made in my name.

NINIAN: We realize all that, Abe—but the fact remains that you're winning. Why, you're even beating the coalition in Rhode Island!

ABE: I've got to step out for a moment. [*He goes out at the right.*]

NINIAN [*cheerfully*]: Poor Abe.

CRIMMIN: You gentlemen have all been close friends of our Candidate for a long time, so perhaps you could answer a question that's been puzzling me considerably. Can I possibly be correct in supposing that he doesn't want to win?

JOSH: The answer is—yes.

CRIMMIN: [*looking toward the right*]: Well—I can only say that, for me, this is all a refreshingly new experience.

BILLY [*belligerently*]: Would *you* want to become President of the United States at this time? Haven't you been reading the newspapers lately?

CRIMMIN: Why, yes—I try to follow the events of the day.

BILLY [*in a rage*]: Don't you realize that they've raised ten thousand volunteers in South Carolina? They're arming them! The Governor has issued a proclamation saying that if Mr. Lincoln is elected, the State will secede tomorrow, and every other state south of the Dixon line will go with it. Can you see what that means? War! Civil War! And *he'll* have the whole terrible responsibility for it—a man who has never wanted anything in his life but to be let alone, in peace!

NINIAN: Calm down, Billy. Go get yourself another drink.

[JED *rushes in.*]

JED: Mr. Edwards, here it is! [*He hands a news despatch to* NINIAN, *then rushes to the window to attract* PHIL's *attention and communicate the big news.*]

NINIAN [*reads*]: "At 10:30 tonight the New York *Herald* conceded that Mr. Lincoln has carried the state by a majority of at least twenty-five thousand and has won the election!" [*He tosses the despatch in the air.*] He's won! He's won! Hurrah!

[*All on the stage shout, cheer, embrace, and slap each other.*]

BILLY: God be praised! God be praised!

CRIMMIN: I knew it! I never had a doubt of it!

[JED *is on the balcony, shouting through a megaphone.*]

JED: Lincoln is elected! Honest Old Abe is our next President!

[*A terrific cheer ascends from the crowd below.* ABE *returns. They rush at him.* BILLY *shakes hands with him, too deeply moved to speak.*]

NINIAN: You've carried New York, Abe! You've won! Congratulations!

CRIMMIN: My congratulations, Mr. President. This is a mighty achievement for all of us.

[JED *comes in and goes to* ABE.]

JED: My very best, Mr. Lincoln!

ABE [*solemnly*]: Thank you—thank you all very much. [*He comes to the left.* JOSH *is the last to shake his hand.*]

JOSH: I congratulate you, Abe.

ABE: Thanks, Josh.

NINIAN: Listen to them. Abe. Listen to that crazy, howling mob down there.

CRIMMIN: It's all for you, Mr. Lincoln.

NINIAN: Abe, get out there and let 'em see you!

ABE: No. I don't want to go out there. I—I guess I'll be going on home, to tell Mary. [*He starts toward the door. A short, stocky officer named* KAVANAGH *comes in from the right. He is followed by two* SOLDIERS.]

CRIMMIN: This is Captain Kavanagh, Mr. *President*.

KAVANAGH [*salutes*]: I've been detailed to accompany you, Mr. Lincoln, in the event of your election.

ABE: I'm grateful, Captain. But I don't need you.

KAVANAGH: I'm afraid you've got to have us, Mr. Lincoln. I don't like to be alarming, but I guess you know as well as I do what threats have been made.

ABE [*wearily*]: I see... Well—Good night, Josh—Ninian— Mr. Crimmin—Billy. Thank you for your good wishes. [*He starts for the door. The others bid him good night, quietly.*]

KAVANAGH: One moment, Sir. With your permission, I'll go first. [*He goes out,* ABE *after him, the two other* SOLDIERS *follow. The light fades.*]

SCENE 12

The yards of the railroad station at Springfield. The date is February 11, 1861.

At the right, at an angle toward the audience, is the back of a railroad car. From behind this, off to the upper left, runs a ramp. Flags and bunting are draped above.

In a row downstage are SOLDIERS, *with rifles and bayonets fixed, and packs on their backs, standing at ease. Off to the left is a large* CROWD, *whose excited murmuring can be heard.*

Kavanagh is in the foreground. A BRAKEMAN *with a lantern is inspecting the wheels of the car, at the left. A* WORKMAN *is at the right, polishing the rails of the car.* KAVANAGH *is pacing up and down, chewing a dead cigar. He looks at his watch. A swaggering* MAJOR *of militia comes down the ramp from the left.*]

MAJOR: I want you men to form up against this ramp. [*To* KAVANAGH, *with a trace of scorn.*] You seem nervous, Mr. Kavanagh.

KAVANAGH: Well—I am nervous. For three months I've been guarding the life of a man who doesn't give a damn what happens to him. I heard today that they're betting two to one in Richmond that he won't be alive to take the oath of office on March the 4th.

MAJOR: I'd like to take some of that money. The State Militia is competent to protect the person of our Commander-in-Chief.

KAVANAGH: I hope the United States Army is competent to help. But those Southerners are mighty good shots. And I strongly suggest that your men be commanded to keep watch through every window of every car, especially whenever the train stops—at a town, or a tank, or anywhere. And if any alarm is sounded, at any point along the line . . .

MAJOR [*a trifle haughty*]: There's no need to command my men to show courage in an emergency.

KAVANAGH: No slur was intended, Major—but we must be prepared in advance for everything.

[*A brass band off to the left strikes up the campaign song, "Old Abe Lincoln came out of the wilderness." The crowd starts to sing it, more and more voices taking it up. A* CONDUCTOR *comes out of the car and looks at his watch. There is a commotion at the left as* NINIAN *and* ELIZABETH EDWARDS, *and* JOSH, BILLY, *and* CRIMMIN *come in and are stopped by the* SOLDIERS. *The* MAJOR *goes forward, bristling with importance.*]

MAJOR: Stand back, there! Keep the crowd back there, you men!

NINIAN: I'm Mr. Lincoln's brother-in-law.

MAJOR: What's your name?

KAVANAGH: I know him, Major. That's Mr. and Mrs. Edwards, and Mr. Speed and Mr. Herndon with them. I know them all. You can let them through.

MAJOR: Very well. You can pass.

[*They come down to the right. The* MAJOR *goes off at the left.*]

CRIMMIN: How is the President feeling today? Happy?

NINIAN: Just as gloomy as ever.

BILLY [*emotionally*]: He came down to the office, and when I asked him what I should do about the sign, "Lincoln and

Herndon," he said, "Let it hang there. Let our clients understand that this election makes no difference to the firm. If I live, I'll be back some time, and then we'll go right on practising just as if nothing had happened."

ELIZABETH: He's always saying that—"If I live" ...

[*A tremendous cheer starts and swells offstage at the left. The* MAJOR *comes on briskly.*]

MAJOR [*to* KAVANAGH]: The President has arrived! [*To his men.*] Attention! [*The* MAJOR *strides down the platform and takes his position by the car, looking off to the left.*]

KAVANAGH [*to* NINIAN *and the others*]: Would you mind stepping back there? We want to keep this space clear for the President's party.

[*They move upstage, at the right. The cheering is now very loud.*]

MAJOR: Present—Arms!

[*The* SOLDIERS *come to the Present. The* MAJOR *salutes. Preceded by* SOLDIERS *who are looking sharply to the right and left,* ABE *comes in from the left, along the platform. He will be fifty-two years old tomorrow. He wears a beard. Over his shoulders is his plaid shawl. In his right hand, he carries his carpetbag; his left hand is leading* TAD. *Behind him are* MARY, ROBERT, *and* WILLIE, *and the* MAID. *All, except* MARY, *are also carrying bags. She carries a bunch of flowers. When they come to the car,* ABE *hands his bag up to the* CONDUCTOR, *then lifts* TAD *up.* MARY, ROBERT, WILLIE, *and the* MAID *get on board, while* ABE *steps over to talk to* NINIAN *and the others. During this, there is considerable commotion at the left, as the* CROWD *tries to surge forward.*]

MAJOR [*rushing forward*]: Keep 'em back! Keep 'em back, men!

[*The* SOLDIERS *have broken their file on the platform and are in line, facing the* CROWD. KAVANAGH *and his* MEN *are close to* ABE. *Each of them has his hand on his revolver, and is keeping a sharp lookout.*]

KAVANAGH: Better get on board, Mr. President.

[ABE *climbs up on to the car's back platform. There is a*

great increase in the cheering when the CROWD *sees him.
They shout:* "Speech! Speech! Give us a speech, Abe! Speech,
Mr. President! Hurray for Old Abe!" *etc.* . . . . ABE *turns to the*
CROWD, *takes his hat off and waves it with a half-hearted
gesture. The cheering dies down.*]

NINIAN: They want you to say something, Abe.

[*For a moment,* ABE *stands still, looking off to the left.*]

ABE: My dear friends—I have to say good-by to you. I am
going now to Washington, with my new whiskers—of which
I hope you approve.

[*The* CROWD *roars with laughter at that. More shouts of*
"Good Old Abe!" *In its exuberant enthusiasm, the* CROWD
again surges forward, at and around the SOLDIERS, *who shout,*
"Get back, there! Stand back, you!"]

ABE [*to the* MAJOR]: It's all right—let them come on.
They're all old friends of mine.

[*The* MAJOR *allows his* MEN *to retreat so that they form
a ring about the back of the car.* KAVANAGH *and his* MEN *are
on the car's steps, watching. The* CROWD—*an assortment of
townspeople, including some Negroes—fills the stage.*]

ABE: No one, not in my situation, can appreciate my feelings of sadness at this parting. To this place, and the kindness
of you people, I owe everything. I have lived here a quarter
of a century, and passed from a young to an old man. Here
my children have been born and one is buried. I now leave,
not knowing when or whether ever I may return. I am called
upon to assume the Presidency at a time when eleven of our
sovereign states have announced their intention to secede
from the Union, when threats of war increase in fierceness
from day to day. It is a grave duty which I now face. In
preparing for it, I have tried to enquire: what great principle
or ideal is it that has kept this Union so long together? And
I believe that it was not the mere matter of separation of the
colonies from the motherland, but that sentiment in the Declaration of Independence which gave liberty to the people
of this country and hope to all the world. This sentiment was
the fulfillment of an ancient dream, which men have held

through all time, that they might one day shake off their chains and find freedom in the brotherhood of life. We gained democracy, and now there is the question whether it is fit to survive. Perhaps we have come to the dreadful day of awakening, and the dream is ended. If so, I am afraid it must be ended forever. I cannot believe that ever again will men have the opportunity we have had. Perhaps we should admit that, and concede that our ideals of liberty and equality are decadent and doomed. I have heard of an eastern monarch who once charged his wise men to invent him a sentence which would be true and appropriate in all times and situations. They presented him the words, "And this too shall pass away." That is a comforting thought in time of affliction— "And this too shall pass away." And yet—[*Suddenly he speaks with quiet but urgent authority.*]—let us believe that it is not true! Let us live to prove that we can cultivate the natural world that is about us, and the intellectual and moral world that is within us, so that we may secure an individual, social, and political prosperity, whose course shall be forward, and which, while the earth endures, shall not pass away.... I commend you to the care of the Almighty, as I hope that in your prayers you will remember me.... Good-by, my friends and neighbors. [*He leans over the railing of the car platform to say good-by to* NINIAN, ELIZABETH, JOSH, BILLY, *and* CRIMMIN, *shaking each by the hand. The band off-stage strikes up "John Brown's Body." The cheering swells. The* CONDUCTOR *looks at his watch and speaks to the* MAJOR, *who gets on board the train. The* CROWD *on stage is shouting* "Good-by, Abe," "Good-by, Mr. Lincoln," "Good luck, Abe," "We trust you, Mr. Lincoln."

As the band swings into the refrain, "Glory, Glory Hallelujah," the CROWD *starts to sing, the number of voices increasing with each word.*

KAVANAGH *tries to speak to* ABE, *but can't be heard. He touches* ABE's *arm, and* ABE *turns on him quickly.*]

KAVANAGH: Time to pull out, Mr. President. Better get inside the car.

[*These words cannot be heard by the audience in the general uproar of singing.* NINIAN, ELIZABETH, JOSH, *and* BILLY *are up on the station platform. The* SOLDIERS *are starting to climb up on to the train.* ABE *gives one last wistful wave of his hat to the* CROWD, *then turns and goes into the car, followed by* KAVANAGH, *the* MAJOR *and the* SOLDIERS. *The band reaches the last line of the song.*]

ALL [*singing*]: "His soul goes marching on."

[*The* BRAKEMAN, *downstage, is waving his lantern. The* CONDUCTOR *swings aboard. The* CROWD *is cheering, waving hats and handkerchiefs. The shrill screech of the engine whistle sounds from the right.*]

[*Curtain*]

ROBERT E. SHERWOOD

Though not a copious writer, Robert Sherwood is an accomplished dramatist who has had hardly a stage failure in twenty years. His plays have more than dramatic sureness, however, for Sherwood is always thoughtful and sometimes powerful in his commentary on our times.

Born on April 4, 1896, in New Rochelle, New York, he began writing as a small child. He edited the magazine, *Children's Life,* for a year at the age of seven, and by the age of ten had written his first play, *Tom Ruggles' Surprise.* Much of his encouragement to write came from his mother, Rosina Emmet Sherwood, an artist.

He was graduated from Milton Academy in 1914 and the following year entered Harvard, where he edited *Lampoon,* the humor magazine. When the United States entered the First World War, he tried to enlist but was rejected repeatedly because he was too tall. He finally joined the Canadian Black Watch, with which he served in France in 1917. He was gassed and wounded, and these experiences in war have come out later in his plays.

From 1919 to 1928 he wrote for periodicals, first as dramatic critic for *Vanity Fair,* then as staff writer for the former humor magazine, *Life,* as literary editor of *Scribner's,* and as motion picture editor of the *New York Herald.* He found success on the stage from the first with *The Road to Rome,* a comedy about the trials of Hannibal in his unsuccessful campaign against the Roman capital. He first won the Pulitzer Prize in 1936 for *Idiot's Delight,* a mixture of comedy, romance, and hard realism, showing what the outbreak of war would mean.

For *Abe Lincoln in Illinois* Sherwood won the Drama Critics' Award and his second Pulitzer Prize. It has been said that no one can fail with a play about Lincoln, but Sherwood's success has been more positive than that. In no other play is his dramaturgic ability better seen, since his problem is not in creating a story but in constructing an effective drama from a huge mass of historical material.

Sherwood's *There Shall Be No Night* (1940) was one of the best plays of the war. It pleaded passionately the cause of the Finns in defending their homeland against the Russians.

Sherwood has also written a novel, *The Virtuous Knight* (1931), and has rewritten plays and stories of other authors. During World War II he served as Head of the Office of War Information and assisted in the writing of some of the speeches of President Roosevelt. When he is not in Hollywood writing for the screen he lives in New York.

His plays and the dates of their first production:

The Road to Rome, January 31, 1927.
The Queen's Husband, January 25, 1928.
Reunion in Vienna, November 16, 1931.
The Petrified Forest, January 7, 1935.
Idiot's Delight, March 24, 1936.
Abe Lincoln in Illinois, October 15, 1938.
There Shall Be No Night, April 29, 1940.
The Rugged Path, November 10, 1945.

CRITICAL COMMENTS

ABE LINCOLN IN ILLINOIS

Mr. Sherwood has built the action of his play around the familiar crises of Lincoln's life—the tragic love affair with Ann Rutledge, the marriage with Mary Todd, the debates against Douglas, and the assumption of the Presidency at a moment whose dreadful ominousness no one realized more fully than he himself. But despite what seems a conventional outline the emphasis is original, and the interpretation of Lincoln's character at least not exactly that of the story books. As a man, Mr. Sherwood's Lincoln is by nature almost pathologically irresolute, and so reluctant to assume the burden of any responsibility that only the remorseless ambition of Mary Todd could have driven him into action. As a political thinker he is dominated by the realization that democracy is threatened chiefly by those who want to render it lip service alone, and consequently he sees the institutions of slavery less as an affront to humanitarian feelings than as the most obvious challenge to the sincerity of that democratic faith upon which the government is nominally founded. To him the question is not primarily whether our black brothers have hearts and souls like our own but whether the admission of an exception in the application of democracy does not set a dangerous precedent and mean that the theoretical right of all to liberty and equal opportunity will come to be actually enjoyed by fewer and fewer rather than by more and more American citizens. Perhaps—I do not pretend to know—Mr. Sherwood is attributing to Lincoln a deeper prophetic insight than he actually had into what was to become one of the most desperate problems of democracy, but in any event the result intended and achieved is to give the historical events of his play a clear modern application and to make it almost as much of an exhortation as it is a pageant.

There are obvious dangers in the attempt to combine in one play two appeals of a radically different sort. The audience here is asked to draw in its own mind the historical parallel, and while it is occupied with this intellectual process, to respond to a peculiarly complex emotional stimulus, to sense the pathos (in the technical sense) which surrounds those figures concerning whose fame and whose fate we know much more than the particular play in which they appear pretends to tell us. That Mr. Sherwood's drama is actually effective both as legend and as lesson is a tribute to his skill, and "Abe Lincoln in Illinois" is always impressive as well as always stately. Despite an extraordinarily fine performance by Raymond Massey, it is not, however, always exciting. Its forward march is sometimes slow, and if the didacticism is never fatuous the stateliness does not always escape a certain ponderosity. In the past Mr. Sherwood has frequently been almost too lively. That is not a fault likely to be charged against him in a play whose most serious defect is a certain lack of vivacity.

[Joseph Wood Krutch, "A Good Beginning," in *The Nation*, 147 (Nov. 5, 1938) 488. Reprinted by permission.]

ABE LINCOLN IN ILLINOIS

Thanks to his talent, Mr. Sherwood has conceived here a story that goes only up to the point of Lincoln's election to the presidency and departure for Washington. As a result, the poignancy that we see in the face of the Lincoln who sat for Brady, the photographer, in the final years, the almost mystical forebodings, and the powers of feeling and imagination that marked him then, are quietly redistributed over the past, and are made to appear at what we are to believe is their earlier source, more pressing, mute, elusive and unforgettable. Such qualities as these Mr. Massey in his acting completely achieves, and to them he adds a recognizable but curiously indefinable distress, a sort of blind alley in the heart somehow, the heart itself young.

Thousands of years before Lincoln was born, it was already impossible, in the pursuit of a certain realistic candor, to write fully of anyone in the least heroic. This play of Mr. Sherwood's, for all our confident freedom of matter and speech, suffers in its own way from this same cause. Lincoln was undoubtedly more varied, contagious, given to dirty stories, native, sharp, bold, shy, glowing, than any stage portrait of him ever was or ever was likely to be. To include the incident's detail, the local comment, the almost scandal, if you like, would merely interfere with the completeness of creation in the character that the play wishes to present. The episodes that are strung together in "Abe Lincoln in Illinois" vary in the extent to which they express Lincoln's story and characteristics. Audiences, therefore, will differ as to the theatre methods of the divers scenes and episodes. Mr. Brooks Atkinson finds the whole occasion of this Lincoln play rich with overtones, admirable and even thrilling. Mr. John Anderson finds that some of the scenes drag pretty heavily, especially toward the end of Act I and through Act II. . . . Mr. John Mason Brown touches on the lack of development in the scenes, and says that the best scenes in the play are ghost-written, meaning where Lincoln's words have been adopted by the dramatist. For my part I find that though the play may vary in its levels, and prove unequal in its choices and final values, the region of it is exalted in the dramatist's own private inclination and attitude toward the subject; the effect at times heavy, the tone noble. . . .

[Stark Young, "Lincoln and Huston," in *New Republic*, 97 (Nov. 9, 1938), p. 18. Reprinted by permission.]

CLIFFORD ODETS

———

WAITING FOR LEFTY

CHARACTERS

FATT	AGATE KELLER
JOE MITCHELL	GUNMAN
EDNA	SECRETARY
MILLER	ACTOR (PHILIPS)
FAYETTE	GRADY
IRV	DR. BARNES
FLORRIE	DR. BENJAMIN
SID STEIN	A MAN
CLAYTON	VOICES

WAITING FOR LEFTY

As the curtain goes up we see a bare stage. On it are sitting six or seven men in a semi-circle. Lolling against the proscenium down left is a young man chewing a toothpick: a gunman. A fat man of porcine appearance is talking directly to the audience. In other words he is the head of a union and the men ranged behind him are a committee of workers. They are now seated in interesting different attitudes and present a wide diversity of type, as we shall soon see. The fat man is hot and heavy under the collar, near the end of a long talk, but not too hot: he is well fed and confident. His name is HARRY FATT.

FATT: You're so wrong I ain't laughing. Any guy with eyes to read knows it. Look at the textile strike—out like lions and in like lambs. Take the San Francisco tie-up—starvation and broken heads. The steel boys wanted to walk out too, but they changed their minds. It's the trend of the times, that's what it is. All we workers got a good man behind us now. He's top man of the country—looking out for our interests—the man in the White House is the one I'm referrin' to. That's why the times ain't ripe for a strike. He's working day and night——

VOICE [*from the audience*]: For who? [*The* GUNMAN *stirs himself.*]

FATT: For you! The records prove it. If this was the Hoover régime, would I say don't go out, boys? Not on your tintype! But things is different now. You read the papers as well as me. You know it. And that's why I'm against the strike. Because we gotta stand behind the man who's standin' behind us! The whole country——

ANOTHER VOICE: Is on the blink! [*The* GUNMAN *looks grave.*]

FATT: Stand up and show yourself, you damn red! Be a man, let's see what you look like! [*Waits in vain.*] Yellow from the word go! Red and yellow makes a dirty color, boys. I got my eyes on four or five of them in the union here. What the hell'll they do for you? Pull you out and run away when trouble starts. Give those birds a chance and they'll have your sisters and wives in the whore houses, like they done in Russia. They'll tear Christ off his bleeding cross. They'll wreck your homes and throw your babies in the river. You think that's bunk? Read the papers! Now listen, we can't stay here all night. I gave you the facts in the case. You boys got hot suppers to go to and——

ANOTHER VOICE: Says you!

GUNMAN: Sit down, Punk!

ANOTHER VOICE: Where's Lefty? [*Now this question is taken up by the others in unison. FATT pounds with gavel.*]

FATT: That's what I wanna know. Where's your pal, Lefty? You elected him chairman—where the hell did he disappear?

VOICES: We want Lefty! Lefty! Lefty!

FATT [*pounding*]: What the hell is this—a circus? You got the committee here. This bunch of cowboys you elected. [*Pointing to man on extreme right end.*]

MAN: Benjamin.

FATT: Yeah, Doc Benjamin. [*Pointing to other men in circle in seated order.*] Benjamin, Miller, Stein, Mitchell, Philips, Keller. It ain't my fault Lefty took a run-out powder. If you guys——

A GOOD VOICE: What's the committee say?

OTHERS: The committee! Let's hear from the committee! [*FATT tries to quiet the crowd, but one of the seated men suddenly comes to the front. The GUNMAN moves over to center stage, but FATT says:*]

FATT: Sure, let him talk. Let's hear what the red boys gotta say!

[*Various shouts are coming from the audience. FATT insolently goes back to his seat in the middle of the circle. He sits on his raised platform and relights his cigar. The GUN-*

MAN *goes back to his post.* JOE, *the new speaker, raises his hand for quiet. Gets it quickly. He is sore.*]

JOE: You boys know me. I ain't a red boy one bit! Here I'm carryin' a shrapnel that big I picked up in the war. And maybe I don't know it when it rains! Don't tell me red! You know what we are? The black and blue boys! We been kicked around so long we're black and blue from head to toes. But I guess anyone who says straight out he don't like it, he's a red boy to the leaders of the union. What's this crap about goin' home to hot suppers? I'm asking to your faces how many's got hot suppers to go home to? Anyone who's sure of his next meal, raise your hand! A certain gent sitting behind me can raise them both. But not in front here! And that's why we're talking strike—to get a living wage!

VOICE: Where's Lefty?

JOE: I honest to God don't know, but he didn't take no run-out powder. That Wop's got more guts than a slaughter house. Maybe a traffic jam got him, but he'll be here. But don't let this red stuff scare you. Unless fighting for a living scares you. We gotta make up our minds. My wife made up my mind last week, if you want the truth. It's plain as the nose on Sol Feinberg's face we need a strike. There's us comin' home every night—eight, ten hours on the cab. "God," the wife says, "eighty cents ain't money—don't buy beans almost. You're workin' for the company," she says to me, "Joe! you ain't workin' for me or the family no more!" She says to me, "If you don't start...."

I. JOE AND EDNA

The lights fade out and a white spot picks out the playing space within the space of seated men. The seated men are very dimly visible in the outer dark, but more prominent is FATT *smoking his cigar and often blowing the smoke in the lighted circle.*

A tired but attractive woman of thirty comes into the room, drying her hands on an apron. She stands there sullenly as JOE

*comes in from the other side, home from work. For a moment
they stand and look at each other in silence.*

JOE: Where's all the furniture, honey?

EDNA: They took it away. No installments paid.

JOE: When?

EDNA: Three o'clock.

JOE: They can't do that.

EDNA: Can't? They did it.

JOE: Why, the palookas, we paid three-quarters.

EDNA: The man said read the contract.

JOE: We must have signed a phoney....

EDNA: It's a regular contract and you signed it.

JOE: Don't be so sour, Edna.... [*Tries to embrace her.*]

EDNA: Do it in the movies, Joe—they pay Clark Gable big
money for it.

JOE: This is a helluva house to come home to. Take my
word!

EDNA: Take MY word! Whose fault is it?

JOE: Must you start that stuff again?

EDNA: Maybe you'd like to talk about books?

JOE: I'd like to slap you in the mouth!

EDNA: No you won't.

JOE [*sheepish*]: Jeez, Edna, you get me sore some time....

EDNA: But just look at me—I'm laughing all over!

JOE: Don't insult me. Can I help it if times are bad? What
the hell do you want me to do, jump off a bridge or something?

EDNA: Don't yell. I just put the kids to bed so they won't
know they missed a meal. If I don't have Emmy's shoes soled
tomorrow, she can't go to school. In the meantime let her
sleep.

JOE: Honey, I rode the wheels off the chariot today. I
cruised around five hours without a call. It's conditions.

EDNA: Tell it to the A & P!

JOE: I booked two-twenty on the clock. A lady with a dog

was lit . . . she gave me a quarter tip by mistake. If you'd only listen to me—we're rolling in wealth.

EDNA: Yeah? How much?

JOE: I had "coffee and—" in a beanery. [*Hands her silver coins.*] A buck four.

EDNA: The second month's rent is due tomorrow.

JOE: Don't look at me that way, Edna.

EDNA: I'm looking through you, not at you. . . . Everything was gonna be so ducky! A cottage by the waterfall, roses in Picardy. You're a four-star-bust! If you think I'm standing for it much longer, you're crazy as a bedbug.

JOE: I'd get another job if I could. There's no work—you know it.

EDNA: I only know we're at the bottom of the ocean.

JOE: What can I do?

EDNA: Who's the man in the family, you or me?

JOE: That's no answer. Get down to brass tacks. Christ, gimme a break, too! A coffee cake and java all day. I'm hungry, too, Babe. I'd work my fingers to the bone if——

EDNA: I'll open a can of salmon.

JOE: Not now. Tell me what to do!

EDNA: I'm not God!

JOE: Jeez, I wish I was a kid again and didn't have to think about the next minute.

EDNA: But you're not a kid and you do have to think about the next minute. You got two blondie kids sleeping in the next room. They need food and clothes. I'm not mentioning anything else— But we're stalled like a flivver in the snow. For five years I laid awake at night listening to my heart pound. For God's sake, do something, Joe, get wise. Maybe get your buddies together, maybe go on strike for better money. Poppa did it during the war and they won out. I'm turning into a sour old nag.

JOE [*defending himself*]: Strikes don't work!

EDNA: Who told you?

JOE: Besides that means not a nickel a week while we're out. Then when it's over they don't take you back.

EDNA: Suppose they don't! What's to lose?

JOE: Well, we're averaging six-seven dollars a week now.

EDNA: That just pays for the rent.

JOE: That is something, Edna.

EDNA: It isn't. They'll push you down to three and four a week before you know it. Then you'll say, "That's somethin'," too!

JOE: There's too many cabs on the street, that's the whole damn trouble.

EDNA: Let the company worry about that, you big fool! If their cabs didn't make a profit, they'd take them off the streets. Or maybe you think they're in business just to pay Joe Mitchell's rent!

JOE: You don't know a-b-c, Edna.

EDNA: I know this—your boss is making suckers outa you boys every minute. Yes, and suckers out of all the wives and the poor innocent kids who'll grow up with crooked spines and sick bones. Sure, I see it in the papers, how good orange juice is for kids. But dammit our kids get colds one on top of the other. They look like little ghosts. Betty never saw a grapefruit. I took her to the store last week and she pointed to a stack of grapefruits. "What's that!" she said. My God, Joe—the world is supposed to be for all of us.

JOE: You'll wake them up.

EDNA: I don't care, as long as I can maybe wake you up.

JOE: Don't insult me. One man can't make a strike.

EDNA: Who says one? You got hundreds in your rotten union!

JOE: The Union ain't rotten.

EDNA: No? Then what are they doing? Collecting dues and patting your back?

JOE: They're making plans.

EDNA: What kind?

JOE: They don't tell us.

EDNA: It's too damn bad about you. They don't tell little Joey what's happening in his bitsie witsie union. What do you think it is—a ping pong game?

JOE: You know they're racketeers. The guys at the top would shoot you for a nickel.

EDNA: Why do you stand for that stuff?

JOE: Don't you wanna see me alive?

EDNA [*after a deep pause*]: No . . . I don't think I do, Joe. Not if you can lift a finger to do something about it, and don't. No, I don't care.

JOE: Honey, you don't understand what——

EDNA: And any other hackie that won't fight . . . let them all be ground to hamburger!

JOE: It's one thing to——

EDNA: Take your hand away! Only they don't grind me to little pieces! I got different plans. [*Starts to take off her apron.*]

JOE: Where are you going?

EDNA: None of your business.

JOE: What's up your sleeve?

EDNA: My arm'd be up my sleeve, darling, if I had a sleeve to wear. [*Puts neatly folded apron on back of chair.*]

JOE: Tell me!

EDNA: Tell you what?

JOE: Where are you going?

EDNA: Don't you remember my old boy friend?

JOE: Who?

EDNA: Bud Haas. He still has my picture in his watch. He earns a living.

JOE: What the hell are you talking about?

EDNA: I heard worse than I'm talking about.

JOE: Have you seen Bud since we got married?

EDNA: Maybe.

JOE: If I thought. . . . [*He stands looking at her.*]

EDNA: See much? Listen, boy friend, if you think I won't do this it just means you can't see straight.

JOE: Stop talking bull!

EDNA: This isn't five years ago, Joe.

JOE: You mean you'd leave me and the kids?

EDNA: I'd leave *you* like a shot!

JOE: No. . . .

EDNA: Yes!

[JOE *turns away, sitting in a chair with his back to her. Outside the lighted circle of the playing stage we hear the other seated members of the strike committee. "She will . . . she will . . . it happens that way," etc. This group should be used throughout for various comments, political, emotional and as general chorus. Whispering. . . . The fat boss now blows a heavy cloud of smoke into the scene.*]

JOE [*finally*]: Well, I guess I ain't got a leg to stand on.

EDNA: No?

JOE [*suddenly mad*]: No, you lousy tart, no! Get the hell out of here. Go pick up that bull-thrower on the corner and stop at some cushy hotel downtown. He's probably been coming here every morning and laying you while I hacked my guts out!

EDNA: You're crawling like a worm!

JOE: You'll be crawling in a minute.

EDNA: You don't scare me that much! [*Indicates a half inch on her finger.*]

JOE: This is what I slaved for!

EDNA: Tell it to your boss!

JOE: He don't give a damn for you or me!

EDNA: That's what I say.

JOE: Don't change the subject!

EDNA: This is the subject, the EXACT SUBJECT! Your boss makes this subject. I never saw him in my life, but he's putting ideas in my head a mile a minute. He's giving your kids that fancy disease called the rickets. He's making a jellyfish outa you and putting wrinkles in my face. This is the subject every inch of the way! He's throwing me into Bud Haas' lap. When in hell will you get wise——

JOE: I'm not so dumb as you think! But you are talking like a Red.

EDNA: I don't know what that means. But when a man knocks you down you get up and kiss his fist! You gutless piece of boloney.

JOE: One man can't——

EDNA [*with great joy*]: I don't say one man! I say a hundred, a thousand, a whole million, I say. But start in your own union. Get those hack boys together! Sweep out those racketeers like a pile of dirt! Stand up like men and fight for the crying kids and wives. Goddammit! I'm tired of slavery and sleepless nights.

JOE [*with her*]: Sure, sure! ...

EDNA: Yes. Get brass toes on your shoes and know where to kick!

JOE [*suddenly jumping up and kissing his wife full on the mouth*]: Listen, Edna. I'm goin' down to 174th Street to look up Lefty Costello. Lefty was saying the other day.... [*He suddenly stops.*] How about this Haas guy?

EDNA: Get out of here!

JOE: I'll be back! [*Runs out.*]

[*For a moment* EDNA *stands triumphant.*]

[*There is a blackout and when the regular lights come up,* JOE MITCHELL *is concluding what he has been saying:*]

JOE: You guys know this stuff better than me. We gotta walk out! [*Abruptly he turns and goes back to his seat and blackout.*]

[*Blackout*]

II. LAB ASSISTANT EPISODE

Discovered: MILLER, *a lab assistant, looking around; and* FAYETTE, *an industrialist.*

FAY.: Like it?

MILL.: Very much. I've never seen an office like this outside the movies.

FAY.: Yes, I often wonder if interior decorators and bathroom fixture people don't get all their ideas from Hollywood. Our country's extraordinary that way. Soap, cosmetics, electric refrigerators—just let Mrs. Consumer know they're used by the Crawfords and Garbos—more volume of sale than one plant can handle!

MILL.: I'm afraid it isn't that easy, Mr. Fayette.

FAY.: No, you're right—gross exaggeration on my part. Competition is cut-throat today. Markets up flush against a stone wall. The astronomers had better hurry—open Mars to trade expansion.

MILL.: Or it will be just too bad!

FAY.: Cigar?

MILL.: Thank you, don't smoke.

FAY.: Drink?

MILL.: Ditto, Mr. Fayette.

FAY.: I like sobriety in my workers... the trained ones, I mean. The Pollacks and niggers, they're better drunk—keeps them out of mischief. Wondering why I had you come over?

MILL.: If you don't mind my saying—very much.

FAY. [*patting him on the knee*]: I like your work.

MILL.: Thanks.

FAY.: No reason why a talented young man like yourself shouldn't string along with us—a growing concern. Loyalty is well repaid in our organization. Did you see Siegfried this morning?

MILL.: He hasn't been in the laboratory all day.

FAY.: I told him yesterday to raise you twenty dollars a month. Starts this week.

MILL.: You don't know how happy my wife'll be.

FAY.: Oh, I can appreciate it. [*He laughs.*]

MILL.: Was that all, Mr. Fayette?

FAY.: Yes, except that we're switching you to laboratory A tomorrow. Siegfried knows about it. That's why I had you in. The new work is very important. Siegfried recommended you very highly as a man to trust. You'll work directly under Dr. Brenner. Make you happy?

MILL.: Very. He's an important chemist!

FAY. [*leaning over seriously*]: We think so, Miller. We think so to the extent of asking you to stay within the building throughout the time you work with him.

MILL.: You mean sleep and eat in?

FAY.: Yes. . . .

MILL.: It can be arranged.

FAY.: Fine. You'll go far, Miller.

MILL.: May I ask the nature of the new work?

FAY. [*looking around first*]: Poison gas. . . .

MILL.: Poison!

FAY.: Orders from above. I don't have to tell you from where. New type poison gas for modern warfare.

MILL.: I see.

FAY.: You didn't know a new war was that close, did you?

MILL.: I guess I didn't.

FAY.: I don't have to stress the importance of absolute secrecy.

MILL.: I understand!

FAY.: The world is an armed camp today. One match sets the whole world blazing in forty-eight hours. Uncle Sam won't be caught napping!

MILL.: [*addressing his pencil*]: They say 12 million men were killed in that last one and 20 million more wounded or missing.

FAY.: That's not our worry. If big business went sentimental over human life there wouldn't be big business of any sort!

MILL.: My brother and two cousins went in the last one.

FAY.: They died in a good cause.

MILL.: My mother says "no!"

FAY.: She won't worry about you this time. You're too valuable behind the front.

MILL.: That's right.

FAY.: All right, Miller. See Siegfried for further orders.

MILL.: You should have seen my brother—he could ride a bike without hands. . . .

FAY.: You'd better move some clothes and shaving tools in tomorrow. Remember what I said—you're with a growing organization.

MILL.: He could run the hundred yards in 9:8 flat. . . .

FAY.: Who?

MILL.: My brother. He's in the Meuse-Argonne Cemetery. Momma went there in 1926. . . .

FAY.: Yes, those things stick. How's your handwriting, Miller, fairly legible?

MILL.: Fairly so.

FAY.: Once a week I'd like a little report from you.

MILL.: What sort of report?

FAY.: Just a few hundred words once a week on Dr. Brenner's progress.

MILL.: Don't you think it might be better coming from the Doctor?

FAY.: I didn't ask you that.

MILL.: Sorry.

FAY.: I want to know what progress he's making, the reports to be purely confidential—between you and me.

MILL.: You mean I'm to watch him?

FAY.: Yes!

MILL.: I guess I can't do that. . . .

FAY.: Thirty a month raise . . .

MILL.: You said twenty. . . .

FAY.: Thirty!

MILL.: Guess I'm not built that way.

FAY.: Forty. . . .

MILL.: Spying's not in my line, Mr. Fayette!

FAY.: You use ugly words, Mr. Miller!

MILL.: For ugly activity? Yes!

FAY.: Think about it, Miller. Your chances are excellent. . . .

MILL.: No.

FAY.: You're doing something for your country. Assuring the United States that when those goddam Japs start a ruckus we'll have offensive weapons to back us up! Don't you read your newspapers, Miller?

MILL.: Nothing but Andy Gump.

FAY.: If you were on the inside you'd know I'm talking cold sober truth! Now, I'm not asking you to make up your mind on the spot. Think about it over your lunch period.

MILL.: No. . . .

FAY.: Made up your mind already?

MILL.: Afraid so.

FAY.: You understand the consequences?

MILL.: I lose my raise——

[*Simultaneously*] {MILL.: And my job!
{FAY.: And your job!

FAY.:You misunderstand——

MILL.: Rather dig ditches first!

FAY.: That's a big job for foreigners.

MILL.: But sneaking—and making poison gas—that's for Americans?

FAY.: It's up to you.

MILL.: My mind's made up.

FAY.: No hard feelings?

MILL.: Sure hard feelings! I'm not the civilized type, Mr. Fayette. Nothing suave or sophisticated about me. Plenty of hard feelings! Enough to want to bust you and all your kind square in the mouth!

[*Does exactly that.*]

[*Blackout*]

III. *THE YOUNG HACK AND HIS GIRL*

Opens with girl and brother. FLORRIE *waiting for* SID *to take her to a dance.*

FLOR.: I gotta right to have something out of life. I don't smoke, I don't drink. So if Sid wants to take me to a dance, I'll go. Maybe if you was in love you wouldn't talk so hard.

IRV: I'm saying it for your good.

FLOR.: Don't be so good to me.

IRV: Mom's sick in bed and you'll be worryin' her to the grave. She don't want that boy hanging around the house and she don't want you meeting him in Crotona Park.

FLOR.: I'll meet him anytime I like!

IRV: If you do, yours truly'll take care of it in his own way. With just one hand, too!

FLOR.: Why are you all so set against him?

IRV: Mom told you ten times—it ain't him. It's that he ain't got nothing. Sure, we know he's serious, that he's stuck on you. But that don't cut no ice.

FLOR.: Taxi drivers used to make good money.

IRV: Today they're makin' five and six dollars a week. Maybe you wanta raise a family on that. Then you'll be back here living with us again and I'll be supporting two families in one. Well . . . over my dead body.

FLOR.: Irv, I don't care—I love him!

IRV: You're a little kid with half-baked ideas!

FLOR.: I stand there behind the counter the whole day. I think about him——

IRV: If you thought more about Mom it would be better.

FLOR.: Don't I take care of her every night when I come home? Don't I cook supper and iron your shirts and . . . you give me a pain in the neck, too. Don't try to shut me up! I bring a few dollars in the house, too. Don't you see I want something else out of life. Sure, I want romance, love, babies. I want everything in life I can get.

IRV: You take care of Mom and watch your step!

FLOR.: And if I don't?

IRV: Yours truly'll watch it for you!

FLOR.: You can talk that way to a girl . . .

IRV: I'll talk that way to your boy friend, too, and it won't be with words! Florrie, if you had a pair of eyes you'd see it's for your own good we're talking. This ain't no time to get married. Maybe later——

FLOR.: "Maybe Later" never comes for me, though. Why don't we send Mom to a hospital? She can die in peace there instead of looking at the clock on the mantelpiece all day.

IRV: That needs money. Which we don't have!

FLOR.: Money, Money, Money!

IRV: Don't change the subject.

FLOR.: This is the subject!

IRV: You gonna stop seeing him? [*She turns away.*] Jesus, kiddie, I remember when you were a baby with curls down your back. Now I gotta stand here yellin' at you like this.

FLOR.: I'll talk to him, Irv.

IRV: When?

FLOR.: I asked him to come here tonight. We'll talk it over.

IRV: Don't get soft with him. Nowadays is no time to be soft. You gotta be hard as a rock or go under.

FLOR.: I found that out. There's the bell. Take the egg off the stove I boiled for Mom. Leave us alone, Irv.

[SID *comes in—the two men look at each other for a second.* IRV *exits.*]

SID [*enters*]: Hello, Florrie.

FLOR.: Hello, Honey. You're looking tired.

SID: Naw, I just need a shave.

FLOR.: Well, draw your chair up to the fire and I'll ring for brandy and soda . . . like in the movies.

SID: If this was the movies I'd bring a big bunch of roses.

FLOR.: How big?

SID: Fifty or sixty dozen—the kind with long, long stems—big as that. . . .

FLOR.: You dope. . . .

SID: Your Paris gown is beautiful.

FLOR.: [*acting grandly*]: Yes, Percy, velvet panels are coming back again. Madame La Farge told me today that Queen Marie herself designed it.

SID: Gee . . . !

FLOR.: Every princess in the Balkans is wearing one like this. [*Poses grandly.*]

SID: Hold it. [*Does a nose camera—thumbing nose and imitating grinding of camera with other hand. Suddenly she falls out of the posture and swiftly goes to him, to embrace him, to kiss him with love. Finally:*]

SID: You look tired, Florrie.

FLOR.: Naw, I just need a shave. [*She laughs tremorously.*]

SID: You worried about your mother?

FLOR.: No.

SID: What's on your mind?

FLOR.: The French and Indian War.

SID: What's on your mind?

FLOR.: I got us on my mind, Sid. Night and day, Sid!

SID: I smacked a beer truck today. Did I get hell! I was driving along thinking of US, too. You don't have to say it— I know what's on your mind. I'm rat poison around here.

FLOR.: Not to me. . . .

SID: I know to who . . . and I know why. I don't blame them. We're engaged now for three years. . . .

FLOR.: That's a long time. . . .

SID: My brother Sam joined the navy this morning—get a break that way. They'll send him down to Cuba with the hootchy-kootchy girls. He don't know from nothing, that dumb basket ball player!

FLOR.: Don't you do that.

SID: Don't you worry, I'm not the kind who runs away. But I'm so tired of being a dog, Baby, I could choke. I don't even have to ask what's going on in your mind. I know from the word go, 'cause I'm thinking the same things, too.

FLOR.: It's yes or no—nothing in between.

SID: The answer is no—a big electric sign looking down on Broadway!

FLOR.: We wanted to have kids. . . .

SID: But that sort of life ain't for the dogs which is us. Christ, Baby! I get like thunder in my chest when we're together. If we went off together I could maybe look the world straight in the face, spit in its eye like a man should do. Goddammit, it's trying to be a man on the earth. Two in life together.

FLOR.: But something wants us to be lonely like that— crawling alone in the dark. Or they want us trapped.

SID: Sure, the big shot money men want us like that.

FLOR.: Highly insulting us——

SID: Keeping us in the dark about what is wrong with us in the money sense. They got the power and mean to be damn sure they keep it. They know if they give in just an inch, all the dogs like us will be down on them together—an ocean knocking them to hell and back and each singing cuckoo with stars coming from their nose and ears. I'm not raving, Florrie——

FLOR.: I know you're not, I know.

SID: I don't have the words to tell you what I feel. I never finished school. . . .

FLOR.: I know. . . .

SID: But it's relative, like the professors say. We worked like hell to send him to college—my kid brother Sam, I mean —and look what he done—joined the navy! The damn fool don't see the cards is stacked for all of us. The money man dealing himself a hot royal flush. Then giving you and me a phoney hand like a pair of tens or something. Then keep on losing the pots 'cause the cards is stacked against you. Then he says, what's the matter you can't win—no stuff on the ball, he says to you. And kids like my brother believe it 'cause they don't know better. For all their education, they don't know from nothing.

But wait a minute! Don't he come around and say to you—this millionaire with a jazz band—listen Sam or Sid or what's-your-name, you're no good, but here's a chance. The whole world'll know who you are. Yes sir, he says, get up on that ship and fight those bastards who's making the world a lousy place to live in. The Japs, the Turks, the Greeks. Take this gun—kill the slobs like a real hero, he says, a real American. Be a hero!

And the guy you're poking at? A real louse, just like you, 'cause they don't let him catch more than a pair of tens, too. On that foreign soil he's a guy like me and Sam, a guy who wants his baby like you and hot sun on his face! They'll teach Sam to point the guns the wrong way, that dumb basket ball player!

FLOR.: I got a lump in my throat, Honey.

SID: You and me—we never even had a room to sit in somewhere.

FLOR.: The park was nice . . .

SID: In Winter? The hallways . . . I'm glad we never got together. This way we don't know what we missed.

FLOR. [*in a burst*]: Sid, I'll go with you—we'll get a room somewhere.

SID: Naw . . . they're right. If we can't climb higher than this together—we better stay apart.

FLOR.: I swear to God I wouldn't care.

SID: You would, you would—in a year, two years, you'd curse the day. I seen it happen.

FLOR.: Oh, Sid. . . .

SID: Sure, I know. We got the blues, Babe—the 1935 blues. I'm talkin' this way 'cause I love you. If I didn't, I wouldn't care. . . .

FLOR.: We'll work together, we'll——

SID: How about the backwash? Your family needs your nine bucks. My family——

FLOR.: I don't care for them!

SID: You're making it up, Florrie. Little Florrie Canary in a cage.

FLOR.: Don't make fun of me.

SID: I'm not, Baby.

FLOR.: Yes, you're laughing at me.

SID: I'm not.

[*They stand looking at each other, unable to speak. Finally, he turns to a small portable phonograph and plays a cheap, sad, dance tune. He makes a motion with his hand; she comes to him. They begin to dance slowly. They hold each other tightly, almost as though they would merge into each other. The music stops, but the scratching record continues to the end of the scene. They stop dancing. He finally unlooses her clutch and seats her on the couch, where she sits, tense and expectant.*]

SID: Hello, Babe.

FLOR.: Hello. [*For a brief time they stand as though in a dream.*]

SID [*finally*]: Good-by, Babe.

[*He waits for an answer, but she is silent. They look at each other.*]

SID: Did you ever see my Pat Rooney imitation? [*He whistles Rosy O'Grady and soft shoes to it. Stops. He asks:*]

SID: Don't you like it?

FLOR. [*finally*]: No. [*Buries her face in her hands.*]

[*Suddenly he falls on his knees and buries his face in her lap.*]

[*Blackout*]

IV. LABOR SPY EPISODE

FATT: You don't know how we work for you. Shooting off your mouth won't help. Hell, don't you guys ever look at the records like me? Look in your own industry. See what happened when the hacks walked out in Philly three months ago! Where's Philly? A thousand miles away? An hour's ride on the train.

VOICE: Two hours!!

FATT.: Two hours . . . what the hell's the difference. Let's hear from someone who's got the practical experience to back him up. Fellers, there's a man here who's seen the whole parade in Philly, walked out with his pals, got knocked down like the rest—and blacklisted after they went back. That's why he's here. He's got a mighty interestin' word to say. [*Announces.*] TOM CLAYTON!

[*As CLAYTON starts up from the audience, FATT gives him a hand which is sparsely followed in the audience. CLAYTON comes forward.*]

Fellers, this is a man with practical strike experience—Tom Clayton from little ole Philly.

CLAYTON [*a thin, modest individual*]: Fellers, I don't mind your booing. If I thought it would help us hacks get better living conditions, I'd let you walk all over me, cut me up to little pieces. I'm one of you myself. But what I wanna say is that Harry Fatt's right. I only been working here in the big town five weeks, but I know conditions just like the rest of you. You know how it is—don't take long to feel the sore spots, no matter where you park.

CLEAR VOICE [*from audience*]: Sit down!

CLAYTON: But Fatt's right. Our officers is right. The time ain't ripe. Like a fruit don't fall off the tree until it's ripe.

CLEAR VOICE: Sit down, you fruit!

FATT [*on his feet*]: Take care of him, boys.

VOICE [*in audience, struggling*]: No one takes care of me.

[*Struggle in house and finally the owner of the voice runs up on stage, says to speaker.*]

SAME VOICE: Where the hell did you pick up that name! Clayton! This rat's name is Clancy, from the old Clancys, way back! Fruit! I almost wet myself listening to that one!

FATT [GUNMAN *with him*]: This ain't a barn! What the hell do you think you're doing here!

SAME VOICE: Exposing a rat!

FATT: You can't get away with this. Throw him the hell outa here.

VOICE [*preparing to stand his ground*]: Try it yourself.... When this bozo throws that slop around. You know who he is? That's a company spy.

FATT: Who the hell are you to make——

VOICE: I paid dues in this union for four years, that's who's me! I gotta right and this pussy-footed rat ain't coming in here with ideas like that. You know his record. Lemme say it out——

FATT: You'll prove all this or I'll bust you in every hack outfit in town!

VOICE: I gotta right. I gotta right. Looka *him*, he don't say boo!

CLAYTON: You're a liar and I never seen you before in my life!

VOICE: Boys, he spent two years in the coal fields breaking up any organization he touched. Fifty guys he put in jail. He's ranged up and down the east coast—shipping, textiles, steel—he's been in everything you can name. Right now——

CLAYTON: That's a lie!

VOICE: Right now he's working for that Bergman outfit on Columbus Circle who furnishes rats for any outfit in the country before, during, and after strikes.

[*The man who is the hero of the next episode goes down to his side with other committee men.*]

CLAYTON: He's trying to break up the meeting, fellers!

VOICE: We won't search you for credentials. . . .

CLAYTON: I got nothing to hide. Your own secretary knows I'm straight.

VOICE: Sure. Boys, you know who this sonovabitch is?

CLAYTON: I never seen you before in my life!

VOICE: Boys, I slept with him in the same bed sixteen years. HE'S MY OWN LOUSY BROTHER!!

FATT [*after pause*]: Is this true? [*No answer from* CLAYTON.]

VOICE [*to* CLAYTON]: Scram, before I break your neck!

[CLAYTON *scrams down center aisle.* VOICE *says, watching him:*]

Remember his map—he can't change that—Clancy!

[*Standing in his place says:*]

Too bad you didn't know about this, Fatt! [*After a pause.*] The Clancy family tree is bearing nuts!

[*Standing isolated clear on the stage is the hero of the next episode.*]

[*Blackout*]

V. THE YOUNG ACTOR

A New York theatrical producer's office. Present are a stenographer and a young actor. She is busy typing; he, waiting with card in hand.

STEN.: He's taking a hot bath . . . says you should wait.

PHILIPS [*the actor*]: A bath did you say? Where?

STEN.: See that door? Right through there—leads to his apartment.

PHIL.: Through there?

STEN.: Mister, he's laying there in a hot perfumed bath. Don't say I said it.

PHIL.: You don't say!

STEN.: An oriental den he's got. Can you just see this big Irishman burning Chinese punk in the bedroom? And a big old rose canopy over his casting couch....

PHIL.: What's that—casting couch?

STEN.: What's that? You from the sticks?

PHIL.: I beg your pardon?

STEN. [*rolls up her sleeves, makes elaborate deaf and dumb signs*]: No from side walkies of New Yorkie...savvy?

PHIL.: Oh, you're right. Two years of dramatic stock out of town. One in Chicago.

STEN.: Don't tell him, Baby Face. He wouldn't know a good actor if he fell over him in the dark. Say you had two years with the Group, two with the Guild.

PHIL.: I'd like to get with the Guild. They say——

STEN.: He won't know the difference. Don't say I said it!

PHIL.: I really did play with Watson Findlay in "Early Birds."

STEN. [*withering him*]: Don't tell him!

PHIL.: He's a big producer, Mr. Grady. I wish I had his money. Don't you?

STEN.: Say, I got a clean heart, Mister. I love my fellow man! [*About to exit with typed letters.*] Stick around—Mr. Philips. You might be the type. If you were a woman——

PHIL.: Please. Just a minute...please...I need the job.

STEN.: Look at him!

PHIL.: I mean...I don't know what buttons to push, and you do. What my father used to say—we had a gas station in Cleveland before the crash—"Know what buttons to push," Dad used to say, "and you'll go far."

STEN.: You can't push me, Mister! I don't ring right these last few years!

PHIL.: We don't know where the next meal's coming from. We——

STEN.: Maybe ... I'll lend you a dollar?

PHIL.: Thanks very much: it won't help.

STEN.: One of the old families of Virginia? Proud?

PHIL.: Oh, not that. You see, I have a wife. We'll have our first baby next month ... so ... a dollar isn't much help.

STEN.: Roped in?

PHIL.: I love my wife!

STEN.: Okay, you love her! Excuse me! You married her. Can't support her. No ... not blaming you. But you're fools, all you actors. Old and young! Watch you parade in and out all day. You still got apples in your cheeks and pins for buttons. But in six months you'll be like them—putting on an act: Phony strutting "pishers"—that's French for dead codfish! It's not their fault. Here you get like that or go under. What kind of job is this for an adult man!

PHIL.: When you have to make a living——

STEN.: I know, but——

PHIL.: Nothing else to do. If I could get something else——

STEN.: You'd take it!

PHIL.: Anything!

STEN.: Telling me! With two brothers in my hair! [MR. GRADY *now enters; played by* FATT.] Mr. Brown sent this young man over.

GRADY: Call the hospital: see how Boris is. [*She assents and exits.*]

PHIL.: Good morning, Mr. Grady....

GRADY: The morning is lousy!

PHIL.: Mr. Brown sent me. [*Hands over card.*]

GRADY: I heard that once already.

PHIL.: Excuse me....

GRADY: What experience?

PHIL.: Oh, yes....

GRADY: Where?

PHIL.: Two years in stock, sir. A year with the Goodman Theatre in Chicago.

GRADY: That all?

PHIL. [*abashed*]: Why no ... with the Theatre Guild ... I was there....

GRADY: Never saw you in a Guild show!

PHIL.: On the road, I mean ... understudying Mr. Lunt ...

GRADY: What part? [PHILIPS *cannot answer.*] You're a lousy liar, son.

PHIL.: I did....

GRADY: You don't look like what I want. Can't understand that Brown. Need a big man to play a soldier. Not a lousy soldier left on Broadway! All in pictures, and we get the nances! [*Turns to work on desk.*]

PHIL. [*immediately playing the soldier*]: I was in the ROTC in college ... Reserve Officers' Training Corps. We trained twice a week....

GRADY: Won't help.

PHIL.: With real rifles. [*Waits.*] Mr. Grady, I weigh a hundred and fifty-five!

GRADY: How many years back? Been eating regular since you left college?

PHIL. [*very earnestly*]: Mr. Grady, I could act this soldier part. I could build it up and act it. Make it up——

GRADY: Think I run a lousy acting school around here?

PHIL.: Honest to God I could! I need the job—that's why I could do it! I'm strong. I know my business! YOU'll get an A-1 performance. Because I need this job! My wife's having a baby in a few weeks. We need the money. Give me a chance!

GRADY: What do I care if you can act it! I'm sorry about your baby. Use your head, son. Tank Town stock is different. Here we got investments to be protected. When I sink fifteen thousand in a show I don't take chances on some youngster. We cast to type!

PHIL.: I'm an artist! I can——

GRADY: That's your headache. Nobody interested in artists here. Get a big bunch for a nickel on any corner. Two flops in a row on this lousy street nobody loves you—only God, and He don't count. We protect investments: we cast to type.

Your face and height we want, not your soul, son. And Jesus Christ himself couldn't play a soldier in this show ... with all his talent. [*Crosses himself in quick repentance for this remark.*]

PHIL.: Anything ... a bit, a walk-on?

GRADY: Sorry: small cast. [*Looking at papers on his desk.*] You try Russia, son. I hear it's hot stuff over there.

PHIL.: Stage manager? Assistant?

GRADY: All filled, sonny. [*Stands up; crumples several papers from the desk.*] Better luck next time.

PHIL.: Thanks. ...

GRADY: Drop in from time to time. [*Crosses and about to exit.*] You never know when something— [*The* STENOGRAPHER *enters with papers to put on desk.*] What did the hospital say?

STEN.: He's much better, Mr. Grady.

GRADY: Resting easy?

STEN.: Dr. Martel said Boris is doing even better than he expected.

GRADY: A damn lousy operation!

STEN.: Yes. ...

GRADY [*belching*]: Tell the nigger boy to send up a bromo seltzer.

STEN.: Yes, Mr. Grady. [*He exits.*] Boris wanted lady friends.

PHIL.: What?

STEN.: So they operated ... poor dog!

PHIL.: A dog?

STEN.: His Russian Wolf Hound! They do the same to you, but you don't know it! [*Suddenly.*] Want advice? In the next office, don't let them see you down in the mouth. They don't like it—makes them shiver.

PHIL.: You treat me like a human being. Thanks. ...

STEN.: You're human!

PHIL.: I used to think so.

STEN.: He wants a bromo for his hangover. [*Goes to door.*] Want that dollar?

PHIL.: It won't help much.

STEN.: One dollar buys ten loaves of bread, Mister. Or one dollar buys nine loaves of bread and one copy of The Communist Manifesto. Learn while you eat. Read while you run. . . .

PHIL.: Manifesto? What's that? [*Takes dollar.*] What is that, what you said. . . . Manifesto?

STEN.: Stop off on your way out—I'll give you a copy. From Genesis to Revelation, Comrade Philips! "And I saw a new earth and a new heaven; for the first earth and the first heaven were passed away; and there was no more sea."

PHIL.: I don't understand that. . . .

STEN.: I'm saying the meek shall not inherit the earth!

PHIL.: No?

STEN.: The MILITANT! Come out in the light, Comrade.

[*Blackout*]

VI. INTERNE EPISODE

DR. BARNES, *an elderly distinguished man, is speaking on the telephone. He wears a white coat.*

DR. BARNES: No, I gave you my opinion twice. You outvoted me. You did this to Dr. Benjamin yourself. That is why you can tell him yourself.

[*Hangs up phone, angrily. As he is about to pour himself a drink from a bottle on the table, a knock is heard.*]

BARNES: Who is it?

BENJAMIN [*without*]: Can I see you a minute, please?

BARNES [*hiding the bottle*]: Come in, Dr. Benjamin, come in.

BENJ.: It's important—excuse me—they've got Leeds up there in my place—He's operating on Mrs. Lewis—the hysterectomy—it's my job. I washed up, prepared . . . they told me at the last minute. I don't mind being replaced, Doctor, but Leeds is a damn fool! He shouldn't be permitted——

BARNES [*dryly*]: Leeds is the nephew of Senator Leeds.

BENJ.: He's incompetent as hell.

BARNES [*obviously changing subjects, picks up lab jar*]: They're doing splendid work in brain surgery these days. This is a very fine specimen. . . .

BENJ.: I'm sorry, I thought you might be interested.

BARNES [*still examining jar*]: Well, I am, young man, I am! Only remember it's a charity case!

BENJ.: Of course. They wouldn't allow it for a second, otherwise.

BARNES: Her life is in danger?

BENJ.: Of course! You know how serious the case is!

BARNES: Turn your gimlet eyes elsewhere, Doctor. Jigging around like a cricket on a hot grill won't help. Doctors don't run these hospitals. He's the Senator's nephew and there he stays.

BENJ.: It's too bad.

BARNES: I'm not calling you down either. [*Plopping down jar suddenly.*] Goddammit, do you think it my fault?

BENJ. [*about to leave*]: I know . . . I'm sorry.

BARNES: Just a minute. Sit down.

BENJ.: Sorry, I can't sit.

BARNES: Stand then!

BENJ. [*sits*]: Understand, Dr. Barnes, I don't mind being replaced at the last minute this way, but . . . well, this flagrant bit of class distinction—because she's poor——

BARNES: Be careful of words like that—"class distinction." Don't belong here. Lots of energy, you brilliant young men, but idiots. Discretion! Ever hear that word?

BENJ.: Too radical?

BARNES: Precisely. And some day like in Germany, it might cost you your head.

BENJ.: Not to mention my job.

BARNES: So they told you?

BENJ.: Told me what?

BARNES: They're closing Ward C next month. I don't have to tell you the hospital isn't self supporting. Until last year that board of trustees met deficits. . . . You can guess the rest. At a board meeting Tuesday, our fine feathered friends discovered they couldn't meet the last quarter's deficit—a neat little sum well over $100,000. If the hospital is to continue at all, its damn——

BENJ.: Necessary to close another charity ward!

BARNES: So they say. . . . [*A wait.*]

BENJ.: But that's not all?

BARNES [*ashamed*]: Have to cut down on staff too. . . .

BENJ.: That's too bad. Does it touch me?

BARNES: Afraid it does.

BENJ.: But after all I'm top man here. I don't mean I'm better than others, but I've worked harder.

BARNES: And shown more promise. . . .

BENJ.: I always supposed they'd cut from the bottom first.

BARNES: Usually.

BENJ.: But in this case?

BARNES: Complications.

BENJ.: For instance? [BARNES *hesitant.*]

BARNES: I like you, Benjamin. It's one ripping shame.

BENJ.: I'm no sensitive plant—what's the answer?

BARNES: An old disease, malignant, tumescent. We need an anti-toxin for it.

BENJ.: I see.

BARNES: What?

BENJ.: I met that disease before—at Harvard first.

BARNES: You have seniority here, Benjamin.

BENJ.: But I'm a Jew! [BARNES *nods his head in agreement.* BENJ. *stands there a moment and blows his nose.*]

BARNES [*blows his nose*]: Microbes!

BENJ.: Pressure from above?

BARNES: Don't think Kennedy and I didn't fight for you!

BENJ.: Such discrimination, with all those wealthy brother Jews on the board?

BARNES: I've remarked before—don't seem to be much difference between wealthy Jews and rich Gentiles. Cut from the same piece!

BENJ.: For myself I don't feel sorry. My parents gave up an awful lot to get me this far. They ran a little dry goods shop in the Bronx until their pitiful savings went in the crash last year. Poppa's peddling neckties. . . . Saul Ezra Benjamin—a man who's read Spinoza all his life.

BARNES: Doctors don't run medicine in this country. The men who know their jobs don't run anything here, except the motormen on trolley cars. I've seen medicine change—plenty—anesthesia, sterilization—but not because of rich men —in *spite* of them! In a rich man's country your true self's buried deep. Microbes! Less. . . . Vermin! See this ankle, this delicate sensitive hand? Four hundred years to breed that. Out of a revolutionary background! Spirit of '76! Ancestors froze at Valley Forge! What's it all mean! Slops! The honest workers were sold out then, in '76. The Constitution's for rich men then and now. Slops! [*The phone rings.*]

BARNES [*angrily*]: Dr. Barnes. [*Listens a moment, looks at* BENJAMIN]: I see. [*Hangs up, turns slowly to the younger Doctor.*] They lost your patient.

[BENJ. *stands solid with the shock of this news but finally hurls his operation gloves to the floor.*]

BARNES: That's right . . . that's right. Young, hot, go and do it! I'm very ancient, fossil, but life's ahead of you, Dr. Benjamin, and when you fire the first shot say, "This one's for old Doc Barnes!" Too much dignity—bullets. Don't shoot vermin! Step on them! If I didn't have an invalid daughter——

BARNES [*goes back to his seat, blows his nose in silence*]: I have said my piece, Benjamin.

BENJ.: Lots of things I wasn't certain of. Many things these radicals say . . . you don't believe theories until they happen to you.

BARNES: You lost a lot today, but you won a great point.

BENJ.: Yes, to know I'm right? To really begin believing in something? Not to say, "What a world!" but to say, "Change the world!" I wanted to go to Russia. Last week I was thinking about it—the wonderful opportunity to do good work in their socialized medicine——

BARNES: Beautiful, beautiful!

BENJ.: To be able to work——

BARNES: Why don't you go? I might be able——

BENJ.: Nothing's nearer what I'd like to do!

BARNES: Do it!

BENJ.: No! our work's here—America! I'm scared. . . . What future's ahead, I don't know. Get some job to keep alive—maybe drive a cab—and study and work and learn my place——

BARNES: And step down hard!

BENJ.: Fight! Maybe get killed, but goddam! We'll go ahead! [BENJAMIN *stands with clenched fist raised high.*]

[*Blackout*]

AGATE: LADIES AND GENTLEMEN, and don't let any-one tell you we ain't got some ladies in this sea of upturned faces! Only they're wearin' pants. Well, maybe I don't know a thing; maybe I fell outa the cradle when I was a kid and ain't been right since—you can't tell!

VOICE: Sit down, cockeye!

AGATE: Who's paying you for those remarks, Buddy?—Moscow Gold? Maybe I got a *glass eye*, but it come from working in a factory at the age of eleven. They hooked it out because they didn't have a shield on the works. But I wear it like a medal 'cause it tells the world where I belong—deep down in the working class! We had delegates in the union there—all kinds of secretaries and treasurers . . . walkin' delegates, but not with blisters on their feet! Oh no! On their fat little ass from sitting on cushions and raking in mazuma. [SECRETARY *and* GUNMAN *remonstrate in words and actions here*] Sit down, boys, I'm just sayin' that about unions in general. I know it ain't true here! Why no, our officers is all aces. Why, I seen our own secretary Fatt walk outa his way not to step on a cockroach. No boys, don't think——

FATT [*breaking in*]: You're out of order!

AGATE [*to audience*]: Am I outa order?

ALL: No, no. Speak. Go on, etc.

AGATE: Yes, our officers is all aces. But I'm a member here—and no experience in Philly either! Today I couldn't wear my union button. The damnest thing happened. When I take the old coat off the wall, I see she's smoking. I'm a sonovagun if the old union button isn't on fire! Yep, the old celluloid was makin' the most god-awful stink: the landlady came up and give me hell! You know what happened?—that old union button just blushed itself to death! Ashamed! Can you beat it?

FATT: Sit down, Keller! Nobody's interested!

AGATE: Yes they are!

GUNMAN: Sit down like he tells you!

AGATE [*continuing to audience*]: And when I finish——

[*His speech is broken by* FATT *and* GUNMAN *who physically handle him. He breaks away and gets to other side of stage. The two are about to make for him when some of the committee men come forward and get in between the struggling parties.* AGATE's *shirt has been torn.*]

AGATE [*to audience*]: What's the answer, boys? The answer is, if we're reds because we wanna strike, then we take over their salute too! Know how they do it? [*Makes Communist salute*] What is it? An uppercut! The good old uppercut to the chin! Hell, some of us boys ain't even got a shirt to our backs. What's the boss class tryin' to do—make a nudist colony outa us?

[*The audience laughs and suddenly* AGATE *comes to the middle of the stage so that the other cabmen back him up in a strong clump.*]

AGATE: Don't laugh! Nothing's funny! This is your life and mine! It's skull and bones every incha the road! Christ, we're dyin' by inches! For what? For the debutant-ees to have their sweet comin' out parties in the Ritz! Poppa's got a daughter she's gotta get her picture in the papers. Christ, they make 'em with our blood. Joe said it. Slow death or fight. It's war.

[*Throughout this whole speech* AGATE *is backed up by the*

*other six workers, so that from their activity it is plain that
the whole group of them are saying these things. Several of
them may take alternate lines out of this long last speech.*]

You Edna, God love your mouth! Sid and Florrie, the other
boys, old Doc Barnes—fight with us for right! It's war! Working class, unite and fight! Tear down the slaughter house of
our old lives! Let freedom really ring.

These slick slobs stand here telling us about bogeymen.
That's a new one for the kids—the reds is bogeymen! But the
man who got me food in 1932, he called me Comrade! The
one who picked me up where I bled—he called me Comrade
too! What are we waiting for.... Don't wait for Lefty! He
might never come. Every minute——

[*This is broken into by a man who has dashed up the center
aisle from the back of the house. He runs up on stage, says*]:

MAN: Boys, they just found Lefty!

OTHERS: What? What? What?

SOME: Shhh.... Shh....

MAN: They found Lefty....

AGATE: Where?

MAN: Behind the car barns with a bullet in his head!

AGATE [*crying*]: Hear it, boys, hear it? Hell, listen to me!
Coast to coast! HELLO AMERICA! HELLO. WE'RE
STORMBIRDS OF THE WORKING-CLASS. WORKERS
OF THE WORLD.... OUR BONES AND BLOOD! And
when we die they'll know what we did to make a new world!
Christ, cut us up to little pieces. We'll die for what is right!
Put fruit trees where our ashes are!

[*To audience*] Well, what's the answer?

ALL: STRIKE!

AGATE: LOUDER!

ALL: STRIKE!

AGATE and OTHERS on Stage. AGAIN!

ALL: STRIKE, STRIKE, STRIKE!!!

[*Curtain*]

CLIFFORD ODETS

A writer of plays about people who are trapped materially or psychologically, Clifford Odets does not deal with pleasant material. But no critic has ever denied his real power on the stage or his keen sense of the human tragedy.

Born on July 18, 1906, in Philadelphia, he grew up and went to school in the Bronx, New York. He became impatient with high school, which he said was a waste of time, and did not graduate.

His desire to write met family opposition, but he persisted in going his own way. He became a radio gag writer and announcer and toured the East doing character roles with a theatrical stock company. From 1928 to 1930 he acted with the Theatre Guild and then joined the Group Theater. His first play, *Awake and Sing,* was completed by 1933 but he could not find a producer.

The following year, having heard that the New Theatre League was having a one-act-play contest, he decided to enter. Using a recent New York taxi-driver's strike as his subject and locking himself away for three days in a hotel room, he wrote *Waiting for Lefty,* which won the contest. The League production of the play made a sensation. Its dramatic invention, its force, and its use of the stage as a "living newspaper" made it stand out among propaganda pieces. For its leftist opinions it has been banned oftener than any other American play.

Odets wrote his other plays in rapid succession. In 1937, he went to Hollywood where he has remained writing for the screen, though not all of his scripts have been produced.

His plays and the dates of their first production:

Awake and Sing, February 19, 1935.
Till the Day I Die, March 26, 1935.
Waiting for Lefty, March 26, 1935. (Previously produced at a benefit performance.)
Paradise Lost, December 9, 1935.
Golden Boy, November 4, 1937.
Rocket to the Moon, November 24, 1938.

Night Music, February 22, 1940.
Clash by Night, December 27, 1941.

CRITICAL COMMENTS

WAITING FOR LEFTY

A new production by the Group Theater supplies the answer to a question I asked in this column three weeks ago. Mr. Clifford Odets, the talented author of "Awake and Sing," has come out for the revolution and thrown in his artistic lot with those who use the theater for direct propaganda. The earlier play, it seems, was written some three years ago before his convictions had crystallized, and it owes to that fact a certain contemplative and brooding quality. The new ones—there are two on a double bill at the Longacre—waste no time on what the author now doubtless regards as side issues, and they hammer away with an unrelenting insistency upon a single theme: Workers of the World Unite!

"Waiting for Lefty," a brief sketch suggested by the recent strike of taxi drivers, is incomparably the better of the two, and whatever else one may say of it, there is no denying its effectiveness as a tour de force. It begins *in medias res* on the platform at a strikers' meeting, and "plants" interrupting from the audience create the illusion that the meeting is actually taking place at the very moment of representation. Brief flashbacks reveal crucial moments in the lives of the drivers, but the scene really remains in the hall itself, and the piece ends when the strike is voted. The pace is swift, the characterization is for the most part crisp, and the points are made one after another, with bold simplicity. What Mr. Odets is trying to do could hardly be done more economically or more effectively.

Cold analysis, to be sure, clearly reveals the fact that such simplicity must be paid for at a certain price. The villains are mere caricatures and even the very human heroes occasionally freeze into stained-glass attitudes, as, for example, a certain lady secretary in one of the flashbacks does when she suddenly stops in her tracks to pay a glowing tribute to "The Communist Manifesto" and to urge its perusal upon all and sundry. No one, however, expects subtleties from a soap-box, and the interesting fact is that

Mr. Odets has invented a form which turns out to be a very effective dramatic equivalent of soap-box oratory.

Innumerable other "proletarian" dramatists have tried to do the same thing with far less success. Some of them have got bogged in futuristic symbolism which could not conceivably do more than bewilder "the worker"; others have stuck close to the usual form of the drama without realizing that this form was developed for other uses and that their attempt to employ it for directly hortatory purposes can only end in what appears to be more than exceedingly crude dramaturgy. Mr. Odets, on the other hand, has made a clean sweep of the conventional form along with the conventional intentions. He boldly accepts as his scene the very platform he intends to use, and from it permits his characters to deliver speeches which are far more convincing there than they would be if elaborately worked into a conventional dramatic story. Like many of his fellows he has evidently decided that art is a weapon, but unlike many who proclaim the doctrine, he has the full courage of his conviction. To others he leaves the somewhat nervous determination to prove that direct exhortation can somehow be made compatible with "art" and that "revolutionary" plays can be two things at once. The result of his downrightness is to succeed where most of the others have failed. He does not ask to be judged by any standards except those which one would apply to the agitator, but by those standards his success is very nearly complete.

[Joseph Wood Krutch, "Mr. Odets Speaks His Mind," in *The Nation*, 140 (April 10, 1935), pp. 427-8. Reprinted by permission.]

WAITING FOR LEFTY

The general theatre public did not get very excited about proletarian drama until Clifford Odets wrote *Waiting for Lefty*.

First presented at a benefit for the New Theatre League in Manhattan, *Waiting for Lefty* got to Broadway by way of the Group Theatre (TIME, April 8). With lines as pointed as a stiletto, with a unique technical trick which used the theatre audience as spectators at a taxi union's mass meeting, *Waiting for Lefty* turned out to be a crashing success in tolerant Manhattan. Thereupon, one by one, 32 League groups produced the show in the country at large and the trouble began. Plays of the calibre of *Mr. Morgan's Nightmare* had evidently been beneath the notice of the American Legion, Friends of New Germany and other illiberal groups. But *Waiting for Lefty,* aside from forcefully presenting the case of capitalist labor racketeering, was such a whacking good show that it became the target of a suppression campaign unequaled since the great Red Scare of 1920.

By last week *Waiting for Lefty* had been banned in seven cities on one ambiguous pretext or another. In Boston the police ran the New Theatre Players out of two houses, finally locked up four actors on charges of "profanity and blasphemy." After winning the George Pierce Baker Cup at the Yale Drama School for their performance of the play, the Unity Players were forbidden in future to act *Waiting for Lefty* anywhere in New Haven. It took a concerted move by University liberals to smash the ban. When the Collective Theatre tried to put on *Waiting for Lefty* in Newark, the troupe was ousted from a school building, then moved to a hall which was promptly condemned by the Building Department, finally went to another hall where nine introductory speakers were successively arrested. In Hollywood the New Theatre Group was presenting *Waiting for Lefty* together with Odets' anti-Nazi *Till The Day I Die* when the director was kidnapped, badly beaten by thugs.

This systematic campaign against a play acknowledged as high art regardless of its political significance reached such nation-wide proportions last week that the strictly non-radical Authors' League of America was moved to come to the defense of the harassed New Theatre League. Declared Vice President Elmer Davis ... of the Authors' League: "The tactics employed to suppress presentation of *Waiting for Lefty* are familiar and timeworn. Technicalities of the fire laws, obsolete statutes from the old 'blue laws' period, red tape in connection with licenses—all of these are used to bar the play from theatres or to stop performances. But the real issue of freedom of opinion and the right to express it is clearly the crux of the matter. Not only those who are concerned with the theatre but everyone who wants to preserve the American heritage of civil liberties will bitterly resent this arbitrary suppression of a play which has been widely acclaimed."

["Agit-Prop," in *Time,* 35 (June 17, 1935), p. 38. Courtesy of *Time.* Copyright, Time Inc., 1935.]

MAXWELL ANDERSON

WINTERSET

CHARACTERS

TROCK	HERMAN
SHADOW	LUCIA
GARTH	PINY
MIRIAMNE	A SAILOR
ESDRAS	STREET URCHIN
THE HOBO	POLICEMAN
1ST GIRL	RADICAL
2ND GIRL	SERGEANT
JUDGE GAUNT	*Non-speaking*
MIO	URCHINS
CARR	TWO MEN IN BLUE SERGE

WINTERSET

ACT ONE

SCENE 1

SCENE: *The scene is the bank of a river under a bridgehead. A gigantic span starts from the rear of the stage and appears to lift over the heads of the audience and out to the left. At the right rear is a wall of solid supporting masonry. To the left an apartment building abuts against the bridge and forms the left wall of the stage with a dark basement window and a door in the brick wall. To the right, and in the foreground, an outcropping of original rock makes a barricade behind which one may enter through a cleft. To the rear, against the masonry, two sheds have been built by waifs and strays for shelter. The river bank, in the foreground, is black rock worn smooth by years of trampling. There is room for exit and entrance to the left around the apartment house, also around the rock to the right. A single street lamp is seen at the left—and a glimmer of apartment lights in the background beyond. It is an early, dark December morning.*

TWO YOUNG MEN IN SERGE *lean against the masonry matching bills.* TROCK ESTRELLA *and* SHADOW *come in from the left.*

TROCK: Go back and watch the car.

[*The* TWO YOUNG MEN *go out.* TROCK *walks to the corner and looks toward the city.*]

You roost of punks and gulls! Sleep, sleep it off,
whatever you had last night, get down in warm,
one big ham-fat against another—sleep,
cling, sleep and rot! Rot out your pasty guts
with diddling, you had no brain to begin. If you had
there'd be no need for us to sleep on iron
who had too much brains for you.

SHADOW: Now look, Trock, look,
　what would the warden say to talk like that?
TROCK: May they die as I die!
　By God, what life they've left me
　they shall keep me well! I'll have that out of them—
　these pismires that walk like men!
SHADOW: Because, look, chief,
　it's all against science and penology
　for you to get out and begin to cuss that way
　before your prison vittles are out of you. Hell,
　you're supposed to leave the pen full of high thought,
　kind of noble-like, loving toward all mankind,
　ready to kiss their feet—or whatever parts
　they stick out toward you. Look at me!
TROCK: I see you.
　And even you may not live as long as you think.
　You think too many things are funny. Well, laugh.
　But it's not so funny.
SHADOW: Come on, Trock, you know me.
　Anything you say goes, but give me leave
　to kid a little.
TROCK: Then laugh at somebody else!
　It's a lot safer! They've soaked me once too often
　in that vat of poisoned hell they keep up-state
　to soak men in, and I'm rotten inside, I'm all
　one liquid puke inside where I had lungs
　once, like yourself! And now they want to get me
　and stir me in again—and that'd kill me—
　and that's fine for them. But before that happens to me
　a lot of these healthy boys'll know what it's like
　when you try to breathe and have no place to put air—
　they'll learn it from me!
SHADOW: They've got nothing on you, chief.
TROCK: I don't know yet. That's what I'm here to find out.
　If they've got what they might have
　it's not a year this time—
　no, nor ten. It's screwed down under a lid.—

I can die quick enough, without help.
SHADOW: You're the skinny kind
   that lives forever.
TROCK: He gave me a half a year,
   the doc at the gate.
SHADOW: Jesus.
TROCK: Six months I get
   and the rest's dirt, six feet.

   [LUCIA, *the street-piano man, comes in right from behind
   the rock and goes to the shed where he keeps his piano.* PINY,
   the apple-woman, follows and stands in the entrance. LUCIA
   speaks to ESTRELLA, *who still stands facing* SHADOW.]
LUCIA: Morning.

   [TROCK *and* SHADOW *go out round the apartment house
   without speaking.*]
PINY: Now what would you call them?
LUCIA: Maybe someting da river washed up.
PINY: Nothing ever washed him—that black one.
LUCIA: Maybe not, maybe so. More like his pa and ma raise-a
   heem in da cellar.

   [*He wheels out the piano.*]
PINY: He certainly gave me a turn.

   [*She lays a hand on the rock.*]
LUCIA: You don' live-a right, ol' gal. Take heem easy. Look
   on da bright-a side. Never say-a die. Me, every day in every
   way I getta be da regular heller.

   [*He starts out.*]

SCENE 2

SCENE: *A cellar apartment under the apartment building,
floored with cement and roofed with huge boa constrictor pipes
that run slantwise from left to right, dwarfing the room. An outside door opens to the left and a door at the right rear leads to
the interior of the place. A low squat window to the left. A table
at the rear and a few chairs and books make up the furniture.*

GARTH, *son of* ESDRAS, *sits alone, holding a violin upside down to inspect a crack at its base. He lays the bow on the floor and runs his fingers over the joint.* MIRIAMNE *enters from the rear, a girl of fifteen.* GARTH *looks up, then down again.*

MIRIAMNE: Garth—

GARTH: The glue lets go. It's the steam, I guess.
　　It splits the hair on your head.

MIRIAMNE: It can't be mended?

GARTH: I can't mend it.
　　No doubt there are fellows somewhere
　　who'd mend it for a dollar—and glad to do it.
　　That is if I had a dollar.—Got a dollar?
　　No, I thought not.

MIRIAMNE: Garth, you've sat at home here
　　three days now. You haven't gone out at all.
　　Something frightens you.

GARTH: Yes?

MIRIAMNE: And father's frightened.
　　He reads without knowing where. When a shadow falls
　　across the page he waits for a blow to follow
　　after the shadow. Then in a little while
　　he puts his book down softly and goes out
　　to see who passed.

GARTH: A bill collector, maybe.
　　We haven't paid the rent.

MIRIAMNE: No.

GARTH: You're a bright girl, sis.—
　　You see too much. You run along and cook.
　　Why don't you go to school?

MIRIAMNE: I don't like school.
　　They whisper behind my back.

GARTH: Yes? About what?

MIRIAMNE: What did the lawyer mean
　　that wrote to you?

GARTH [*rising*]: What lawyer?

MIRIAMNE: I found a letter
on the floor of your room. He said, "Don't get me wrong,
but stay in out of the rain the next few days,
just for instance."
GARTH: I thought I burned that letter.
MIRIAMNE: Afterward you did. And then what was printed
about the Estrella gang—you hid it from me,
you and father. What is it—about this murder—?
GARTH: Will you shut up, you fool!
MIRIAMNE: But if you know
why don't you tell them, Garth?
If it's true—what they say—
you knew all the time Romagna wasn't guilty,
and could have said so—
GARTH: Everybody knew
Romagna wasn't guilty! But they weren't listening
to evidence in his favor. They didn't want it.
They don't want it now.
MIRIAMNE: But was that why
they never called on you?—
GARTH: So far as I know
they never'd heard of me—and I can assure you
I knew nothing about it—
MIRIAMNE: But something's wrong—
and it worries father—
GARTH: What could be wrong?
MIRIAMNE: I don't know.
    [*A pause.*]
GARTH: And I don't know. You're a good kid, Miriamne,
but you see too many movies. I wasn't mixed up
in any murder, and I don't mean to be.
If I had a dollar to get my fiddle fixed
and another to hire a hall, by God I'd fiddle
some of the prodigies back into Sunday School
where they belong, but I won't get either, and so
I sit here and bite my nails—but if you hoped

I had some criminal romantic past
you'll have to look again!
MIRIAMNE: Oh, Garth, forgive me—
But I want you to be so far above such things
nothing could frighten you. When you seem to shrink
and be afraid, and you're the brother I love,
I want to run there and cry, if there's any question
they care to ask, you'll be quick and glad to answer,
for there's nothing to conceal!
GARTH: And that's all true—
MIRIAMNE: But then I remember—
how you dim the lights—
and we go early to bed—and speak in whispers—
and I could think there's a death somewhere behind us—
an evil death—
GARTH [*hearing a step*]: Now for God's sake, be quiet!
   [ESDRAS, *an old rabbi with a kindly face, enters from the*
outside. He is hurried and troubled.]
ESDRAS: I wish to speak alone with someone here
if I may have this room. Miriamne—
MIRIAMNE [*turning to go*]: Yes, father.
   [*The outer door is suddenly thrown open.* TROCK *ap-*
pears.]
TROCK [*after a pause*]: You'll excuse me for not knocking.
   [SHADOW *follows* TROCK *in.*]
Sometimes it's best to come in quiet. Sometimes
it's a good way to go out. Garth's home, I see.
He might not have been here if I made a point
of knocking at doors.
GARTH: How are you, Trock?
TROCK: I guess
you can see how I am.
   [*To* MIRIAMNE]
Stay here. Stay where you are.
We'd like to make your acquaintance.
—if you want the facts
I'm no better than usual, thanks. Not enough sun,

my physician tells me. Too much close confinement.
A lack of exercise and an overplus
of beans in the diet. You've done well, no doubt?
GARTH: I don't know what makes you think so.
TROCK: Who's the family?
GARTH: My father and my sister.
TROCK: Happy to meet you.
  Step inside a minute. The boy and I
  have something to talk about.
ESDRAS: No,'no—he's said nothing—
  nothing, sir, nothing!
TROCK: When I say go out, you go—
ESDRAS [*pointing to the door*]: Miriamne—
GARTH: Go on out, both of you!
ESDRAS: Oh, sir—I'm old—
  old and unhappy—
GARTH: Go on!
    [MIRIAMNE *and* ESDRAS *go inside.*]
TROCK: And if you listen
  I'll riddle that door!
    [SHADOW *shuts the door behind them and stands against*
it.]
  I just got out, you see,
  and I pay my first call on you.
GARTH: Maybe you think
  I'm not in the same jam you are.
TROCK: That's what I do think.
  Who started looking this up?
GARTH: I wish I knew,
  and I wish he was in hell! Some damned professor
  with nothing else to do. If you saw his stuff
  you know as much as I do.
TROCK: It wasn't you
  turning state's evidence?
GARTH: Hell, Trock, use your brain!
  The case was closed. They burned Romagna for it

and that finished it. Why should I look for trouble
and maybe get burned myself?

TROCK: Boy, I don't know,
but I just thought I'd find out.

GARTH: I'm going straight, Trock.
I can play this thing, and I'm trying to make a living.
I haven't talked and nobody's talked to me.
Christ—it's the last thing I'd want!

TROCK: Your old man knows.

GARTH: That's where I got the money that last time
when you needed it. He had a little saved up,
but I had to tell him to get it. He's as safe
as Shadow there.

TROCK [*looking at* SHADOW]: There could be people safer
than that son-of-a-bitch.

SHADOW: Who?

TROCK: You'd be safer dead
along with some other gorillas.

SHADOW: It's beginning to look
as if you'd feel safer with everybody dead,
the whole god-damn world.

TROCK: I would. These Jesus-bitten
professors! Looking up their half-ass cases!
We've got enough without that.

GARTH: There's no evidence.
to reopen the thing.

TROCK: And suppose they called on you
and asked you to testify?

GARTH: Why then I'd tell 'em
that all I know is what I read in the papers.
And I'd stick to that.

TROCK: How much does your sister know?

GARTH: I'm honest with you, Trock. She read my name
in the professor's pamphlet, and she was scared
the way anybody would be. She got nothing
from me, and anyway she'd go to the chair
herself before she'd send me there.

TROCK: Like hell.

GARTH: Besides, who wants to go to trial again
except the radicals?—You and I won't spill
and unless we did there's nothing to take to court
as far as I know. Let the radicals go on howling
about getting a dirty deal. They always howl
and nobody gives a damn. This professor's red—
everybody knows it.

TROCK: You're forgetting the judge.
Where's the damn judge?

GARTH: What judge?

TROCK: Read the morning papers.
It says Judge Gaunt's gone off his nut. He's got
that damn trial on his mind, and been going round
proving to everybody he was right all the time
and the radicals were guilty—stopping people
in the street to prove it—and now he's nuts entircly
and nobody knows where he is.

GARTH: Why don't they know?

TROCK: Because he's on the loose somewhere! They've got
the police of three cities looking for him.

GARTH: Judge Gaunt?

TROCK: Yes. Judge Gaunt.

SHADOW: Why should that worry you?
He's crazy, ain't he? And even if he wasn't
he's arguing on your side. You're jittery, chief.
God, all the judges are looney. You've got the jitters,
and you'll damn well give yourself away some time
peeing yourself in public.

[TROCK *half turns toward* SHADOW *in anger.*]
Don't jump the gun now,
I've got pockets in my clothes, too.
[*His hand is in his coat pocket.*]

TROCK: All right. Take it easy.
[*He takes his hand from his pocket, and* SHADOW *does the
same.*]
[*To* GARTH]:

Maybe you're lying to me and maybe you're not.
Stay at home a few days.
GARTH: Sure thing. Why not?
TROCK: And when I say stay home I mean stay home.
  If I have to go looking for you you'll stay a long time
  wherever I find you.
  [*To* SHADOW]:
  Come on. We'll get out of here.
  [*To* GARTH]:
  Be seeing you.
  [SHADOW *and* TROCK *go out. After a pause* GARTH *walks
over to his chair and picks up the violin. Then he puts it
down and goes to the inside door, which he opens.*]
GARTH: He's gone.
  [MIRIAMNE *enters,* ESDRAS *behind her.*]
MIRIAMNE [*going up to* GARTH]: Let's not stay here.
  [*She puts her hands on his arms.*]
  I thought he'd come for something—horrible.
  Is he coming back?
GARTH: I don't know.
MIRIAMNE: Who is he, Garth?
GARTH: He'd kill me if I told you who he is,
  that is, if he knew.
MIRIAMNE: Then don't say it—
GARTH: Yes, and I'll say it! I was with a gang one time
  that robbed a pay roll. I saw a murder done,
  and Trock Estrella did it. If that got out
  I'd go to the chair and so would he—that's why
  he was here today—
MIRIAMNE: But that's not true—
ESDRAS: He says it
  to frighten you, child.
GARTH: Oh, no I don't! I say it
  because I've held it in too long! I'm damned
  if I sit here forever, and look at the door,
  waiting for Trock with his sub-machine gun, waiting
  for police with a warrant!—I say I'm damned, and I am,

no matter what I do! These piddling scales
on a violin—first position, third, fifth,
arpeggios in E—and what I'm thinking
is Romagna dead for the murder—dead while I sat here
dying inside—dead for the thing Trock did
while I looked on—and I could have saved him, yes—
but I sat here and let him die instead of me
because I wanted to live! Well, it's no life,
and it doesn't matter who I tell, because
I mean to get it over!
MIRIAMNE: Garth, it's not true!
GARTH: I'd take some scum down with me if I died—
    that'd be one good deed—
ESDRAS: Son, son, you're mad—
    someone will hear—
GARTH: Then let them hear! I've lived
    with ghosts too long, and lied too long. God damn you
    if you keep me from the truth!—
        [*He turns away.*]
    Oh, God damn the world!
    I don't want to die!
        [*He throws himself down.*]
ESDRAS: I should have known.
    I thought you hard and sullen,
    Garth, my son. And you were a child, and hurt
    with a wound that might be healed.
    —All men have crimes,
    and most of them are hidden, and many are heavy
    as yours must be to you.
        [GARTH *sobs.*]
    They walk the streets
    to buy and sell, but a spreading crimson stain
    tinges the inner vestments, touches flesh,
    and burns the quick. You're not alone.
GARTH: I'm alone
    in this.
ESDRAS: Yes, if you hold with the world that only

those who die suddenly should be revenged.
But those whose hearts are cancered, drop by drop
in small ways, little by little, till they've borne
all they can bear, and die—these deaths will go
unpunished now as always. When we're young
we have faith in what is seen, but when we're old
we know that what is seen is traced in air
and built on water. There's no guilt under heaven,
just as there's no heaven, till men believe it—
no earth, till men have seen it, and have a word
to say this is the earth.

GARTH: Well, I say there's an earth,
and I say I'm guilty on it, guilty as hell.

ESDRAS: Yet till it's known you bear no guilt at all—
unless you wish. The days go by like film,
like a long written scroll, a figured veil
unrolling out of darkness into fire
and utterly consumed. And on this veil
running in sounds and symbols of men's minds
reflected back, life flickers and is shadow
going toward flame. Only what men can see
exists in that shadow. Why must you rise and cry out:
That was I, there in the ravelled tapestry,
there, in that pistol flash, when the man was killed.
I was there, and was one, and am bloodstained!
Let the wind
and fire take that hour to ashes out of time
and out of mind! This thing that men call justice,
this blind snake that strikes men down in the dark,
mindless with fury, keep your hand back from it,
pass by in silence—let it be forgotten, forgotten!—
Oh, my son, my son—have pity!

MIRIAMNE: But if it was true
and someone died—then it was more than shadow—
and it doesn't blow away—

GARTH: Well, it was true.

ESDRAS: Say it if you must. If you have heart to die,

say it, and let them take what's left—there was little
to keep, even before—
GARTH: Oh, I'm a coward—
I always was. I'll be quiet and live. I'll live
even if I have to crawl. I know.
   [*He gets up and goes into the inner room.*]
MIRIAMNE: Is it better
to tell a lie and live?
ESDRAS: Yes, child. It's better.
MIRIAMNE: But if I had to do it—
I think I'd die.
ESDRAS: Yes, child. Because you're young.
MIRIAMNE: Is that the only reason?
ESDRAS: The only reason.

SCENE 3

SCENE: *Under the bridge, evening of the same day. When the
curtain rises* MIRIAMNE *is sitting alone on the ledge at the rear of
the apartment house. A spray of light falls on her from a street
lamp above. She shivers a little in her thin coat, but sits still as
if heedless of the weather. Through the rocks on the other side a*
TRAMP *comes down to the river bank, hunting a place to sleep.
He goes softly to the apple-woman's hut and looks in, then turns
away, evidently not daring to preëmpt it. He looks at* MIRIAMNE
*doubtfully. The door of the street-piano man is shut. The vaga-
bond passes it and picks carefully among some rags and shavings
to the right.* MIRIAMNE *looks up and sees him but makes no sign.
She looks down again, and the man curls himself up in a makeshift bed in the corner, pulling a piece of sacking over his shoulders.* TWO GIRLS *come in from round the apartment house.*

1ST GIRL: Honest, I never heard of anything so romantic.
Because you never liked him.
2ND GIRL: I certainly never did.
1ST GIRL: You've got to tell me how it happened. You've got
to.

2ND GIRL: I couldn't. As long as I live I couldn't. Honest, it was terrible. It was terrible.

1ST GIRL: What was so terrible?

2ND GIRL: The way it happened.

1ST GIRL: Oh, please—not to a soul, never.

2ND GIRL: Well, you know how I hated him because he had such a big mouth. So he reached over and grabbed me, and I began all falling to pieces inside, the way you do—and I said, "Oh, no you don't mister," and started screaming and kicked a hole through the windshield and lost a shoe, and he let go and was cursing and growling because he borrowed the car and didn't have money to pay for the windshield, and he started to cry, and I got so sorry for him I let him, and now he wants to marry me.

1ST GIRL: Honest, I never heard of anything so romantic!

[*She sees the sleeping* TRAMP.]

My God, what you won't see!

[*They give the* TRAMP *a wide berth, and go out right. The* TRAMP *sits up looking about him.* JUDGE GAUNT, *an elderly, quiet man, well dressed but in clothes that have seen some weather, comes in uncertainly from the left. He holds a small clipping in his hand and goes up to the Hobo.*]

GAUNT [*tentatively*]: Your pardon, sir. Your pardon, but perhaps you can tell me the name of this street.

HOBO: Huh?

GAUNT: The name of this street?

HOBO: This ain't no street.

GAUNT: There, where the street lamps are.

HOBO: That's the alley.

GAUNT: Thank you. It has a name, no doubt?

HOBO: That's the alley.

GAUNT: I see. I won't trouble you. You wonder why I ask, I daresay.—I'm a stranger.—Why do you look at me?

[*He steps back.*]

I—I'm not the man you think. You've mistaken me, sir.

HOBO: Huh?

JUDGE: Perhaps misled by a resemblance. But you're mistaken

—I had an errand in this city. It's only by accident that I'm
here—

HOBO [*muttering*]: You go to hell.

JUDGE [*going nearer to him, bending over him*]: Yet why
should I deceive you? Before God, I held the proofs in my
hands. I hold them still. I tell you the defense was cunning
beyond belief, and unscrupulous in its use of propaganda—
they gagged at nothing—not even—

[*He rises.*]

No, no—I'm sorry—this will hardly interest you. I'm sorry.
I have an errand.

[*He looks toward the street.* ESDRAS *enters from the basement and goes to* MIRIAMNE. *The* JUDGE *steps back into the
shadows.*]

ESDRAS: Come in, my daughter. You'll be cold here.

MIRIAMNE: After a while.

ESDRAS: You'll be cold. There's a storm coming.

MIRIAMNE: I didn't want him to see me crying. That was all.

ESDRAS: I know.

MIRIAMNE: I'll come soon.

[ESDRAS *turns reluctantly and goes out the way he came.*
MIRIAMNE *rises to go in, pausing to dry her eyes.* MIO *and*
CARR, *road boys of seventeen or so, come round the apartment
house. The* JUDGE *has disappeared.*]

CARR: Thought you said you were never coming east again.

MIO: Yeah, but—I heard something changed my mind.

CARR: Same old business?

MIO: Yes. Just as soon not talk about it.

CARR: Where did you go from Portland?

MIO: Fishing—I went fishing. God's truth.

CARR: Right after I left?

MIO: Fell in with a fisherman's family on the coast and went
after the beautiful mackerel fish that swim in the beautiful
sea. Family of Greeks—Aristides Marinos was his lovely
name. He sang while he fished. Made the pea-green Pacific
ring with his bastard Greek chanties. Then I went to Hollywood High School for a while.

CARR: I'll bet that's a seat of learning.

MIO: It's the hind end of all wisdom. They kicked me out after a time.

CARR: For cause?

MIO: Because I had no permanent address, you see. That means nobody's paying school taxes for you, so out you go.
[*To* MIRIAMNE]
What's the matter, kid?

MIRIAMNE: Nothing.
[*She looks up at him, and they pause for a moment.*]
Nothing.

MIO: I'm sorry.

MIRIAMNE: It's all right.
[*She withdraws her eyes from his and goes out past him. He turns and looks after her.*]

CARR: Control your chivalry.

MIO: A pretty kid.

CARR: A baby.

MIO: Wait for me.

CARR: Be a long wait?
[MIO *steps swiftly out after* MIRIAMNE, *then returns.*]
Yeah?

MIO: She's gone.

CARR: Think of that.

MIO: No, but I mean—vanished. Presto—into nothing— prodigioso.

CARR: Damn good thing, if you ask me. The homely ones are bad enough, but the lookers are fatal.

MIO: You exaggerate, Carr.

CARR: I doubt it.

MIO: Well, let her go. This river bank's loaded with typhus rats, too. Might as well die one death as another.

CARR: They say chronic alcoholism is nice but expensive. You can always starve to death.

MIO: Not always. I tried it. After the second day I walked thirty miles to Niagara Falls and made a tour of the plant to get the sample of shredded wheat biscuit on the way out.

CARR: Last time I saw you you couldn't think of anything you wanted to do except curse God and pass out. Still feeling low?

MIO: Not much different.

[*He turns away, then comes back.*]

Talk about the lost generation, I'm the only one fits that title. When the State executes your father, and your mother dies of grief, and you know damn well he was innocent, and the authorities of your home town politely inform you they'd consider it a favor if you lived somewhere else—that cuts you off from the world—with a meat-axe.

CARR: They asked you to move?

MIO: It came to that.

CARR: God, that was white of them.

MIO: It probably gave them a headache just to see me after all that agitation. They knew as well as I did my father never staged a holdup. Anyway, I've got a new interest in life now.

CARR: Yes—I saw her.

MIO: I don't mean the skirt.—No, I got wind of something, out west, some college professor investigating the trial and turning up new evidence. Couldn't find anything he'd written out there, so I beat it east and arrived on this blessed island just in time to find the bums holing up in the public library for the winter. I know now what the unemployed have been doing since the depression started. They've been catching up on their reading in the main reference room. Man, what a stench! Maybe I stank, too, but a hobo has the stench of ten because his shoes are poor.

CARR: Tennyson.

MIO: Right. Jeez, I'm glad we met up again! Never knew anybody else that could track me through the driven snow of Victorian literature.

CARR: Now you're cribbing from some half-forgotten criticism of Ben Jonson's Roman plagiarisms.

MIO: Where did you get your education, sap?

CARR: Not in the public library, sap. My father kept a news-stand.

MIO: Well, you're right again.

[*There is a faint rumble of thunder.*]

What's that? Winter thunder?

CARR: Or Mister God, beating on His little tocsin. Maybe announcing the advent of a new social order.

MIO: Or maybe it's going to rain coffee and doughnuts.

CARR: Or maybe it's going to rain.

MIO: Seems more likely.

[*Lowering his voice*]

Anyhow, I found Professor Hobhouse's discussion of the Romagna case. I think he has something. It occurred to me I might follow it up by doing a little sleuthing on my own account.

CARR: Yes?

MIO: I have done a little. And it leads me to somewhere in that tenement house that backs up against the bridge. That's how I happen to be here.

CARR: They'll never let you get anywhere with it, Mio. I told you that before.

MIO: I know you did.

CARR: The State can't afford to admit it was wrong, you see. Not when there's been that much of a row kicked up over it. So for all practical purposes the State was right and your father robbed the pay roll.

MIO: There's still such a thing as evidence.

CARR: It's something you can buy. In fact, at the moment I don't think of anything you can't buy, including life, honor, virtue, glory, public office, conjugal affection and all kinds of justice, from the traffic court to the immortal nine. Go out and make yourself a pot of money and you can buy all the justice you want. Convictions obtained, convictions averted. Lowest rates in years.

MIO: I know all that.

CARR: Sure.

MIO: This thing didn't happen to you.

They've left you your name
and whatever place you can take. For my heritage
they've left me one thing only, and that's to be
my father's voice crying up out of the earth
and quicklime where they stuck him. Electrocution
doesn't kill, you know. They eviscerate them
with a turn of the knife in the dissecting room.
The blood spurts out. The man was alive. Then into
the lime pit, leave no trace. Make it short shrift
and chemical dissolution. That's what they thought
of the man that was my father. Then my mother—
I tell you these county burials are swift
and cheap and run for profit! Out of the house
and into the ground, you wife of a dead dog. Wait,
here's some Romagna spawn left.
Something crawls here—
something they called a son. Why couldn't he die
along with his mother? Well, ease him out of town,
ease him out, boys, and see you're not too gentle.
He might come back. And, by their own living Jesus,
I will go back, and hang the carrion
around their necks that made it!
Maybe I can sleep then.
Or even live.

CARR: You have to try it?

MIO: Yes.
Yes. It won't let me alone. I've tried to live
and forget it—but I was birthmarked with hot iron
into the entrails. I've got to find out who did it
and make them see it till it scalds their eyes
and make them admit it till their tongues are blistered
with saying how black they lied!

[HERMAN, *a gawky shoe salesman, enters from the left.*]

HERMAN: Hello. Did you see a couple of girls go this way?

CARR: Couple of girls? Did we see a couple of girls?

MIO: No.

CARR: No. No girls.

[HERMAN *hesitates, then goes out right.* LUCIA *comes in from the left, trundling his piano.* PINY *follows him, weeping.*]

PINY: They've got no right to do it—

LUCIA: All right, hell what, no matter, I got to put him away, I got to put him away, that's what the hell!

[TWO STREET URCHINS *follow him in.*]

PINY: They want everybody on the relief rolls and nobody making a living?

LUCIA: The cops, they do what the big boss says. The big boss, that's the mayor, he says he heard it once too often, the sextette—

PINY: They want graft, that's all. It's a new way to get graft—

LUCIA: Oh, no, no, no! He's a good man, the mayor. He's just don't care for music, that's all.

PINY: Why shouldn't you make a living on the street? The National Biscuit Company ropes off Eighth Avenue—and does the mayor do anything? No, the police hit you over the head if you try to go through!

LUCIA: You got the big dough, you get the pull, fine. No big dough, no pull, what the hell, get off the city property! To-morrow I start cooking chestnuts...

[*He strokes the piano fondly. The* TWO GIRLS *and* HERMAN *come back from the right.*]

She's a good little machine, this baby. Cost plenty—and two new records I only played twice. See, this one.

[*He starts turning the crank, talking while he plays.*]

Two weeks since they play this one in a picture house.

[*A* SAILOR *wanders in from the left. One of the* STREET URCHINS *begins suddenly to dance a wild rumba, the others watch.*]

Good boy—see, it's a lulu—it itches in the feet!

[HERMAN, *standing with his girl, tosses the boy a penny. He bows and goes on dancing; the other* URCHIN *joins him. The* SAILOR *tosses a coin.*]

SAILOR: Go it, Cuba! Go it!

[LUCIA *turns the crank, beaming.*]

2ND GIRL: Oh, Herman!

[*She throws her arms around* HERMAN *and they dance.*]

1ST URCHIN: Hey, pipe the professionals!

1ST GIRL: Do your glide, Shirley. Do your glide!

LUCIA: Maybe we can't play in front, maybe we can play behind!

[*The* HOBO *gets up from his nest and comes over to watch. A* YOUNG RADICAL *wanders in.*]

Maybe you don't know, folks! Tonight we play good-bye to the piano! Good-bye forever! No more piano on the streets! No more music! No more money for the music-man! Last time, folks! Good-bye to the piano—good-bye forever!

[MIRIAMNE *comes out of the rear door of the apartment and stands watching. The* SAILOR *goes over to the* 1ST GIRL *and they dance together.*]

Maybe you don't know, folks! Tomorrow will be sad as hell, tonight we dance! Tomorrow no more Verdi, no more rumba, no more good time! Tonight we play good-bye to the piano, good-bye forever!

[*The* RADICAL *edges up to* MIRIAMNE *and asks her to dance. She shakes her head and he goes to* PINY *who dances with him. The* HOBO *begins to do a few lonely curvets on the side above.*]

Hoy! Hoy! Pick 'em up and take 'em around! Use the head, use the feet! Last time forever!

[*He begins to sing to the air.*]

MIO: Wait for me, will you?

CARR: Now's your chance.

[MIO *goes over to* MIRIAMNE *and holds out a hand, smiling. She stands for a moment uncertain, then dances with him.* ESDRAS *comes out to watch.* JUDGE GAUNT *comes in from the left. There is a rumble of thunder.*]

LUCIA: Hoy! Hoy! Maybe it rains tonight, maybe it snows tomorrow! Tonight we dance good-bye.

[*He sings the air lustily. A* POLICEMAN *comes in from the left and looks on.* TWO OR THREE PEDESTRIANS *follow him.*]

POLICEMAN: Hey you!

    [LUCIA *goes on singing.*]

    Hey, you!

LUCIA [*still playing*]: What you want?

POLICEMAN: Sign off!

LUCIA: What you mean? I get off the street!

POLICEMAN: Sign off!

LUCIA [*still playing*]: What you mean?

    [*The* POLICEMAN *walks over to him.* LUCIA *stops playing and the* DANCERS *pause.*]

POLICEMAN: Cut it.

LUCIA: Is this a street?

POLICEMAN: I say cut it out.

    [*The* HOBO *goes back to his nest and sits in it, watching.*]

LUCIA: It's the last time. We dance good-bye to the piano.

POLICEMAN: You'll dance good-bye to something else if I catch you cranking that thing again.

LUCIA: All right.

PINY: I'll bet you don't say that to the National Biscuit Company!

POLICEMAN: Lady, you've been selling apples on my beat for some time now, and I said nothing about it—

PINY: Selling apples is allowed—

POLICEMAN: You watch yourself—

    [*He takes a short walk around the place and comes upon the* HOBO.]

    What are you doing here?

    [*The* HOBO *opens his mouth, points to it, and shakes his head.*]

    Oh, you are, are you?

    [*He comes back to* LUCIA.]

So you trundle your so-called musical instrument to wherever you keep it, and don't let me hear it again.

[*The* RADICAL *leaps on the base of the rock at right. The* 1ST GIRL *turns away from the* SAILOR *toward the* 2ND GIRL *and* HERMAN.]

SAILOR: Hey, captain, what's the matter with the music?

POLICEMAN: Not a thing, admiral.

SAILOR: Well, we had a little party going here—

POLICEMAN: I'll sav you did.

2ND GIRL: Please, officer, we want to dance.

POLICEMAN: Go ahead. Dance.

2ND GIRL: But we want music!

POLICEMAN [*turning to go*]: Sorry. Can't help you.

RADICAL: And there you see it, the perfect example of capitalistic oppression! In a land where music should be free as air and the arts should be encouraged, a uniformed minion of the rich, a guardian myrmidon of the Park Avenue pleasure hunters, steps in and puts a limit on the innocent enjoyments of the poor! We don't go to theatres! Why not? We can't afford it! We don't go to night clubs, where women dance naked and the music drips from saxophones and leaks out of Rudy Vallee—we can't afford that either!— But we might at least dance on the river bank to the strains of a barrel organ—!

[GARTH *comes out of the apartment and listens.*]

POLICEMAN: It's against the law!

RADICAL: What law? I challenge you to tell me what law of God or man—what ordinance—is violated by this spontaneous diversion? None! I say none! An official whim of the masters who should be our servants!—

POLICEMAN: Get down! Get down and shut up!

RADICAL: By what law, by what ordinance do you order me to be quiet?

POLICEMAN: Speaking without a flag. You know it.

RADICAL [*pulling out a small American flag*]: There's my flag! There's the flag of this United States which used to guarantee the rights of man—the rights of man now violated by every third statute of the commonweal—

POLICEMAN: Don't try to pull tricks on me! I've seen you before! You're not making any speech, and you're climbing down—

JUDGE GAUNT [*who has come quietly forward*]: One moment, officer. There is some difference of opinion even on the bench as to the elasticity of police power when applied in minor emergencies to preserve civil order. But the weight of authority would certainly favor the defendant in any equitable court, and he would be upheld in his demand to be heard.

POLICEMAN: Who are you?

JUDGE GAUNT: Sir, I am not accustomed to answer that question.

POLICEMAN: I don't know you.

GAUNT: I am a judge of some standing, not in your city but in another with similar statutes. You are aware, of course, that the bill of rights is not to be set aside lightly by the officers of any municipality—

POLICEMAN [*looking over* GAUNT's *somewhat bedraggled costume*]: Maybe they understand you better in the town you come from, but I don't get your drift.—

[*To the* RADICAL]

I don't want any trouble, but if you ask for it you'll get plenty. Get down!

RADICAL: I'm not asking for trouble, but I'm staying right here.

[*The* POLICEMAN *moves toward him.*]

GAUNT [*taking the policeman's arm, but shaken off roughly*]: I ask this for yourself, truly, not for the dignity of the law nor the maintenance of precedent. Be gentle with them when their threats are childish—be tolerant while you can— for your least harsh word will return on you in the night —return in a storm of cries!—

[*He takes the policeman's arm again.*]

Whatever they may have said or done, let them disperse in peace! It is better that they go softly, lest when they are dead you see their eyes pleading, and their outstretched

hands touch you, fingering cold on your heart!—I have been
harsher than you. I have sent men down that long corridor
into blinding light and blind darkness!

[*He suddenly draws himself erect and speaks defiantly.*]
And it was well that I did so! I have been an upright judge!
They are all liars! Liars!

POLICEMAN [*shaking* GAUNT *off so that he falls*]: Why, you
fool, you're crazy!

GAUNT: Yes, and there are liars on the force! They came to
me with their shifty lies!

[*He catches at the policeman, who pushes him away with
his foot.*]

POLICEMAN: You think I've got nothing better to do than
listen to a crazy fool?

1ST GIRL: Shame, shame!

POLICEMAN: What have I got to be ashamed of? And what's
going on here, anyway? Where in hell did you all come
from?

RADICAL: Tread on him! That's right! Tread down the poor
and the innocent!

[*There is a protesting murmur in the crowd.*]

SAILOR [*moving in a little*]: Say, big boy, you don't have to
step on the guy.

POLICEMAN [*facing them, stepping back*]: What's the matter
with you? I haven't stepped on anybody!

MIO [*at the right, across from the* POLICEMAN]: Listen now,
fellows, give the badge a chance.
He's doing his job, what he gets paid to do,
The same as any of you. They're all picked men,
these metropolitan police, hand picked
for loyalty and a fine up-standing pair
of shoulders on their legs—it's not so easy
to represent the law. Think what he does
for all of us, stamping out crime!
Do you want to be robbed and murdered in your beds?

SAILOR: What's eating you?

RADICAL: He must be a capitalist.

MIO: They pluck them fresh
   from Ireland, and a paucity of head-piece
   is a prime prerequisite. You from Ireland, buddy?
POLICEMAN [*surly*]: Where are you from?
MIO: Buddy, I tell you flat
   I wish I was from Ireland, and could boast
   some Tammany connections. There's only one drawback
   about working on the force. It infects the brain,
   it eats the cerebrum. There've been cases known,
   fine specimens of manhood, too, where autopsies,
   conducted in approved scientific fashion,
   revealed conditions quite incredible
   in policemen's upper layers. In some, a trace,
   in others, when they've swung a stick too long,
   there was nothing there!—but nothing! Oh, my friends,
   this fine athletic figure of a man
   that stands so grim before us, what will they find
   when they saw his skull for the last inspection?
   I fear me a little puffball dust will blow away
   rejoining earth, our mother—and this same dust,
   this smoke, this ash on the wind, will represent
   all he had left to think with!
HOBO: Hooray!
      [*The* POLICEMAN *turns on his heel and looks hard at the*
HOBO, *who slinks away.*]
POLICEMAN: Oh, yeah?
MIO: My theme
   gives ears to the deaf and voice to the dumb! But now
   forgive me if I say you were most unkind
   in troubling the officer. He's a simple man
   of simple tastes, and easily confused
   when faced with complex issues. He may reflect
   on returning home, that is, so far as he
   is capable of reflection, and conclude
   that he was kidded out of his uniform pants,
   and in his fury when this dawns on him
   may smack his wife down!

POLICEMAN: That'll be about enough from you, too, professor!

MIO: May I say that I think you have managed this whole situation rather badly, from the beginning?—

POLICEMAN: You may not!

[TROCK *slips in from the background. The* TWO YOUNG MEN IN SERGE *come with him.*]

MIO: Oh, but your pardon, sir! It's apparent to the least competent among us that you should have gone about your task more subtly—the glove of velvet, the hand of iron, and all that sort of thing—

POLICEMAN: Shut that hole in your face!

MIO: Sir, for that remark I shall be satisfied with nothing less than an unconditional apology! I have an old score to settle with policemen, brother, because they're fools and fatheads, and you're one of the most fatuous fat-heads that ever walked his feet flat collecting graft! Tell that to your sergeant back in the booby-hatch.

POLICEMAN: Oh, you want an apology, do you? You'll get an apology out of the other side of your mouth!

[*He steps toward* MIO. CARR *suddenly stands in his path.*] Get out of my way!

[*He pauses and looks round him; the crowd looks less and less friendly. He lays a hand on his gun and backs to a position where there is nobody behind him.*] Get out of here, all of you! Get out! What are you trying to do—start a riot?

MIO: There now, that's better! That's in the best police tradition. Incite a riot yourself and then accuse the crowd.

POLICEMAN: It won't be pleasant if I decide to let somebody have it! Get out!

[*The onlookers begin to melt away. The* SAILOR *goes out left with the* GIRLS *and* HERMAN. CARR *and* MIO *go out right,* CARR *whistling "The Star Spangled Banner." The* HOBO *follows them. The* RADICAL *walks past with his head in the air.* PINY *and* LUCIA *leave the piano where it stands and slip away to the left. At the end the* POLICEMAN *is left standing in the center, the* JUDGE *near him.* ESDRAS *stands in the doorway.* MIRIAMNE *is left sitting half in shadows and unseen by* ESDRAS.]

JUDGE GAUNT [*to the* POLICEMAN]: Yes, but should a man die, should it be necessary that one man die for the good of many, make not yourself the instrument of death, lest you sleep to wake sobbing! Nay, it avails nothing that you are the law—this delicate ganglion that is the brain, it will not bear these things—!

[*The* POLICEMAN *gives the* JUDGE *the once-over, shrugs, decides to leave him there and starts out left.* GARTH *goes to his father—a fine sleet begins to fall through the street lights.* TROCK *is still visible.*]

GARTH: Get him in here, quick.

ESDRAS: Who, son?

GARTH: The Judge, damn him!

ESDRAS: It is Judge Gaunt?

GARTH: Who did you think it was? He's crazy as a bedbug and telling the world. Get him inside!

[*He looks round.*]

ESDRAS: [*going up to* GAUNT]: Will you come in, sir?

GAUNT: You will understand, sir. We old men know how softly we must proceed with these things.

ESDRAS: Yes, surely, sir.

GAUNT: It was always my practice—always. They will tell you that of me where I am known. Yet even I am not free of regret—even I. Would you believe it?

ESDRAS: I believe we are none of us free of regret.

GAUNT: None of us? I would it were true. I would I thought it were true.

ESDRAS: Shall we go in, sir? This is sleet that's falling.

GAUNT: Yes. Let us go in.

[ESDRAS, GAUNT *and* GARTH *enter the basement and shut the door.* TROCK *goes out with his men. After a pause* MIO *comes back from the right, alone. He stands at a little distance from* MIRIAMNE.]

Mio: Looks like rain.
>   [*She is silent.*]
>   You live around here?
>   [*She nods gravely.*]
>   I guess
>   you thought I meant it—about waiting here to meet me.
>   [*She nods again.*]
>   I'd forgotten about it till I got that winter
>   across the face. You'd better go inside.
>   I'm not your kind. I'm nobody's kind but my own.
>   I'm waiting for this to blow over.
>   [*She rises.*]
>   I lied. I meant it—
>   I meant it when I said it—but there's too much black
>   whirling inside me—for any girl to know.
>   So go on in. You're somebody's angel child
>   and they're waiting for you.
Miriamne: Yes. I'll go.
>   [*She turns.*]
Mio: And tell them
>   when you get inside where it's warm,
>   and you love each other,
>   and mother comes to kiss her darling, tell them
>   to hang on to it while they can, believe while they can
>   it's a warm safe world, and Jesus finds his lambs
>   and carries them in his bosom.—I've seen some lambs
>   that Jesus missed. If they ever want the truth
>   tell them that nothing's guaranteed in this climate
>   except it gets cold in winter, nor on this earth
>   except you die sometime.
>   [*He turns away.*]
Miriamne: I have no mother.
>   And my people are Jews.
Mio: Then you know something about it.
Miriamne: Yes.
Mio: Do you have enough to eat?

MIRIAMNE: Not always.
MIO: What do you believe in?
MIRIAMNE: Nothing.
MIO: Why?
MIRIAMNE: How can one?
MIO: It's easy if you're a fool. You see the words
in books. Honor, it says there, chivalry, freedom,
heroism, enduring love—and these
are words on paper. It's something to have them there.
You'll get them nowhere else.
MIRIAMNE: What hurts you?
MIO: Just that.
You'll get them nowhere else.
MIRIAMNE: Why should you want them?
MIO: I'm alone, that's why. You see those lights,
along the river, cutting across the rain—?
those are the hearths of Brooklyn, and up this way
the love-nests of Manhattan—they turn their points
like knives against me—outcast of the world,
snake in the streets.—I don't want a hand-out.
I sleep and eat.
MIRIAMNE: Do you want me to go with you?
MIO: Where?
MIRIAMNE: Where you go.
    [*A pause. He goes nearer to her.*]
MIO: Why, you god-damned little fool—
what made you say that?
MIRIAMNE: I don't know.
MIO: If you have a home
stay in it. I ask for nothing. I've schooled myself
to ask for nothing, and take what I can get,
and get along. If I fell for you, that's my look-out,
and I'll starve it down.
MIRIAMNE: Wherever you go, I'd go.
MIO: What do you know about loving?
How could you know?
Have you ever had a man?

MIRIAMNE [*after a slight pause*]: No. But I know.
　Tell me your name.
MIO: Mio. What's yours?
MIRIAMNE: Miriamne.
MIO: There's no such name.
MIRIAMNE: But there's no such name as Mio!
　M.I.O. It's no name.
MIO: It's for Bartolomeo.
MIRIAMNE: My mother's name was Miriam,
　so they called me Miriamne.
MIO: Meaning little Miriam?
MIRIAMNE: Yes.
MIO: So now little Miriamne will go in
　and take up quietly where she dropped them all
　her small housewifely cares.—When I first saw you,
　not a half-hour ago, I heard myself saying,
　this is the face that launches ships for me—
　and if I owned a dream—yes, half a dream—
　we'd share it. But I have no dream. This earth
　came tumbling down from chaos, fire and rock,
　and bred up worms, blind worms that sting each other
　here in the dark. These blind worms of the earth
　took out my father—and killed him, and set a sign
　on me—the heir of the serpent—and he was a man
　such as men might be if the gods were men—
　but they killed him—
　as they'll kill all others like him
　till the sun cools down on the stabler molecules,
　yes, till men spin their tent-worm webs to the stars
　and what they think is done, even in the thinking,
　and they are the gods, and immortal, and constellations
　turn for them all like mill wheels—still as they are
　they will be, worms and blind. Enduring love,
　oh gods and worms, what mockery!—And yet
　I have blood enough in my veins. It goes like music,
　singing, because you're here. My body turns
　as if you were the sun, and warm. This men called love

in happier times, before the Freudians taught us
to blame it on the glands. Only go in
before you breathe too much of my atmosphere
and catch death from me.

MIRIAMNE: I will take my hands
and weave them to a little house, and there
you shall keep a dream—

MIO: God knows I could use a dream
and even a house.

MIRIAMNE: You're laughing at me, Mio!

MIO: The worms are laughing.
I tell you there's death about me
and you're a child! And I'm alone and half mad
with hate and longing. I shall let you love me
and love you in return, and then, why then
God knows what happens!

MIRIAMNE: Something most unpleasant?

MIO: Love in a box car—love among the children.
I've seen too much of it. Are we to live
in this same house you make with your two hands
mystically, out of air?

MIRIAMNE: No roof, no mortgage!
Well, I shall marry a baker out in Flatbush,
it gives hot bread in the morning! Oh, Mio, Mio,
in all the unwanted places and waste lands
that roll up into the darkness out of sun
and into sun out of dark, there should be one empty
for you and me.

MIO: No.

MIRIAMNE: Then go now and leave me.
I'm only a girl you saw in the tenements,
and there's been nothing said.

MIO: Miriamne.
    [*She takes a step toward him.*]

MIRIAMNE: Yes.
    [*He kisses her lips lightly.*]

MIO: Why, girl, the transfiguration on the mount
   was nothing to your face. It lights from within—
   a white chalice holding fire, a flower in flame,
   this is your face.
MIRIAMNE: And you shall drink the flame
   and never lessen it. And round your head
   the aureole shall burn that burns there now,
   forever. This I can give you. And so forever
   the Freudians are wrong.
MIO: They're well-forgotten
   at any rate.
MIRIAMNE: Why did you speak to me
   when you first saw me?
MIO: I knew then.
MIRIAMNE: And I came back
   because I must see you again. And we danced together
   and my heart hurt me. Never, never, never,
   though they should bind me down and tear out my eyes,
   would I ever hurt you now. Take me with you, Mio,
   let them look for us, whoever there is to look,
   but we'll be away.
      [MIO *turns away toward the tenement.*]
MIO: When I was four years old
   we climbed through an iron gate, my mother and I,
   to see my father in prison. He stood in the death-cell
   and put his hand through the bars and said, My Mio,
   I have only this to leave you, that I love you,
   and will love you after I die. Love me then, Mio,
   when this hard thing comes on you, that you must live
   a man despised for your father. That night the guards,
   walking in flood-lights brighter than high noon,
   led him between them with his trousers slit
   and a shaven head for the cathodes. This sleet and rain
   that I feel cold here on my face and hands
   will find him under thirteen years of clay
   in prison ground. Lie still and rest, my father,

for I have not forgotten. When I forget
may I lie blind as you. No other love,
time passing, nor the spaced light-years of suns
shall blur your voice, or tempt me from the path
that clears your name—
till I have these rats in my grip
or sleep deep where you sleep.
  [*To* Miriamne]
  I have no house,
nor home, nor love of life, nor fear of death,
nor care for what I eat, or who I sleep with,
or what color of calcimine the Government
will wash itself this year or next to lure
the sheep and feed the wolves. Love somewhere else,
and get your children in some other image
more acceptable to the State! This face of mine
is stamped for sewage!
  [*She steps back, surmising.*]
Miriamne: Mio—
Mio: My road is cut
  in rock, and leads to one end. If I hurt you, I'm sorry.
  One gets over hurts.
Miriamne: What was his name—
  your father's name?
Mio: Bartolomeo Romagna.
  I'm not ashamed of it.
Miriamne: Why are you here?
Mio: For the reason
  I've never had a home. Because I'm a cry
  out of a shallow grave, and all roads are mine
  that might revenge him!
Miriamne: But Mio—why here—why here?
Mio: I can't tell you that.
Miriamne: No—but—there's someone
  lives here—lives not far—and you mean to see him—
  you mean to ask him—
    [*She pauses.*]

MIO: Who told you that?

MIRIAMNE: His name
is Garth—Garth Esdras—

MIO: [*after a pause, coming nearer*]: Who are you, then? You seem
to know a good deal about me.—Were you sent
to say this?

MIRIAMNE: You said there was death about you! Yes,
but nearer than you think! Let it be as it is—
let it all be as it is, never see this place
nor think of it—forget the streets you came
when you're away and safe! Go before you're seen
or spoken to!

MIO: Will you tell me why?

MIRIAMNE: As I love you
I can't tell you—and I can never see you—

MIO: I walk where I please—

MIRIAMNE: Do you think it's easy for me
to send you away?
[*She steps back as if to go.*]

MIO: Where will I find you then
if I should want to see you?

MIRIAMNE: Never—I tell you
I'd bring you death! Even now. Listen!
[SHADOW *and* TROCK *enter between the bridge and the
tenement house.* MIRIAMNE *pulls* MIO *back into the shadow of
the rock to avoid being seen.*]

TROCK: Why, fine.

SHADOW: You watch it now—just for the record, Trock—
you're going to thank me for staying away from it
and keeping you out. I've seen men get that way,
thinking they had to plug a couple of guys
and then a few more to cover it up, and then
maybe a dozen more. You can't own all
and territory adjacent, and you can't
slough all the witnesses, because every man
you put away has friends—

TROCK: I said all right.
  I said fine.
SHADOW: They're going to find this judge,
  and if they find him dead it's just too bad,
  and I don't want to know anything about it—
  and you don't either.
TROCK: You all through?
SHADOW: Why sure.
TROCK: All right.
  We're through too, you know.
SHADOW: Yeah?
  [*He becomes wary.*]
TROCK: Yeah, we're through.
SHADOW: I've heard that said before, and afterwards
  somebody died.
  [TROCK *is silent.*]
  Is that what you mean?
TROCK: You can go.
  I don't want to see you.
SHADOW: Sure, I'll go.
  Maybe you won't mind if I just find out
  what you've got on you. Before I turn my back
  I'd like to know.
  [*Silently and expertly he touches* TROCK'S *pockets, ex-
tracting a gun.*]
  Not that I'd distrust you,
  but you know how it is.
  [*He pockets the gun.*]
  So long, Trock.
TROCK: So long.
SHADOW: I won't talk.
  You can be sure of that.
TROCK: I know you won't.
  [SHADOW *turns and goes out right, past the rock and
along the bank. As he goes the* TWO YOUNG MEN IN BLUE
SERGE *enter from the left and walk slowly after* SHADOW. *They
look toward* TROCK *as they enter and he motions with his*

thumb in the direction taken by SHADOW. *They follow*
SHADOW *out without haste.* TROCK *watches them disappear,*
then slips out the way he came. MIO *comes a step forward,*
looking after the two men. Two or three shots are heard, then
silence. MIO *starts to run after* SHADOW.]
MIRIAMNE: Mio!
MIO: What do you know about this?
MIRIAMNE: The other way,
　Mio—quick!
　　[CARR *slips from the right, in haste.*]
CARR: Look, somebody's just been shot.
　He fell in the river. The guys that did the shooting
　ran up the bank.
MIO: Come on.
　　[MIO *and* CARR *run out right.* MIRIAMNE *watches un-*
certainly, then slowly turns and walks to the rear door of the
tenement. She stands there a moment, looking after Mio, then
goes in, closing the door. CARR *and* MIO *return.*]
CARR: There's a rip tide past the point. You'd never find him.
MIO: No.
CARR: You know a man really ought to carry insurance living
　around here.—God, it's easy, putting a fellow away. I never
　saw it done before.
MIO [*looking at the place where Miriamne stood*]: They have
　it all worked out.
CARR: What are you doing now?
MIO: I have a little business to transact in this neighborhood.
CARR: You'd better forget it.
MIO: No.
CARR: Need any help?
MIO: Well, if I did I'd ask you first. But I don't see how it
　would do any good. So you keep out of it and take care of
　yourself.
CARR: So long, then.
MIO: So long, Carr.
CARR [*looking down-stream*]: He was drifting face up. Must
　be half-way to the island the way the tide runs.

[*He shivers.*]
God, it's cold here. Well—
[*He goes out to the left.* Mio *sits on the edge of the rock.*
Lucia *comes stealthily back from between the bridge and the
tenement, goes to the street-piano and wheels it away.* Piny
comes in. They take a look at Mio, but say nothing. Lucia
goes into his shelter and Piny *into hers.* Mio *rises, looks up
at the tenement, and goes out to the left.*]

ACT TWO

SCENE: *The basement as in Scene 2 of Act One. The same evening.* ESDRAS *sits at the table reading,* MIRIAMNE *is seated at the left, listening and intent. The door of the inner room is half open and* GARTH'S *violin is heard. He is playing the theme from the third movement of Beethoven's Archduke Trio.* ESDRAS *looks up.*

ESDRAS: I remember when I came to the end
  of all the Talmud said, and the commentaries,
  then I was fifty years old—and it was time
  to ask what I had learned. I asked this question
  and gave myself the answer. In all the Talmud
  there was nothing to find but the names of things,
  set down that we might call them by those names
  and walk without fear among things known. Since then
  I have had twenty years to read on and on
  and end with Ecclesiastes. Names of names,
  evanid days, evanid nights and days
  and words that shift their meaning. Space is time,
  that which was is now—the men of tomorrow
  live, and this is their yesterday. All things
  that were and are and will be, have their being
  then and now and to come. If this means little
  when you are young, remember it. It will return
  to mean more when you are old.
MIRIAMNE: I'm sorry—I
  was listening for something.
ESDRAS: It doesn't matter.
  It's a useless wisdom. It's all I have,
  but useless. It may be there is no time,
  but we grow old. Do you know his name?
MIRIAMNE: Whose name?

ESDRAS: Why, when we're young and listen for a step
   the step should have a name—
      [MIRIAMNE, *not hearing, rises and goes to the window.*
GARTH *enters from within, carrying his violin and carefully
closing the door.*]
GARTH [*as* ESDRAS *looks at him*]: Asleep.
ESDRAS: He may
   sleep on through the whole night—then in the morning
   we can let them know.
GARTH: We'd be wiser to say nothing—
   let him find his own way back.
ESDRAS: How did he come here?
GARTH: He's not too crazy for that. If he wakes again
   we'll keep him quiet and shift him off tomorrow.
   Somebody'd pick him up.
ESDRAS: How have I come
   to this sunken end of a street, at a life's end—?
GARTH: It was cheaper here—not to be transcendental—
   So—we say nothing—?
ESDRAS: Nothing.
MIRIAMNE: Garth, there's no place
   in this whole city—not one—
   where you wouldn't be safer
   than here—tonight—or tomorrow.
GARTH [*bitterly*]: Well, that may be.
   What of it?
MIRIAMNE: If you slipped away and took
   a place somewhere where Trock couldn't find you—
GARTH: Yes—
   using what for money? and why do you think
   I've sat here so far—because I love my home
   so much? No, but if I stepped round the corner
   it'd be my last corner and my last step.
MIRIAMNE: And yet—
   if you're here—they'll find you here—
   Trock will come again—
   and there's worse to follow—

GARTH: Do you want to get me killed?
MIRIAMNE: No.
GARTH: There's no way out of it. We'll wait
and take what they send us.
ESDRAS: Hush! You'll wake him.
GARTH: I've done it.
I hear him stirring now.
[*They wait quietly.* JUDGE GAUNT *opens the door and
enters.*]
GAUNT [*in the doorway*]: I beg your pardon—
no, no, be seated—keep your place—I've made
your evening difficult enough, I fear;
and I must thank you doubly for your kindness,
for I've been ill—I know it.
ESDRAS: You're better, sir?
GAUNT: Quite recovered, thank you. Able, I hope,
to manage nicely now. You'll be rewarded
for your hospitality—though at this moment
[*He smiles.*]
I'm low in funds.
[*He inspects his billfold.*]
Sir, my embarrassment
is great indeed—and more than monetary,
for I must own my recollection's vague
of how I came here—how we came together—
and what we may have said. My name is Gaunt,
Judge Gaunt, a name long known in the criminal courts,
and not unhonored there.
ESDRAS: My name is Esdras—
and this is Garth, my son. And Miriamne,
the daughter of my old age.
GAUNT: I'm glad to meet you.
Esdras. Garth Esdras.
[*He passes a hand over his eyes.*]
It's not a usual name.
Of late it's been connected with a case—
a case I knew. But this is hardly the man.

Though it's not a usual name.
[*They are silent.*]
Sir, how I came here,
as I have said, I don't well know. Such things
are sometimes not quite accident.
ESDRAS: We found you
outside our door and brought you in.
GAUNT: The brain
can be overworked, and weary, even when the man
would swear to his good health. Sir, on my word
I don't know why I came here, nor how, nor when,
nor what would explain it. Shall we say the machine
begins to wear? I felt no twinge of it.—
You will imagine how much more than galling
I feel it, to ask my way home—and where I am—
but I do ask you that.
ESDRAS: This is New York City—
or part of it.
GAUNT: Not the best part, I presume?
[*He smiles grimly.*]
No, not the best.
ESDRAS: Not typical, no.
GAUNT: And you—
[*To* GARTH]
you are Garth Esdras?
GARTH: That's my name.
GAUNT: Well, sir.
[*To* ESDRAS]
I shall lie under the deepest obligation
if you will set an old man on his path,
for I lack the homing instinct, if the truth
were known. North, east and south mean nothing to me
here in this room.
ESDRAS: I can put you in your way.
GARTH: Only you'd be wiser to wait a while—
if I'm any judge.—

GAUNT: It happens I'm the judge—
   [*With stiff humor*]
  in more ways than one. You'll forgive me if I say
  I find this place and my predicament somewhat distasteful.
   [*He looks round him.*]
GARTH: I don't doubt you do;
  but you're better off here.
GAUNT: Nor will you find it wise
  to cross my word as lightly as you seem
  inclined to do. You've seen me ill and shaken—
  and you presume on that.
GARTH: Have it your way.
GAUNT: Doubtless what information is required
  we'll find nearby.
ESDRAS: Yes, sir—the terminal,—
  if you could walk so far.
GAUNT: I've done some walking—
  to look at my shoes.
   [*He looks down, then puts out a hand to steady himself.*]
   That—that was why I came—
  never mind—it was there—and it's gone.
   [*To* GARTH]
  Professor Hobhouse—
  that's the name—he wrote some trash about you
  and printed it in a broadside.
  —Since I'm here I can tell you
  it's a pure fabrication—lacking facts
  and legal import. Senseless and impudent,
  written with bias—with malicious intent
  to undermine the public confidence
  in justice and the courts. I knew it then—
  all he brings out about this testimony
  you might have given. It's true I could have called you,
  but the case was clear—Romagna was known guilty,
  and there was nothing to add. If I've endured
  some hours of torture over their attacks
  upon my probity—and in this torture

have wandered from my place, wandered perhaps
in mind and body—and found my way to face you—
why, yes, it is so—I know it—I beg of you
say nothing. It's not easy to give up
a fair name after a full half century
of service to a state. It may well rock
the surest reason. Therefore I ask of you
say nothing of this visit.

GARTH: I'll say nothing.

ESDRAS: Nor any of us.

GAUNT: Why, no—for you'd lose, too.
You'd have nothing to gain.

ESDRAS: Indeed we know it.

GAUNT: I'll remember you kindly. When I've returned,
there may be some mystery made of where I was—
we'll leave it a mystery?

GARTH: Anything you say.

GAUNT: Why, now I go with much more peace of mind—
if I can call you friends.

ESDRAS: We shall be grateful
for silence on your part, Your Honor.

GAUNT: Sir—
if there were any just end to be served
by speaking out, I'd speak! There is none. No—
bear that in mind!

ESDRAS: We will, Your Honor.

GAUNT: Then—
I'm in some haste. If you can be my guide,
we'll set out now.

ESDRAS: Yes, surely.

[*There is a knock at the door. The four look at each other
with some apprehension.* MIRIAMNE *rises.*]

I'll answer it.

MIRIAMNE: Yes.

[*She goes into the inner room and closes the door.*
ESDRAS *goes to the outer door. The knock is repeated. He
opens the door.* MIO *is there.*]

ESDRAS: Yes, sir.

MIO: May I come in?

ESDRAS: Will you state your business, sir?
It's late—and I'm not at liberty—

MIO: Why, I might say
that I was trying to earn my tuition fees
by peddling magazines. I could say that,
or collecting old newspapers—paying cash—
highest rates—no questions asked—
[*He looks round sharply.*]

GARTH: We've nothing to sell.
What do you want?

MIO: Your pardon, gentlemen.
My business is not of an ordinary kind,
and I felt the need of this slight introduction
while I might get my bearings. Your name is Esdras,
or they told me so outside.

GARTH: What do you want?

MIO: Is that the name?

GARTH: Yes.

MIO: I'll be quick and brief.
I'm the son of a man who died many years ago
for a pay roll robbery in New England. You
should be Garth Esdras, by what I've heard. You have
some knowledge of the crime, if one can believe
what he reads in the public prints, and it might be
that your testimony, if given, would clear my father
of any share in the murder. You may not care
whether he was guilty or not. You may not know.
But I do care—and care deeply, and I've come
to ask you face to face.

GARTH: To ask me what?

MIO: What do you know of it?

ESDRAS: This man Romagna,
did he have a son?

MIO: Yes, sir, this man Romagna,

as you choose to call him, had a son, and I
am that son, and proud.

ESDRAS: Forgive me.

MIO: Had you known him,
and heard him speak, you'd know why I'm proud, and why
he was no malefactor.

ESDRAS: I quite believe you.
If my son can help he will. But at this moment,
as I told you—could you, I wonder, come tomorrow,
at your own hour?

MIO: Yes.

ESDRAS: By coincidence
we too of late have had this thing in mind—
there have been comments printed, and much discussion
which we could hardly avoid.

MIO: Could you tell me then
in a word?—What you know—
is it for him or against him?—
that's all I need.

ESDRAS: My son knows nothing.

GARTH: No.
The picture-papers lash themselves to a fury
over any rumor—make them up when they're short
of bedroom slops.—This is what happened. I
had known a few members of a gang one time
up there—and after the murder they picked me up
because I looked like someone that was seen
in what they called the murder car. They held me
a little while, but they couldn't identify me
for the most excellent reason I wasn't there
when the thing occurred. A dozen years later now
a professor comes across this, and sees red
and asks why I wasn't called on as a witness
and yips so loud they syndicate his picture
in all the rotos. That's all I know about it.
I wish I could tell you more.

ESDRAS: Let me say too

that I have read some words your father said,
and you were a son fortunate in your father,
whatever the verdict of the world.

MIO: There are few
who think so, but it's true, and I thank you. Then—
that's the whole story?

GARTH: All I know of it.

MIO: They cover their tracks well, the inner ring
that distributes murder. I came three thousand miles
to this dead end.

ESDRAS: If he was innocent
and you know him so, believe it, and let the others
believe as they like.

MIO: Will you tell me how a man's
to live, and face his life, if he can't believe
that truth's like a fire,
and will burn through and be seen
though it takes all the years there are?
While I stand up and have breath in my lungs
I shall be one flame of that fire;
it's all the life I have.

ESDRAS: Then you must live so.
One must live as he can.

MIO: It's the only way
of life my father left me.

ESDRAS: Yes? Yet it's true
the ground we walk on is impacted down
and hard with blood and bones of those who died
unjustly. There's not one title to land or life,
even your own, but was built on rape and murder,
back a few years. It would take a fire indeed
to burn out all this error.

MIO: Then let it burn down,
all of it!

ESDRAS: We ask a great deal of the world
at first—then less—and then less.
We ask for truth

and justice. But this truth's a thing unknown
in the lightest, smallest matter—and as for justice,
who has once seen it done? You loved your father,
and I could have loved him, for every word he spoke
in his trial was sweet and tolerant, but the weight
of what men are and have, rests heavy on
the graves of those who lost. They'll not rise again,
and their causes lie there with them.
GAUNT: If you mean to say
that Bartolomeo Romagna was innocent,
you are wrong. He was guilty.
There may have been injustice
from time to time, by regrettable chance, in our courts,
but not in that case, I assure you.
MIO: Oh, you assure me!
You lie in your scrag teeth, whoever you are!
My father was murdered!
GAUNT: Romagna was found guilty
by all due process of law, and given his chance
to prove his innocence.
MIO: What chance? When a court
panders to mob hysterics, and the jury
comes in loaded to soak an anarchist
and a foreigner, it may be due process of law
but it's also murder!
GAUNT: He should have thought of that
before he spilled blood.
MIO: He?
GAUNT: Sir, I know too well
that he was guilty.
MIO: Who are you? How do you know?
I've searched the records through, the trial and what
came after, and in all that million words
I found not one unbiased argument
to fix the crime on him.
GAUNT: And you yourself,
were you unprejudiced?

MIO: Who are you?

ESDRAS: Sir,
this gentleman is here, as you are here,
to ask my son, as you have asked, what ground
there might be for this talk of new evidence
in your father's case. We gave him the same answer
we've given you.

MIO: I'm sorry. I'd supposed
his cause forgotten except by myself. There's still
a defense committee then?

GAUNT: There may be. I
am not connected with it.

ESDRAS: He is my guest,
and asks to remain unknown.

MIO [*after a pause, looking at* GAUNT]: The judge at the trial
was younger, but he had your face. Can't be
that you're the man?—Yes—Yes.—The jury charge—
I sat there as a child and heard your voice,
and watched that Brahminical mouth. I knew even then
you meant no good to him. And now you're here
to winnow out truth and justice—the fountain-head
of the lies that slew him! Are you Judge Gaunt?

GAUNT: I am.

MIO: Then tell me what damnation to what inferno
would fit the toad that sat in robes and lied
when he gave the charge, and knew he lied! Judge that,
and then go to your place in that hell!

GAUNT: I know and have known
what bitterness can rise against a court
when it must say, putting aside all weakness,
that a man's to die. I can forgive you that,
for you are your father's son, and you think of him
as a son thinks of his father. Certain laws
seem cruel in their operation; it's necessary
that we be cruel to uphold them. This cruelty
is kindness to those I serve.

MIO: I don't doubt that.
　　I know who it is you serve.
GAUNT: Would I have chosen
　　to rack myself with other men's despairs,
　　stop my ears, harden my heart, and listen only
　　to the voice of law and light, if I had hoped
　　some private gain for serving? In all my years
　　on the bench of a long-established commonwealth
　　not once has my decision been in question
　　save in this case. Not once before or since.
　　For hope of heaven or place on earth, or power
　　or gold, no man has had my voice, nor will
　　while I still keep the trust that's laid on me
　　to sentence and define.
MIO: Then why are you here?
GAUNT: My record's clean. I've kept it so. But suppose
　　with the best intent, among the myriad tongues
　　that come to testify, I had missed my way
　　and followed a perjured tale to a lethal end
　　till a man was forsworn to death? Could I rest or sleep
　　while there was doubt of this,
　　even while there was question in a layman's mind?
　　For always, night and day,
　　there lies on my brain like a weight, the admonition:
　　see truly, let nothing sway you; among all functions
　　there's but one godlike, to judge. Then see to it
　　you judge as a god would judge, with clarity,
　　with truth, with what mercy is found consonant
　　with order and law. Without law men are beasts,
　　and it's a judge's task to lift and hold them
　　above themselves. Let a judge be once mistaken
　　or step aside for a friend, and a gap is made
　　in the dykes that hold back anarchy and chaos,
　　and leave men bond but free.
MIO: Then the gap's been made,
　　and you made it.

GAUNT: I feared that too. May you be a judge
   sometime, and know in what fear,
   through what nights long
   in fear, I scanned and verified and compared
   the transcripts of the trial.
MIO: Without prejudice,
   no doubt. It was never in your mind to prove
   that you'd been right.
GAUNT: And conscious of that, too—
   that that might be my purpose—watchful of that,
   and jealous as his own lawyer of the rights
   that should hedge the defendant!
   And still I found no error,
   shook not one staple of the bolts that linked
   the doer to the deed! Still following on
   from step to step, I watched all modern comment,
   and saw it centered finally on one fact—
   Garth Esdras was not called. This is Garth Esdras,
   and you have heard him. Would his deposition
   have justified a new trial?
MIO: No. It would not.
GAUNT: And there I come, myself. If the man were still
   in his cell, and waiting, I'd have no faint excuse
   for another hearing.
MIO: I've told you that I read
   the trial from beginning to end. Every word you spoke
   was balanced carefully to keep the letter
   of the law and still convict—convict, by Christ,
   if it tore the seven veils! You stand here now
   running cascades of casuistry, to prove
   to yourself and me that no judge of rank and breeding
   could burn a man out of hate! But that's what you did
   under all your varnish!
GAUNT: I've sought for evidence,
   and you have sought. Have you found it? Can you cite
   one fresh word in defense?
MIO: The trial itself

was shot full of legerdemain, prearranged to lead
the jury astray—

GAUNT: Could you prove that?

MIO: Yes!

GAUNT: And if
the jury were led astray, remember it's
the jury, by our Anglo-Saxon custom,
that finds for guilt or innocence. The judge
is powerless in that matter.

MIO: Not you! Your charge
misled the jury more than the evidence,
accepted every biased meaning, distilled
the poison for them!

GAUNT: But if that were so
I'd be the first, I swear it, to step down
among all men, and hold out both my hands
for manacles—yes, publish it in the streets,
that all I've held most sacred was defiled
by my own act. A judge's brain becomes
a delicate instrument to weigh men's lives
for good and ill—too delicate to bear
much tampering. If he should push aside
the weights and throw the beam, and say, this once
the man is guilty, and I will have it so
though his mouth cry out from the ground,
and all the world
revoke my word, he'd have a short way to go
to madness. I think you'd find him in the squares,
stopping the passers-by with arguments,—
see, I was right, the man was guilty there—
this was brought in against him, this—and this—
and I was left no choice! It's no light thing
when a long life's been dedicate to one end
to wrench the mind awry!

MIO: By your own thesis
you should be mad, and no doubt you are.

GAUNT: But my madness

is only this—that I would fain look back
on a life well spent—without one stain—one breath
of stain to flaw the glass—not in men's minds
nor in my own. I take my God as witness
I meant to earn that clearness, and believe
that I have earned it. Yet my name is clouded
with the blackest, fiercest scandal of our age
that's touched a judge. What I can do to wipe
that smutch from my fame I will. I think you know
how deeply I've been hated, for no cause
that I can find there. Can it not be—and I ask this
quite honestly—that the great injustice lies
on your side and not mine? Time and time again
men have come before me perfect in their lives,
loved by all who knew them, loved at home,
gentle, not vicious, yet caught so ripe red-handed
in some dark violence there was no denying
where the onus lay.

MIO: That was not so with my father!

GAUNT: And yet it seemed so to me. To other men
who sat in judgment on him. Can you be sure—
I ask this in humility—that you,
who were touched closest by the tragedy,
may not have lost perspective—may have brooded
day and night on one theme—till your eyes are tranced
and show you one side only?

MIO: I see well enough.

GAUNT: And would that not be part of the malady—
to look quite steadily at the drift of things
but see there what you wish—not what is there—
not what another man to whom the story
was fresh would say is there?

MIO: You think I'm crazy.
Is that what you meant to say?

GAUNT: I've seen it happen
with the best and wisest men. I but ask the question.
I can't speak for you. Is it not true wherever

you walk, through the little town where you knew him well,
or flying from it, inland or by the sea,
still walking at your side, and sleeping only
when you too sleep, a shadow not your own
follows, pleading and holding out its hands
to be delivered from shame?

MIO: How you know that
by God I don't know.

GAUNT: Because one spectre haunted you and me—
and haunts you still, but for me it's laid to rest
now that my mind is satisfied. He died
justly and not by error.
      [*A pause.*]

MIO [*stepping forward*]: Do you care to know
you've come so near to death it's miracle
that pulse still beats in your splotchy throat?
Do you know
there's murder in me?

GAUNT: There was murder in your sire,
and it's to be expected! I say he died
justly, and he deserved it!

MIO: Yes, you'd like too well
to have me kill you! That would prove your case
and clear your name, and dip my father's name
in stench forever! You'll not get that from me!
Go home and die in bed, get it under cover,
your lux-et-lex putrefaction of the right thing,
you man that walks like a god!

GAUNT: Have I made you angry
by coming too near the truth?

MIO: This sets him up,
this venomous slug, this sets him up in a gown,
deciding who's to walk above the earth
and who's to lie beneath! And giving reasons!
The cobra giving reasons; I'm a god,
by Buddha, holy and worshipful my fang,
and can I sink it in!

[*He pauses, turns as if to go, then sits.*]
This is no good.
   This won't help much.
   [*The* JUDGE *and* ESDRAS *look at each other.*]
GAUNT: We should be going.
ESDRAS: Yes.
   [*They prepare to go.*]
   I'll lend you my coat.
GAUNT [*looking at it with distaste*]: No, keep it. A little rain
   shouldn't matter to me.
ESDRAS: It freezes as it falls,
   and you've a long way to go.
GAUNT: I'll manage, thank you.
   [GAUNT *and* ESDRAS *go out,* ESDRAS *obsequious, closing
   the door.*]
GARTH: [*looking at* MIO's *back*]: Well?
MIO [*not moving*]: Let me sit here a moment.
   [GARTH *shrugs his shoulders and goes toward the inner
   door.* MIRIAMNE *opens it and comes out.* GARTH *looks at her,
   then at* MIO, *then lays his fingers on his lips. She nods.* GARTH
   goes out. MIRIAMNE *sits and watches* MIO. *After a little he
   turns and sees her.*]
MIO: How did you come here?
MIRIAMNE: I live here.
MIO: Here?
MIRIAMNE: My names is Esdras. Garth
   is my brother. The walls are thin.
   I heard what was said.
MIO [*stirring wearily*]: I'm going. This is no place for me.
MIRIAMNE: What place
   would be better?
MIO: None. Only it's better to go.
   Just to go.
   [*She comes over to him, puts her arm round him and
   kisses his forehead.*]
MIRIAMNE: Mio.
MIO: What do you want?

Your kisses burn me—and your arms. Don't offer
what I'm never to have! I can have nothing. They say
they'll cross the void sometime to the other planets
and men will breathe in that air.
Well, I could breathe there,
but not here now. Not on this ball of mud.
I don't want it.

MIRIAMNE: They can take away so little
with all their words. For you're a king among them.
I heard you, and loved your voice.

MIO: I thought I'd fallen
so low there was no further, and now a pit
opens beneath. It was bad enough that he
should have died innocent, but if he were guilty—
then what's my life—what have I left to do—?
The son of a felon—and what they spat on me
was earned—and I'm drenched with the stuff.
Here on my hands
and cheeks, their spittle hanging! I liked my hands
because they were like his. I tell you I've lived
by his innocence, lived to see it flash
and blind them all—

MIRIAMNE: Never believe them, Mio,
never.

[*She looks toward the inner door.*]

MIO: But it was truth I wanted, truth—
not the lies you'd tell yourself, or tell a woman,
or a woman tells you! The judge with his cobra mouth
may have spat truth—and I may be mad! For me—
your hands are too clean to touch me. I'm to have
the scraps from hotel kitchens—and instead of love
those mottled bodies that hitch themselves through alleys
to sell for dimes or nickels. Go, keep yourself chaste
for the baker bridegroom—baker and son of a baker,
let him get his baker's dozen on you!

MIRIAMNE: No—
say once you love me—say it once; I'll never

ask to hear it twice, nor for any kindness,
and you shall take all I have!

[GARTH *opens the inner door and comes out.*]

GARTH: I interrupt
a love scene, I believe. We can do without
your adolescent mawkishness.
[*To* MIRIAMNE]
You're a child.
You'll both remember that.

MIRIAMNE: I've said nothing to harm you—
and will say nothing.

GARTH: You're my sister, though,
and I take a certain interest in you. Where
have you two met?

MIRIAMNE: We danced together.

GARTH: Then
the dance is over, I think.

MIRIAMNE: I've always loved you
and tried to help you, Garth. And you've been kind.
Don't spoil it now.

GARTH: Spoil it how?

MIRIAMNE: Because I love him.
I didn't know it would happen. We danced together.
And the world's all changed. I see you through a mist,
and our father, too. If you brought this to nothing
I'd want to die.

GARTH [*to Mio*]: You'd better go.

MIO: Yes, I know.

[*He rises. There is a trembling knock at the door.* MIRI-
AMNE *goes to it. The* HOBO *is there shivering.*]

HOBO: Miss, could I sleep under the pipes tonight, miss?
Could I, please?

MIRIAMNE: I think—not tonight.

HOBO: There won't be any more nights—
if I don't get warm, miss.

MIRIAMNE: Come in.

[*The* HOBO *comes in, looks round deprecatingly, then*

goes to a corner beneath a huge heating pipe, which he crawls under as if he'd been there before.]

HOBO: Yes, miss, thank you.

GARTH: Must we put up with that?

MIRIAMNE: Father let him sleep there—
   last winter.

GARTH: Yes, God, yes.

MIO: Well, good night.

MIRIAMNE: Where will you go?

MIO: Yes, where? As if it mattered.

GARTH: Oh, sleep here, too.
   We'll have a row of you under the pipes.

MIO: No, thanks.

MIRIAMNE: Mio, I've saved a little money. It's only
   some pennies, but you must take it.
      [*She shakes some coins out of a box into her hand.*]

MIO: No, thanks.

MIRIAMNE: And I love you.
   You've never said you love me.

MIO: Why wouldn't I love you
   when you're clean and sweet,
   and I've seen nothing sweet or clean
   this last ten years? I love you. I leave you that
   for what good it may do you. It's none to me.

MIRIAMNE: Then kiss me.

MIO [*looking at* GARTH]: With that scowling over us? No.
   When it rains, some spring
   on the planet Mercury, where the spring comes often,
   I'll meet you there, let's say. We'll wait for that.
   It may be some time till then.
      [*The outside door opens and* ESDRAS *enters with* JUDGE
GAUNT, *then, after a slight interval,* TROCK *follows.* TROCK
surveys the interior and its occupants one by one, carefully.]

TROCK: I wouldn't want to cause you inconvenience,
   any of you, and especially the Judge.
   I think you know that. You've all got things to do—
   trains to catch, and so on. But trains can wait.

Hell, nearly anything can wait, you'll find,
only I can't. I'm the only one that can't
because I've got no time. Who's all this here?
Who's that?
   [*He points to the* HOBO.]
ESDRAS: He's a poor half-wit, sir,
that sometimes sleeps there.
TROCK: Come out. I say come out,
whoever you are.
   [*The* HOBO *stirs and looks up.*]
Yes, I mean you. Come out.
   [*The* HOBO *emerges.*]
What's your name?
HOBO: They mostly call me Oke.
TROCK: What do you know?
HOBO: No, sir.
TROCK: Where are you from?
HOBO: I got a piece of bread.
   [*He brings it out, trembling.*]
TROCK: Get back in there!
   [*The* HOBO *crawls back into his corner.*]
Maybe you want to know why I'm doing this.
Well, I've been robbed, that's why—
robbed five or six times;
the police can't find a thing—so I'm out for myself—
if you want to know.
   [*To* MIO]
Who are you?
MIO: Oh, I'm a half-wit,
came in here by mistake. The difference is
I've got no piece of bread.
TROCK: What's your name?
MIO: My name?
Theophrastus Such. That's respectable.
You'll find it all the way from here to the coast
on the best police blotters.
Only the truth is we're a little touched in the head,

Oke and me. You'd better ask somebody else.

TROCK: Who is he?

ESDRAS: His name's Romagna. He's the son.

TROCK: Then what's he doing here? You said you were on the level.

GARTH: He just walked in. On account of the stuff in the papers. We didn't ask him.

TROCK: God, we are a gathering. Now if we had Shadow we'd be all here, huh? Only I guess we won't see Shadow. No, that's too much to ask.

MIO: Who's Shadow?

TROCK: Now you're putting questions. Shadow was just nobody, you see. He blew away. It might happen to anyone.

[*He looks at* GARTH.]

Yes, anyone at all.

MIO: Why do you keep your hand in your pocket, friend?

TROCK: Because I'm cold, punk. Because I've been outside and it's cold as the tomb of Christ.

[*To* GARTH]

Listen, there's a car waiting at the street to take the Judge home. We'll take him to the car.

GARTH: That's not necessary.

ESDRAS: No.

TROCK: I say it is, see? You wouldn't want to let the Judge walk, would you? The Judge is going to ride where he's going, with a couple of chauffeurs, and everything done in style. Don't you worry about the Judge. He'll be taken care of. For good.

GARTH: I want no hand in it.

TROCK: Anything happens to me happens to you too, musician.

GARTH: I know that.

TROCK: Keep your mouth out of it then. And you'd better keep the punk here tonight, just for luck.

[*He turns toward the door. There is a brilliant lightning flash through the windows, followed slowly by dying thunder.* TROCK *opens the door. The rain begins to pour in sheets.*]

Jesus, somebody tipped it over again!

[*A cough racks him.*]

Wait till it's over. It takes ten days off me every time I step
into it.

[*He closes the door.*]

Sit down and wait.

[*Lightning flashes again. The thunder is fainter.* ESDRAS,
GARTH *and the* JUDGE *sit down.*]

GAUNT: We were born too early. Even you who are young
are not of the elect. In a hundred years
man will put his finger on life itself, and then
he will live as long as he likes. For you and me
we shall die soon—one day, one year more or less,
when or where, it's no matter. It's what we call
an indeterminate sentence. I'm hungry.

[GARTH *looks at* MIRIAMNE.]

MIRIAMNE: There was nothing left
tonight.

HOBO: I've got a piece of bread,

[*He breaks his bread in two and hands half to the* JUDGE.]

GAUNT: I thank you, sir.

[*He eats.*]

This is not good bread.

[*He rises.*]

Sir, I am used
to other company. Not better, perhaps, but their clothes
were different. These are what it's the fashion to call
the underprivileged.

TROCK: Oh, hell!

[*He turns toward the door.*]

MIO [*to* TROCK]: It would seem that you and the Judge know
each other.

TROCK: [TROCK *faces him.*] I've been around.

MIO: Maybe you've met before.

TROCK: Maybe we have.

MIO: Will you tell me where?

TROCK: How long do you want to live?

MIO: How long? Oh, I've got big ideas about that.

TROCK: I thought so. Well, so far I've got nothing against you but your name, see? You keep it that way.

[*He opens the door. The rain still falls in torrents. He closes the door. As he turns from it, it opens again, and* SHADOW, *white, bloodstained and dripping, stands in the doorway.* GARTH *rises.* TROCK *turns.*]

GAUNT [*to the* HOBO]: Yet if one were careful of his health, ate sparingly, drank not at all, used himself wisely, it might be that even an old man could live to touch immortality. They may come on the secret sooner than we dare hope. You see? It does no harm to try.

TROCK [*backing away from* SHADOW]: By God, he's out of his grave!

SHADOW [*leaning against the doorway, holding a gun in his hands*]: Keep your hands where they belong, Trock.
You know me.

TROCK: Don't! Don't! I had nothing to do with it!

[*He backs to the opposite wall.*]

SHADOW: You said the doctor gave you six months to live—
well, I don't give you that much. That's what you had,
six months, and so you start bumping off your friends
to make sure of your damn six months. I got it from you.
I know where I got it.
Because I wouldn't give it to the Judge.
So he wouldn't talk.

TROCK: Honest to God—

SHADOW: What God?
The one that let you put three holes in me
when I was your friend? Well, He let me get up again
and walk till I could find you. That's as far as I get,
but I got there, by God! And I can hear you
even if I can't see!
[*He takes a staggering step forward.*]
A man needs blood
to keep going.—I got this far.—And now I can't see!
It runs out too fast—too fast—

when you've got three slugs
clean through you.
Show me where he is, you fools! He's in here!
I got here!
[*He drops the gun.*]
Help me! Help me! Oh, God! Oh, God!
I'm going to die! Where does a man lie down?
I want to lie down!
[Mɪʀɪᴀᴍɴᴇ *starts toward* Sʜᴀᴅᴏᴡ. Gᴀʀᴛʜ *and* Esᴅʀᴀs
help him into the next room, Mɪʀɪᴀᴍɴᴇ *following.* Tʀᴏᴄᴋ
squats in his corner, breathing hard, looking at the door. Mɪᴏ
stands, watching Tʀᴏᴄᴋ. Gᴀʀᴛʜ *returns, wiping his hand with
a handkerchief.* Mɪᴏ *picks up and pockets the gun.* Mɪʀɪᴀᴍɴᴇ
comes back and leans against the door jamb.]
Gᴀᴜɴᴛ: You will hear it said that an old man makes a good
judge, being calm, clear-eyed, without passion. But this is
not true. Only the young love truth and justice. The old
are savage, wary, violent, swayed by maniac desires, cynical
of friendship or love, open to bribery and the temptations
of lust, corrupt and dastardly to the heart. I know these
old men. What have they left to believe, what have they left
to lose? Whorers of daughters, lickers of girls' shoes, con-
trivers of nastiness in the night, purveyors of perversion,
worshippers of possession! Death is the only radical. He
comes late, but he comes at last to put away the old men
and give the young their places. It was time.
[*He leers.*]
Here's one I heard yesterday:
    Marmaduke behind the barn
        got his sister in a fix;
    he says damn instead of darn;
        ain't he cute? He's only six!
Hᴏʙᴏ: He, he, he!
Gᴀᴜɴᴛ: And the hoot-owl hoots all night,
        and the cuckoo cooks all day,
    and what with a minimum grace of God
        we pass the time away.

Hobo: He, he, he—I got ya!
  [*He makes a sign with his thumb.*]
Gaunt [*sings*]: And he led her all around
            and he laid her on the ground
            and he ruffled up the feathers of her
            cuckoo's nest!
Hobo: Ho, ho, ho!
Gaunt: I am not taken with the way you laugh.
  You should cultivate restraint.
    [Esdras *reënters.*]
Trock: Shut the door.
Esdras: He won't come back again.
Trock: I want the door shut! He was dead, I tell you!
    [Esdras *closes the door.*]
  And Romagna was dead, too, once! Can't they keep a man
  under ground?
Mio: No. No more! They don't stay under ground any more,
  and they don't stay under water! Why did you have him
  killed?
Trock: Stay away from me! I know you!
Mio: Who am I, then?
Trock: I know you, damn you! Your name's Romagna!
Mio: Yes! And Romagna was dead, too, and Shadow was dead,
  but the time's come when you can't keep them down, these
  dead men! They won't stay down! They come in with
  their heads shot off and their entrails dragging! Hundreds
  of them! One by one—all you ever had killed! Watch the
  door! See!—It moves!
Trock [*looking, fascinated, at the door*]: Let me out of here!
    [*He tries to rise.*]
Mio [*the gun in his hand*]: Oh, no! You'll sit there and wait
  for them! One by one they'll come through that door, pulling their heads out of the gunny-sacks where you tied them
  —glauming over you with their rotten hands! They'll see
  without eyes and crawl over you—Shadow and the paymaster and all the rest of them—putrescent bones without
  eyes! Now! Look! Look! For I'm first among them!

TROCK: I've done for better men than you! And I'll do for you!

GAUNT [*rapping on the table*]: Order, gentlemen, order! The witness will remember that a certain decorum is essential in the court-room!

MIO: By God, he'll answer me!

GAUNT [*thundering*]: Silence! Silence! Let me remind you of courtesy toward the witness! What case is this you try?

MIO: The case of the state against Bartolomeo Romagna for the murder of the paymaster!

GAUNT: Sir, that was disposed of long ago!

MIO: Never disposed of, never, not while I live!

GAUNT: Then we'll have done with it now! I deny the appeal! I have denied the appeal before and I do so again!

HOBO: He, he!—He thinks he's in the moving pictures!

[*A flash of lightning.*]

GAUNT: Who set that flash! Bailiff, clear the court! This is not Flemington, gentlemen! We are not conducting this case to make a journalistic holiday!

[*The thunder rumbles faintly.* GARTH *opens the outside door and faces a solid wall of rain.*]

Stop that man! He's one of the defendants!

[*Garth closes the door.*]

MIO: Then put him on the stand!

GARTH: What do you think you're doing?

MIO: Have you any objection?

GAUNT: The objection is not sustained. We will hear the new evidence. Call your witness.

MIO: Garth Esdras!

GAUNT: He will take the stand!

GARTH: If you want me to say what I said before I'll say it!

MIO: Call Trock Estrella then!

GAUNT: Trock Estrella to the stand!

TROCK: No, by God!

MIO: Call Shadow, then! He'll talk! You thought he was dead, but he'll get up again and talk!

TROCK [*screaming*]: What do you want of me?

Mio: You killed the paymaster! You!
Trock: You lie! It was Shadow killed him!
Mio: And now I know! Now I know!
Gaunt: Again I remind you of courtesy toward the witness!
Mio: I know them now!
  Let me remind you of courtesy toward the dead!
  He says that Shadow killed him! If Shadow were here
  he'd say it was Trock! There were three men involved
  in the new version of the crime for which
  my father died! Shadow and Trock Estrella
  as principals in the murder—Garth as witness!—
  Why are they here together?—and you—the Judge—
  why are you here? Why, because you were all afraid
  and you drew together out of that fear to arrange
  a story you could tell! And Trock killed Shadow
  and meant to kill the Judge out of that same fear—
  to keep them quiet! This is the thing I've hunted
  over the earth to find out, and I'd be blind
  indeed if I missed it now!
    [*To* Gaunt]
    You heard what he said:
  It was Shadow killed him! Now let the night conspire
  with the sperm of hell! It's plain beyond denial
  even to this fox of justice—and all his words
  are curses on the wind! You lied! You lied!
  You knew this too!
Gaunt [*low*]: Let me go. Let me go!
Mio: Then why
  did you let my father die?
Gaunt: Suppose it known,
  but there are things a judge must not believe
  though they should head and fester underneath
  and press in on his brain. Justice once rendered
  in a clear burst of anger, righteously,
  upon a very common laborer,
  confessed an anarchist, the verdict found
  and the precise machinery of law

invoked to know him guilty—think what furor
would rock the state if the court then flatly said
all this was lies—must be reversed? It's better,
as any judge can tell you, in such cases,
holding the common good to be worth more
than small injustice, to let the record stand,
let one man die. For justice, in the main,
is governed by opinion. Communities
will have what they will have, and it's quite as well,
after all, to be rid of anarchists. Our rights
as citizens can be maintained as rights
only while we are held to be the peers
of those who live about us. A vendor of fish
is not protected as a man might be
who kept a market. I own I've sometimes wished
this was not so, but it is. The man you defend
was unfortunate—and his misfortune bore
almost as heavily on me.—I'm broken—
broken across. You're much too young to know
how bitter it is when a worn connection chars
and you can't remember—can't remember.
  [*He steps forward.*]
  You
will not repeat this? It will go no further?
MIO: No.
  No further than the moon takes the tides—no further
  than the news went when he died—
  when you found him guilty
  and they flashed that round the earth. Wherever men
  still breathe and think, and know what's done to them
  by the powers above, they'll know. That's all I ask.
  That'll be enough.
    [TROCK *has risen and looks darkly at* MIO.]
GAUNT: Thank you. For I've said some things
  a judge should never say.
TROCK: Go right on talking.
  Both of you. It won't get far, I guess.

MIO: Oh, you'll see to that?

TROCK: I'll see to it. Me and some others.
Maybe I lost my grip there just for a minute.
That's all right.

MIO: Then see to it! Let it rain!
What can you do to me now when the night's on fire
with this thing I know? Now I could almost wish
there was a god somewhere—I could almost think
there was a god—and he somehow brought me here
and set you down before me here in the rain
where I could wring this out of you! For it's said,
and I've heard it, and I'm free! He was as I thought him,
true and noble and upright, even when he went
to a death contrived because he was as he was
and not your kind! Let it rain! Let the night speak fire
and the city go out with the tide, for he was a man
and I know you now, and I have my day!

[*There is a heavy knock at the outside door.* MIRIAMNE
opens it, at a glance from GARTH. *The* POLICEMAN *is there in
oilskins.*]

POLICEMAN: Evening.
[*He steps in, followed by a* SERGEANT, *similarly dressed.*]
We're looking for someone
might be here. Seen an old man around acting a little off?
[*To* ESDRAS]
You know the one
I mean. You saw him out there. Jeez! You've got
a funny crowd here!
[*He looks round. The* HOBO *shrinks into his corner.*]
That's the one I saw.
What do you think?

SERGEANT: That's him. You mean to say
you didn't know him by his pictures?
[*He goes to* GAUNT]
Come on, old man.
You're going home.

GAUNT: Yes, sir. I've lost my way.
  I think I've lost my way.
SERGEANT: I'll say you have.
  About three hundred miles. Now don't you worry
  We'll get you back.
GAUNT: I'm a person of some rank
  in my own city.
SERGEANT: We know that. One look at you
  and we'd know that.
GAUNT: Yes, sir.
POLICEMAN: If it isn't Trock!
  Trock Estrella. How are you, Trock?
TROCK: Pretty good,
  thanks.
POLICEMAN: Got out yesterday again, I hear?
TROCK: That's right.
SERGEANT: Hi'ya, Trock?
TROCK: O.K.
SERGEANT: You know we got orders
  to watch you pretty close. Be good now, baby,
  or back you go. Don't try to pull anything,
  not in my district.
TROCK: No, sir.
SERGEANT: No bumping off.
  If you want my advice quit carrying a gun.
  Try earning your living for once.
TROCK: Yeah.
SERGEANT: That's an idea.
  Because if we find any stiffs on the river bank
  we'll know who to look for.
MIO: Then look in the other room!
  I accuse that man of murder! Trock Estrella!
  He's a murderer!
POLICEMAN: Hello. I remember you.
SERGEANT: Well, what murder?
MIO: It was Trock Estrella
  that robbed the pay roll thirteen years ago

and did the killing my father died for! You know
the Romagna case! Romagna was innocent,
and Trock Estrella guilty!

SERGEANT: [*disgusted*]: Oh, what the hell!
That's old stuff—the Romagna case.

POLICEMAN: Hey, Sarge!
[*The* SERGEANT *and* POLICEMAN *come closer together.*]
The boy's a professional kidder. He took me over
about half an hour ago. He kids the police
and then ducks out!

SERGEANT: Oh, yeah?

MIO: I'm not kidding now.
You'll find a dead man there in the next room
and Estrella killed him!

SERGEANT: Thirteen years ago?
And nobody smelled him yet?

MIO [*pointing*]: I accuse this man
of two murders! He killed the paymaster long ago
and had Shadow killed tonight. Look, look for yourself!
He's there all right!

POLICEMAN: Look boy. You stood out there
and put the booby sign on the dumb police
because they're fresh out of Ireland. Don't try it twice.

SERGEANT [*to* GARTH]: Any corpses here?

GARTH: Not that I know of.

SERGEANT: I thought so.
[MIO *looks at* MIRIAMNE.]
[*To* MIO]
Think up a better one.

MIO: Have I got to drag him
out here where you can see him?
[*He goes toward the inner door.*]
Can't you scent a murder
when it's under your nose? Look in!

MIRIAMNE: No, no—there's no one—there's no one there!

SERGEANT [*looking at* MIRIAMNE]: Take a look inside.

POLICEMAN: Yes, sir.

[*He goes into the inside room. The* SERGEANT *goes up to the door. The* POLICEMAN *returns.*]

　　He's kidding, Sarge. If there's a cadaver
　　in here I don't see it.

MIO: You're blind then!

　　[*He goes into the room, the* SERGEANT *following him.*]

SERGEANT: What do you mean?

　　[*He comes out,* MIO *following him.*]

　　When you make a charge of murder it's better to have
　　the corpus delicti, son. You're the kind puts in
　　fire alarms to see the engine!

MIO: By God, he was there!
　　He went in there to die.

SERGEANT: I'll bet he did.
　　And I'm Haile Selassie's aunt! What's your name?

MIO: Romagna.

　　[*To* GARTH]

　　What have you done with him?

GARTH: I don't know what you mean.

SERGEANT [*to* GARTH]: What's he talking about?

GARTH: I wish I could tell you.
　　I don't know.

SERGEANT: He must have seen something.

POLICEMAN: He's got
　　the Romagna case on the brain. You watch yourself,
　　chump, or you'll get run in.

MIO: Then they're in it together!
　　All of them!

　　[*To* MIRIAMNE]

　　Yes, and you!

GARTH: He's nuts, I say.

MIRIAMNE [*gently*]: You have dreamed something—isn't it
　　true?
　　You've dreamed—
　　But truly, there was no one—

　　[MIO *looks at her comprehendingly.*]

MIO: You want me to say it.
   [*He pauses.*]
   Yes, by God, I was dreaming.
SERGEANT [*to* POLICEMAN]: I guess you're right.
   We'd better be going. Haven't you got a coat?
GAUNT: No, sir.
SERGEANT: I guess I'll have to lend you mine.
   [*He puts his oilskins on* GAUNT.]
   Come on, now. It's getting late.
   [GAUNT, *the* POLICEMAN *and the* SERGEANT *go out.*]
TROCK: They're welcome to him.
   His fuse is damp. Where is that walking fool
   with the three slugs in him?
ESDRAS: He fell in the hall beyond
   and we left him there.
TROCK: That's lucky for some of us. Is he out this time
   or is he still butting around?
ESDRAS: He's dead.
TROCK: That's perfect.
   [*To* MIO]
   Don't try using your firearms, amigo baby,
   the Sarge is outside.
   [*He turns to go.*]
   Better ship that carrion
   back in the river! The one that walks when he's dead;
   maybe he'll walk the distance for you.
GARTH: Coming back?
TROCK: Well, if I come back,
   you'll see me. If I don't, you won't. Let the punk
   go as far as he likes. Turn him loose and let him go.
   And may you all rot in hell.
   [*He pulls his coat around him and goes to the left.* MIRI-
AMNE *climbs up to look out a window.*]
MIRIAMNE: He's climbing up to the street,
   along the bridgehead.
   [*She turns.*]
   Quick, Mio! It's safe now! Quick!

GARTH: Let him do as he likes.

MIRIAMNE: What do you mean? Garth! He means to kill him!
You know that!

GARTH: I've no doubt Master Romagna
can run his own campaign.

MIRIAMNE: But he'll be killed!

MIO: Why did you lie about Shadow?

[*There is a pause.* GARTH *shrugs, walks across the room,
and sits.*]

You were one of the gang!

GARTH: I can take a death if I have to! Go tell your story,
only watch your step, for I warn you, Trock's out gunning
and you may not walk very far. Oh, I could defend it
but it's hardly worth while.
If they get Trock they get me too.
Go tell them. You owe me nothing.

ESDRAS: This Trock you saw,
no one defends him. He's earned his death so often
there's nobody to regret it. But his crime,
his same crime that has dogged you, dogged us down
from what little we had, to live here among the drains,
where the waterbugs break out like a scrofula
on what we eat—and if there's lower to go
we'll go there when you've told your story. And more
that I haven't heart to speak—

MIO [*to* GARTH]: My father died
in your place. And you could have saved him!
You were one of the gang!

GARTH: Why, there you are.
You certainly owe me nothing.

MIRIAMNE: [*moaning*]: I want to die.
I want to go away.

MIO: Yes, and you lied!
And trapped me into it!

MIRIAMNE: But Mio, he's my brother.
I couldn't give them my brother.

MIO: No. You couldn't.

You were quite right. The gods were damned ironic
tonight, and they've worked it out.

ESDRAS: What will be changed
if it comes to trial again? More blood poured out
to a mythical justice, but your father lying still
where he lies now.

MIO: The bright, ironical gods!
What fun they have in heaven! When a man prays hard
for any gift, they give it, and then one more
to boot that makes it useless.
    [*To* MIRIAMNE]
    You might have picked
some other stranger to dance with!

MIRIAMNE: I know.

MIO: Or chosen
some other evening to sit outside in the rain.
But no, it had to be this. All my life long
I've wanted only one thing, to say to the world
and prove it: the man you killed was clean and true
and full of love as the twelve-year-old that stood
and taught in the temple. I can say that now
and give my proofs—and now you stick a girl's face
between me and the rites I've sworn the dead
shall have of me! You ask too much! Your brother
can take his chance! He was ready enough to let
an innocent man take certainty for him
to pay for the years he's had. That parts us, then,
but we're parted anyway, by the same dark wind
that blew us together. I shall say what I have to say.
    [*He steps back.*]
And I'm not welcome here.

MIRIAMNE: But don't go now! You've stayed
too long! He'll be waiting!

MIO: Well, is this any safer?
Let the winds blow, the four winds of the world,
and take us to the four winds.
    [*The three are silent before him. He turns and goes out.*]

ACT THREE

SCENE: *The river bank outside the tenement, a little before the close of the previous act. The rain still falls through the street lamps. The* TWO NATTY YOUNG MEN IN SERGE AND GRAY *are leaning against the masonry in a ray of light, concentrating on a game of chance. Each holds in his hand a packet of ten or fifteen crisp bills. They compare the numbers on the top notes and immediately a bill changes hands. This goes on with varying fortune until the tide begins to run toward the* 1ST GUNMAN, *who has accumulated nearly the whole supply. They play on in complete silence, evidently not wishing to make any noise. Occasionally they raise their heads slightly to look carefully about. Luck begins to favor the* 2ND GUNMAN, *and the notes come his way. Neither evinces the slightest interest in how the game goes. They merely play on, bored, half-absorbed. There is a slight noise at the tenement door. They put the bills away and watch.* TROCK *comes out, pulls the door shut and comes over to them. He says a few words too low to be heard, and without changing expression the* YOUNG MEN *saunter toward the right.* TROCK *goes out to the left, and the* 2ND PLAYER, *catching that out of the corner of his eye, lingers in a glimmer of light to go on with the game. The* 1ST, *with an eye on the tenement door, begins to play without ado, and the bills again shift back and forth, then concentrate in the hands of the* 1ST GUNMAN. *The* 2ND *shrugs his shoulders, searches his pockets, finds one bill, and playing with it begins to win heavily. They hear the door opening, and putting the notes away, slip out in front of the rock.* MIO *emerges, closes the door, looks round him and walks to the left. Near the corner of the tenement he pauses, reaches out his hand to try the rain, looks up toward the street, and stands uncertainly a moment. He returns and leans against the tenement wall.* MIRIAMNE *comes out.* MIO *continues to look off into space as if unaware of her. She looks away.*

Mio: This rather takes one off his high horse.—What 1 mean, tough weather for a hegira. You see, this is my sleeping suit, and if I get it wet—basta!

Miriamne: If you could only hide here.

Mio: Hide?

Miriamne: Lucia would take you in. The street-piano man.

Mio: At the moment, I'm afflicted with claustrophobia. I prefer to die in the open, seeking air.

Miriamne: But you could stay there till daylight.

Mio: You're concerned about me.

Miriamne: Shall I ask him?

Mio: No. On the other hand there's a certain reason in your concern. I looked up the street and our old friend Trock hunches patiently under the warehouse eaves.

Miriamne: I was sure of that.

Mio: And here I am, a young man on a cold night, waiting the end of the rain. Being read my lesson by a boy, a blind boy—you know the one I mean. Knee-deep in the salt-marsh, Miriamne, bitten from within, fought.

Miriamne: Wouldn't it be better if you came back in the house?

Mio: You forget my claustrophobia.

Miriamne: Let me walk with you, then. Please. If I stay beside you he wouldn't dare.

Mio: And then again he might.—We don't speak the same language, Miriamne.

Miriamne: I betrayed you. Forgive me.

Mio: I wish I knew this region. There's probably a path along the bank.

Miriamne: Yes. Shadow went that way.

Mio: That's true, too. So here I am, a young man on a wet night, and blind in my weather eye. Stay and talk to me.

Miriamne: If it happens—it's my fault.

Mio: Not at all, sweet. You warned me to keep away. But I would have it. Now I have to find a way out. It's like a chess game. If you think long enough there's always a way out.—For one or the other.—I wonder why white always

wins and black always loses in the problems. White to move
and mate in three moves. But what if white were to lose—
ah, what then? Why, in that case, obviously black would
be white and white would be black.—As it often is.—As we
often are.—Might makes white. Losers turn black. Do you
think I'd have time to draw a gun?

MIRIAMNE: No.

MIO: I'm a fair shot. Also I'm fair game.

[*The door of the tenement opens and* GARTH *comes out
to look about quickly. Seeing only* MIO *and* MIRIAMNE *he goes
in and comes out again almost immediately carrying one end
of a door on which a body lies covered with a cloth. The* HOBO
*carries the other end. They go out to the right with their
burden.*]

This is the burial of Shadow, then;
feet first he dips, and leaves the haunts of men.
Let us make mourn for Shadow, wetly lying,
in elegiac stanzas and sweet crying.
Be gentle with him, little cold waves and fishes;
nibble him not, respect his skin and tissues—

MIRIAMNE: Must you say such things?

MIO: My dear, some requiem is fitting over the dead, even
for Shadow. But the last rhyme was bad.
Whittle him not, respect his dying wishes.
That's better. And then to conclude:
His aromatic virtues, slowly rising
will circumnamb the isle, beyond disguising.
He clung to life beyond the wont of men.
Time and his silence drink us all. Amen.
How I hate these identicals. The French allow them, but
the French have no principles anyway. You know, Miri-
amne, there's really nothing mysterious about human life.
It's purely mechanical, like an electric appliance. Stop the
engine that runs the generator and the current's broken.
When we think the brain gives off a small electric dis-
charge—quite measurable, and constant within limits. But
that's not what makes your hair stand up when frightened.

MIRIAMNE: I think it's a mystery.

MIO: Human life? We'll have to wear veils if we're to keep
it a mystery much longer. Now if Shadow and I were made
up into sausages we'd probably make very good sausages.

MIRIAMNE: Don't—

MIO: I'm sorry. I speak from a high place, far off, long ago,
looking down. The cortège returns.

[GARTH *and the* HOBO *return, carrying the door, the
cloth lying loosely over it.*]

I hope you placed an obol in his mouth to pay the ferry-
man? Even among the Greeks a little money was prerequisite to Elysium.

[GARTH *and the* HOBO *go inside, silent.*]

No? It's grim to think of Shadow lingering among lesser
shades on the hither side. For lack of a small gratuity.

[ESDRAS *comes out the open door and closes it behind
him.*]

ESDRAS: You must wait here, Mio, or go inside. I know
you don't trust me, and I haven't earned your trust.
You're young enough to seek truth—
and there is no truth;
and I know that—
but I shall call the police and see that you
get safely off.

MIO: It's a little late for that.

ESDRAS: I shall try.

MIO: And your terms? For I daresay you make terms?

ESDRAS: No.

MIO: Then let me remind you what will happen.
The police will ask some questions.
When they're answered
they'll ask more, and before they're done with it
your son will be implicated.

ESDRAS: Must he be?

MIO: I shall not keep quiet.

[*A pause.*]

ESDRAS: Still, I'll go.

MIO: I don't ask help, remember. I make no truce.
He's not on my conscience, and I'm not on yours.
ESDRAS: But you
could make it easier, so easily.
He's my only son. Let him live.
MIO: His chance of survival's
better than mine, I'd say.
ESDRAS: I'll go.
MIO: I don't urge it.
ESDRAS: No. I put my son's life in your hands.
When you're gone,
that may come to your mind.
MIO: Don't count on it.
ESDRAS: Oh,
I count on nothing.
[*He turns to go.* MIRIAMNE *runs over to him and silently kisses his hands.*]
Not mine, not mine, my daughter!
They're guilty hands.
[*He goes out left.* GARTH's *violin is heard within.*]
MIO: There was a war in heaven
once, all the angels on one side, and all
the devils on the other, and since that time
disputes have raged among the learned, concerning
whether the demons won, or the angels. Maybe
the angels won, after all.
MIRIAMNE: And again, perhaps
there are no demons or angels.
MIO: Oh, there are none.
But I could love your father.
MIRIAMNE: I love him. You see,
He's afraid because he's old. The less one has
to lose the more he's afraid.
MIO: Suppose one had
only a short stub end of life, or held
a flashlight with the batteries run down
till the bulb was dim, and knew that he could live

while the glow lasted. Or suppose one knew
that while he stood in a little shelter of time
under a bridgehead, say, he could live, and then,
from then on, nothing. Then to lie and turn
with the earth and sun, and regard them not in the least
when the bulb was extinguished or he stepped beyond
his circle into the cold? How would he live
that last dim quarter-hour, before he went,
minus all recollection, to grow in grass between cobble-
stones?

MIRIAMNE: Let me put my arms round you, Mio.
Then if anything comes, it's for me, too.
[*She puts both arms round him.*]

MIO: Only suppose
this circle's charmed! To be safe until he steps
from this lighted space into dark! Time pauses here
and high eternity grows in one quarter-hour
in which to live.

MIRIAMNE: Let me see if anyone's there—
there in the shadows.
[*She looks toward the right.*]

MIO: It might blast our eternity—
blow it to bits. No, don't go. This is forever,
here where we stand. And I ask you, Miriamne,
how does one spend a forever?

MIRIAMNE: You're frightened?

MIO: Yes.
So much that time stands still.

MIRIAMNE: Why didn't I speak—
tell them—when the officers were here? I failed you
in that one moment!

MIO: His life for mine? Oh, no.
I wouldn't want it, and you couldn't give it.
And if I should go on living we're cut apart
by that brother of yours.

MIRIAMNE: Are we?

MIO: Well, think about it.

A body lies between us, buried in quicklime.
Your allegiance is on the other side of that grave
and not to me.
MIRIAMNE: No, Mio! Mio, I love you!
MIO: I love you, too, but in case my life went on
beyond that barrier of dark—then Garth
would run his risk of dying.
MIRIAMNE: He's punished, Mio.
His life's been torment to him. Let him go,
for my sake, Mio.
MIO: I wish I could. I wish
I'd never seen him—or you. I've steeped too long
in this thing. It's in my teeth and bones. I can't
let go or forget. And I'll not add my lie
to the lies that cumber his ground. We live our days
in a storm of lies that drifts the truth too deep
for a path or shovel; but I've set my foot on a truth
for once, and I'll trail it down!
   [*A silence.* MIRIAMNE *looks out to the right.*]
MIRIAMNE: There's someone there—
I heard—
   [CARR *comes in from the right.*]
MIO: It's Carr.
CARR: That's right. No doubt about it.
Excuse me.
MIO: Glad to see you. This is Miriamne.
Carr's a friend of mine.
CARR: You're better employed
than when I saw you last.
MIO: Bow to the gentleman,
Miriamne. That's meant for you.
MIRIAMNE: Thank you, I'm sure.
Should I leave you, Mio? You want to talk?
MIO: Oh, no,
we've done our talking.
MIRIAMNE: But—
CARR: I'm the one's out of place—

I wandered back because I got worried about you,
that's the truth.—Oh—those two fellows with the hats
down this way, you know, the ones that ran
after we heard the shooting—they're back again,
lingering or malingering down the bank,
revisiting the crime, I guess. They may mean well.

MIO: I'll try to avoid them.

CARR: I didn't care
for the way they looked at me.—No luck, I suppose,
with that case history? The investigation
you had on hand?

MIO: I can't say. By the way,
the stiff that fell in the water and we saw swirling
down the eddy, he came trudging up, later on,
long enough to tell his name. His name was Shadow,
but he's back in the water now. It's all in an evening.
These things happen here.

CARR: Good God!

MIO: I know.
I wouldn't believe it if you told it.

CARR: But—
the man was alive?

MIO: Oh, not for long! He's dunked
for good this time. That's all that's happened.

CARR: Well,
if you don't need me—

MIRIAMNE: You had a message to send—
have you forgotten—?

MIO: I?—Yes, I had a message—
but I won't send it—not now.

MIRIAMNE: Then I will—!

MIO: No.
Let it go the way it is! It's all arranged
another way. You've been a good scout, Carr,
the best I ever knew on the road.

CARR: That sounds
like making your will.

MIO: Not yet, but when I do
   I've thought of something to leave you. It's the view
   of Mt. Rainier from the Seattle jail,
   snow over cloud. And the rusty chain in my pocket
   from a pair of handcuffs my father wore. That's all
   the worldly goods I'm seized of.
CARR: Look, Mio—hell—
   if you're in trouble—
MIO: I'm not. Not at all. I have
   a genius that attends me where I go,
   and guards me now. I'm fine.
CARR: Well, that's good news.
   He'll have his work cut out.
MIO: Oh, he's a genius.
CARR: I'll see you then.
   I'll be at the Grand Street place. I'm lucky tonight,
   and I can pay. I could even pay for two.
MIO: Thanks, I may take you up.
CARR: Good night.
MIO: Right, Carr.
CARR [*to* MIRIAMNE]: Good night.
MIRIAMNE [*after a pause*]: Good night.
      [CARR *goes out to the left.*]
   Why did you do that? He's your genius, Mio,
   and you let him go.
MIO: I couldn't help it.
MIRIAMNE: Call him.
   Run after him and call him!
MIO: I tried to say it
   and it strangled in my throat. I might have known
   you'd win in the end.
MIRIAMNE: Is it for me?
MIO: For you?
   It stuck in my throat, that's all I know.
MIRIAMNE: Oh, Mio,
   I never asked for that! I only hoped
   Garth could go clear.

MIO: Well, now he will.

MIRIAMNE: But you—
  It was your chance!

MIO: I've lost
  my taste for revenge if it falls on you. Oh, God,
  deliver me from the body of this death
  I've dragged behind me all these years! Miriamne!
  Miriamne!

MIRIAMNE: Yes!

MIO: Miriamne, if you love me
  teach me a treason to what I am, and have been,
  till I learn to live like a man! I think I'm waking
  from a long trauma of hate and fear and death
  that's hemmed me from my birth—and glimpse a life
  to be lived in hope—but it's young in me yet, I can't
  get free, or forgive! But teach me how to live
  and forget to hate!

MIRIAMNE: He would have forgiven.

MIO: He?

MIRIAMNE: Your father.
  [*A pause.*]

MIO: Yes.
  [*Another pause.*]
  You'll think it strange, but I've never
  remembered that.

MIRIAMNE: How can I help you?

MIO: You have.

MIRIAMNE: If I were a little older—if I knew
  the things to say! I can only put out my hands
  and give you back the faith you bring to me
  by being what you are. Because to me
  you are all hope and beauty and brightness drawn
  across what's black and mean!

MIO: He'd have forgiven—
  Then there's no more to say—I've groped long enough
  through this everglades of old revenges—here
  the road ends.—Miriamne. Miriamne.

the iron I wore so long—it's eaten through
and fallen from me. Let me have your arms.
They'll say we're children—Well—the world's made up
of children.
MIRIAMNE: Yes.
MIO: But it's too late for me.
MIRIAMNE: No.
[*She goes into his arms, and they kiss for the first time.*]
Then we'll meet again?
MIO: Yes.
MIRIAMNE: Where?
MIO: I'll write—
or send Carr to you.
MIRIAMNE: You won't forget?
MIO: Forget?
Whatever streets I walk, you'll walk them, too,
from now on, and whatever roof or stars
I have to house me, you shall share my roof
and stars and morning, I shall not forget.
MIRIAMNE: God keep you!
MIO: And keep you. And this to remember!
If I should die, Miriamne, this half-hour
is our eternity. I came here seeking
light in darkness, running from the dawn,
and stumbled on a morning.
[*One of the* YOUNG MEN IN SERGE *strolls in casually from
the right, looks up and down without expression, then, seem-
ingly having forgotten something, retraces his steps and goes
out.* ESDRAS *comes in slowly from the left. He has lost his hat,
and his face is bleeding from a slight cut on the temple. He
stands abjectly near the tenement.*]
MIRIAMNE: Father—what is it?
[*She goes towards* ESDRAS.]
ESDRAS: Let me alone.
[*He goes nearer to* MIO.]
He wouldn't let me pass.
The street's so icy up along the bridge

I had to crawl on my knees—he kicked me back
three times—and then he held me there—I swear
what I could do I did! I swear to you
I'd save you if I could.
MIO: What makes you think
that I need saving?
ESDRAS: Child, save yourself if you can!
He's waiting for you.
MIO: Well, we knew that before.
ESDRAS: He won't wait much longer. He'll come here—
he told me so. Those damned six months of his—
he wants them all—and you're to die—you'd spread
his guilt—I had to listen to it—
MIO: Wait—
     [*He walks forward and looks casually to the right, then
returns.*]
There must be some way up through the house and out
across the roof—
ESDRAS: He's watching that. But come in—
and let me look.—
MIO: I'll stay here, thanks. Once in
and I'm a rat in a deadfall—I'll stay here—
look for me if you don't mind.
ESDRAS: Then watch for me—
I'll be on the roof—
     [*He goes in hurriedly.*]
MIO [*looking up*]: Now all you silent powers
that make the sleet and dark, and never yet
have spoken, give us a sign, let the throw be ours
this once, on this longest night, when the winter sets
his foot on the threshold leading up to spring
and enters with remembered cold—let fall
some mercy with the rain. We are two lovers
here in your night, and we wish to live.
MIRIAMNE: Oh, Mio—
if you pray that way, nothing good will come!
You're bitter, Mio.

Mio: How many floors has this building?

Miriamne: Five or six. It's not as high as the bridge.

Mio: No, I thought not. How many pomegranate seeds
did you eat, Persephone?

Miriamne: Oh, darling, darling,
if you die, don't die alone.

Mio: I'm afraid I'm damned
to hell, and you're not damned at all. Good God,
how long he takes to climb!

Miriamne: The stairs are steep.

[*A slight pause.*]

Mio: I'll follow him.

Miriamne: He's there—at the window—now.
He waves you to go back, not to go in.
Mio, see, that path between the rocks—
they're not watching that—they're out at the river—
I can see them there—they can't watch both—
it leads to a street above.

Mio: I'll try it, then.
Kiss me. You'll hear. But if you never hear—
then I'm the king of hell, Persephone,
and I'll expect you.

Miriamne: Oh, lover, keep safe.

Mio: Good-bye.

[*He slips out quickly between the rocks. There is a quick
machine gun rat-tat. The violin stops.* Miriamne *runs toward
the path.* Mio *comes back slowly, a hand pressed under his
heart.*]
It seems you were mistaken.

Miriamne: Oh, God, forgive me!

[*She puts an arm round him. He sinks to his knees.*]
Where is it, Mio? Let me help you in! Quick, quick,
let me help you!

Mio: I hadn't thought to choose—this—ground—
but it will do.

[*He slips down.*]

Miriamne: Oh, God, forgive me!

MIO: Yes?
>The king of hell was not forgiven then,
>Dis is his name, and Hades is his home—
>and he goes alone—

MIRIAMNE: Why does he bleed so? Mio, if you go
>I shall go with you.

MIO: It's better to stay alive.
>I wanted to stay alive—because of you—
>I leave you that—and what he said to me dying:
>I love you, and will love you after I die.
>Tomorrow, I shall still love you, as I've loved
>the stars I'll never see, and all the mornings
>that might have been yours and mine. Oh, Miriamne,
>you taught me this.

MIRIAMNE: If only I'd never seen you
>then you could live—

MIO: That's blasphemy—Oh, God,
>there might have been some easier way of it.
>You didn't want me to die, did you, Miriamne—?
>You didn't send me away—?

MIRIAMNE: Oh, never, never—

MIO: Forgive me—kiss me—I've got blood on your lips—
>I'm sorry—it doesn't matter—I'm sorry—
>>[ESDRAS *and* GARTH *come out.*]

MIRIAMNE: Mio—
>I'd have gone to die myself—you must hear this, Mio,
>I'd have died to help you—you must listen, sweet,
>you must hear it—
>>[*She rises.*]
>I can die, too, see! You! There!
>You in the shadows!—You kill him to silence him!
>>[*She walks toward the path.*]
>But I'm not silenced! All that he knew I know,
>and I'll tell it tonight; Tonight—
>tell it and scream it
>through all the streets—that Trock's a murderer
>and he hired you for this murder!

Your work's not done—
and you won't live long! Do you hear?
You're murderers, and I know who you are!
   [*The machine gun speaks again. She sinks to her knees.*
GARTH *runs to her.*]
GARTH: You little fool!
   [*He tries to lift her.*]
MIRIAMNE: Don't touch me!
   [*She crawls toward* MIO.]
Look, Mio! They kill me, too. Oh, you can believe me
now, Mio. You can believe I wouldn't hurt you,
because I'm dying! Why doesn't he answer me?
Oh, now he'll never know!
   [*She sinks down, her hand over her mouth, choking.*
GARTH *kneels beside her, then rises, shuddering. The* HOBO
comes out. LUCIA *and* PINY *look out.*]
ESDRAS: It lacked only this.
GARTH: Yes.
   [ESDRAS *bends over* MIRIAMNE, *then rises slowly.*]
Why was the bastard born? Why did he come here?
ESDRAS: Miriamne—Miriamne—yes, and Mio,
one breath shall call you now—forgive us both—
forgive the ancient evil of the earth
that brought you here—
GARTH: Why must she be a fool?
ESDRAS: Well, they were wiser than you and I. To die
when you are young and untouched, that's beggary
to a miser of years, but the devils locked in synod
shake and are daunted when men set their lives
at hazard for the heart's love, and lose. And these,
who were yet children, will weigh more than all
a city's elders when the experiment
is reckoned up in the end. Oh, Miriamne,
and Mio—Mio, my son—know this where you lie,
this is the glory of earth-born men and women,
not to cringe, never to yield, but standing,
take defeat implacable and defiant,

die unsubmitting. I wish that I'd died so,
long ago; before you're old you'll wish
that you had died as they have. On this star,
in this hard star-adventure, knowing not
what the fires mean to right and left, nor whether
a meaning was intended or presumed,
man can stand up, and look out blind, and say:
in all these turning lights I find no clue,
only a masterless night, and in my blood
no certain answer, yet is my mind my own,
yet is my heart a cry toward something dim
in distance, which is higher than I am
and makes me emperor of the endless dark
even in seeking! What odds and ends of life
men may live otherwise, let them live, and then
go out, as I shall go, and you. Our part
is only to bury them. Come, take her up.
They must not lie here.

    [LUCIA *and* PINY *come near to help.* ESDRAS *and* GARTH
stoop to carry MARIAMNE.]

MAXWELL ANDERSON

With more than twenty-five plays to his credit, the Pulitzer Prize and two Drama Critics' Awards, Maxwell Anderson is one of America's first-ranking playwrights and enjoys an international reputation. He stands today as one who has sought to express in his work the bases of real value in the drama as an art form.

Born on December 15, 1888, in Atlantic, Pennsylvania, the son of a Baptist minister, Anderson moved about with his family until they settled in North Dakota. He was graduated at the University of North Dakota in 1911, and received his master's degree at Leland Stanford in 1914. He taught school for a while but, wishing to write, he turned to journalism and worked successively for papers in Grand Forks, San Francisco, and New York, to which he came in 1918. Until 1924 he contributed to the *New Republic,* the *New York Evening Globe* and the *New York World.*

In the meantime he turned to playwriting. Following his own ideas rather than those in current fashion, he wrote in verse and mixed comedy with tragedy. His first play, *White Desert,* was not a popular success though it was favorably reviewed.

Collaborating with Laurence Stallings, Anderson found his first stage successs with *What Price Glory?*—a war play whose realism, coming after the romantic and sentimental treatments of World War I, made it the hit of the season. Today, after World War II, it still reads well.

Anderson continued writing both alone and in collaboration but did not have another real success until 1930, with the production of *Elizabeth the Queen,* a historical drama in verse in which the Lunts starred. In 1933 he won the Pulitzer Prize for *Both Your Houses,* which attacked malpractices in our national political life.

Anderson's outstanding achievement in the theater, however, is *Winterset,* for which he won the Drama Critics' Award in 1935. Here he attempts the feat of writing a tragedy in verse on a contemporary theme. Few American plays have attracted so much critical commentary. *Winterset* has fully established Anderson's stature as a dramatist of serious artistic integrity.

In 1937, he won the Drama Critics' Award the second time for *High Tor,* a whimsically ironic comedy with serious touches. He has also written short dramas for the radio, and a critical work, *The Essence of Tragedy* (1939). His recent plays have fallen below his former level, though there are fine things in *The Eve of St. Mark* and *Joan of Lorraine.* He continues to live in New York, is a hard and steady worker, and has made his place through originality and sincere devotion to the drama.

His plays and the dates of their first production:

The White Desert, October 18, 1923.

What Price Glory?, September 3, 1924. (With Laurence Stallings.)

Outside Looking In, September 7, 1925.

First Flight, September 17, 1925. (With Laurence Stallings.)

The Buccaneer, October 2, 1925. (With Laurence Stallings.)

Saturday's Children, January 26, 1927.

Gods of the Lightning, October 24, 1928. (With Harold Hickerson.)

Gypsy, January 14, 1929.

Elizabeth the Queen, November 3, 1930.

Night over Taos, March 9, 1932.

Both Your Houses, March 6, 1933.

Mary of Scotland, November 27, 1933.

Valley Forge, December 10, 1934.

Winterset, September 25, 1935.

The Wingless Victory, December 23, 1936.

High Tor, January 9, 1937.

The Masque of Kings, February 8, 1937.

The Star-Wagon, September 29, 1937.

Knickerbocker Holiday, October 19, 1938.

Key Largo, November 27, 1939.

Journey to Jerusalem, October 5, 1940.

Candle in the Wind, October 22, 1941.

Storm Operation, January 11, 1944.

Truckline Café, February 27, 1946.

Joan of Lorraine, November 18, 1946.

CRITICAL COMMENTS

WINTERSET

There are at least two reasons why I believe "Winterset" a play of more than usual significance.

To begin with, it is verse drama of a very special kind. I do not mean to assume that a play in verse, even a commercially successful play in verse, would necessarily be noteworthy merely because it was at once "poetic" and successful. Mr. Anderson himself has written "poetic drama" before now, and despite the popularity of his "Mary of Scotland" I could never feel that that play, as a play, was more than respectable. Indeed, the very fact that its author, who had collaborated in "What Price Glory?" and independently written at least one excellent comedy, turned to a historical subject when he wished to write a play in verse was distinctly dispiriting. It seemed to confirm the almost universal if tacit assumption that only the past can be conceived in poetic terms, that the poetic drama has ceased to exist, not because we have left poetry, but because poetry has left us— because modern life and our conception of it are radically unsuited to that degree of elevation which makes verse a natural medium of sincere expression. To a considerable degree at least, "Mary of Scotland" partook of the nature of a pastiche, and a pastiche is not merely the opposite of a work of art. It also usually amounts to a confession on the part of its maker that he was compelled to use fragments of other men's art because he found it impossible to transmute his experience into art of his own creation.

"Winterset," on the other hand, is a contemporary theme treated in connection with contemporary life. The important fact is not that its language is metered. Furthermore, when one stresses the fact that the scene is contemporary, one does not, of course, mean to assume that only in connection with contemporary events can anything significant be said. But verse is an outward sign that the author proposes to reach a certain degree of elevation. And the choice of the contemporary scene is an outward sign that he proposes to attack in the directest possible manner the problem of demonstrating that the life of today affords themes inviting treatment in the poetic form. The measure of his success is just the fact that the impressiveness of the drama is nowhere diminished by any sense on the spectator's part that the matter and manner are radically incongruous.

"Winterset" exhibits most of the usual technical characteristics of the poetic drama. Its personages not only speak verse but are endowed with that supernormal power of expression which sacrifices realistic representation to completeness of communication. The meanest of them takes on a dignity which belongs to him not as a person but as a necessary participant in an action the sum total of which is grand in its implications. The most important are capable of philosophic reflections which, as individuals, they would never be competent to formulate but which are permitted them by virtue of a convention endowing the chief figures in poetic drama with the power to understand the significance of their own character and actions. Yet to anyone not unduly disturbed by the mere unfamiliarity of such a play the fact that twentieth-century persons should speak in the form and manner of poetry soon becomes as readily acceptable as the fact that a twelfth-century Danish prince or a fourteen-year-old Italian girl of the Renaissance should do so. To say all this is not to say that "Winterset" is perfect or everywhere completely realized. For example, the deaths which constitute the catastrophe seem annoyingly fortuitous. But it does indicate why it demonstrates more successfully than any other American play that the poetic drama is not dead beyond hope of resurrection.

The second great virtue of "Winterset" lies in its illustration of the manner in which a "socially significant" theme may be treated in genuinely dramatic and genuinely poetic fashion. Obviously the situation was suggested by the Sacco-Vanzetti trial, but Mr. Anderson has realized that the attempt to use such a subject in imaginative literature is justifiable only if imaginative literature can produce an effect or reach a depth of understanding beyond the scope of the essay, the speech, or the polemic. There is no excuse for saying in the dramatic form what can be said in a simpler manner, and Mr. Anderson has justified himself, first, by his brilliant generalization of the subject and, secondly, by the success with which he has explored its deepest implications—the question of the nature of justice and the question of the effect upon various human beings of their success or failure in the search for it. By dealing not with the event itself but with the reverberations of that event in after years, he sacrificed journalistic immediacy but gained to an immeasurable degree in emotional and philosophic richness.

[Joseph Wood Krutch, " 'Winterset'—Critics' Prize-Winner," in *The Nation*, 142 (April 15, 1936), pp. 484-5. Reprinted by permission.]

WINTERSET

Mr. Maxwell Anderson in "Winterset" fights one of the chief causes that the American theatre needs to fight for. The increasing audiences for the play are, therefore, a matter for great encouragement. I have already said, in a previous review, that "Winterset" is not only the most important play of this season so far; it is, also, the most notable effort in the poetic-dramatic medium that, up to now, we have had in the American theatre.

In the introduction Mr. Anderson sets forth some of his points of view and purposes in the choice of the poetic medium for this drama. "I have," he says, "a strong and chronic hope that the theatre of this country will outgrow the phase of journalistic social comment and reach occasionally into the upper air of poetic tragedy. I believe with Goethe that dramatic poetry is man's greatest achievement on this earth so far, and I believe with the early Bernard Shaw that the theatre is essentially a cathedral of the spirit, devoted to the exaltation of men...." The best prose in the world, he says, is inferior on the stage to the best poetry. Though it is the fashion to say that poetry is a matter of content and emotion, not of form, this argument is said in an age of prose by prose writers who have not studied the effect of form on content. The majority of present-day playgoers have never seen any other kind of play except that in which the method rests on realism. From this has proceeded the cult of understatement, hence the realistic drama in which the climax is reached in an eloquent gesture or a moment of meaningful silence. This feeling is so emphatic that one is doubtful of being able to explain to this majority that verse was once the accepted convention on the stage, as prose is now. It is not easy to explain to them that prose fought its way into the playbooks with difficulty at the beginning of the scientific era in which we live and will hold its place there only so long as men make a religion of fact and believe that information, conveyed in statistical language, can make them free.

The poet-dramatist in this case is certain that our existing condition in the theatre, for all its illusion of permanence, will change. An age of reason will be followed once more, as has happened in the past, by an age of faith in things unseen. "What faith men will then have, when they have lost their certainty of salvation through laboratory work, I don't know, having myself only a faith that men will have a faith." He believes that many in the theatre audiences have anticipated his conclusions by one of those intuitional short-cuts that confound the devotees of pure reason, and that they are not only ready but impatient for plays that will undertake again the consideration of man's place and destiny in prophetic rather than prosaic terms. He believes that the theatre, more than any other art, "has the power to weld and determine what the race dreams into what the race will become." All of which, as he says, may sound rather far-fetched in the face of our present Broadway, and Broadway may laugh at it unconscionably, but Broadway is itself as transient as the real-estate values under its feet. Those who fail to outlive the street in which they work will fail because they have accepted its valuations and measured their product by these valuations.

Reading "Winterset" after seeing it so well acted on the stage— especially by Mr. Richard Bennett and Mr. Burgess Meredith— not to speak of the two superlative settings, is an experience. Certainly the second act, with all its conflicting motifs and vibrations, excellent in the printed form just as they were on the stage, is one of the best acts in the range of modern English drama. In the printed play it is also interesting to see that the dramatist was not able quite to slow down the last act to the lyric interlude he wanted it to be. Obviously, the melodrama—an honorable form, or quality, in drama, certainly—hung, as it had to do, on the tensity of waiting for a death. If, here, we had instead a short scene, the problem of the poetic medium would not have been noticed. A long scene, here, to be successful, must have a complete fusion of the dramatic content and the poetic form employed to contain and convey it. The dramatist's purpose in this part of the play was to complete the psychology of his young hero; and so a double danger appeared—one danger in the duration of the analysis, and proceeding from that, another in the poetic medium itself. In these passages a good deal of the poetic medium is not *per se* wholly successful. It needs condensation at times, and in the metrical form there is at times a soft tendency, not unfamiliar to readers of English poetry thirty years ago, a kind of fluting along. Severe tests applied to these passages as spoken in rehearsals might have helped.

Even in the light of the less successful passages, however, Mr. Anderson appears plausible enough in his contention that verse has value for the theatre in that it is almost always written under more emotional stress than prose. The writing of verse generates more emotion in the writer, and this heightening is likely to come over to the audience—a point which may be true even though it be often evident in verse passages that are forced and, as poetry, bad. The difference, however, between poetry in general and poetry that is strictly intended for the stage, is something to be thought about, and that Mr. Anderson does not discuss. For example, there are many passages in Seneca's dramas that are obviously intended to accomplish, in the closet and without benefit of stage production, a dramatic result similar to what these passages, in a less intensified and decorated expression, would have given when performed on the stage. The descendants of these Senecan excitations are plentiful enough among the Elizabethans, who both wrote and acted them out. We may, finally, consider the general relation of poetry to its being spoken. This brings us back again to the theatre. Mr. T. S. Eliot's conviction is that the ideal medium for poetry is the theatre—"for the simplest auditors there is the plot, for the more thoughtful the character and conflict of character, for the more literary the words and phrasing, for the more musically sensitive the rhythm, and for the auditors of greater sensitiveness and understanding a meaning which reveals itself gradually."

[Stark Young, "Preface to Medium," in *The New Republic*, 85 (Jan. 8, 1936) p. 257. Reprinted by permission.]

LILLIAN HELLMAN

―――

WATCH ON THE RHINE

CHARACTERS

ANISE

JOSEPH

FANNY FARRELLY

DAVID FARRELLY

MARTHE DE BRANCOVIS

TECK DE BRANCOVIS

SARA MÜLLER

JOSHUA MÜLLER

BODO MÜLLER

BABETTE MÜLLER

KURT MÜLLER

SCENE

The scene of the play is the living room of the Farrelly country house, about twenty miles from Washington.

The time is late spring, 1940.

ACT ONE

Early on a Wednesday morning.

ACT TWO

Ten days later.

ACT THREE

A half hour later.

WATCH ON THE RHINE

ACT ONE

SCENE—*The living room of the Farrelly house, about twenty miles from Washington, D. C., on a warm spring morning.*

Center stage are large French doors leading to an elevated open terrace. On the terrace are chairs, tables, a large table for dining. Some of this furniture we can see; most of it is on the left side of the terrace, beyond our sight. Left stage is an arched entrance, leading to the oval reception hall. We can see the main staircase as it goes off to the back of the hall. Right stage is a door leading to a library. The Farrelly house was built in the early nineteenth century. It has space, simplicity, style. The living room is large. Up stage right is a piano; down stage left, a couch; down stage right, a couch and chairs; up stage a few smaller chairs. Four or five generations have furnished this room and they have all been people of taste. There are no styles, no periods; the room has never been refurnished. Each careless aristocrat has thrown into the room what he or she liked as a child, what he or she brought home when grown up. Therefore the furniture is of many periods: the desk is English, the couch is Victorian, some of the pictures are modern, some of the ornaments French. The room has too many things in it: vases, clocks, miniatures, boxes, china animals. On the right wall is a large portrait of a big kind-faced man in an evening suit of 1900. On another wall is a large, very ugly landscape. The room is crowded. But it is cool and clean and its fabrics and woods are in soft colors.

*At Rise—*ANISE, *a thin Frenchwoman of about sixty, in a dark housekeeper's dress, is standing at a table sorting mail. She takes the mail from a small basket, holds each letter to the light, reads each postal card, then places them in piles. On the terrace,* JOSEPH, *a tall middle-aged Negro butler, wheels a breakfast wagon. As he appears,* FANNY FARRELLY *comes in from the hall.*

She is a handsome woman of about sixty-three. She has on a fancy, good-looking dressing-gown.

   Left and right are the audience's left and right.

FANNY [*stops to watch* ANISE. *Sees* JOSEPH *moving about on terrace. Calls*]: Joseph! [*To* ANISE.] Morning.

ANISE [*continues examining mail*]: Good morning, Madame.

JOSEPH [*comes to terrace door*]: Yes'm?

FANNY: Everybody down?

JOSEPH: No'm. Nobody. I'll get your tea. [*He returns to breakfast wagon on terrace.*]

FANNY: Mr. David isn't down yet? But he knows he is to meet the train.

JOSEPH [*comes in from the terrace with the cup of tea*]: He's got plenty of time, Miss Fanny. The train ain't in till noon.

FANNY: Breakfast is at nine o'clock in this house and will be until the day after I die. Ring the bell.

JOSEPH: It ain't nine yet, Miss Fanny. It's eight-thirty.

FANNY: Well, put the clocks up to nine and ring the bell.

JOSEPH: Mr. David told me not to ring it any more. He says it's got too mean a ring, that bell. It disturbs folks.

FANNY: That's what it was put there for. I like to disturb folks.

JOSEPH: Yes'm.

FANNY: You slept well, Anise. You were asleep before I could dismantle myself.

ANISE: I woke several times during the night.

FANNY: Did you? Then you were careful not to stop snoring. We must finally get around to rearranging your room. [ANISE *hands her three or four letters.*] Even when you don't snore, it irritates me. [FANNY *opens a letter, begins to read it. After a minute:*] What time is it?

ANISE: It is about eight-thirty. Joseph just told you.

FANNY: I didn't hear him. I'm nervous. Naturally. My mail looks dull. [*Reading the letter.*] Jenny always tells you a piece of gossip three times, as if it grew fresher with the telling. Did you put flowers in their rooms?

ANISE: Certainly.

FANNY: David ought to get to the station by eleven-thirty.

ANISE [*patiently*]: The train does not draw in until ten minutes past noon.

FANNY: But it might come in early. It's been known.

ANISE: Never. Not in the Union Station in Washington, the District of Columbia.

FANNY [*irritably*]: But it might. It might. Don't argue with me about everything. What time is it?

ANISE: It's now twenty-seven minutes before nine. It will be impossible to continue telling you the time every three minutes from now until Miss Sara arrives. I think you are having a nervous breakdown. Compose yourself.

FANNY: It's been twenty years. Any mother would be nervous. If your daughter were coming home and you hadn't seen her, and a husband, *and* grandchildren—

ANISE: I do not say that it is wrong to be nervous. I, too, am nervous. I say only that you are.

FANNY: Very well. I heard you. *I* say that I am. [*She goes back to reading her letter. Looks up.*] Jenny's still in California. She's lost her lavallière again. Birdie Chase's daughter is still faire l'amouring with that actor. Tawdry, Jenny says it is. An actor. Fashions in sin change. In my day, it was Englishmen. I don't understand infidelity. If you love a man, then why? If you don't love him, then why stay with him? [*Without turning, she points over her head to Joshua Farrelly's portrait.*] Thank God, I was in love. I thought about Joshua last night. Three grandchildren. He would have liked that. I hope I will. [*Points to other letters.*] Anything in anybody else's mail?

ANISE: Advertisements for Mr. David and legal things. For our Count and Countess, there is nothing but what seems an invitation to a lower-class embassy tea and letters asking for bills to get paid.

FANNY: That's every morning. [*Thoughtfully.*] In the six

weeks the Balkan nobility have been with us, they seem to have run up a great many bills.

ANISE: Yes. *I* told you that. Then there was a night-letter for Mr. David.

[*A very loud, very unpleasant bell begins to ring.*]

FANNY [*through the noise*]: Really? From whom?

ANISE: From her. I took it on the telephone, and—

[*Bell drowns out her voice.*]

FANNY: Who is "her?" [*Bell becomes very loud.*] Go tell him to stop that noise—

ANISE [*goes toward terrace, calling*]: Joseph! Stop that bell. Miss Fanny says to stop it.

JOSEPH [*calls*]: Miss Fanny said to start it.

FANNY [*shouts out to him*]: I didn't tell you to hang yourself with it.

JOSEPH [*appears on terrace*]: I ain't hung. Your breakfast is ready. [*Disappears.*]

FANNY [*to* ANISE]: Who is "her"?

ANISE: That Carter woman from Lansing, Michigan.

FANNY: Oh, my. Is she back in Washington again? What did the telegram say?

ANISE: It said the long sickness of her dear Papa had terminated in full recovery.

FANNY: That's too bad.

ANISE: She was returning, and would Mr. David come for dinner a week from Thursday? "Love," it said, "to you and your charming mother." [*To* FANNY.] That's you. I think Miss Carter from Lansing, Michigan, was unwise in attending the illness of her Papa.

FANNY: I hope so. Why?

ANISE [*shrugs*]: There is much winking of the eyes going on between our Countess and Mr. David.

FANNY [*eagerly*]: I know that. Anything new happen?

ANISE [*too innocently*]: Happen? I don't know what you mean.

FANNY: You know damn well what I mean.

ANISE: *That?* Oh, no, I don't think that.

JOSEPH [*appears in the door*]: The sausage cakes is shrinking.

FANNY [*rises. To* ANISE]: I want everybody down here immediately. Is the car ready? [ANISE *nods.*] Did you order a good dinner? [*Shrieks.*] David! Oh.

[DAVID FARRELLY, *a pleasant-looking man of thirty-nine, comes in from the entrance hall, almost bumps into* FANNY.]

DAVID: Good morning, everybody.

ANISE [*to* FANNY]: Everything is excellent. You have been asking the same questions for a week. You have made the kitchen very nervous.

DAVID [*to* JOSEPH]: Why did you ring that air-raid alarm again?

JOSEPH: Ain't me, Mr. David. I don't like no noise. Miss Fanny told me.

FANNY: Good morning, David.

DAVID [*to* JOSEPH]: Tell Fred to leave the car. I'll drive to the station.

JOSEPH [*nods*]: Yes, sir. [*Exits.*]

DAVID [*to* FANNY, *half amused, half annoyed, as he begins to read his mail*]: Mama, I think we'll fix up the chickenhouse for you as a playroom. We'll hang the room with bells and you can go into your second childhood in the proper privacy.

FANNY: I find it very interesting. You sleep soundly, you rise at your usual hour—although your sister, whom you haven't seen in years, is waiting at the station—

DAVID: She is not waiting at the station. [*Laughs.*] The train does not come in until ten minutes past twelve.

FANNY [*airily*]: It's almost that now.

ANISE [*turns to look at her*]: Really, Miss Fanny, contain yourself. It is twenty minutes before nine.

DAVID: And I have *not* slept soundly. And I've been up since six o'clock.

FANNY: The Balkans aren't down yet. Where are they?

DAVID: I don't know.

ANISE: There's nothing in your mail, Mr. David. Only the usual advertisements.

DAVID: And for me, that is all that is ever likely to come— here.

ANISE [*haughtily, as she starts toward hall*]: I cannot, of course, speak for Miss Fanny. *I* have never opened a letter in my life.

DAVID: I know. You don't have to. For you they fly open.

FANNY [*giggles*]: It's true. You're a snooper, Anise. [ANISE *exits.* FANNY *talks as* ANISE *moves out.*] I rather admire it. It shows an interest in life. [*She looks up at Joshua's portrait.*] You know, I've been lying awake most of the night wondering what Papa would have thought about Sara. He'd have been very pleased, wouldn't he? I always find myself wondering what Joshua would have felt.

DAVID: Yes. But maybe it would be just as well if you didn't expect me to be wondering about it, too. I wasn't married to him, Mama. He was just my father.

FANNY: My. You got up on the wrong side of the bed. [*She moves past him. Points to the mail which he is still opening.*] The bills are for our noble guests. Interesting, how many there are every morning. How much longer are they going to be with us?

DAVID [*without looking at her*]: I don't know.

FANNY: It's been six weeks. Now that Sara and her family are coming, even this house might be a little crowded— [*He looks up at her. Quickly.*] Yes. I know I invited them. I felt sorry for Marthe, and Teck rather amused me. He plays good cribbage, and he tells good jokes. But that's not enough for a lifetime guest. If you've been urging her to stay, I wish you'd stop it. They haven't any money; all right, lend them some—

DAVID: I have been urging them to stay?

FANNY: I'm not so old I don't recognize flirting when I see it.

DAVID: But you're old enough not to be silly.

FANNY: I'm not silly. I'm charming.

[MARTHE DE BRANCOVIS, *an attractive woman of thirty-one or thirty-two, enters.*]

MARTHE: Good morning, Fanny. Morning, David.

FANNY: Good morning, Marthe.

DAVID [*warmly*]: Good morning.

MARTHE: Fanny, darling, couldn't you persuade yourself to let me have a tray in bed and some cotton for my ears?

DAVID: Certainly not. My father ate breakfast at nine; and whatever my father did . . .

FANNY [*carefully, to* DAVID]: There was a night-letter for you from that Carter woman in Lansing, Michigan. She is returning and you are to come to dinner next Thursday. [*As she exits on terrace.*] C-A-R-T-E-R. [*Pronounces it carefully.*] Lansing, Michigan.

DAVID [*laughs*]: I know how to spell Carter, but thank you. [FANNY *exits.* DAVID *looks up at* MARTHE.] Do you understand my mother?

MARTHE: Sometimes.

DAVID: Miss Carter was done for your benefit.

MARTHE [*smiles*]: That means she has guessed that I would be jealous. And she has guessed right.

DAVID [*looks at her*]: Jealous?

MARTHE: I know I've no right to be, but I am. And Fanny knows it.

DAVID [*carelessly*]: Don't pay any attention to Mama. She has a sure instinct for the women I like, and she begins to hammer away early. Marthe— [*Goes to decanter on side-table.*] I'm going to have a drink. I haven't had a drink before breakfast since the day I took my bar examination. [*Pours himself a drink, gulps it down.*] What's it going to be like to stand on a station platform and see your sister after all these years? I'm afraid, I guess.

MARTHE: Why?

DAVID: I don't know. Afraid she won't like me— [*Shrugs.*] We were very fond of each other, but it's been a long time.

MARTHE: I remember Sara. Mama brought me one day when your father was stationed in Paris. I was about six and Sara was about fifteen and you were—

DAVID: You were a pretty little girl.

MARTHE: Do you really remember me? You never told me before.

FANNY [*yelling from the terrace*]: David! Come to breakfast.

DAVID [*as if he had not been listening*]: You know, I've never met Sara's husband. Mama did. I think the first day Sara met him, in Munich. Mama didn't like the marriage much in those days—and Sara didn't care, and Mama didn't like Sara not caring. Mama cut up about it, bad.

MARTHE: Why?

DAVID: Probably because they didn't let her arrange it. Why does Mama ever act badly? She doesn't remember ten minutes later.

MARTHE: Wasn't Mr. Müller poor?

DAVID: Oh, Mama wouldn't have minded that. If they'd only come home and let her fix their lives for them— [*Smiles.*] But Sara didn't want it that way.

MARTHE: You'll have a house full of refugees—us and—

DAVID: Are you and Teck refugees? I'm not sure I know what you're refugees from.

MARTHE: From Europe.

DAVID: From what Europe?

MARTHE [*smiles, shrugs*]: I don't know. I don't know myself, really. Just Europe. [*Quickly comes to him.*] Sara will like you. I like you. [*Laughs.*] That doesn't make sense, does it?

[*On her speech,* TECK DE BRANCOVIS *appears in the hall. He is a good-looking man of about forty-five. She stops quickly.*]

TECK [*to* MARTHE *and* DAVID]: Good morning.

[*The bell gives an enormous ring.*]

DAVID [*goes to terrace*]: Good morning, Teck. For years I've been thinking they were coming for Mama with a net.

I'm giving up hope. I may try catching her myself. [*Disappears, calling:*] Mama! Stop that noise.

TECK: I wonder if science has a name for women who enjoy noise? [*Goes to table, picks up his mail.*] Many mistaken people, Marthe, seem to have given you many charge accounts.

MARTHE: The Countess de Brancovis. That still does it. It would be nice to be able to pay bills again—

TECK: Do not act as if I refused to pay them. I did not sleep well last night. I was worried. We have eighty-seven dollars in American Express checks. [*Pleasantly, looking at her.*] That's all we have, Marthe.

MARTHE [*shrugs*]: Maybe something will turn up. It's due.

TECK [*carefully*]: David? [*Then, as she turns to look at him*] The other relatives will arrive this morning?

MARTHE: Yes.

TECK [*points to porch*]: I think Madame Fanny and Mr. David may grow weary of accents and charity guests. Or is the husband of the sister a rich one?

MARTHE: No. He's poor. He had to leave Germany in '33.

TECK: A Jew?

MARTHE: No. I don't think so.

TECK: Why did he have to leave Germany?

MARTHE [*still reading*]: Oh, I don't know, Teck. He's an anti-Nazi.

TECK: A political?

MARTHE: No, I don't think so. He was an engineer. I don't know. I don't know much about him.

TECK: Did you sleep well?

MARTHE: Yes. Why not?

TECK: Money does not worry you?

MARTHE: It worries me very much. But I just lie still now and hope. I'm glad to be here. [*Shrugs.*] Maybe something good will happen. We've come to the end of a road. That's been true for a long time. Things will have to go one way or the other. Maybe they'll go well, for a change.

TECK: I have not come to the end of any road.

MARTHE [*looks at him*]: No? I admire you.

TECK: I'm going into Washington tonight. Phili has a poker game every Wednesday evening. He has arranged for me to join it.

MARTHE [*after a pause*]: Have you been seeing Phili?

TECK: Once or twice. Why not? Phili and I are old friends. He may be useful. I do not want to stay in this country forever.

MARTHE: You can't leave them alone. Your favorite dream, isn't it, Teck? That they will let you play with them again? I don't think they will, and I don't think you should be seeing Phili, or that you should be seen at the Embassy.

TECK [*smiles*]: You have political convictions now?

MARTHE: I don't know what I have. I've never liked Nazis, as you know, and you should have had enough of them. They seem to have had enough of you, God knows. It would be just as well to admit they are smarter than you are and let them alone.

TECK [*looking at her carefully, after a minute*]: That is interesting.

MARTHE: What is interesting?

TECK: I think you are trying to say something to me. What is it?

MARTHE: That you ought not to be at the Embassy, and that it's insane to play cards in a game with Von Seitz with eighty-seven dollars in your pocket. I don't think he'd like your not being able to pay up. Suppose you lose?

TECK: I shall try not to lose.

MARTHE: But if you do lose and can't pay, it will be all over Washington in an hour. [*Points to terrace.*] They'll find out about it, and we'll be out of here when they do.

TECK: I think I want to be out of here. I find that I do not like the picture of you and our host.

MARTHE [*carefully*]: There is no picture, as you put it, to like or dislike.

TECK: Not yet? I am glad to hear that. [*Comes toward her slowly.*] Marthe, you understand that I am not really a fool?

You understand that it is unwise to calculate me that way?

MARTHE [*slowly, as if it were an effort*]: Yes, I understand that. And I understand that I am getting tired. Just plain tired. The whole thing's too much for me. I've always meant to ask you, since you play on so many sides, why we don't come out any better. I've always wanted to ask you how it happened. [*Sharply.*] I'm tired, see? And I just want to sit down. Just to sit down in a chair and stay.

TECK [*carefully*]: Here?

MARTHE: I don't know. Any place—

TECK: You have thus arranged it with David?

MARTHE: I've arranged nothing.

TECK: But you are trying, eh? [*He comes close to her.*] I think not. I would not like that. Do not make any arrangements, Marthe. I may not allow you to carry them through. [*Smiles.*] Come to breakfast now. [*He passes her, disappears on the terrace. She stands still and thoughtful. Then she, too, moves to the terrace, disappears.*]

[JOSEPH *appears on the terrace, carrying a tray toward the unseen breakfast table. The stage is empty. After a minute, there are sounds of footsteps in the hall.* SARA MÜLLER *appears in the doorway, comes toward the middle of the room as if expecting to find somebody, stops, looks around, begins to smile. Behind her in the doorway, are three children; behind them,* KURT MÜLLER. *They stand waiting, watching* SARA. SARA *is forty-one or forty-two, a good-looking woman, with a well-bred, serious face. She is very badly dressed. Her dress is too long, her shoes were bought a long time ago and have no relation to the dress, and the belt of her dress has become untied and is hanging down. She looks clean and dowdy. As she looks around the room, her face is gay and surprised. Smiling, without turning, absently, she motions to the children and* KURT. *Slowly, the children come in.* BODO MÜLLER, *a boy of nine, comes first. He is carrying coats. Behind him, carrying two cheap valises, is* JOSHUA MÜLLER, *a boy of fourteen. Behind him is* BABETTE MÜLLER, *a pretty little girl of twelve. They are dressed for a much colder climate. They come forward, look at their mother, then move to a couch. Behind them is* KURT MÜLLER, *a large, powerful, German-looking man of about forty-seven. He is carrying a shabby valise and a brief-case. He stands watching* SARA. JOSHUA *puts down the valises, goes to his father, takes the valise from* KURT, *puts it neatly near his, and puts the brief-case near* KURT. BABETTE *goes to* SARA, *takes a package from her, places it near the valise. Then she turns to* BODO, *takes the coats he is carrying, puts them neatly on top of the valises. After a second,* KURT *sits down. As he does so, we see that his movements are slow and careful, as if they are made with effort.*]

BABETTE [*points to a couch near which they are standing. She has a slight accent*]: Is it allowed?

KURT [*smiles. He has an accent*]: Yes. It is allowed.

[BABETTE *and* BODO *sit stiffly on the couch.*]

JOSHUA [*nervously. He has a slight accent*]: But we did not sound the bell—

SARA [*idly, as she wanders around the room, her face excited*]: The door isn't locked. It never was. Never since I can remember.

BODO [*softly, puzzled*]: The entrance of the home is never locked. So.

KURT [*looks at him*]: You find it curious to believe there are people who live and do not need to watch, eh, Bodo?

BODO: Yes, Papa.

KURT [*smiles*]: You and I.

JOSHUA [*smiles*]: It is strange. But it must be good, I think.

KURT: Yes.

SARA: Sit back. Be comfortable. I—I wonder where Mama and David— [*Delighted, sees portrait of Joshua Farrelly, points to it.*] And that was my Papa. That was the famous Joshua Farrelly. [*They all look up at it. She wanders around the room.*] My goodness, isn't it a fine room? I'd almost forgotten— [*Picks up a picture from the table.*] And this was my grandmother. [*Very nervously.*] Shall I go and say we're here? They'd be having breakfast, I think. Always on the side terrace in nice weather. I don't know. Maybe— [*Picks up another picture.*] "To Joshua and Fanny Farrelly. With admiration. Alfonso, May 7, 1910." I had an ermine boa and a pink coat. I was angry because it was too warm in Madrid to wear it.

BODO: Alfons von Spanien? Der hat immer Bilder von sich verschenkt. Ein schlechtes Zeichen für einen Mann.

JOSHUA: Mama told you it is good manners to speak the language of the country you visit. Therefore, speak in English.

BODO: I said he seemed always to give his photograph. I said that is a bad flag on a man. Grow fat on the poor people and give pictures of the face.

[JOSHUA *sits down.*]

SARA: I remember a big party and cakes and a glass of champagne for me. I was ten, I guess— [*Suddenly laughs.*] That was when Mama said the first time a king got shot at, he was a romantic, but the fifth time he was a comedian. And when my father gave his lecture in Madrid, he repeated it— right in Madrid. It was a great scandal. You know, Alfonso was always getting shot at or bombed.

BODO [*shrugs*]: Certainement.

JOSHUA: Certainement? As-tu perdu la tête?

BABETTE: Speak in English, please.

KURT [*without turning*]: You are a terrorist, Bodo?

BODO [*slowly*]: No.

JOSHUA: Then since when has it become *natural* to shoot upon people?

BODO: Do not give me lessons. It is neither right or natural to shoot upon people. I know that.

SARA [*looks at* BABETTE, *thoughtfully*]: An ermine boa. A boa is a scarf. I should like to have one for you, Babbie. Once, in Prague, I saw a pretty one. I wanted to buy it for you. But we had to pay our rent. [*Laughs.*] But I almost bought it.

BABETTE: Yes, Mama. Thank you. Tie your sash, Mama.

SARA [*thoughtfully*]: Almost twenty years.

BODO: You were born here, Mama?

SARA: Upstairs. And I lived here until I went to live with your father. [*Looks out beyond terrace.*] Your Uncle David and I used to have a garden, behind the terrace, I wonder if it's still there. I like a garden. I've always hoped we'd have a house some day and settle down— [*Stops, nervously, turns to stare at* KURT, *who is looking at her.*] I am talking so foolish. Sentimental. At my age. Gardens and ermine boas. I haven't wanted anything—

KURT [*comes toward her, takes her hand*]: Sara. Stop it. This is a fine room. A fine place to be. Everything is so pleasant and full of comfort. This will be a good piano on which to play again. And it is all so clean. I like that. Now, you shall not be a baby. You must enjoy your house, and not be afraid that you hurt me with it. Yes?

BABETTE: Papa, tie Mama's sash, please.

SARA [*shyly smiles at him as he leans down to tie the belt*]: Yes, of course. It's strange, that's all. We've never been in a place like this together—

KURT: That does not mean, and should not mean, that we do not remember how to enjoy what comes our way. We are on a holiday.

JOSHUA: A holiday? But for how long? And what plans afterwards?

KURT [*quietly*]: We will have plans when the hour arrives to make them.

[ANISE *appears from the hall. She starts into the room, stops, bewildered. The* MÜLLERS *have not seen her. Then, as* SARA *turns,* ANISE *speaks. As she speaks, the children rise.*]

ANISE: What? What?

SARA [*softly*]: Anise. It's me. It's Sara.

ANISE [*coming forward slowly*]: What? [*Then as she approaches* SARA, *she begins to run toward her.*] Miss Sara! Miss Sara! [*They reach each other, both laugh happily.* SARA *kisses* ANISE.] I would have known you. Yes, I would. I would have known— [*Excited, bewildered, nervous, she looks toward* KURT.] How do you do, sir? How do you do? [*Turns toward the children.*] How do you do?

JOSHUA: Thank you, Miss Anise. We are in good health.

SARA [*very happily*]: You look the same. I think you look the same. Just the way I've always remembered. [*To the others.*] This is the Anise I have told you about. She was here before I was born.

ANISE: But how— Did you just come in? What a way to come home! And after all the plans we've made! But you were to come on the twelve o'clock train, and Mr. David was to meet you—

BABETTE: The twelve o'clock train was most expensive. We could not have come with that train. We liked the train we came on. It was most luxurious.

ANISE [*very nervously, very rattled*]: But Madame Fanny will have a fit. I will call her— She will not be able to contain herself. She—

SARA [*softly*]: I wanted a few minutes. I'm nervous about coming home, I guess.

BODO [*conversationally*]: You are French, Madame Anise?

ANISE: Yes, I am from the Bas Rhin. [*She looks past* SARA, *and bobs her head idiotically at* KURT.] Sara's husband. That's nice. That is nice.

BODO: Yes. Your accent is from the North. That is fine country. We were in hiding there once.

[BABETTE *quickly pokes him.*]

ANISE: Hiding? You— [*Turns nervously to* KURT.] But here we stand and talk. You have not had your breakfast, sir!

BABETTE [*simply, eagerly*]: It would be nice to have breakfast.

ANISE: Yes, of course— I will go and order it.

SARA [*to the children*]: What would you like for breakfast?

BABETTE [*surprised*]: What would we like? Why, Mama, we will have anything that can be spared. If eggs are not too rare or too expensive—

ANISE [*amazed*]: Rare? Why— Oh, I—I must call Miss Fanny now. It is of a necessity. [*Excited, rushing toward terrace, calling:*] Miss Fanny. Miss Fanny. [*Back to* SARA.] Have you forgotten your Mama's nature? She cannot bear not knowing things. Miss Fanny! What a way to come home! After twenty years and nobody at the station—

FANNY'S VOICE: Don't yell at me. What is the matter with you?

ANISE [*excitedly, as* FANNY *draws near*]: She's here. They're here. Miss Sara. She's here, I tell you.

[FANNY *comes up to her, stares at her, then looks slowly around until she sees* SARA.]

SARA [*softly*]: Hello, Mama.

FANNY [*after a long pause, softly, coming toward her*]: Sara. Sara, darling. You're here. You're really here. [*She reaches her, takes her arms, stares at her, smiles.*] Welcome. Welcome. Welcome to your house. [*Slowly.*] You're not young, Sara.

SARA [*smiles*]: No, Mama. I'm forty-one.

FANNY [*softly*]: Forty-one. Of course. [*Presses her arms again.*] Oh, Sara, I'm— [*Then quickly.*] You look more like Papa now. That's good. The years have helped you. [*Turns to look at* KURT.] Welcome to this house, sir.

KURT [*warmly*]: Thank you, Madame.

FANNY [*turns to look at* SARA *again, nervously pats her arm. Nods, turns again to stare at* KURT. *She is nervous and chatty.*] You are a good-looking man, for a German. I didn't remember you that way. I like a good-looking man. I always have.

KURT [*smiles*]: I like a good-looking woman. I always have.

FANNY: Good. That's the way it should be.

BODO [*to* SARA]: Ist das Grossmama?

FANNY [*looks down*]: Yes. I am your grandmother. Also, I speak German, so do not talk about me. I speak languages very well. But there is no longer anybody to speak with. Anise has half-forgotten her French, which was always bad; and I have nobody with whom to speak my Italian or German or— Sara, it's very good to have you home. I'm chattering away, I—

JOSHUA: Now you have us, Madame. We speak ignorantly, but fluently, in German, French, Italian, Spanish—

KURT: And boastfully in English.

BODO: There is never a need for boasting. If we are to fight for the good of all men, it is to be accepted that we must be among the most advanced.

ANISE: My God.

FANNY [*to* SARA]: Are these your *children?* Or are they dressed up midgets?

SARA [*laughs*]: These are my children, Mama. This, Babette. [BABETTE *bows.*] This, Joshua. [JOSHUA *bows.*] This is Bodo. [BODO *bows.*]

FANNY: Joshua was named for Papa. You wrote me. [*Indicates picture of Joshua Farrelly.*] You bear a great name, young man.

JOSHUA [*smiles, indicates his father*]: My name is MÜLLER.

FANNY [*looks at him, laughs*]: Yes. You look a little like your grandfather. [*To* BABETTE.] And so do you. You are a nice-looking girl. [*To* BODO.] You look like nobody.

BODO [*proudly*]: I am not beautiful.

FANNY [*laughs*]: Well, Sara, well. Three children. You have done well. [*To* KURT.] You, too, sir, of course. Are you quite recovered? Sara wrote that you were in Spain and—

BODO: Did Mama write that Papa was a great hero? He was brave, he was calm, he was expert, he was resourceful, he was—

KURT [*laughs*]: My biographer. And as unprejudiced as most of them.

SARA: Where is David? I am so anxious— Has he changed much? Does he ...

FANNY [*to* ANISE]: Don't stand there. Go and get him right away. Go get David. [*As* ANISE *exits.*] He's out having breakfast with the titled folk. Do you remember Marthe Randolph? I mean, do you remember Hortie Randolph, her mother, who was my friend? Can you follow what I'm saying? I'm not speaking well today.

SARA [*laughs*]: Of course I remember Marthe and Hortie. You and she used to scream at each other.

FANNY: Well, Marthe, her daughter, married Teck de Brancovis. *Count* de Brancovis. He was fancy when she married him. Not so fancy now, I suspect. Although still chic and tired. You know what I mean, the way they are in Europe. Well, they're here.

SARA: What's David like now? I—

FANNY: Like? Like? I don't know. He's a lawyer. You know that. Papa's firm. He's never married. You know that, too—

SARA: Why hasn't he married?

FANNY: Really, I don't know. I don't think he likes his own taste. Which is very discriminating of him. He's had a lot of girls, of course, one more ignorant and silly than the other— [*Goes toward terrace, begins to scream.*] And where is he? David! David!

ANISE's VOICE: He's coming, Miss Fanny. He's coming. Contain yourself. He was down at the garage getting ready to leave—

FANNY: I don't care where he is. Tell him to come.— David! [*Suddenly points to picture of Joshua.*] That's my Joshua. Handsome, eh? We were very much in love. Hard to believe of people nowadays, isn't it?

SARA: Kurt and I love each other.

FANNY: Oh. You do? I daresay. But there are ways and ways of loving.

SARA: How dare you, Mama—

KURT [*laughs*]: Ladies, ladies.

SARA [*giggles*]: Why, I almost got mad then. You know, I don't think I've been mad since I last saw you.

BODO: My! You and Mama must not get angry. Anger is protest. And so you must direction it to the proper channels and then harness it for the good of other men. That is correct, Papa?

FANNY [*peers down at him*]: If you grow up to talk like that, and stay as ugly as you are, you are going to have one of these successful careers on the lecture platform.

[JOSHUA *and* BABETTE *laugh.*]

JOSHUA: Ah. It is a great pleasure to hear Grandma talk with you.

BODO [*to* FANNY, *tenderly*]: We will not like each other.

[KURT *has wandered to the piano. Standing, he touches the keys in the first bars of a Mozart Rondo.*]

FANNY: You are wrong. I think we are rather alike; if that is so, let us at least remember to admire each other.

[DAVID *comes running in from the entrance hall. At the door he stops, stares at* SARA.]

DAVID [*to* SARA]: Sara. Darling—

SARA [*wheels, goes running toward him. She moves into his arms. He leans down, kisses her with great affection*]: David. David.

DAVID [*softly*]: It's been a long, long time. I got to thinking it would never happen. [*He leans down, kisses her hair. After a minute, he smiles, presses her arm.*]

SARA [*excited*]: David, I'm excited. Isn't it strange? To be here, to see each other— But I am forgetting. This is my husband. These are my children. Babette, Joshua, Bodo.

[*They all three advance, stand in line to shake hands.*]

BODO [*shaking hands*]: How do you do, Uncle David?

DAVID: How do you do, Bodo? [DAVID *shakes hands with* JOSHUA.] Boys can shake hands. But so pretty a girl must be kissed. [*He kisses* BABETTE. *She smiles, very pleased, and crosses to the side of* SARA.]

BABETTE: Thank you. Fix your hairpin, Mama.

[SARA *shoves back a falling hairpin.*]

DAVID [*crossing to* KURT]: I'm happy to meet you, sir, and to have you here.

KURT: Thank you. Sara has told me so much from you. You have a devoted sister.

DAVID [*very pleased*]: Have I? Still? That's mighty good to hear.

[ANISE *comes in from the library.*]

ANISE: Your breakfast is coming. Shall I wash the children, Miss Sara?

JOSHUA [*amazed*]: Wash us? Do people wash each other?

SARA: No, but the washing is a good idea. Go along now, and hurry. [*All three start for the hall.*] And then we'll all have a fine, big breakfast again.

[*The children exit.*]

FANNY: Again? Don't you usually have a good breakfast?

KURT [*smiles*]: No, Madame. Only sometimes.

SARA [*laughs*]: Oh, we do all right, usually. [*Very happily, very gaily.*] Ah, it's good to be here. [*Puts her arm in DAVID's.*] We were kids. Now we're all grown up! I've got children, you're a lawyer, and a fine one, I bet—

FANNY: The name of Farrelly on the door didn't, of course, hurt David's career.

DAVID [*smiles*]: Sara, you might as well know Mama thinks of me only as a monument to Papa and a not very well-made monument at that. I am not the man Papa was.

SARA [*to FANNY, smiles*]: How do you know he's not?

FANNY [*carefully*]: I beg your pardon. That is the second time you have spoken disrespectfully of your father. [SARA *and* DAVID *laugh.* FANNY *turns to* KURT.] I hope you will like me.

KURT: I hope so.

SARA [*pulls him to the couch, sits down with him*]: Now I want to hear about you— [*Looks at him, laughs.*] I'm awfully nervous about seeing you. Are you, about me?

DAVID: Yes, I certainly am.

SARA [*looks around*]: I'm like an idiot. I want to see everything right away. The lake, and my old room—and I want to talk and ask questions . . .

KURT [*laughs*]: More slow, Sara. It is most difficult to have twenty years in a few minutes.

SARA: Yes, I know, but— Oh, well. Kurt's right. We'll say it all slowly. It's just nice being back. Haven't I fine children?

DAVID: Very fine. You're lucky. I wish I had them.

FANNY: How could you have them? All the women you like are too draughty, if you know what I mean. I'm sure that girl from Lansing, Michigan, would be sterile. Which is as God in his wisdom would have it.

SARA: Oh. So you have a girl?

DAVID: I have no girl. This amuses Mama.

FANNY: He's very attractive to some women. [TO KURT.]

Both my children are attractive, whatever else they're not. Don't you think so? [*Points to* DAVID.] He's flirting with our Countess now, Sara. You will see for yourself.

DAVID [*sharply*]: You are making nervous jokes this morning, Mama. And they're not very good ones.

FANNY [*gaily*]: I tell the truth. If it turns out to be a joke, all the better.

SARA [*affectionately*]: Ah, Mama hasn't changed. And that's good, too.

FANNY: Don't mind me, Sara, I, too, am nervous about seeing you. [*To* KURT.] You'll like it here. You are an engineer?

KURT: Yes.

FANNY: Do you remember the day we met in München? The day Sara brought you to lunch? I thought you were rather a clod and that Sara would have a miserable life. I think I was wrong. [*To* DAVID.] You see? I always admit when I'm wrong.

DAVID: You are a woman who is noble in all things, at all times.

FANNY: Oh, you're mad at me. [*To* KURT.] As I say, you'll like it here. I've already made some plans. The new wing will be for you and Sara. The old turkey-house we'll fix up for the children. A nice, new bathroom, and we'll put in their own kitchen, and Anise will move in with them—

SARA: That's kind of you, Mama. But—but—we won't make any plans for a while— [*Very quietly.*] A good, long vacation; God knows Kurt needs it—

FANNY: A vacation? You'll be staying here, of course. You don't have to worry about work— Engineers can always get jobs, David says, and he's already begun to inquire—

KURT: I have not worked as an engineer since many years, Madame.

DAVID: Haven't you? I thought—Didn't you work for Dornier?

KURT: Yes. Before '33.

FANNY: But you have worked in other places. A great many

other places, I should say. Every letter of Sara's seemed to have a new postmark.

KURT [*smiles*]: We move most often.

DAVID: You gave up engineering?

KURT: I gave it up? [*Smiles.*] One could say it that way.

FANNY: What do you do?

SARA: Mama, we—

KURT: It is difficult to explain.

DAVID [*after a slight pause*]: If you'd rather not.

FANNY: No, I—I'm trying to find out something. [*To* KURT.] May I ask it, sir?

KURT: Let me help you, Madame. You wish to know whether not being an engineer buys adequate breakfasts for my family. It does not. I have no wish to make a mystery of what I have been doing; it is only that it is awkward to place neatly. [*Smiles, motions with his hand.*] It sounds so big: it is so small. I am an Anti-Fascist. And that does not pay well.

FANNY: Do you mind questions?

SARA: Yes.

KURT [*sharply*]: Sara. [*To* FANNY.] Perhaps I shall not answer them. But I shall try.

FANNY: Are you a radical?

KURT: You would have to tell me what that word means to you, Madame.

FANNY [*after a slight pause*]: That is just. Perhaps we all have private definitions. We all are Anti-Fascists, for example—

SARA: Yes. But Kurt works at it.

FANNY: What kind of work?

KURT: Any kind. Anywhere.

FANNY [*sharply*]: I will stop asking questions.

SARA [*very sharply*]: That would be sensible, Mama.

DAVID: Darling, don't be angry. We've been worried about you, naturally. We knew so little, except that you were having a bad time.

SARA: I didn't have a bad time. We never—

KURT: Do not lie for me, Sara.

SARA: I'm not lying. I didn't have a bad time, the way they mean. I—

FANNY [*slowly*]: You had a bad time just trying to live, didn't you? That's obvious, Sara, and foolish to pretend it isn't. Why wouldn't you take money from us? What kind of nonsense—

SARA [*slowly*]: We've lived the way we wanted to live. I don't know the language of rooms like this any more. And I don't want to learn it again.

KURT: Do not bristle about it.

SARA: I'm not bristling. [*To* FANNY.] I married because I fell in love. You can understand that.

FANNY [*slowly*]: Yes.

SARA: For almost twelve years, Kurt went to work every morning and came home every night, and we lived modestly, and happily— [*Sharply.*] As happily as people could in a starved Germany that was going to pieces—

KURT: Sara, please. You're angry. I do not like it that way. I will try to find a way to tell you with quickness. Yes. [SARA *turns, looks at him, starts to speak, stops.*] I was born in a town called Fürth. [*Pauses. Looks up, smiles.*] There is a holiday in my town. We call it Kirchweih. It was a gay holiday with games and music and a hot white sausage to eat with the wine. I grow up, I move away—to school, to work—but always I come back to Kirchweih. It is for me, the great day of the year. [*Slowly.*] But after the war, that day begins to change. The sausage is made from bad stuff, the peasants come in without shoes, the children are too sick— [*Carefully.*] It is bad for my people, those years, but always I have hope. In the festival of August, 1931, more than a year before the storm, I give up that hope. On that day, I see twenty-seven men murdered in a Nazi street fight. I cannot stay by now and watch. My time has come to move. I say with Luther, "Here I stand. I can do nothing else. God help me. Amen."

SARA: It doesn't pay well to fight for what we believe in. But I wanted it the way Kurt wanted it. [*Shrugs.*] They don't like us in Europe; I guess they never did. So Kurt brought us home. You've always said you wanted us. If you don't, I will understand.

DAVID: Darling, of course we want you—

FANNY [*rises*]: I am old. And made of dry cork. And bad-mannered. Please forgive me.

SARA [*goes quickly to* FANNY]: Shut up, Mama. We're all acting like fools. I'm glad to be home. That's all I know. So damned glad.

DAVID: And we're damned glad to have you. Come on. Let's walk to the lake. We've made it bigger and planted the island with blackberries—

[*She smiles and goes to him. Together they move out the hall entrance.*]

FANNY [*after a silence*]: They've always liked each other. We're going to have Zwetschgen-Knoedel for dinner. You like them?

KURT: Indeed.

FANNY: I hope you like decent food.

KURT: I do.

FANNY: That's a good sign in a man.

MARTHE [*coming in from the terrace. Stops in the doorway*]: Oh, I'm sorry, Fanny. We were waiting. I didn't want to interrupt the family reunion. I—

FANNY: This is my son-in-law, Herr Müller. The Countess de Brancovis.

KURT AND MARTHE [*together*]: How do you do?

MARTHE: And how is Sara, Herr Müller? I haven't seen her since I was a little girl. She probably doesn't remember me at all. [TECK *comes in from the hall. She turns.*] This is my husband, Herr Müller.

KURT: How do you do?

TECK: How do you do, sir? [KURT *bows. They shake hands*]. Would it be impertinent for one European to make welcome another?

KURT [*smiles*]: I do not think so. It would be friendly.

BODO [*appears at the hall door*]: Papa— [*Sees* TECK *and* MARTHE, *bows.*] Oh, good morning. Miss Anise says you are the Count and Countess. Once before we met a Count and Countess. They had a small room bordering on ours in Copenhagen. They were more older than you, and more poor. We shared with them our newspaper.

MARTHE [*laughs*]: It wasn't us, but it might have been. What's your name?

TECK [*laughs*]: We hope you will be as kind to us.

BODO: My name is Bodo. It's a strange name. No? [*To KURT.*] Papa, this is the house of great wonders. Each has his bed, each has his bathroom. The arrangement of it, that is splendorous.

FANNY [*laughs*]: You are a fancy talker, Bodo.

KURT: Oh, yes. In many languages.

BODO [*to FANNY*]: Please to correct me when I am wrong. Papa, the plumbing is such as you have never seen. Each implement is placed on the floor, and all are simultaneous in the same room. You will therefore see that being placed most solidly on the floor allows of no rats, rodents or crawlers, and is most sanitary. [*To the others.*] Papa will be most interested. He likes to know how each thing of everything is put together. And he is so fond of being clean—

KURT [*laughs. To FANNY*]: I am a hero to my children. It bores everybody but me.

TECK: It is most interesting, Herr Müller. I thought I had a good ear for the accents of your country. But yours is most difficult to place. It is Bayrisch? Or is it—

BODO: That's because Papa has worked in so many—

KURT [*quickly*]: German accents are the most difficult to identify. I, myself, when I try, am usually incorrect. It would be particularly difficult with me because I speak other languages. Yours would be Roumanian?

MARTHE [*laughs*]: My God, is it that bad?

KURT [*smiles*]: I am showing off. I know the Count de Brancovis is Roumanian.

TECK [*heartily*]: So? We have met before? I thought so, but I cannot remember—

KURT: No, sir. We have not met before. I read your name in the newspapers.

TECK [*to* KURT]: Strange. I was sure I had met you. I was in the Paris Legation for many years, and I thought perhaps—

KURT: Oh, no. If it is possible to believe, I am the exile who is not famous. [*To* FANNY.] I have been thinking with pleasure, Madame Fanny, of breakfast on your porch. [*He points to the picture of Joshua Farrelly.*] Your husband once wrote: "I am getting older now and Europe seems far away. Fanny and I will have an early breakfast on the porch and then I shall drive the bays into Washington." [*Remembering.*] And then he goes on: "Henry Adams tells me he has been reading Karl Marx. I shall have to tell him my father made me read Marx many years ago and that, since he proposes to exhibit himself to impress me, will spoil Henry's Sunday."

FANNY [*laughs, delighted. Takes* KURT'S *arm*]: And so it did. I had forgotten that. I am pleased with you. I shall come and serve your food myself. I had forgotten Joshua ever wrote it.

[*They start out of the terrace doors together, followed by* BODO.]

KURT [*as they disappear*]: I try to impress you. I learned it last night.

[FANNY *laughs. They disappear.*]

TECK [*smiles*]: He is a clever man. A quotation from Joshua Farrelly is a sure road to Fanny's heart. Where did you say Herr Müller was from?

MARTHE: Germany.

TECK: I know that. [*Goes to a valise. He leans over, stares at it, looks at the labels, pushes the lock. The lock opens; he closes it. Then he turns and, as he speaks, picks up the briefcase.*] What part of Germany?

MARTHE: I don't know. And I never knew you were an expert on accents.

TECK: I never knew it either. Are you driving into Washington with David this morning?

MARTHE: I was going to. But he may not be going to the office, now that Sara's here. I was to have lunch with Sally Tyne. [TECK *puts down the briefcase.*] What are you doing?

TECK: Wondering why luggage is unlocked and a shabby brief-case is so carefully locked.

MARTHE: You're very curious about Mr. Müller.

TECK: Yes. And I do not know why. Something far away ... I am curious about a daughter of the Farrelly's who marries a German who has bullet scars on his face and broken bones in his hands.

MARTHE [*sharply*]: Has he? There are many of them now, I guess.

TECK: So there are. But this one is in this house. [*He goes to the bell cord, pulls it. She watches him nervously.*]

MARTHE: Is it—is he any business of yours?

TECK: What is my business? Anything might be my business now.

MARTHE: Yes—unfortunately. You might inquire from your friend Von Seitz. They always know their nationals.

TECK [*pleasantly, ignoring the sharpness with which she has spoken*]. Oh, yes, I will do that, of course. But I do not like to ask questions without knowing the value of the answers.

MARTHE: Teck. This man is a little German Sara married years ago. I remember Mama talking about it. He was nothing then and he isn't now. They've had a tough enough time already without—

TECK: Have you— Have you been sleeping with David?

MARTHE [*stops, stares at him, then simply*]: No. I have not been. And that hasn't been your business for a good many years now.

TECK: You like him?

MARTHE [*nervously*]: What's this for, Teck?

TECK: Answer me, please.

MARTHE: I— [*She stops.*]

TECK: Yes? Answer me.

MARTHE: I do like him.

TECK: What does he feel about you?

MARTHE: I don't know.

TECK: But you are trying to find out. You have made any plans with him?

MARTHE: Of course not. I—

TECK: You will try to make him have plans. I have recognized it. Well, we have been together a long— [JOSEPH *enters.* TECK *stops.*] Joseph, Miss Fanny wishes you to take the baggage upstairs.

JOSEPH: Yes, sir. I was going to. [*He begins to pick up the baggage.* MARTHE *has turned sharply and is staring at* TECK. *Then she rises, watches* JOSEPH *pick up the baggage, turns again to look at* TECK.]

TECK: As I was saying. It is perhaps best that we had this talk.

MARTHE [*she stops, waits for* JOSEPH *to move off. He exits, carrying the valises.*]: Why did you do that? Why did you tell Joseph that Fanny wanted him to take the baggage upstairs?

TECK: Obviously it is more comfortable to look at baggage behind closed doors.

MARTHE [*very sharply*]: What kind of silliness is this now? Leave these people alone— [*As he starts to exit.*] I won't let you—

TECK: What? [*As he moves again, she comes after him.*]

MARTHE: I said I won't let you. You are not—

TECK: How many times have you seen me angry? [MARTHE *looks up, startled.*] You will not wish to see another. Run along now and have lunch with something you call Sally Tyne. But do not make plans with David. You will not be able to carry them out. You will go with me, when I am ready to go. You understand. [*He exits during his speech. The last words come as he goes through the door, and as the curtain falls.*]

ACT TWO

SCENE—*The same as Act One, about ten days later. During the act it will begin to grow dark; but the evening is warm and the terrace doors are open.*

AT RISE—SARA *is sitting on the couch, crocheting.* FANNY *and* TECK *are sitting at a small table playing cribbage.* BODO *is sitting near them, at a large table, working on a heating pad. The cord is torn from the bag, the bag is ripped open.* ANISE *sits next to him, anxiously watching him. Outside on the terrace,* JOSHUA *is going through baseball motions, coached by* JOSEPH. *From time to time they move out of sight, reappear, move off again.*

FANNY [*playing a card*]: One.

BODO [*after a minute, to* TECK]: The arrangement of this heating pad grows more complex.

TECK [*smiles, moves on the cribbage board*]: And the more wires you remove, the more complex it will grow.

BODO [*points to bag*]: Man has learned to make man comfortable. Yet all cannot have the comforts. [*To* ANISE.] How much did this cost you?

ANISE: It cost me ten dollars. And you have made a ruin of it.

BODO: That is not yet completely true. [*To* FANNY.] Did I not install for you a twenty-five-cent button-push for your radio?

TECK [*playing a card*]: Two and two. [*Moves pegs on the cribbage board.*]

FANNY: Yes, you're quite an installer.

BODO [*to* TECK]: As I was wishing to tell you, Count de Brancovis, comfort and plenty exist. Yet all cannot have it. Why?

TECK: I do not know. It has worried many men. Why?

ANISE [*to* BODO]: Yes, why?

353

BODO [*takes a deep breath, raises his finger as if about to lecture*]: Why? [*Considers a moment, then deflates himself.*] I am not as yet sure.

ANISE: I thought not.

FANNY [*turns to look at* JOSHUA *and* JOSEPH *on the terrace*]. Would you mind doing that dancing some place else?

JOSEPH [*looking in*]: Yes'm. That ain't dancing. I'm teaching Josh baseball.

FANNY: Then maybe he'd teach you how to clean the silver.

JOSEPH: I'm a good silver-cleaner, Miss Fanny.

FANNY: But you're getting out of practice.

JOSEPH [*after a moment's thought*]: Yes'm I see what you mean. [*He exits.*]

FANNY [*playing a card*]: Three.

JOSHUA: It is my fault. I'm crazy about baseball.

BODO: Baseball players are among the most exploited people in this country. I read about it.

FANNY: You never should have learned to read.

BODO: Their exploited condition is foundationed on the fact that—

JOSHUA [*bored*]: All right, all right. I still like baseball.

SARA: Founded, Bodo, not foundationed.

JOSHUA: He does it always. He likes long words. In all languages.

TECK: How many languages do you children speak?

BODO: Oh, we do not really know any very well, except German and English. We speak bad French and—

SARA: And bad Danish and bad Czech.

TECK: You seem to have stayed close to the borders of Germany. Did Herr Müller have hopes, as so many did, that National Socialism would be overthrown on every tomorrow?

SARA: We have not given up that hope. Have you, Count de Brancovis?

TECK: I never had it.

JOSHUA [*pleasantly*]: Then it must be most difficult for you to sleep.

TECK: I beg your pardon?

SARA: Schweig doch, Joshua!

FANNY [*to* TECK]: Sara told Joshua to shut up. [*Playing a card.*] Twelve.

TECK: I have offended you, Mrs. Müller. I am most sorry.

SARA [*pleasantly*]: No, sir, you haven't offended me. I just don't like polite political conversations any more.

TECK [*nods*]: All of us, in Europe, had too many of them.

SARA: Yes. Too much talk. By this time all of us must know where we are and what we have to do. It's an indulgence to sit in a room and discuss your beliefs as if they were a juicy piece of gossip.

FANNY: You know, Sara, I find it very pleasant that Kurt, considering his history, doesn't make platform speeches. He hasn't tried to convince anybody of anything.

SARA [*smiles*]: Why should he, Mama? You are quite old enough to have your own convictions—or Papa's.

FANNY [*turns to look at her*]: I am proud to have Papa's convictions.

SARA: Of course. But it might be well to have a few new ones, now and then.

FANNY [*peers over at her*]: Are you criticizing me?

SARA [*smiles*]: Certainly not.

BABETTE [*comes running in from right entrance door. She has on an apron and she is carrying a plate. She goes to* FANNY]: Eat it while it's hot, Grandma.

[FANNY *peers down, takes the fork, begins to eat.* ANISE *and* BODO *both rise, move to* FANNY, *inspect the plate.*]

FANNY [*to them*]: Go away.

ANISE: It is a potato pancake.

FANNY: And the first good one I've eaten in many, many years. I love a good potato pancake.

BODO: I likewise.

BABETTE: I am making a great number for dinner. Move away, Bodo.

TECK [*playing a card*]: Fifteen and two.

ANISE [*who has followed* BODO *back to the chair*]: You've ruined it! I shall sue you.

JOSHUA: I told you not to let him touch it.

SARA [*laughs*]: I remember you were always saying that, Anise—that you were going to sue. That's very French. I was sick once in Paris, and Babbie stayed up for a whole night and day and finished a dress I was making for a woman on the Rue Jacob. I told her to tell the woman she'd done it—I thought perhaps the woman would give her a candy or something—and anyway, I was very proud of her work. But no. The woman admitted the dress was well done, but said she was going to sue because I hadn't done it myself. Fancy that.

FANNY [*slowly*]: You sewed for a living?

SARA: Not a very good one. But Babbie and I made a little something now and then. Didn't we, darling?

FANNY [*sharply*]: Really, Sara, were these—these things necessary? Why couldn't you have written?

SARA [*laughs*]: You've asked me that a hundred times in the last week.

JOSHUA [*gently*]: I think it is only that Grandma feels sorry for us. Grandma has not seen much of the world.

FANNY: Don't you start giving me lectures, Joshua. I'm fond of you. And of you, Babbie. [*To* ANISE.] Are there two desserts for dinner? And are they sweet?

ANISE: Yes.

FANNY [*turns to* BODO]: I wish I were fond of you.

BODO: You are. [*Happily.*] You are very fond of me.

FANNY [*playing a card*]: Twenty-five.

BABETTE: This is for you, Grandma. I'm making a bed-jacket. It is nice lace. Papa brought it to me from Spain and I mean for you to have it.

FANNY [*kisses* BABETTE]: Thank you, darling. A sequence and three. A pair and five. [*To* TECK, *as they finish the cribbage game.*] There. That's two dollars off. I owe you eight-fifty.

TECK: Let us carry it until tomorrow. You shall give it to me as a going-away token.

FANNY [*too pleased*]: You're going away?

TECK [*laughs*]: Ah, Madame Fanny. Do not sound *that* happy.

FANNY: Did I? That's rude of me. When are you going?

TECK: In a few days, I think. [*Turns to look at* SARA.] We're too many refugees, eh, Mrs. Müller?

SARA [*pleasantly*]: Perhaps.

TECK: Will you be leaving, also?

SARA: I beg your pardon?

TECK: I thought perhaps you, too, would be moving on. Herr Müller does not give me the feeling of a man who settles down. Men who have done his work, seldom leave it. Not for a quiet country house.

[*All three children look up.*]

SARA [*very quietly*]: What work do you think my husband has done, Count de Brancovis?

TECK: Engineering?

SARA [*slowly*]: Yes. Engineering.

FANNY [*very deliberately to* TECK]: I don't know what you're saying. They shall certainly not be leaving—ever. Is that understood, Sara?

SARA: Well, Mama—

FANNY: There are no wells about it. You've come home to see me die and you will wait until I'm ready.

SARA [*laughs*]: Really, Mama, that isn't the reason I came home.

FANNY: It's a good enough reason. I shall do a fine death. I intend to be a great deal of trouble to everybody.

ANISE: I daresay.

FANNY: I shall take to my bed early and stay for years. In great pain.

ANISE: I am sure of it. You will duplicate the disgrace of the birth of Miss Sara.

SARA [*laughs*]: Was I born in disgrace?

ANISE: It was not your fault. But it was disgusting. Three weeks before you were to come—all was excellent, of course, in so healthy a woman as Madame Fanny—a great dinner was given here and, most unexpectedly, attended by a beautiful lady from England.

FANNY: Do be still. You are dull and fanciful—

ANISE: Mr. Joshua made the great error of waltzing the beauty for two dances, Madame Fanny being unfitted for the waltz and under no circumstances being the most graceful of dancers.

FANNY [*her voice rising*]: Are you crazy? I danced magnificently.

ANISE: It is well you thought so. A minute did not elapse between the second of the waltzes and a scream from Madame Fanny. She was in labor. Two hundred people, and if we had left her alone, she would have remained in the ballroom—

FANNY: How you invent! How you invent!

ANISE: Do not call to me that I am a liar. For three weeks you are in the utmost agony—

FANNY: And so I was. I remember it to this day—

ANISE [*to* SARA, *angrily*]: Not a pain. Not a single pain. She would lie up there in state, stealing candy from herself. Then, when your Papa would rest himself for a minute at the dinner or with a book, a scream would dismantle the house— it was revolting. [*Spitefully to* FANNY.] And now the years have passed and I may disclose to you that Mr. Joshua knew you were going through the play-acting—

FANNY [*rises*]: He did not. You are a malicious—

ANISE: Once he said to me, "Anise, it is well that I am in love. This is of a great strain and her Great-uncle Freddie was not right in the head, neither."

FANNY [*screaming*]: You will leave this house— You are a liar, a woman of—

SARA: Mama, sit down.

ANISE: I will certainly leave this house. I will—

SARA [*sharply*]: Both of you. Sit down. And be still.

ANISE: She has intimated that I lie—

FANNY [*screaming*]: Intimated! Is that what I was doing— [ANISE *begins to leave the room.*] All right. I beg your pardon. I apologize.

[ANISE *turns.*]

SARA: Both of you. You are acting like children.

BODO: Really, Mama. You insult us.

ANISE: I accept your apology. Seat yourself.

[*They both sit down.*]

FANNY: [*after a silence*]: I am unloved.

BABETTE: I love you, Grandma.

FANNY: Do you, Babbie?

JOSHUA: And I.

FANNY [*nods very pleased. To* BODO]: And you?

BODO: *I* loved you the primary second I saw you.

FANNY: You are a charlatan.

ANISE: As for me, I am fond of all the living creatures. It is true that the children cause me greater work, which in turn more greatly inconveniences the feet. However, I do not complain. I believe in children.

FANNY: Rather like believing in the weather, isn't it? [DAVID *and* KURT *come in from the terrace. Both are in work clothes, their sleeves rolled up.*] Where have you been?

DAVID: Oh, we've been helping Mr. Chabeuf spray the fruit trees.

ANISE: Mr. Chabeuf says that Herr Müller has the makings of a good farmer. From a Frenchman that is a large thing to say.

KURT [*who has looked around the room, looked at* TECK, *strolled over to* BODO]: Mr. Chabeuf and I have an excellent time exchanging misinformation. My father was a farmer. I have a wide knowledge of farmer's misinformation.

FANNY. This is good farm land. Perhaps, in time—

DAVID [*laughs*]. Mama would give you the place, Kurt, if you guaranteed that your great-grandchildren would die here.

KURT [*smiles*]. I would like to so guarantee.

TECK: A farmer. That is very interesting. Abandon your ideals, Herr Müller?

KURT: Ideals? [*Carefully.*] Sara, heisst das auf deutsch "Ideale"?

SARA: Yes.

KURT: Is that what I have now? I do not like the word. It gives to me the picture of a small, pale man at a seaside resort. [*To* BODO.] What are you doing?

BODO: Preparing an elderly electric pad for Miss Anise. I am confused.

KURT [*wanders toward the piano*]: So it seems.

BODO: Something has gone wrong with the principle on which I have been working. It is probably that I will ask your assistance.

KURT [*bows to him*]: Thank you. Whenever you are ready. [*Begins to pick out notes with one hand.*]

FANNY: We shall have a little concert tomorrow evening. In honor of Babbie's birthday. [*To* KURT.] Kurt, you and I will play "The Clock Symphony." Then Joshua and I will play the duet we've learned, and Babbie will sing. And I shall finish with a Chopin Nocturne.

DAVID [*laughs*]: I thought you'd be the last on the program.

TECK: Where is Marthe?

FANNY: She'll be back soon. She went into town to do an errand for me. [*To* DAVID.] Did you buy presents for everybody?

DAVID: I did.

SARA [*smiles, to* BABETTE]: We always did that here. If somebody had a birthday, we all got presents. Nice, isn't it?

DAVID [*to* ANISE]: I shall buy you an electric pad. You will need it.

ANISE: Indeed.

FANNY: Did you buy me a good present?

DAVID: Pretty good. [*Pats* BABETTE's *head*.] The best present goes to Babbie; it's *her* birthday.

FANNY: Jewelry?

DAVID: No, not jewelry.

FANNY: Oh. Not jewelry.

DAVID: Why? Why should you want jewelry? You've got too many bangles now.

FANNY: I didn't say I wanted it. I just asked you.

TECK [*gets up*]: It was a natural mistake, David. You see, Mrs. Mellie Sewell told your mother that she had seen you and Marthe in Barstow's. And your mother said you were probably buying her a present, or one for Babbie.

DAVID [*too sharply*]: Yes.

TECK [*laughs*]: Yes what?

DAVID [*slowly*]: Just yes.

FANNY [*too hurriedly*]: Mellie gets everything wrong. She's very anxious to meet Marthe because she used to know Francie Cabot, her aunt. Marthe's aunt, I mean, not Mellie's.

SARA [*too hurriedly*]: She really came to inspect Kurt and me. But I saw her first. [*She looks anxiously at* DAVID, *who has turned his back on the room and is facing the terrace.*] You were lucky to be out, David.

DAVID: Oh, she calls every Saturday afternoon, to bring Mama all the Washington gossip of the preceding week. She gets it all wrong, you understand, but that doesn't make any difference to either Mama or her. Mama then augments it, wits it up, Papa used to say—

FANNY: Certainly. I sharpen it a little. Mellie has no sense of humor.

DAVID: So Mama sharpens it a little, and delivers it to-morrow afternoon to old lady Marcy down the road. Old lady Marcy hasn't heard a word in ten years, so she un-sharpens it again, and changes the names. By Wednesday afternoon—

TECK [*smiles*]: By Wednesday afternoon it will not be you who were in Barstow's, and it will be a large diamond pin with four sapphires delivered to Gaby Deslys.

DAVID [*turns, looks at him*]: Exactly.

FANNY [*very nervously*]: Francie Cabot, Marthe's aunt, you understand— [*To* KURT.] Did you ever know Paul von Seitz, a German?

KURT: I have heard of him.

FANNY [*speaking very rapidly*]: Certainly. He was your Ambassador to somewhere, I've forgotten. Well Francie Cabot married him. I could have. Any American, not crippled, whose father had money— He was crazy about me. I was better-looking than Francie. Well, years later when he was your Ambassador—my father was, too, as you probably know—not your Ambassador, of course, ours—but I am talking about Von Seitz.

DAVID [*laughs to* KURT]: You can understand how it goes. Old lady Marcy is not entirely to blame.

FANNY: Somebody asked me if I didn't regret not marrying him. I said, "Madame, je le regrette tous les jours et j'en suis heureuse chaque soir." [FANNY *turns to* DAVID.] That means I regret it every day and am happy about it every night. You understand what I meant, by *night?* Styles in wit change so.

DAVID: I understood it, Mama.

JOSHUA: We, too, Grandma.

BABETTE [*approvingly*]: It is most witty.

BODO: I do not know that I understood. You will explain to me, Grandma?

SARA: Later.

FANNY: [*turns to look at* TECK]: You remember the old Paul von Seitz?

TECK [*nods*]: He was stationed in Paris when I first was there.

FANNY: Of course. I always forgot you were a diplomat.

TECK: It is just as well.

FANNY: There's something insane about a Roumanian diplomat. Pure insane. I knew another one, once. He wanted to marry me, too.

SARA [*laughs*]: All of Europe.

FANNY: Not all. Some. Naturally. I was rich, I was witty, my family was of the best. I was handsome, unaffected—

DAVID: And noble and virtuous and kind and elegant and fashionable and simple—it's hard to remember everything you were. I've often thought it must have been boring for Papa to have owned such perfection.

FANNY [*shrieks*]: What! Your father bored with me! Not for a second of our life—

DAVID [*laughs*]: Oh God, when will I learn?

BODO: Do not shriek, Grandma. It is an unpleasant sound for the ear.

FANNY: Where was I? Oh, yes. What I started out to say was— [*She turns, speaks carefully to* TECK.] Mellie Sewell told me, when you left the room, that she had heard from Louis Chandler's child's governess that you had won quite a bit of money in a poker game with Sam Chandler and some Germans at the Embassy. [KURT, *who has been playing the piano, stops playing very abruptly.* TECK *turns to look at him.*] *That's* how I thought of Von Seitz. His nephew Philip was in on the game.

DAVID [*looks at* TECK]: It must have been a big game. Sam Chandler plays in big games.

TECK: Not big enough.

DAVID: Have you known Sam long?

TECK: For years. Every Embassy in Europe knew him.

DAVID [*sharply*]: Sam and Nazis must make an unpleasant poker game.

[KURT *begins to play a new melody.*]

TECK [*who has not looked away from* KURT]: I do not play poker to be amused.

DAVID [*irritably*]: What's Sam selling now?

TECK: Bootleg munitions. He always has.

DAVID: You don't mind?

TECK: Mind? I have not thought about it.

FANNY: Well, you ought to think about it. Sam Chandler has always been a scoundrel. All of the Chandlers are. They're cousins of mine. Mama used to say they never should have learned to walk on two feet. They would have been more comfortable on four.

TECK: Do you know the young Von Seitz, Herr Müller? He was your military attaché in Spain.

KURT: He was the German government attaché in Spain. I know his name, of course. He is a famous artillery expert. But the side on which I fought was not where he was stationed, Count de Brancovis.

ANISE [BABETTE and JOSHUA *begin to hum the song* KURT *is playing.* SARA *begins to hum*]: It is time for the bath and the change of clothes. I will give you five minutes—

FANNY: What is the song?

TECK: It was a German soldier's song. They sang it as they straggled back in '18. I remember hearing it in Berlin. Were you there then, Herr Müller?

KURT [*the playing and the humming continue*]: I was not in Berlin.

TECK: But you were in the war, of course?

KURT: Yes. I was in the war.

FANNY: You didn't think then you'd live to see another war.

KURT: Many of us were afraid we would.

FANNY: What are the words?

SARA: The Germans in Spain, in Kurt's Brigade, wrote new words for the song.

KURT: This was what you heard in Berlin, in 1918. [*Begins to sing in German.*]

> "Wir zieh'n Heim, wir zieh'n Heim,
> Mancher kommt nicht mit,
> Mancher ging verschütt,
> Aber Freunde sind wir stets."

[*In English.*]

"We come home. We come home.
  Some of us are gone, and some of us are lost, but we are
      friends:
  Our blood is on the earth together.
  Some day. Some day we shall meet again.
  Farewell."

[*Stops singing.*] At a quarter before six on the morning of November 7th, 1936, eighteen years later, five hundred Germans walked through the Madrid streets on their way to defend the Manzanares River. We felt good that morning. You know how it is to be good when it is needed to be good?

So we had need of new words to say that. I translate with awkwardness, you understand. [*Begins to sing in English.*]

"And so we have met again.
The blood did not have time to dry.
We lived to stand and fight again.
This time we fight for people.
This time the bastards will keep their hands away.
Those who sell the blood of other men, this time,
They keep their hands away.
For us to stand.
For us to fight.
This time, no farewell, no farewell."

[*Music dies out. There is silence for a minute.*] We did not win. [*Looks up, gently.*] It would have been a different world if we had.

SARA: Papa said so years ago. Do you remember, Mama? "For every man who lives without freedom, the rest of us must face the guilt."

FANNY: Yes. "We are liable in the conscience-balance for the tailor in Lodz, the black man in our South, the peasant in—" [*Turns to* TECK. *Unpleasantly.*] Your country, I think.

ANISE [*rises*]: Come. Baths for everybody. [*To* BODO.] Gather the wires. You have wrecked my cure.

BODO: If you would allow me a few minutes more—

ANISE: Come along. I have been duped for long enough. Come Joshua. Babette. Baths.

JOSHUA [*starts out after* ANISE. BABETTE *begins to gather up the sewing*]: My tub is a thing of glory. But I do not like it so prepared for me and so announced by Miss Anise. [*He exits.*]

BODO [*to* ANISE]: You are angry about this. I do not blame you with my heart or my head. I admit I have failed. But Papa will repair it, Anise. Will you not, Papa? In a few minutes—

TECK [*to* BODO]: Your father is an expert electrician?

BODO: Oh yes, sir.

TECK: And as good with radio—

[BODO *begins to nod.*]

KURT [*sharply*]: Count de Brancovis. Make your questions to me, please. Not to my children.

[*The others look up, surprised.*]

TECK [*pleasantly*]: Very well, Herr Müller.

ANISE [*as she exits with* BODO]: Nobody can fix it. You have made a pudding of it.

BODO [*as he follows her*]: Do not worry. In five minutes tonight, you will have a pad far better— [*As* BODO *reaches the door he bumps into* MARTHE *who is carrying large dress boxes.*] Oh. Your pardon. Oh, hello. [*He disappears.*]

MARTHE [*gaily*]: Hello. [*To* FANNY.] I waited for them. I was afraid they wouldn't deliver this late in the day. [*To* SARA.] Come on, Sara. I can't wait to see them.

SARA: What?

MARTHE: Dresses. From Fanny. A tan linen, and a dark green with wonderful buttons, a white net for Babbie, and a suit for you, and play dresses for Babbie, and a dinner dress in gray to wear for Babbie's birthday—gray should be good for you, Sara—all from Savitt's. We sneaked the measurements, Anise and I—

SARA [*she goes toward* FANNY]: How nice of you, Mama. How very kind of you. And of you, Marthe, to take so much trouble— [*She leans down, kisses* FANNY.] You're a sweet woman, Mama.

DAVID: That's the first time Mama's ever heard that word. [*He takes the boxes from* MARTHE, *puts them near the staircase.* MARTHE *smiles at him, touches his hand, as* TECK *watches them.*]

FANNY [*giggles*]: I have a bottom sweetness, if you understand what I mean.

DAVID: I have been too close to the bottom to see it.

FANNY: That should be witty. I don't know why it isn't.

[BABETTE *goes over to stare at the boxes.*]

SARA: From Savitt's. Extravagant of you. They had such lovely clothes. I remember my coming-out dress— [*Goes to*

KURT.] Do you remember the black suit with the braid, and the Milan hat? Not the *first* day we met, but the picnic day? [*He smiles up at her.*] Well, they were from Savitt's. That was over twenty years ago—I've known you a long time. Me, in an evening dress. Now you'll have to take me into Washington. I want to show off. Next week, and we'll dance, maybe— [*Sees that he is not looking at her.*] What's the matter, darling? [*No answer. Slowly he turns to look at her.*] What's the matter, Kurt? [*Takes his arms, very unhappily.*] What have I done? It isn't that dresses have ever mattered to me, it's just that—

KURT: Of course, they have mattered to you. As they should. I do not think of the dress. [*Draws her to him.*] How many years have I loved that face?

SARA [*her face very happy*]: So?

KURT: So. [*He leans down, kisses her, as if it were important.*]

SARA [*pleased, unembarrassed*]: There are other people here.

MARTHE [*slowly*]: And good for us to see.

TECK: Nostalgia?

MARTHE: No. Nostalgia is for something you have known. [*FANNY coughs.*]

BABETTE [*comes to* FANNY]: Grandma, is it allowed to look at my dresses?

FANNY: Of course, child. Run along.

BABETTE [*picks up the boxes, goes toward the hall entrance, stops near* FANNY]: I love dresses, I have a great fondness for materials and colors. Thank you, Grandma. [*She runs out of the room.*]

[JOSEPH *appears in the doorway.*]

JOSEPH: There is a long-distance operator with a long-distance call for Mr. Müller. She wants to talk with him on the long-distance phone.

KURT: Oh— Excuse me, please— [KURT *rises quickly.* SARA *turns sharply to look at him.* TECK *looks up.* KURT *goes quickly out.* TECK *watches him go.* SARA *stands staring after him.*]

MARTHE [*laughs*]: I feel the same way as Babbie. Come on, Sara. Let's try them on.

[SARA *does not turn.*]

TECK: You also have a new dress?

MARTHE [*looks at him*]: Yes. Fanny was kind to me, too.

TECK: You are a very generous woman, Madame Fanny. Did you also give her a sapphire bracelet from Barstow's?

FANNY: I beg your—

DAVID [*slowly*]: No. I gave Marthe the bracelet. And I understand that it is not any business of yours.

[FANNY *rises.* SARA *turns.*]

FANNY: Really, David—

DAVID: Be still, Mama.

TECK [*after a second*]: Did you tell him that, Marthe?

MARTHE: Yes.

TECK [*looks up at her*]: I shall not forgive you for that. [*Looks at* DAVID.] It is a statement which no man likes to hear from another man. You understand? [*Playfully.*] That is the type of thing about which we used to play at duels in Europe.

DAVID [*comes toward him*]: We are not so musical comedy here. And you are not in Europe.

TECK: Even if I were, I would not suggest any such action. I would have reasons for not wishing it.

DAVID: It would be well for you not to suggest *any* action. And the reason for *that* is you might get hurt.

TECK [*slowly*]: That would not be my reason. [*To* MARTHE.] Your affair has gone far enough—

MARTHE [*sharply*]: It is not an affair—

TECK: I do not care what it is. The time has come to leave here. Go upstairs and pack your things. [*She does not move.* DAVID *turns toward her.*] Go on, Marthe.

MARTHE [*to* DAVID]: I am not going with him. I told you that.

DAVID: I don't want you to go with him.

FANNY [*carefully*]: Really, David, aren't you interfering in all this a good deal—

DAVID [*carefully*]: Yes, Mama. I am.

TECK [*to* MARTHE]: When you are speaking to me, please say what you have to say to me.

MARTHE [*comes to him*]: You are trying to frighten me. But you are not going to frighten me any more. I will say it to you: I am not going with you. I am never going with you again.

TECK [*softly*]: If you do not fully mean what you say, or if you might change your mind, you are talking unwisely, Marthe.

MARTHE: I know that.

TECK: Shall we talk about it alone?

MARTHE: You can't make me go, can you, Teck?

TECK: No, I can't make you.

MARTHE: Then there's no sense talking about it.

TECK: Are you in love with him?

MARTHE: Yes.

FANNY [*sharply*]: Marthe! What is all this?

MARTHE [*sharply*]: I'll tell *you* about it in a minute.

DAVID: You don't have to explain anything to anybody.

TECK [*ignores him*]: Is he in love with you?

MARTHE: I don't think so. You won't believe it, because you can't believe anything that hasn't got tricks to it, but David hasn't much to do with this. I told you I would leave some day, and I remember where I said it—[*slowly*]—and why I said it.

TECK: I also remember. But I did not believe you. I have not had much to offer you these last years. But if now we had some money and could go back—

MARTHE: No. I don't like you, Teck. I never have.

TECK: And I have always known it.

FANNY [*stiffly*]: I think your lack of affections should be discussed with more privacy. Perhaps—

DAVID: Mama—

MARTHE: There is nothing to discuss. Strange. I've talked

to myself about this scene for almost fifteen years. I knew a lot of things to say to you and I used to lie awake at night or walk along the street and say them. Now I don't want to. I guess you only want to talk that way, when you're not sure what you can do. When you're sure, then what's the sense of saying it? "This is why and this is why and this—" [*Very happily.*] But when you know you can do it, you don't have to say anything; you can just go. And I'm going. There is nothing you can do. I would like you to believe that now.

TECK: Very well, Marthe. I think I made a mistake. I should not have brought you here. I believe you now.

MARTHE [*after a pause, she looks at* DAVID]: I'll move into Washington, and—

DAVID: Yes. Later. But I'd like you to stay here for a while, with us, if you wouldn't mind.

SARA: It would be better for you, Marthe—

FANNY: It's very interesting that I am not being consulted about this. [*To* MARTHE.] I have nothing against you, Marthe. I am sorry for you, but I don't think—

MARTHE: Thank you, Sara, David. But I'd rather move in now. [*Turns, comes toward* FANNY.] But perhaps I have something against you. Do you remember my wedding?

FANNY: Yes.

MARTHE: Do you remember how pleased Mama was with herself? Brilliant Mama, handsome Mama—everybody thought so, didn't they? A seventeen-year-old daughter, marrying a pretty good title, about to secure herself in a world that Mama liked—she didn't ask me what I liked. And the one time I tried to tell her, she frightened me— [*Looks up.*] Maybe I've always been frightened. All my life.

TECK: Of course.

MARTHE [*to* FANNY, *as if she had not heard* TECK]: I remember Mama's face at the wedding—it was *her* wedding, really, not mine.

FANNY [*sharply*]: You are very hard on your mother.

MARTHE: Nineteen hundred and twenty-five. No, I'm not hard on her. I only tell the truth. She wanted a life for me,

I suppose. It just wasn't the life I wanted for myself. [*Sharply.*] And that's what you have tried to do. With your children. In another way. Only Sara got away. And that made you angry—until so many years went by that you forgot.

FANNY: I don't usually mind people saying anything they think, but I find that—

MARTHE: I don't care what you mind or don't mind. I'm in love with your son—

FANNY [*very sharply*]: That's unfortunate—

MARTHE: And I'm sick of watching you try to make him into his father. I don't think you even know you do it any more and I don't think he knows it any more, either. And that's what's most dangerous about it.

FANNY [*very angrily*]: I don't know what you are talking about.

DAVID: I think you do. [*Smiles.*] You shouldn't mind hearing the truth—and neither should I.

FANNY [*worried, sharply*]: David! What does all this nonsense mean? I—

MARTHE [*to* FANNY]: Look. That pretty world Mama got me into was a tough world, see? I'm used to trouble. So don't try to interfere with me, because I won't let you. [*She goes to* DAVID.] Let's just have a good time. [*He leans down, takes both her hands, kisses them. Then slowly, she turns away, starts to exit. To* TECK.] You will also be going today?

TECK: Yes.

MARTHE: Then let us make sure we go in different directions, and do not meet again. Good-bye, Teck.

TECK: Good-bye, Marthe. You will not believe me, but I tried my best, and I am now most sorry to lose you.

MARTHE: Yes. I believe you. [*She moves out. There is silence for a minute.*]

FANNY: Well, a great many things have been said in the last few minutes.

DAVID [*crosses to bell cord. To* TECK]: I will get Joseph to pack for you.

TECK: Thank you. Do not bother. I will ring for him when

I am ready. [KURT *comes in from the study door.* SARA *turns, stares at him, waits. He does not look at her.*] It will not take me very long. [*He starts for the door, looking at* KURT.]

SARA: What is it, Kurt?

KURT: It is nothing of importance, darling— [*He looks quickly at* TECK, *who is moving very slowly.*]

SARA: Don't tell me it's nothing. I know the way you look when—

KURT [*sharply*]: I said it was of no importance. I must get to California for a few weeks. That is all.

SARA: I—

TECK [*turns*]: It is in the afternoon newspaper, Herr Müller. [*Points to paper on table.*] I was waiting to find the proper moment to call it to your attention. [*He moves toward the table, as they all turn to watch him. He picks up the paper, turns it over, begins to read.*] "Zurich, Switzerland: The Zurich papers today reprinted a despatch from the *Berliner Tageblatt*—on the capture of Colonel Max Freidank. Freidank is said [SARA *begins to move toward him*]—to be the chief of the Anti-Nazi Underground Movement. Colonel Freidank has long been an almost legendary figure. The son of the famous General Freidank, he was a World War officer and a distinguished physicist before the advent of Hitler." That is all.

SARA: Max—

KURT: Be still, Sara.

TECK: They told me of it at the Embassy last night. They also told me that with him, they had taken a man who called himself Ebber, and a man who called himself Triste. They could not find a man called Gotter. [*He starts again toward the door.*] I shall be a lonely man without Marthe. I am also a very poor one. I should like to have ten thousand dollars before I go.

DAVID [*carefully*]: You will make no loans in this house.

TECK: I was not speaking of a loan.

FANNY [*carefully*]: God made you not only a scoundrel but a fool. That is a dangerous combination.

DAVID [*suddenly leaps toward* TECK]: Damn you, you—

KURT [*suddenly pounds on the top of the piano, as* DAVID *almost reaches* TECK]: Leave him alone. [*Moves quickly to stop* DAVID.] Leave him alone! *David! Leave him alone!*

DAVID [*angrily to* KURT]: Keep out of it. [*Starts toward* TECK *again.*] I'm beginning to see what Marthe meant. Blackmailing with your wife— You—

KURT [*very sharply*]: He is not speaking of his wife. Or you. He means me. [*Looks at* TECK.] Is that correct?

[SARA *moves toward* KURT. DAVID *draws back, bewildered.*]

TECK: Good. It was necessary for me to hear you say it. You understand that?

KURT: I understand it.

SARA [*frightened, softly*]: Kurt—

DAVID: What is all this about? What the hell are you talking about?

TECK [*sharply for the first time*]: Be still. [*To* KURT.] At your convenience. Your hands are shaking, Herr Müller.

KURT [*quietly*]: My hands were broken: they are bad when I have fear.

TECK: I am sorry. I can understand that. It is not pleasant. [*Motions toward* FANNY *and* DAVID.] Perhaps you would like a little time to— I will go and pack, and be ready to leave. We will all find that more comfortable, I think. You should get yourself a smaller gun, Herr Müller. That pistol you have been carrying is big and awkward.

KURT: You saw the pistol when you examined our bags?

TECK: You knew that?

KURT: Oh, yes. I have the careful eye, through many years of needing it. And then you have not the careful eye. The pistol was lying to the left of a paper package and when you leave, it is to the right of the package.

SARA: Kurt! Do you mean that—

KURT [*sharply*]: Please, darling, do not do that.

TECK: It is a German Army Luger?

KURT: Yes.

TECK: Keep it in your pocket, Herr Müller. You will have

no need to use it. And, in any case, I am not afraid of it. You understand that?

KURT [*slowly*]: I understand that you are not a man of fears. That is strange to me, because I am a man who has so many fears.

TECK [*laughs, as he exits*]: Are you? That is most interesting. [*He exits.*]

DAVID [*softly*]: What is this about, Kurt?

KURT: He knows who I am and what I do and what I carry with me.

SARA [*carefully*]: What about Max?

KURT: The telephone was from Mexico. Ilse received a cable. Early on the morning of Monday, they caught Ebber and Triste. An hour after they took Max in Berlin. [*She looks up at him, begins to shake her head. He presses her arm.*] Yes. It is hard.

FANNY [*softly*]: You said he knew who you were and what you carried with you. I don't understand.

KURT: I am going to tell you: I am a German outlaw. I work with many others in an illegal organization. I have so worked for seven years. I am on what is called a desired list. But I did not know I was worth ten thousand dollars. My price has risen.

DAVID [*slowly*]: And what do you carry with you?

KURT: Twenty-three thousand dollars. It has been gathered from the pennies and nickels of the poor who do not like Fascism, and who believe in the work we do. I came here to bring Sara home and to get the money. I had hopes to rest here for a while, and then—

SARA [*slowly*]: And I had hopes someone else would take it back and you would stay with us— [*She shakes her head, then.*] Max is not dead?

KURT: No. The left side of his face is dead. [*Softly.*] It was a good face.

SARA [*to* FANNY *and* DAVID, *as if she were going to cry*]: It was a very good face. He and Kurt—in the old days— [*To*

KURT.] After so many years. If Max got caught, then nobody's got a chance. Nobody. [*She suddenly sits down.*]

DAVID [*points upstairs*]: He wants to sell what he knows to you? Is that right?

KURT: Yes.

FANNY: Wasn't it careless of you to leave twenty-three thousand dollars lying around to be seen?

KURT: No, it was not careless of me. It is in a locked brief-case. I have thus carried money for many years. There seemed no safer place than Sara's home. It was careless of you to have in your house a man who opens baggage and blackmails.

DAVID [*sharply*]: Yes. It was very careless.

FANNY: But you said you knew he'd seen it—

KURT: Yes. I knew it the first day we were here. What was I to do about it? He is not a man who steals. This is a safer method. I knew that it would come some other way. I have been waiting to see what the way would be. That is all I could do.

DAVID [*to* FANNY]: What's the difference? It's been done. [*To* KURT.] If he wants to sell to you, he must have another buyer. Who?

KURT: The Embassy. Von Seitz, I think.

DAVID: You mean he has told Von Seitz about you and—

KURT: No. I do not think he has told him anything. As yet. It would be foolish of him. He has probably only asked most guarded questions.

DAVID: But you're here. You're in this country. They can't do anything to you. They wouldn't be crazy enough to try it. Is your passport all right?

KURT: Not quite.

FANNY: Why not? Why isn't it?

KURT [*wearily, as if he were bored*]: Because people like me are not given visas with such ease. And I was in a hurry to bring my wife and my children to safety. [*Sharply.*] Madame Fanny, you must come to understand it is no longer the world you once knew.

DAVID: It doesn't matter. You're a political refugee. We

don't turn back people like you. People who are in danger.
You will give me your passport and tomorrow morning I'll
see Barnes. We'll tell him the truth— [*Points to the door.*]
Tell de Brancovis to go to hell. There's not a damn thing
he or anybody else can do.

SARA [*looks up at* KURT, *who is staring at her*]: You don't
understand, David.

DAVID: There's a great deal I don't understand. But there's
nothing to worry about.

SARA: Not much to worry about as long as Kurt is in this
house. But he's not going to—

KURT: The Count has made the guess that—

SARA: That you will go back to get Ebber and Triste and
Max. Is that right, Kurt? Is that right?

KURT: Yes, darling, I will try. They were taken to Sonnenburg. Guards can be bribed— It has been done once before
at Sonnenburg. We will try for it again. I must go back,
Sara. I must start.

SARA: Of course, you must go back. I guess I was trying to
think it wouldn't come. But— [*To* FANNY *and* DAVID.] Kurt's
got to go back. He's got to go home. He's got to buy them out.
He'll do it, too. You'll see. [*She stops, breathes.*] It's hard
enough to get back. Very hard. But if they knew he was
coming— They want Kurt bad. Almost as much as they wanted
Max— And then there are hundreds of others, too— [*She gets
up, comes to him. He holds her, puts his face in her hair. She
stands holding him, trying to speak without crying. She puts
her face down on his head.*] Don't be scared, darling. You'll
get back. You'll see. You've done it before—you'll do it again.
Don't be scared. You ll get Max out all right. [*Gasps.*] And
then you'll do his work, won't you? That's good. That's fine.
You'll do a good job, the way you've always done. [*She is crying very hard. To* FANNY.] Kurt doesn't feel well. He was
wounded and he gets tired— [*To* KURT.] You don't feel well,
do you? [*Slowly. She is crying too hard now to be heard
clearly.*] Don't be scared, darling. You'll get home. Don't
worry, you'll get home. Yes, you will.

ACT THREE

SCENE—*The same. A half hour later.*
AT RISE—FANNY *is sitting in a chair.* KURT *is at the piano, his head resting on one hand. He is playing softly with the other hand.* SARA *is sitting very quietly on the couch.* DAVID *is pacing on the terrace.*

FANNY [*to* DAVID]: David, would you stop that pacing, please? [DAVID *comes in.*] And would you stop that one-hand piano playing? Either play, or get up. [KURT *gets up, crosses to the couch, sits.* SARA *looks at him, gets up, crosses to the decanters, begins to make a drink.*]

SARA [*to* DAVID]: A drink?

DAVID: What? Yes, please. [*To* KURT.] Do you intend to buy your friends out of jail?

KURT: I intend to try.

FANNY: It's all very strange to me. I thought things were so well run that bribery and—

KURT [*smiles*]: What a magnificent work Fascists have done in convincing the world that they are men from legends.

DAVID: They have done very well for themselves—unfortunately.

KURT: Yes. But not by themselves. Does it make us all uncomfortable to remember that they came in on the shoulders of the most powerful men in the world? Of course. And so we would prefer to believe they are men from the planets. They are not. Let me reassure you. They are smart, they are sick, and they are cruel. But given men who know what they fight for— [*Shrugs.*] You saw it in Spain. [*Laughs.*] I will console you, A year ago last month, at three o'clock in the morning, Freidank and I, with two elderly pistols, raided the home of the Gestapo chief in Konstanz, got what we wanted and the following morning Freidank was eating his breakfast three blocks away, and I was over the Swiss border.

FANNY [*slowly*]: You are brave men.

KURT: I do not tell you the story to prove we are remarkable, but to prove they are *not*.

[SARA *brings him a drink. Gives one to* DAVID.]

SARA [*Softly, touching* KURT's *shoulder*]: Kurt loves Max.

KURT: Always since I came here I have a dream: that he will come in this room some day. How he would like it here, eh, Sara? He loves good food and wine, and you have books— [*Laughs happily.*] He is fifty-nine years of age. And when he was fifty-seven, he carried me on his back, seven miles across the border. I had been hurt— That takes a man, does it not?

FANNY [*to* KURT]: You look like a sick man to me.

KURT: No. I'm only tired. I do not like to wait. It will go.

SARA [*sharply*]: Oh, it's more than that. This is one of the times you wonder why everything has to go against you.

KURT: Waiting. It is waiting that is bad.

DAVID [*points upstairs*]: Damn him! He's doing it deliberately.

KURT: It is then the corruption begins. Once in Spain I waited for two days until the planes would exhaust themselves. I think then why must our side fight always with naked hands. The spirit and the hands. All is against us but ourselves. Sometimes, it was as if you must put up your hands and tear the wings from the planes—and then it is bad.

SARA: You will not think that when the time comes. It will go.

KURT: Of a certainty.

FANNY: But does it have to go on being your hands?

KURT: For each man, his own hands. He has to sleep with them.

DAVID [*uncomfortably, as if he did not like to say it*]: That's right. I guess it's the way all of us should feel. But—but you have a family. Isn't there somebody else who hasn't a wife and children—

KURT: Each could have his own excuse. Some love for the

first time, some have bullet holes, some have fear of the camps, some are sick, many are getting older. [*Shrugs.*] Each could find a reason. And many find it. My children are not the only children in the world, even to me.

FANNY: That's noble of you, of course. But they are your children, nevertheless. And Sara, she—

SARA. Mama—

KURT [*after a slight pause*]: One means always in English to insult with that word noble?

FANNY: Of course not, I—

KURT: It is not noble. It is the way I must live. Good or bad, it is what I am. [*Turns deliberately to look at* FANNY.] And what I am is not what you wanted for your daughter, twenty years ago or now.

FANNY: You are misunderstanding me.

KURT [*smiles*]: For our girl, too, we want a safe and happy life. And it is thus I try to make it for her. We each have our way. I do not convert you to mine.

DAVID: You are very certain of your way.

KURT [*smiles*]: I seem so to you? Good.

[JOSEPH *appears in the hall doorway. He is carrying valises and overcoats.*]

JOSEPH: What'll I do with these, Miss Fanny?

FANNY: They're too large for eating, aren't they? What were you thinking of doing with them?

JOSEPH: I mean, it's Fred's day off.

DAVID: All right. You drive him into town.

JOSEPH: Then who's going to serve at dinner?

FANNY [*impatiently*]: Belle can do it alone tonight.

JOSEPH: No she can't. Belle's upstairs packing with Miss Marthe. My, there's quite a lot of departing, ain't there?

FANNY [*very impatiently*]: All right, then cook can bring in dinner.

JOSEPH: I wouldn't ask her to do that, if I were you. She's mighty mad: the sink pipe is leaking again. You just better wait for your dinner till I get back from Washington.

FANNY [*shouting*]: We are not cripples and we were eating

dinner in this house before you arrived to show us how to use the knife and fork. [JOSEPH *laughs*.] Go on. Put his things in the car. I'll ring for you when he's ready.

JOSEPH: You told me the next time you screamed to remind you to ask my pardon.

FANNY: You call that screaming?

JOSEPH: Yes'm.

FANNY: Very well. I ask your pardon. [*Waves him away*.] Go on!

JOSEPH: Yes'm. [*Exits*.]

[TECK *appears in the door. He is carrying his hat and the brief-case we have seen in Act One.* SARA, *seeing the brief-case, looks startled, looks quickly at* KURT. KURT *watches* TECK *as he comes toward him.* TECK *throws his hat on a chair, comes to the table at which* KURT *is sitting, puts the brief-case on the table.* KURT *puts out his hand, puts it on the brief-case, leaves it there.*]

TECK [*smiles at the gesture*]: Nothing has been touched, Herr Müller. I brought it from your room, for your convenience.

FANNY [*angrily*]: Why didn't you steal it? Since you do not seem to—

TECK: That would have been very foolish of me, Madame Fanny.

KURT: Very.

TECK: I hope I have not kept you waiting too long. I wanted to give you an opportunity to make any explanations—

DAVID [*angrily*]: Does your price include listening to this tony conversation?

TECK [*turns to look at him*]: My price will rise if I have to spend the next few minutes being interrupted by your temper. I will do my business with Herr Müller. And you will understand, I will take from you no interruptions, no exclamations, no lectures, no opinions of what I am or what I am doing.

KURT [*quietly*]: You will not be interrupted.

TECK [*sits down at table with* KURT]: I have been curious

about you, Herr Müller. Even before you came here. Because Fanny and David either knew very little about you, which was strange, or wouldn't talk about you, which was just as strange. Have you ever had come to you one of those insistent half-memories of some person or some place?

KURT [*quietly, without looking up*]: You had such a half-memory of me?

TECK: Not even a memory, but something. The curiosity of one European for another, perhaps.

KURT: A most sharp curiosity. You lost no time examining— [*Pats the case.*]—this. You are an expert with locks?

TECK: No, indeed. Only when I wish to be.

FANNY [*angrily, to* TECK]: I would like you out of this house as quickly as—

TECK [*turns to her*]: Madame Fanny, I have just asked Mr. David not to do that. I must now ask you. [*Leans forward to* KURT.] Herr Müller, I got one of the desired lists from Von Seitz, without, of course, revealing anything to him. As you probably know, they are quite easy to get. I simply told him that we refugees move in small circles and I might come across somebody on it. If, however, I have to listen to any more of this from any of you, I shall go immediately to him.

KURT [*to* DAVID *and* FANNY]: Please allow the Count to do this in his own way. It will be best.

TECK [*takes a sheet of paper from his pocket*]: There are sixty-three names on this list. I read them carefully, I narrow the possibilities and under "G" I find Gotter. [*Begins to read*]: "Age, forty to forty-five. About six feet. One hundred seventy pounds. Birthplace unknown to us. Original occupation unknown to us, although he seems to know Munich and Dresden. Schooling unknown to us. Family unknown to us. No known political connections. No known trade-union connections. Many descriptions, few of them in agreement and none of them of great reliability. Equally unreliable, though often asked for, were Paris, Copenhagen, Brussels police descriptions. Only points on which there is agreement: married to a foreign woman, either American or English; three children; has used name of Gotter, Thomas Bodmer, Karl Francis. Thought to have left Germany in 1933, and to have joined Max Freidank shortly after. Worked closely with Freidank, perhaps directly under his orders. Known to have crossed border in 1934—February, May, June, October. Known to have again crossed border with Max Freidank in 1935—August, twice in October, November, January—"

KURT [*smiles*]: The report is unreliable. It would have been impossible for God to have crossed the border that often.

TECK [*looks up, laughs. Then looks back at list*]: "In 1934, outlaw radio station announcing itself as Radio European, begins to be heard. Station was located in Düsseldorf: the house of a restaurant waiter was searched, and nothing was found. Radio heard during most of 1934 and 1935. In an attempt to locate it, two probable Communists killed in the tool-house of a farm near Bonn. In three of the broadcasts, Gotter known to have crossed border immediately before and after. Radio again became active in early part of 1936. Active attempt made to locate Freidank. Gotter believed to have then appeared in Spain with Madrid Government army, in one of the German brigades, and to have been a brigade commander under previously used name of Bodmer. Known to have stayed in France the first months of 1938. Again crossed German border some time during week when Hitler's Hamburg radio speech interrupted and went off the air." [*Looks up.*] That was a daring deed, Herr Müller. It caused a great scandal. I remember. It amused me.

KURT: It was not done for that reason.

TECK: "Early in 1939, informer in Konstanz reported Gotter's entry, carrying money which had been exchanged in Paris and Brussels. Following day, home of Konstanz Gestapo chief raided for spy list by two men—" [KURT *turns to look at* FANNY *and* DAVID, *smiles.*] My God, Herr Müller, that job took two good men.

SARA [*angrily*]: Even you admire them.

TECK: Even I. Now I conclude a week ago that you are Gotter, Karl Francis—

KURT: Please. Do not describe me to myself again.

TECK: And that you will be traveling home—[*points to brief-case*]—with this. But you seem in no hurry, and so I must wait. Last night when I hear that Freidank has been taken, I guess that you will now be leaving. Not for California. I will tell you free of charge, Herr Müller, that they have got no information from Freidank or the others.

KURT: Thank you. But I was sure they would not. I know all three most well. They will take what will be given them.

TECK [*looks down. Softly*]: There is a deep sickness in the German character, Herr Müller. A pain-love, a death-love—

DAVID [*very angrily*]: Oh, for God's sake, spare us *your* moral judgments.

FANNY [*very sharply*]: Yes. They are sickening. Get on!

KURT: Fanny and David are Americans and they do not understand our world—as yet. [*Turns to* DAVID *and* FANNY.] All Fascists are not of one mind, one stripe. There are those who give the orders, those who carry out the orders, those who watch the orders being carried out. Then there are those who are half in, half hoping to come in. They are made to do the dishes and clean the boots. Frequently they come in high places and wish now only to survive. They came late: some because they did not jump in time, some because they were stupid, some because they were shocked at the crudity of the German evil, and preferred their own evils, and some because they were fastidious men. For those last, we may well some day have pity. They are lost men, their spoils are small, their day is gone. [*To* TECK.] Yes?

TECK [*slowly*]: Yes. You have the understanding heart. It will get in your way some day.

KURT [*smiles*]: I will watch it.

TECK: We are both men in trouble, Herr Müller. The world, ungratefully, seems to like your kind even less than it does mine. [*Leans forward.*] Now. Let us do business. You will not get back if Von Seitz knows you are going.

KURT: You are wrong. Instead of crawling a hundred feet an hour in deep night, I will walk across the border with as little trouble as if I were a boy again on a summer walking trip. There are many men they would like to have. I would be allowed to walk directly to them—until they had all the names and all the addresses. [*Laughs, points his finger at* TECK.] *Roumanians* would pick me up ahead of time. *Germans* would not.

TECK [*smiles*]: Still the national pride?

KURT: Why not? For that which is good.

FANNY [*comes over, very angrily, to* TECK]: I have not often in my life felt what I feel now. Whatever you are, and however you became it, the picture of a man selling the lives of other men—

TECK: Is very ugly, Madame Fanny. I do not do it without some shame, and therefore I must sink my shame in large money. [*Puts his hand on the brief-case.*] The money is here. For ten thousand, you go back to save your friends, nobody will know that you go, and I will give you my good wishes. [*Slowly, deliberately,* KURT *begins to shake his head.* TECK *waits, then carefully.*] What?

KURT: This money is going home with me. It was not given to me to save my life, and I shall not so use it. It is to save the lives and further the work of more than I. It is important to me to carry on that work and to save the lives of three valuable men, and to do that with all speed. But— [*sharply*] Count de Brancovis, the first morning we arrived in this house, my children wanted their breakfast with great haste. That is because the evening before we had been able only to buy milk and buns for them. If I would not touch this money for them, I would not touch it for you. [*Very sharply.*] It goes back with me. The way it is. And if it does not get back, it is because I will not get back.

[*There is a long pause.* SARA *gets up, turns away.*]

TECK: Then I do not think you will get back. You are a brave one, Herr Müller, but you will not get back.

KURT [*as if he were very tired*]: I will send to you a postal card and tell you about my bravery.

DAVID [*coming toward* KURT]: Is it true that if this swine talks, you and the others will be—

SARA [*very softly*]: Caught and killed. Of course. If they're lucky enough to get killed quickly. [*Quietly, points to the table.*] You should have seen those hands in 1935.

FANNY [*violently, to* DAVID]: We'll give him the money. For God's sake, let's give it to him and get him out of here.

DAVID [*to* SARA]: Do you want him to go back?

SARA: Yes. I do.

DAVID: All right. [*Goes to her, lifts her face.*] You're a good girl.

KURT: That is true. Brave and good, my Sara. She is everything. She is handsome and gay and— [*Puts his hand over his eyes.* SARA *turns away.*]

DAVID [*after a second, comes to stand near* TECK]: If we give you the money, what is to keep you from selling to Von Seitz?

TECK: I do not like your thinking I would do that. But—

DAVID [*tensely*]: Look here. I'm sick of what you'd like or wouldn't like. And I'm sick of your talk. We'll get this over with now, without any more fancy talk from you, or as far as I am concerned, you can get out of here without any money and sell to any buyer you can find. I can't take much more of you at any cost.

TECK [*smiles*]: It is your anger which delays us. I was about to say that I understood your fear that I would go to Von Seitz, and I would suggest that you give me a small amount of cash now and a check dated a month from now. In a month, Herr Müller should be nearing home, and he can let you know. And if you should not honor the check because Herr Müller is already in Germany, Von Seitz will pay a little something for a reliable description. I will take my chance on that. You will now say that I could do that in any case— and that is the chance you will take.

DAVID [*looks at* KURT, *who does not look up*]: Is a month enough? For you to get back?

KURT [*shrugs*]: I do not know.

DAVID [*to* TECK]: Two months from today. How do you want the cash and how do you want the check?

TECK: *One month from today.* That I will not discuss. One month. Please decide now.

DAVID [*sharply*]: All right. [*To* TECK.] How do you want it?

TECK: Seventy-five hundred dollars in a check. Twenty-five hundred in cash.

DAVID: I haven't anywhere near that much cash in the house. Leave your address and I'll send it to you in the morning.

TECK [*laughs*]: Address? I have no address, and I wish it now. Madame Fanny has cash in her sitting-room safe.

FANNY: Have you investigated that, too?

TECK [*laughs*]: No. You once told me you always kept money in the house.

DAVID [*to* FANNY]: How much have you got upstairs?

FANNY: I don't know. About fifteen or sixteen hundred.

TECK: Very well. That will do. Make the rest in the check.

DAVID: Get it, Mama, please. [*He starts toward the library door.* FANNY *starts for the hall exit.*]

FANNY [*turns, looks carefully at* TECK]: Years ago, I heard somebody say that being Roumanian was not a nationality, but a profession. The years have brought no change.

KURT [*softly*]: Being a Roumanian aristocrat is a profession.

[FANNY *exits. After her exit, there is silence.* KURT *does not look up,* SARA *does not move.*]

TECK [*awkwardly*]: The new world has left the room. [*Looks up at them.*] I feel less discomfort with you. We are Europeans, born to trouble and understanding it.

KURT: My wife is not a European.

TECK: Almost. [*Points upstairs.*] They are young. The world has gone well for most of them. For us— [*Smiles.*] The three of us—we are like peasants watching the big frost. Work, trouble, ruin,— [*Shrugs.*] But no need to call curses at the frost. There it is, it will be again, always—for us.

SARA [*gets up, moves to the window, looks out*]: You mean my husband and I do not have angry words for you. What for? We know how many there are of you. They don't, yet. My mother and brother feel shocked that you are in their house. For us—we have seen you in so many houses.

TECK: I do not say you *want* to understand me, Mrs. Müller. I say only that you do.

SARA: Yes. You are not difficult to understand.

KURT [*slowly gets up, stands stiffly. Then he moves toward the decanter table*]: A whiskey?

TECK: No, thank you. [*He turns his head to watch* KURT *move. He turns back.*]

KURT: Sherry?

TECK [*nods*]: Thank you, I will.

KURT [*as he pours*]: You, too, wish to go back to Europe.

TECK: Yes.

KURT: But they do not much want you. Not since the Budapest oil deal of '31.

TECK: You seem as well informed about me as I am about you.

KURT: That must have been a conference of high comedy, that one. Everybody trying to guess whether Kessler was working for Fritz Thyssen, and what Thyssen *really* wanted— and whether this "National Socialism" was a smart blind of Thyssen's, and where was Wolff—I should like to have seen you and your friends. It is too bad: you guessed an inch off, eh?

TECK: More than an inch.

KURT: And Kessler has a memory? [*Almost playfully.*] I do not think Von Seitz would pay you money for a description of a man who has a month to travel. But I think he would pay you in a visa and a cable to Kessler. I think you want a visa almost as much as you want money. Therefore, I conclude you will try for the money here, and the visa from Von Seitz. [*He comes toward the table carrying the sherry glass.*]

I cannot get anywhere near Germany in a month and you know it. [*He is about to place the glass on the table.*] I have been bored with this talk of paying you money. If they are willing to try you on this fantasy, I am not. Whatever made you think I would take such a chance? Or *any* chance? You're a gambler. But you should not gamble with your life. [TECK *has turned to stare at him, made a half motion as if to rise. As he does so, and on the words, "gamble with your life," KURT drops the glass, hits TECK in the face. Struggling, TECK makes a violent effort to rise. KURT throws himself on TECK, knocking him to the floor. As TECK falls to the floor, KURT hits him on the side of the head. At the fourth blow, TECK does not move. KURT rises, takes the gun from his pocket, begins to lift TECK from the floor. As he does so, JOSHUA appears in the hall entrance. He is washed and ready for dinner. As he reaches the door, he stops, sees the scene, stands quietly as if he were waiting for orders. KURT begins to balance TECK, to balance himself.* [To JOSHUA] Hilf mir. [JOSHUA *comes quickly to* KURT.] Mach die Tür auf! [JOSHUA *runs toward the doors, opens them, standing waiting.*] Bleib da! Mach die Tür zu! [KURT *begins to move out through the terrace. When he is outside the doors,* JOSHUA *closes them quickly, stands looking at his mother.*]

SARA: There's trouble.

JOSHUA: Do not worry. I will go up now. I will pack. In ten minutes all will be ready. I will say nothing. I will get the children ready— [*He starts quickly for the hall, turns for a second to look toward the terrace doors. Then almost with a sob.*] This was a nice house.

SARA [*softly*]: We're not going this time, darling. There's no need to pack.

JOSHUA [*stares at her, puzzled*]: But Papa—

SARA: Go upstairs, Joshua. Take Babbie and Bodo in your room, and close the door. Stay there until I call you. [*He looks at her,* SARA *sits down.*] There's nothing to be frightened of, darling. Papa is all right. [*Then very softly.*] Papa is going home.

JOSHUA: To Germany?

SARA: Yes.

JOSHUA: Oh. Alone?

SARA: Alone. [*Very softly.*] Don't say anything to the children. He will tell them himself.

JOSHUA: I won't.

SARA [*as he hesitates*]: I'm all right. Go upstairs now. [*He moves slowly out, she watches him, he disappears. For a minute she sits quietly. Then she gets up, moves to the terrace doors, stands with her hands pressed against them. Then she crosses, picks up the overturned chair, places it by the table, picks up the glass, puts it on the table. As if without knowing what she is doing, she wipes the table with her handkerchief.*]

[FANNY *comes in from hall. After a second,* DAVID *comes in from library. Stops, looks around room.*]

DAVID: Where is he? Upstairs?

SARA: No. They went outside.

FANNY: Outside? They went outside. What are they doing, picking a bouquet together?

SARA [*without turning*]: They just went outside.

DAVID [*looks at her*]: What's the matter, Sara?

[SARA *shakes her head. Goes to the desk, opens the telephone book, looks at a number, begins to dial the telephone.*]

FANNY: Eleven hundred, eleven hundred and fifty, twelve, twelve-fifty—

DAVID: For God's sake, stop counting that money.

FANNY: All right. I'm nervous. And I don't like to think of giving him too much.

SARA: It's very nice of you and Mama. All that money— [*into the telephone*] Hello. What time is your next plane? Oh. To— South. To El Paso, or— Brownsville. Yes.

DAVID [*to* FANNY]: Is Joseph ready?

FANNY: I don't know. I told him I'd call him.

SARA: To Brownsville? Yes. Yes. That's all right. At what time? Yes. No. The ticket will be picked up at the airport.

[DAVID *begins to cross to the bell cord. She looks up.*] No. David. Don't call Joseph. *David! Please!* [*He draws back,*

stares at her. Looking at him, she goes on the conversation.]
Ritter, R-I-T-T-E-R. From Chicago. Yes. Yes. [*She hangs up,
walks away.*]

DAVID: Sara! What's happening? What is all this? [*She does
not answer.*] Where is Kurt? What— [*He starts for the terrace
door.*]

SARA: David. *Don't go out.*

FANNY [*rises*]: Sara! What's happening—

SARA: For seven years now, day in, day out, men have
crossed the German border. They are always in danger. They
always may be going in to die. Did you ever see the face of a
man who never knows if this day will be the last day? [*Softly.*]
Don't go out on the terrace, David. Leave Kurt alone.

FANNY [*softly*]: Sara! What is—

SARA [*quietly*]: For them, it may be torture, and it may be
death. Some day, when it's all over, maybe there'll be a few
of them left to celebrate. There aren't many of Kurt's age left.
He couldn't take a chance on them. They wouldn't have
liked it. [*Suddenly, violently.*] He'd have had a bad time
trying to explain to them that because of this house and this
nice town and my mother and my brother, he took chances
with their work and with their lives. [*Quietly.*] Sit down,
Mama. I think it's all over now. [*To* DAVID.] There's nothing
you can do about it. It's the way it had to be.

DAVID: Sara—

FANNY: Do you mean what I think you— [*Sinks slowly into
her chair.*]

SARA [*she turns, looks out toward the doors. After a pause*]:
He's going away tonight and he's never coming back any
more. [*In a sing-song.*] Never, never, never. [*She looks down
at her hands, as if she were very interested in them.*] I don't
like to be alone at night. I guess everybody in the world's got
a time in the day they don't like. Me, it's right before I go to
sleep. And now it's going to be for always. All the rest of my
life. [*She looks up as* KURT *comes in from the terrace.*] I've
told them. There is an eighty-thirty plane going as far south

as Brownsville. I've made you a reservation. In the name of Ritter.

KURT [*stands looking at her*]: Liebe Sara! [*Then he goes to the table at which* FANNY *is sitting. To* FANNY.] It is hard for you, eh? [*He pats her hand.*] I am sorry.

FANNY [*without knowing why, she takes her hand away*]: Hard? I don't know. I—I don't— I don't know what I want to say.

KURT [*looks at the hand she has touched, then turns to look at* DAVID]. Before I come in, I stand and think. I say, I will make Fanny and David understand. I say, how can I? Does one understand a killing? No. To hell with it, I say. I do what must be done. I have long sickened of words when I see the men who live by them. What do you wish to make them understand, I ask myself. Wait. Stand here. Just stand here. What are you thinking? Say it to them just as it comes to you. And this is what came to me. When you kill in a war, it is not so lonely; and I remember a cousin I have not seen for many years; and a melody comes back and I begin to make it with my fingers; a staircase in a house in Bonn years ago; an old dog who used to live in our town; Sara in a hundred places—Shame on us. Thousands of years and we cannot yet make a world. Like a child I am. I have stopped a man's life. [*Points to the place on the couch where he had been sitting opposite* TECK.] I sit here. I listen to him. You will not believe—but I pray that I will not have to touch him. Then I know I will have to. I know that if I do not, it is only that I pamper myself, and risk the lives of others. I want you from the room. I know what I must do. [*Loudly*] All right. Do I now pretend sorrow? Do I now pretend it is not I who act thus? No. I do it. I have done it. I will do it again. And I will keep my hope that we may make a world in which all men can die in bed. I have a great hate for the violent. They are the sick of the world. [*Softly.*]Maybe I am sick now, too.

SARA: You aren't sick. Stop that. It's late. You must go soon.

KURT [*looks up at her*]: Maybe all that I have ever wanted is a land that would let me have you. [*Then without looking away from her, he puts out his hands, she touches them.*] I am going to say good-bye now to my children. Then I am going to take your car— [*Motions with his head.*] I will take him with me. After that, it is up to you. Two ways. You can let me go and keep silent. I believe I can hide him and the car. At the end of two days, if they have not been found, you will tell as much of the truth as is safe for you to say. Tell them the last time you saw us we were on our way to Washington. You did not worry at the absence, we might have rested there. Two crazy foreigners fight, one gets killed, you know nothing of the reason. I will have left the gun, there will be no doubt who did the killing. If you will give me those two days, I think I will be far enough away from here. If the car is found before then— [*Shrugs.*] I will still try to move with speed. And all that will make you, for yourselves, part of a murder. For the world, I do not think you will be in bad trouble. [*He pauses.*] There is another way. You can call your police. You can tell them the truth. I will not get home. [*To* SARA.] I wish to see the children now. [*She goes out into the hall and up the stairs. There is silence.*]

FANNY: What are you thinking, David?

DAVID: I don't know. What are you thinking?

FANNY: Me? Oh, I was thinking about my JOSHUA. I was thinking that a few months before he died, we were sitting out there. [*Points to terrace.*] He said, "Fanny, the Renaissance American is dying, the Renaissance man is dying." I said what do you mean, although I knew what he meant, I always knew. "A Renaissance man," he said, "is a man who wants to know. He wants to know how fast a bird will fly, how thick is the crust of the earth, what made Iago evil, how to plow a field. He knows there is no dignity to a mountain, if there is no dignity to man. You can't put that in a man, but when it's *really* there, and he will fight for it, put your trust in him."

DAVID [*gets up, smiles, looks at* FANNY]: You're a smart woman sometimes. [SARA *enters with* JOSHUA. *To* KURT.] Don't worry about things here. My soul doesn't have to be so nice and clean. I'll take care of it. You'll have your two days. And good luck to you.

FANNY: You go with my blessing, too. I like you.

[BODO *enters.*]

SARA: See? I come from good stock.

[KURT *looks at* DAVID. *Then he begins to smile. Nods to* DAVID. *Turns, smiles at* FANNY.]

FANNY: Do you like me?

KURT: I like you, Madame, very much.

FANNY: Would you be able to cash that check?

KURT [*laughs*]: Oh, no.

FANNY: Then take the cash. I, too, would like to contribute to your work.

KURT [*slowly*]: All right. Thank you. [*He takes the money from the table, puts it in his pocket.*]

BODO [*to* KURT]: You like Grandma? I thought you would, with time. I like her, too. Sometimes she dilates with screaming, but— Dilates is correct?

[BABETTE *enters,* JOSHUA *stands away from the others, looking at his father.* KURT *turns to look at him.*]

JOSHUA: Alles in Ordnung?

KURT: Alles in Ordnung.

BODO: What? What does that mean, all is well?

[*There is an awkward silence.*]

BABETTE [*as if she sensed it*]: We are all clean for dinner. But nobody else is clean. And I have on Grandma's dress to me—

FANNY [*very nervously*]: Of course. And you look very pretty. You're a pretty little girl, Babbie.

BODO [*looks around the room*]: What is the matter? Everybody is acting like such a ninny. I got that word from Grandma.

KURT: Come here. [*They look at him. Then slowly* BABETTE *comes toward him, followed by* BODO. JOSHUA *comes more slowly, to stand at the side of* KURT's *chair.*] We have said many good-byes to each other, eh? We must now say another. [*As they stare at him, he smiles, slowly, as if it were difficult.*] This time, I leave you with good people to whom I believe you also will be good. [*Half playfully.*] Would you allow me to give away my share in you, until I come back?

BABETTE [*slowly*]: If you would like it.

KURT: Good. To your mother, her share. My share, to Fanny and David. It is all and it is the most I have to give. [*Laughs.*] There. I have made a will, eh? Now. We will not joke. I have something to say to you. It is important for me to say it.

JOSHUA [*softly*]: You are talking to us as if we were children.

KURT [*turns to look at him*]: Am I, Joshua? I wish you were children. I wish I could say love your mother, do not eat too many sweets, clean your teeth—[*Draws* BODO *to him.*] I cannot say these things. You are not children. I took it all away from you.

BABETTE: We have had a most enjoyable life, Papa.

KURT [*smiles*]: You are a gallant little liar. And I thank you for it. I have done something bad today—

FANNY [*shocked, sharply*]: Kurt—

SARA: Don't, Mama.

[BODO *and* BABETTE *have looked at* FANNY *and* SARA, *puzzled. Then they have turned again to look at* KURT.]

KURT: It is not to frighten you. In a few days, your mother and David will tell you.

BODO: You could not do a bad thing.

BABETTE [*proudly*]: You could not.

KURT [*shakes his head*]: Now let us get straight together. The four of us. Do you remember when we read about "Les Misérables"? Do you remember that we talked about it afterwards and Bodo got candy on Mama's bed?

BODO: I remember.

KURT: Well. He stole bread. The world is out of shape we said, when there are hungry men. And until it gets in shape, men will steal and lie and—[*a little more slowly*]—kill. But for whatever reason it is done, and whoever does it—you understand me—it is all bad. I want you to remember that. Whoever does it, it is bad. [*Then very gaily.*] But you will live to see the day when it will not have to be. All over the world, in every place and every town, there are men who are going to make sure it will not have to be. They want what I want: a childhood for every child. For my children, and I for theirs. [*He picks* BODO *up, rises.*] Think of that. It will make you happy. In every town and every village and every mud hut in the world, there is always a man who loves children and who will fight to make a good world for them. And now good-bye. Wait for me. I shall try to come back for you. [*He moves toward the hall, followed by* BABETTE, *and more slowly, by* JOSHUA.] Or you shall come to me. At Hamburg, the boat will come in. It will be a fine, safe land— I will be waiting on the dock. And there will be the three of you and Mama and Fanny and David. And I will have ordered an extra big dinner and we will show them what our Germany can be like— [*He has put* BODO *down. He leans down, presses his face in* BABETTE's *hair. Tenderly, as her mother has done earlier, she touches his hair.*]

JOSHUA: Of course. That is the way it will be. Of course. But—but if you should find yourself delayed— [*very slowly*]— then I will come to you. Mama.

SARA [*she has turned away*]: I heard you, Joshua.

KURT [*he kisses* BABETTE]: Gute Nacht, Liebling!

BABETTE: Gute Nacht, Papa. Mach's gut!

KURT [*leans to kiss* BODO]: Good night, baby.

BODO: Good night, Papa. Mach's gut!

[BABETTE *runs up the steps. Slowly* BODO *follows her.*]

KURT [*kisses* JOSHUA]: Good night, son.

JOSHUA: Good night, Papa. Mach's gut! [*He begins to climb the steps.* KURT *stands watching them, smiling. When they disappear, he turns to* DAVID.]

KURT: Good-bye, and thank you.

DAVID: Good-bye, and good luck.

KURT [*he moves to* FANNY]: Good-bye. I have good children, eh?

FANNY: Yes, you have.

[KURT *kisses her hand.*]

KURT [*slowly, he turns toward* SARA]: Men who wish to live have the best chance to live. I wish to live. I wish to live with you.

[*She comes toward him.*]

SARA: For twenty years. It is as much for me today. [*Takes his arms.*] Just once, and for all my life. [*He pulls her toward him.*] Come back for me, darling. If you can. [*Takes brief-case from table and gives it to him.*]

KURT [*simply*]: I will try. [*He turns.*] Good-bye, to you all. [*He exits. After a second, there is the sound of a car starting. They sit listening to it. Gradually the noise begins to go off into the distance. A second later,* JOSHUA *appears.*]

JOSHUA: Mama— [*She looks up. He is very tense.*] Bodo cries. Babette looks very queer. I think you should come.

SARA [*gets up, slowly*]: I'm coming.

JOSHUA [*to* FANNY *and* DAVID. *Still very tense*]: Bodo talks so fancy, we forget sometimes he is a baby. [*He waits for* SARA *to come up to him. When she reaches him, she takes his hand, goes up the steps, disappears.* FANNY *and* DAVID *watch them.*]

FANNY [*after a minute*]: Well, here we are shaken out of the magnolias, eh?

DAVID: Yes. So we are.

FANNY: Tomorrow will be a hard day. But we'll have Babbie's birthday dinner. And we'll have music afterwards. You can be the audience. I think you'd better go up to Marthe now. Be as careful as you can. She'd better stay here for a while. I daresay I can stand it.

DAVID [*turns, smiles*]: Even your graciousness is ungracious, Mama.

FANNY: I do my best. Well, I think I shall go and talk to Anise. I like Anise best when I don't feel well. [*She begins to move off.*]

DAVID: Mama. [*She turns.*] We are going to be in for trouble. You understand that?

FANNY: I understand it very well. We will manage. You and I. I'm not put together with flour paste. And neither are you— I am happy to learn.

DAVID: Good night, Mama.

[*As she moves out, the curtains falls.*]

LILLIAN HELLMAN

Of the younger writers for the American stage, Lillian Hellman is one of the best established, with three successes and the Drama Critics' Award for *Watch on the Rhine* (1941). She has real dramatic sense, a fine command of character and dialogue, and underlying seriousness of purpose.

Born on June 20, 1905, in New Orleans, she grew up in New York, studied for three years at New York University and enrolled briefly at Columbia.

In 1924, she began work for the publishing firm of Horace Liveright, Inc., but after a year married the playwright, Arthur Kober, and found herself introduced to the world of writing and writers. For the next several years she was active in many things but chiefly as a play and scenario reader in New York and Hollywood.

Her play, *The Children's Hour,* produced in 1934 under the direction of Herman Shumlin, was a success. *Days to Come* was a failure, but *The Little Foxes,* a fine study of hard-bitten character, was a hit, and *Watch on the Rhine* is easily the best of the anti-Nazi plays.

Miss Hellman continues to live in New York, with periods in Hollywood while she adapts her plays for the screen. Her recent dramas have been less praised, but she is among our most accomplished playwrights and will surely be heard from again.

Her plays and the dates of their first production:

The Children's Hour, November 20, 1934.

Days To Come, December 15, 1936.

The Little Foxes, February 15, 1939.

Watch on the Rhine, April 1, 1941.

The Searching Wind, April 12, 1944.

Another Part of the Forest, November 20, 1946.

CRITICAL COMMENTS

WATCH ON THE RHINE

In "Watch on the Rhine," which was put on at the Martin Beck last evening, Lillian Hellman has brought the awful truth close to home. She has translated the death struggle between ideas in familiar terms we are bound to respect and understand. Curious how much better she has done it than anybody else by forgetting the headlines and by avoiding the obvious approaches to the great news subject of today. After the hardness and coldness of "The Children's Hour" and "The Little Foxes," it is also remarkable that she is now writing with great humanity about people whose native grace she admires.

Her two previous dramas were more perfectly put together, each scene dovetailing with the one preceding. The narrative of "Watch on the Rhine" drifts into generalities before the main action is well started. But that is carping at technicalities, and it does not destroy a general impression that "Watch on the Rhine" is the finest thing she has written. Beautifully directed by Herman Shumlin and magnificently acted by Paul Lukas in the leading part, it is a play of pith and moment and the theatre may be proud of it.

What it says is that the death of fascism is more desirable than the lives and well-being of the people who hate it. Miss Hellman makes that familiar point without political argument and without reproducing in miniature form the struggle between fascism and democracy. . . .

The characters are well drawn out of affection for people of integrity. The writing is enormously skillful—humorous, witty and also forthright when the time comes for plain speaking. Among other things, Miss Hellman draws a vivid contrast between the simple good-will of a normal American family and the dark callousness of Europeans who have grown accustomed to horror, intrigue and desperation.

[Brooks Atkinson, in *The New York Times* (April 2, 1941), p. 26. Reprinted by permission.]

WATCH ON THE RHINE

Miss Lillian Hellman's play ... could be treated as a thriller, or as a politico-propagandist tract; it is in many ways that sort of story. But Miss Hellman has chosen it as the framework for the expression of the European tragedy and of the hidden sense of guilt which those who were too much outside it will never lose; and because she is a dramatist of the first order she has made of it the richest and most moving play we have seen since *Thunder Rock.*

She spares us nothing of the raw European horror of the Thirties. The man, hunted, injured from past tortures, brave as a lion because he is the victim of a terrible fear; the wife, immensely strong in the knowledge of her fate and her faith; the children, so terrifying in their frank and adult wisdom, and their acceptance of the fugitive's lot, but so roundly and truly children—these make up a group, a family whose bonds are not merely those of flesh and blood but of an implicit, never-spoken-of, and perpetual act of faith.

Over against them is placed the world-adventurer—not the direct Nazi, but the assiduous jackal, the Nazi type without the Nazi faith—Nazi enough, however, to remind us, when his wife publicly exposes and deserts him, of a certain Ribbentrop who never forgave the insults he imagined he received at the Court of St. James. The second contrast is, of course, the châtelaine of the country house, growing to a graceful old age, having built for herself a character which combines eccentricity with selfishness, and masks only too often a heart of gold behind a failure to understand.

Apart from a slightly machine-made opening to the first act, the author manipulates her plot and characters with an assurance, an economy, and a sense of human values to which only an exceptionally talented cast could do justice.

[Basil Wright, in *The Spectator*, 168 (May 1, 1942), p. 419. Reprinted by permission.]

HOWARD LINDSAY and
RUSSEL CROUSE

———

LIFE WITH FATHER

CHARACTERS

FATHER—*about* 50
MOTHER (*Vinnie*)—*about* 40
CLARENCE—*about* 17
JOHN—*about* 15
WHITNEY—*about* 13
HARLAN—*about* 6
CORA (*Vinnie's Cousin*)—*about* 30
MARY SKINNER—*about* 16
THE REVEREND DR. LLOYD—*about* 50
DR. HUMPHREYS—*about* 55
DR. SOMERS—*about* 60
MARGARET, *the cook*—*about* 45
ANNIE, *a maid*—*about* 20
DELIA, *a maid*—*about* 25
NORA, *a maid*—*about* 40
MAGGIE, *a maid*—*about* 30

SCENES

The time: late in the 1880's.
The entire action takes place in the Morning Room of the Day
 home on Madison Avenue.

ACT ONE

Scene 1 *Breakfast time. An early summer morning.*
Scene 2 *Tea time. The same day.*

ACT TWO

Scene 1 *Sunday, after church. A week later.*
Scene 2 *Breakfast time. Two days later. [During Scene 2 the
 curtain is lowered to denote a lapse of three hours.]*

ACT THREE

Scene 1 *Mid-afternoon. A month later.*
Scene 2 *Breakfast time. The next morning.*

LIFE WITH FATHER

ACT ONE

SCENE 1

The Morning Room of the Day home at 420 Madison Avenue. In the custom of the Victorian period, this was the room where the family gathered for breakfast, and because it was often the most comfortable room in the house, it served also as a living-room for the family and their intimates.

There is a large arch in the center of the upstage wall of the room, through which we can see the hall and the stairs leading to the second floor, and below them the rail of the stairwell leading to the basement. The room can be closed off from the hall by sliding doors in the archway. The front door of the house, which is stage right, can't be seen, but frequently is heard to slam.

In the Morning Room the sunshine streams through the large window at the right which looks out on Madison Avenue. The room itself is furnished with the somewhat less than comfortable furniture of the period, which is the late 1880's. The general color scheme in drapes and upholstery is green. Below the window is a large comfortable chair where FATHER *generally sits to read his paper. Right of center is the table which serves as a living-room table, with its proper table cover and fruit bowl; but now, expanded by extra leaves, it is doing service as a breakfast table. Against the back wall, either side of the arch, are two console tables which are used by the maid as serving tables. Left of center is a sofa, with a table just above its right end holding a lamp, framed photographs, and other ornaments. In the left wall is a fireplace, its mantel draped with a lambrequin. On the mantel are a clock and other ornaments, and above the mantel is a large mirror in a Victorian frame. The room is cluttered with the min-utiæ of the period, including the inevitable rubber plant, and looking down from the walls are the Day ancestors in painted portraits. The room has the warm quality that comes only from having been lived in by a family which enjoys each other's com-pany—a family of considerable means.*

As the curtain rises, ANNIE, *the new maid, a young Irish girl, is finishing setting the table for breakfast. After an uncertain look at the result she crosses over to her tray on the console table.* VINNIE *comes down the stairs and into the room.* VINNIE *is a charming, lovable, and spirited woman of forty. She has a lively mind which darts quickly away from any practical matter. She has red hair.*

ANNIE: Good morning, ma'am.

VINNIE: Good morning, Annie. How are you getting along?

ANNIE: All right, ma'am, I hope.

VINNIE: Now, don't be worried just because this is your first day. Everything's going to be all right—but I do hope nothing goes wrong. [*Goes to the table.*] Now, let's see, is the table all set? [ANNIE *follows her.*] The cream and the sugar go down at this end.

ANNIE [*placing them where* VINNIE *has indicated*]: I thought in the center, ma'am; everyone could reach them easier.

VINNIE: Mr. Day sits here.

ANNIE [*gets a tray of napkins, neatly rolled and in their rings, from the console table*]: I didn't know where to place the napkins, ma'am.

VINNIE: You can tell which go where by the rings. [*Takes them from the tray and puts them down as she goes around the table.* ANNIE *follows her.*] This one belongs to Whitney —it has his initial on it, "W"; that one with the little dog on it is Harlan's, of course. He's the baby. This "J" is for John and the "C" is for Clarence. This narrow plain one is mine. And this is Mr. Day's. It's just like mine—except that it got bent one morning. And that reminds me—always be sure Mr. Day's coffee is piping hot.

ANNIE: Ah, your man has coffee instead of tea of a morn-ing?

VINNIE: We all have coffee except the two youngest boys. They have their milk. And, Annie, always speak of my husband as Mr. Day.

ANNIE: I will that.

VINNIE [*correcting her*]: "Yes, ma'am," Annie.

ANNIE: Yes, ma'am.

VINNIE: And if Mr. Day speaks to you, just say: "Yes, sir." Don't be nervous—you'll get used to him.

[CLARENCE, *the eldest son, about seventeen, comes down the stairs and into the room. He is a manly, serious, good-looking boy. Because he is starting in at Yale next year, he thinks he is grown-up. He is red-headed.*]

CLARENCE: Good morning, Mother. [*He kisses her.*]

VINNIE: Good morning, Clarence.

CLARENCE: Did you sleep well, Mother?

VINNIE: Yes, thank you, dear. [CLARENCE *goes to* FATHER'S *chair and picks up the morning paper. To* ANNIE.] We always start with fruit, except the two young boys, who have porridge.

[ANNIE *brings the fruit and porridge to the table.* CLARENCE, *looking at the paper, makes a whistling sound.*]

CLARENCE: Jiminy! Another wreck on the New Haven. That always disturbs the market. Father won't like that.

VINNIE: I do wish that New Haven would stop having wrecks. If they knew how it upset your father— [*Sees that* CLARENCE'S *coat has been torn and mended.*] My soul and body. Clarence, what's happened to your coat?

CLARENCE: I tore it. Margaret mended it for me.

VINNIE: It looks terrible. Why don't you wear your blue suit?

CLARENCE: That looks worse than this one. You know, I burnt that hole in it.

VINNIE: Oh, yes—well, you can't go around looking like that. I'll have to speak to your father. Oh, dear!

[JOHN, *who is about fifteen, comes down the stairs and into the room.* JOHN *is gangly and a little overgrown. He is red-headed.*]

JOHN: Good morning, Mother. [*He kisses her.*]

VINNIE: Good morning, John.

JOHN [*to* CLARENCE]: Who won?

CLARENCE: I haven't looked yet.

JOHN: Let me see. [*He tries to take the paper away from* CLARENCE.]

CLARENCE: Be careful!

VINNIE: Boys, don't wrinkle that paper before your father's looked at it.

CLARENCE [*to* JOHN]: Yes!

[VINNIE *turns to* ANNIE.]

VINNIE: You'd better get things started. We want everything ready when Mr. Day comes down. [ANNIE *exits.*] Clarence, right after breakfast I want you and John to move the small bureau from my room into yours.

CLARENCE: What for? Is somebody coming to visit us?

JOHN: Who's coming?

VINNIE: I haven't said anyone was coming. And don't you say anything about it. I want it to be a surprise.

CLARENCE: Oh! Father doesn't know yet?

VINNIE: No. And I'd better speak to him about a new suit for you before he finds out he's being surprised by visitors.

[ANNIE *enters with a tray on which are two glasses of milk, which she puts at* HARLAN's *and* WHITNEY's *places at the table.*]

[WHITNEY *comes down the stairs and rushes into the room. He is about thirteen. Suiting his age, he is a lively active boy. He is red-headed.*]

WHITNEY: Morning. [*He kisses his mother quickly, then runs to* CLARENCE *and* JOHN.] Who won?

JOHN: The Giants, 7 to 3. Buck Ewing hit a home run.

WHITNEY: Let me see!

[HARLAN *comes sliding down the banister. He enters the room, runs to his mother, and kisses her.* HARLAN *is a rolypoly, lovable, good-natured youngster of six. He is red-headed.*

VINNIE: How's your finger, darling?

HARLAN: It itches.

VINNIE [*kissing the finger*]: That's a sign it's getting better. Now don't scratch it. Sit down, boys. Get in your chair, darling. [*The boys move to the table and take their places. CLARENCE puts the newspaper beside his father's plate. JOHN stands waiting to place VINNIE's chair when she sits.*] Now, Annie, watch Mr. Day, and as soon as he finishes his fruit— [*Leaves the admonition hanging in mid-air as the sound of FATHER's voice booms from upstairs.*]

FATHER'S VOICE: Vinnie! Vinnie!

[*All eyes turn toward the staircase. VINNIE rushes to the foot of the stairs, speaking as she goes.*]

VINNIE: What's the matter, Clare?

FATHER'S VOICE: Where's my necktie?

VINNIE: Which necktie?

FATHER'S VOICE: The one I gave you yesterday.

VINNIE: It isn't pressed yet. I forgot to give it to Margaret.

FATHER'S VOICE: I told you distinctly I wanted to wear that necktie today.

VINNIE: You've got plenty of neckties. Put on another one right away and come down to breakfast.

FATHER'S VOICE: Oh, damn! Damnation!

[*VINNIE goes to her place at the table. JOHN places her chair for her, then sits. WHITNEY has started eating.*]

CLARENCE: Whitney!

VINNIE: Wait for your father, Whitney.

WHITNEY: Oh, and I'm in a hurry! John, can I borrow your glove today? I'm going to pitch.

JOHN: If I don't play myself.

WHITNEY: Look, if you need it, we're playing in that big field at the corner of Fifty-seventh and Madison.

VINNIE: 'Way up there!

WHITNEY: They're building a house on that vacant lot on Fiftieth Street.

VINNIE: My! My! My! Here we move to Forty-eighth Street just to get out of the city!

WHITNEY: Can't I start breakfast, Mother? I promised to be there by eight o'clock.

VINNIE: After breakfast, Whitney, you have to study your catechism.

WHITNEY: Mother, can't I do that this afternoon?

VINNIE: Whitney, you have to learn five questions every morning before you leave the house.

WHITNEY: Aw, Mother—

VINNIE: You weren't very sure of yourself when I heard you last night.

WHITNEY: I know them now.

VINNIE: Let's see. [WHITNEY *rises and faces his mother.*] "What is your name?"

WHITNEY: Whitney Benjamin.

VINNIE: "Who gave you this name?"

WHITNEY: "My sponsors in baptism, wherein I was made a member of Christ, the child of God and an inheritor of the Kingdom of Heaven." Mother, if I hadn't been baptized wouldn't I have a name?

VINNIE: Not in the sight of the Church. "What did your sponsors then for you?"

WHITNEY: "They did promise and vow three things in my name—"

[FATHER *makes his appearance on the stairway and comes down into the room.* FATHER *is in his forties, distinguished in appearance, with great charm and vitality, extremely well dressed in a conservative way. He is red-headed.*]

FATHER [*heartily*]: Good morning, boys. [*They rise and answer him.*] Good morning, Vinnie. [*He goes to her and kisses her.*] Have a good night?

VINNIE: Yes, thank you, Clare.

FATHER: Good! Sit down, boys.

[*The doorbell rings and a postman's whistle is heard.*]

VINNIE: That's the doorbell, Annie. [ANNIE *exits.*] Clare, that new suit looks very nice.

FATHER: Too damn tight! [*He sits in his place at the head of the table.*] What's the matter with those fellows over in

London? I wrote them a year ago they were making my clothes too tight!

VINNIE: You've put on a little weight, Clare.

FATHER: I weigh just the same as I always have. [*Attacks his orange. The boys dive into their breakfasts.* ANNIE *enters with the mail, starts to take it to* VINNIE. FATHER *sees her.*] What's that? The mail? That goes to me.

[ANNIE *gives the mail to* FATHER *and exits with her tray.*]

VINNIE: Well, Clarence has just managed to tear the only decent suit of clothes he has.

FATHER [*looking through the mail*]: Here's one for you, Vinnie. John, hand that to your mother. [*He passes the letter on.*]

VINNIE: Clare dear, I'm sorry, but I'm afraid Clarence is going to have to have a new suit of clothes.

FATHER: Vinnie, Clarence has to learn not to be so hard on his clothes.

CLARENCE: Father, I thought—

FATHER: Clarence, when you start in Yale in the fall, I'm going to set aside a thousand dollars just to outfit you, but you'll get no new clothes this summer.

CLARENCE: Can't I have one of your old suits cut down for me?

FATHER: Every suit I own still has plenty of wear in it. I wear my clothes until they're worn out.

VINNIE: Well, if you want your clothes worn out, Clarence can wear them out much faster than you can.

CLARENCE: Yes, and, Father, you don't get a chance to wear them out. Every time you get a new batch of clothes, Mother sends the old ones to the missionary barrel. I guess I'm just as good as any old missionary.

[ANNIE *returns with a platter of bacon and eggs and a pot of coffee.*]

VINNIE: Clarence, before you compare yourself to a missionary, remember the sacrifices they make.

FATHER [*chuckling*]: I don't know, Vinnie, I think my clothes would look better on Clarence than on some Hottentot. [*To* CLARENCE.] Have that black suit of mine cut down to fit you before your mother gets her hands on it.

[ANNIE *clears the fruit.*]

CLARENCE: Thank you, Father. [*To* JOHN.] One of Father's suits! Thank you, sir!

FATHER: Whitney, don't eat so fast.

WHITNEY: Well, Father, I'm going to pitch today and I promised to get there early, but before I go I have to study my catechism.

FATHER: What do you bother with that for?

VINNIE [*with spirit*]: Because if he doesn't know his catechism he can't be confirmed!

WHITNEY [*pleading*]: But I'm going to pitch today.

FATHER: Vinnie, Whitney's going to pitch today and he can be confirmed any old time.

VINNIE: Clare, sometimes it seems to me that you don't care whether your children get to Heaven or not.

FATHER: Oh, Whitney'll get to Heaven all right. [*To* WHITNEY.] I'll be there before you are, Whitney; I'll see that you get in.

VINNIE: What makes you so sure they'll let you in?

FATHER: Well, if they don't I'll certainly raise a devil of a row.

[ANNIE *is at* FATHER'S *side with the platter of bacon and eggs, ready to serve him, and draws back at this astounding declaration, raising the platter.*]

VINNIE [*with shocked awe*]: Clare, I do hope you'll behave when you get to Heaven.

[FATHER *has turned to serve himself from the platter, but* ANNIE, *not yet recovered from the picture of* FATHER *raising a row at the gates of Heaven, is holding it too high for him.*]

FATHER [*storming*]: Vinnie, how many times have I asked you not to engage a maid who doesn't even know how to serve properly?

VINNIE: Clare, can't you see she's new and doing her best?

FATHER: How can I serve myself when she's holding that platter over my head?

VINNIE: Annie, why don't you hold it lower?

[ANNIE *lowers the platter.* FATHER *serves himself, but goes on talking.*]

FATHER: Where'd she come from anyway? What became of the one we had yesterday? I don't see why you can't keep a maid.

VINNIE: Oh, you don't!

FATHER: All I want is service. [ANNIE *serves the others nervously. So far as* FATHER *is concerned, however, the storm has passed, and he turns genially to* WHITNEY.] Whitney, when we get to Heaven we'll organize a baseball team of our own. [*The boys laugh.*]

VINNIE: It would be just like you to try to run things up there.

FATHER: Well, from all I've heard about Heaven, it seems to be a pretty unbusinesslike place. They could probably use a good man like me. [*Stamps on the floor three times. It is his traditional signal to summon* MARGARET, *the cook, from the kitchen below.*]

VINNIE: What do you want Margaret for? What's wrong?

[ANNIE *has reached the sideboard and is sniffing audibly.*]

FATHER [*distracted*]: What's that damn noise?

VINNIE: Shhh—it's Annie.

FATHER: Annie? Who's Annie?

VINNIE: The maid. [ANNIE, *seeing that she has attracted attention, hurries out into the hall where she can't be seen or heard.*] Clare, aren't you ashamed of yourself?

FATHER [*surprised*]: What have I done now?

VINNIE: You made her cry—speaking to her the way you did.

FATHER: I never said a word to her—I was addressing myself to you.

VINNIE: I do wish you'd be more careful. It's hard enough to keep a maid—and the uniforms just fit this one.

[MARGARET, *the cook, a small Irishwoman of about fifty, hurries into the room.*]

MARGARET: What's wanting?

FATHER: Margaret, this bacon is good. [MARGARET *beams and gestures deprecatingly.*] It's good. It's done just right!

MARGARET: Yes, sir! [*She smiles and exits.* ANNIE *returns, recovered, and starts serving the coffee.* VINNIE *has opened her letter and glanced through it.*]

VINNIE: Clare, this letter gives me a good idea. I've decided that next winter I won't give a series of dinners.

FATHER: I should hope not.

VINNIE: I'll give a big musicale instead.

FATHER: You'll give a what?

VINNIE: A musicale.

FATHER [*peremptorily*]: Vinnie, I won't have my peaceful home turned into a Roman arena with a lot of hairy fiddlers prancing about.

VINNIE: I didn't say a word about hairy fiddlers. Mrs. Spiller has written me about this lovely young girl who will come for very little.

FATHER: What instrument does this inexpensive paragon play?

VINNIE: She doesn't play, Clare, she whistles.

FATHER: Whistles? Good God!

VINNIE: She whistles sixteen different pieces. All for twenty-five dollars.

FATHER [*stormily*]: I won't pay twenty-five dollars to any human peanut stand. [*He tastes his coffee, grimaces, and again stamps three times on the floor.*]

VINNIE: Clare, I can arrange this so it won't cost you a penny. If I invite fifty people and charge them fifty cents apiece, there's the twenty-five dollars right there!

FATHER: You can't invite people to your own house and charge them admission.

VINNIE: I can if the money's for the missionary fund.

FATHER: Then where will you get the twenty-five dollars to pay that poor girl for her whistling?

VINNIE: Now, Clare, let's not cross that bridge until we come to it.

FATHER: And if we do cross it, it will cost me twenty-five

dollars. Vinnie, I'm putting my foot down about this musicale, just as I've had to put my foot down about your keeping this house full of visiting relatives. Why can't we live here by ourselves in peace and comfort?

[MARGARET *comes dashing into the room.*]

MARGARET: What's wanting?

FATHER [*sternly*]: Margaret, what is this? [*He holds up his coffee cup and points at it.*]

MARGARET: It's coffee, sir.

FATHER: It is not coffee! You couldn't possibly take water and coffee beans and arrive at that! It's slops, that's what it is—slops! Take it away! Take it away, I tell you!

[MARGARET *takes* FATHER's *cup and dashes out.* ANNIE *starts to take* VINNIE's *cup.*]

VINNIE: Leave my coffee there, Annie! It's perfectly all right!

[ANNIE *leaves the room.*]

FATHER [*angrily*]: It is not! I swear I can't imagine how she concocts such an atrocity. I come down to this table every morning hungry—

VINNIE: Well, if you're hungry, Clare, why aren't you eating your breakfast?

FATHER: What?

VINNIE: If you're hungry, why aren't you eating your breakfast?

FATHER [*thrown out of bounds*]: I am. [*He takes a mouthful of bacon and munches it happily, his eyes falling on* HARLAN.] Harlan, how's that finger? Come over here and let me see it. [HARLAN *goes to his father's side. He shows his finger.*] Well, that's healing nicely. Now don't pick that scab or it will leave a scar, and we don't want scars on our fingers, do we? [*He chuckles.*] I guess you'll remember after this that cats don't like to be hugged. It's all right to stroke them, but don't squeeze them. Now go back and finish your oatmeal.

HARLAN: I don't like oatmeal.

FATHER [*kindly*]: It's good for you. Go back and eat it.

HARLAN: But I don't like it.

FATHER [*quietly, but firmly*]: I'll tell you what you like and what you don't like. You're not old enough to know about such things. You've no business not to like oatmeal. It's good.

HARLAN: I hate it.

FATHER [*firmly, but not quietly*]: That's enough! We won't discuss it! Eat that oatmeal at once!

[*In contrast to* HARLAN, WHITNEY *has been eating his oatmeal at a terrific rate of speed. He pauses and puts down his spoon.*]

WHITNEY: I've finished *my* oatmeal. May I be excused?

FATHER: Yes, Whitney, you may go. [WHITNEY *slides off his chair and hurries to the stairs.*] Pitch a good game.

VINNIE: Whitney!

WHITNEY: I'm going upstairs to study my catechism.

VINNIE: Oh, that's all right. Run along.

WHITNEY [*on the way up*]: Harlan, you'd better hurry up and finish your oatmeal if you want to go with me.

[*Throughout breakfast* FATHER *has been opening and glancing through his mail. He has just reached one letter, however, that bewilders him.*]

FATHER: I don't understand why I'm always getting damn fool letters like this!

VINNIE: What is it, Clare?

FATHER: "Dear Friend Day: We are assigning you the exclusive rights for Staten Island for selling the Gem Home Popper for popcorn—"

CLARENCE: I think that's for me, Father.

FATHER: Then why isn't it addressed to Clarence Day, Jr.? [*He looks at the envelope.*] Oh, it is. Well, I'm sorry. I didn't mean to open your mail.

[MARGARET *returns and slips a cup of coffee to the table beside* FATHER.]

VINNIE: I wouldn't get mixed up in that, Clarence. People like popcorn, but they won't go all the way to Staten Island to buy it.

[FATHER *has picked up the paper and is reading it. He drinks his coffee absentmindedly.*]

FATHER: Chauncey Depew's having another birthday.

VINNIE: How nice.

FATHER: He's always having birthdays. Two or three a year. Damn! Another wreck on the New Haven!

VINNIE: Yes. Oh, that reminds me. Mrs. Bailey dropped in yesterday.

FATHER: Was she in the wreck?

VINNIE: No. But she was born in New Haven. Clarence, you're having tea with Edith Bailey Thursday afternoon.

CLARENCE: Oh, Mother, do I have to?

JOHN [*singing*]: "I like coffee, I like tea. I like the girls and the girls like me."

CLARENCE: Well, the girls don't like me and I don't like them.

VINNIE: Edith Bailey's a very nice girl, isn't she, Clare?

FATHER: Edith Bailey? Don't like her. Don't blame Clarence.

[FATHER *goes to his chair by the window and sits down with his newspaper and a cigar. The others rise.* HARLAN *runs upstairs.* ANNIE *starts clearing the table and exits with the tray of dishes a little later.* VINNIE *speaks in a guarded tone to the two boys.*]

VINNIE: Clarence, you and John go upstairs and do—what I asked you to.

JOHN: You said the small bureau, Mother?

VINNIE: Shh! Run along.

[*The boys go upstairs, somewhat unwillingly.* MARGARET *enters.*]

MARGARET: If you please, ma'am, there's a package been delivered with a dollar due on it. Some kitchen knives.

VINNIE: Oh, yes, those knives from Lewis & Conger's. [*She gets her purse from the drawer in the console table and gives* MARGARET *a dollar.*] Here, give this dollar to the man, Margaret.

FATHER: Make a memorandum of that, Vinnie. One dollar and whatever it was for.

VINNIE [*looking into purse*]: Clare, dear, I'm afraid I'm going to need some more money.

FATHER: What for?

VINNIE: You were complaining of the coffee this morning. Well, that nice French drip coffee pot is broken—and you know how it got broken.

FATHER [*taking out his wallet*]: Never mind that, Vinnie. As I remember, that coffee pot cost five dollars and something. Here's six dollars. [*He gives her six dollars.*] And when you get it, enter the exact amount in the ledger downstairs.

VINNIE: Thank you, Clare.

FATHER: We can't go on month after month having the household accounts in such a mess.

VINNIE [*she sits on the arm of* FATHER's *chair*]: No, and I've thought of a system that will make my bookkeeping perfect.

FATHER: I'm certainly relieved to hear that. What is it?

VINNIE: Well, Clare dear, you never make half the fuss over how much I've spent as you do over my not being able to remember what I've spent it for.

FATHER: Exactly. This house must be run on a business basis. That's why I insist on your keeping books.

VINNIE: That's the whole point, Clare. All we have to do is open charge accounts everywhere and the stores will do my bookkeeping for me.

FATHER: Wait a minute, Vinnie—

VINNIE: Then when the bills come in you'd know exactly where your money had gone.

FATHER: I certainly would. Vinnie, I get enough bills as it is.

VINNIE: Yes, and those bills always help. They show you just where I spent the money. Now if we had charge accounts everywhere—

FATHER: Now, Vinnie, I don't know about that.

VINNIE: Clare dear, don't you hate those arguments we

have every month? I certainly do. Not to have those I should think would be worth something to you.

FATHER: Well, I'll open an account at Lewis & Conger's—and one at McCreery's to start with—we'll see how it works out. [*He shakes his head doubtfully. Her victory gained,* VINNIE *moves away.*]

VINNIE: Thank you, Clare. Oh—the rector's coming to tea today.

FATHER: The rector? I'm glad you warned me. I'll go to the club. Don't expect me home until dinner time.

VINNIE: I do wish you'd take a little more interest in the church. [*Goes behind* FATHER'S *chair and looks down at him with concern.*]

FATHER: Vinnie, getting me into Heaven's your job. If there's anything wrong with my ticket when I get there, you can fix it up. Everybody loves you so much—I'm sure God must, too.

VINNIE: I'll do my best, Clare. It wouldn't be Heaven without you.

FATHER: If you're there, Vinnie, I'll manage to get in some way, even if I have to climb the fence.

JOHN [*from upstairs*]: Mother, we've moved it. Is there anything else?

FATHER: What's being moved?

VINNIE: Never mind, Clare. I'll come right up, John. [*She goes to the arch, stops. Looks back at* FATHER.] Oh, Clare it's eight thirty. You don't want to be late at the office.

FATHER: Plenty of time. [VINNIE *looks nervously toward the door, then goes upstairs.* FATHER *returns to his newspaper.* VINNIE *has barely disappeared when something in the paper arouses* FATHER'S *indignation.*] Oh, God!

[VINNIE *comes running downstairs.*]

VINNIE: What's the matter, Clare? What's wrong?

FATHER: Why did God make so many damn fools and Democrats?

VINNIE [*relieved*]: Oh, politics. [*She goes upstairs again.*]

FATHER [*shouting after her*]: Yes, but it's taking the bread out of our mouths. It's robbery, that's what it is, highway robbery! Honest Hugh Grant! Honest! Bah! A fine mayor you've turned out to be. [FATHER *launches into a vigorous denunciation of Mayor Hugh Grant, addressing that gentleman as though he were present in the room, called upon the Day carpet to listen to* FATHER'S *opinion of Tammany's latest attack on his pocketbook.*] If you can't run this city without raising taxes every five minutes, you'd better get out and let someone who can. Let me tell you, sir, that the real-estate owners of New York City are not going to tolerate these conditions any longer. Tell me this—are these increased taxes going into public improvements or are they going into graft —answer me that, honestly, if you can, Mr. Honest Hugh Grant. You can't! I thought so. Bah! [ANNIE *enters with her tray. Hearing* FATHER *talking, she curtsies and backs into the hall, as if uncertain whether to intrude on* FATHER *and the Mayor.* VINNIE *comes downstairs.*] If you don't stop your plundering of the pocketbooks of the good citizens of New York, we're going to throw you and your boodle Board of Aldermen out of office.

VINNIE: Annie, why aren't you clearing the table?

ANNIE: Mr. Day's got a visitor.

FATHER: I'm warning you for the last time.

VINNIE: Oh, nonsense, he's just reading his paper, Annie. Clear the table. [VINNIE *goes off through the arch.* ANNIE *comes in timidly and starts to clear the table.*]

FATHER [*still lecturing Mayor Grant*]: We pay you a good round sum to watch after our interests, and all we get is inefficiency! [ANNIE *looks around trying to see the Mayor and, finding the room empty, assumes* FATHER'S *remarks are directed at her.*] I know you're a nincompoop and I strongly suspect you of being a scalawag. [ANNIE *stands petrified.* WHITNEY *comes downstairs.*] It's graft—that's what it is— Tammany graft—and if you're not getting it, somebody else is.

WHITNEY: [*to* FATHER]: Where's John? Do you know where John is?

FATHER: Dick Croker's running this town and you're just his cat's-paw.

[VINNIE *comes in from downstairs, and* HARLAN *comes down from upstairs.* FATHER *goes on talking. The others carry on their conversation simultaneously, ignoring* FATHER *and his imaginary visitor.*]

HARLAN: Mother, where's John?

VINNIE: He's upstairs, dear.

FATHER: And as for you, Richard Croker—don't think, just because you're hiding behind these minions you've put in public office, that you're going to escape your legal responsibilities.

WHITNEY [*calling upstairs*]: John, I'm going to take your glove!

JOHN [*from upstairs*]: Don't you lose it! And don't let anybody else have it either!

VINNIE: Annie, you should have cleared the table long ago.

[ANNIE *loads her tray feverishly, eager to escape.*]

FATHER [*rising and slamming down the paper in his chair*]: Legal responsibilities—by gad, sir, I mean *criminal* responsibilities.

[*The boys start toward the front door.*]

VINNIE [*starting upstairs*]: Now you watch Harlan, Whitney. Don't let him be anywhere the ball can hit him. Do what Whitney says, Harlan. And don't be late for lunch.

[FATHER *has reached the arch on his way out of the room, where he pauses for a final shot at Mayor Grant.*]

FATHER: Don't forget what happened to William Marcy Tweed—and if you put our taxes up once more, we'll put you in jail! [*He goes out of the archway to the left. A few seconds later he is seen passing the arch toward the outer door wearing his square derby and carrying his stick and gloves. The door is heard to slam loudly.*]

[ANNIE *seizes her tray of dishes and runs out of the arch to the left toward the basement stairs. A second later there is a scream from* ANNIE *and a tremendous crash.*]

[JOHN *and* CLARENCE *come rushing down and look over*

the rail of the stairs below. VINNIE *follows them almost immediately.*]

VINNIE: What is it? What happened?

CLARENCE: The maid fell downstairs.

VINNIE: I don't wonder, with your Father getting her so upset. Why couldn't she have finished with the table before she fell downstairs?

JOHN: I don't think she hurt herself.

VINNIE: And today of all days! Boys, will you finish the table? And, Clarence, don't leave the house until I talk to you. [*She goes downstairs.*]

[*During the following scene* CLARENCE *and* JOHN *remove* VINNIE'S *best breakfast tablecloth and cram it carelessly into the drawer of the console table, then take out the extra leaves from the table, push it together, and replace the living-room table cover and the bowl of fruit.*]

JOHN: What do you suppose Mother wants to talk to you about?

CLARENCE: Oh, probably about Edith Bailey.

JOHN: What do you talk about when you have tea alone with a girl?

CLARENCE: We don't talk about anything. I say: 'Isn't it a nice day?' and she says: 'Yes,' and I say: 'I think it's a little warmer than yesterday,' and she says: 'Yes, I like warm weather, don't you?' and I say: 'Yes,' and then we wait for the tea to come in. And then she says: 'How many lumps?' and I say: 'Two, thank you,' and she says: 'You must have a sweet tooth,' and I can't say: 'Yes' and I can't say: 'No,' so we just sit there and look at each other for half an hour. Then I say: 'Well, it's time I was going,' and she says: 'Must you?' and I say: 'I've enjoyed seeing you very much,' and she says: 'You must come again,' and I say 'I will,' and get out.

JOHN [*shaking his head*]: Some fellows like girls.

CLARENCE: I don't.

JOHN: And did you ever notice fellows, when they get sweet on a girl—the silly things a girl can make them do? And they don't even seem to know they're acting silly.

CLARENCE: Well, not for Yours Truly!

[VINNIE *returns from downstairs.*]

VINNIE: I declare I don't see how anyone could be so clumsy.

CLARENCE: Did she hurt herself?

VINNIE: No, she's not hurt—she's just hysterical! She doesn't make sense. Your father may have raised his voice; and if she doesn't know how to hold a platter properly, she deserved it—but I know he didn't threaten to put her in jail. Oh, well! Clarence, I want you to move your things into the front room. You'll have to sleep with the other boys for a night or two.

CLARENCE: You haven't told us who's coming.

VINNIE [*happily*]: Cousin Cora. Isn't that nice?

CLARENCE: It's not nice for me. I can't get any sleep in there with those children.

JOHN: Wait'll Father finds out she's here! There'll be a rumpus.

VINNIE: John, don't criticize your father. He's very hospitable after he gets used to the idea.

[*The doorbell rings.* JOHN *and* VINNIE *go to the window.*]

JOHN: Yes, it's Cousin Cora. Look, there's somebody with her.

VINNIE [*looking out*]: She wrote me she was bringing a friend of hers. They're both going to stay here. [*A limping* ANNIE *passes through the hall.*] Finish with the room, boys.

CLARENCE: Do I have to sleep with the other boys and have tea with Edith Bailey all in the same week?

VINNIE: Yes, and you'd better take your father's suit to the tailor's right away, so it will be ready by Thursday.

[VINNIE *goes down the hall to greet* CORA *and* MARY. CLARENCE *hurries off, carrying the table leaves.*]

VINNIE'S VOICE [*in the hall*]: Cora dear—

CORA'S VOICE: Cousin Vinnie, I'm so glad to see you! This is Mary Skinner.

VINNIE'S VOICE: Ed Skinner's daughter! I'm so glad to see you. Leave your bags in the hall and come right upstairs.

[VINNIE *enters, going toward the stairs.* CORA *follows her, but, seeing* JOHN, *enters the room and goes to him.* MARY *follows* CORA *in timidly.* CORA *is an attractive country cousin of about thirty.* MARY *is a refreshingly pretty small-town girl of sixteen.*]

CORA [*seeing* JOHN]: Well, Clarence, it's so good to see you!

VINNIE [*coming into the room*]: Oh, no, that's John.

CORA: John! Why, how you've grown! You'll be a man before your mother! [*She laughs herself at this time-worn quip.*] John, this is Mary Skinner. [*They exchange greetings.*] Vinnie, I have so much to tell you. We wrote you Aunt Carrie broke her hip. That was the night Robert Ingersoll lectured. Of course she couldn't get there; and it was a good thing for Mr. Ingersoll she didn't. [CLARENCE *enters.*] And Grandpa Ebbetts hasn't been at all well.

CLARENCE: How do you do, Cousin Cora? I'm glad to see you.

CORA: This can't be Clarence!

VINNIE: Yes, it is.

CORA: My goodness, every time I see you boys you've grown another foot. Let's see—you're going to St. Paul's now, aren't you?

CLARENCE [*with pained dignity*]: St. Paul's! I was through with St. Paul's long ago. I'm starting in Yale this fall.

MARY: Yale!

CORA: Oh, Mary, this is Clarence—Mary Skinner. [MARY *smiles, and* CLARENCE, *the woman-hater, nods politely and walks away.*] This is Mary's first trip to New York. She was so excited when she saw a horse car.

VINNIE: We'll have to show Mary around. I'll tell you—I'll have Mr. Day take us all to Delmonico's for dinner tonight.

MARY: Delmonico's!

CORA: Oh, that's marvelous! Think of that, Mary—Delmonico's! And Cousin Clare's such a wonderful host.

VINNIE: I know you girls want to freshen up. So come upstairs. Clarence, I'll let the girls use your room now, and when they've finished you can move, and bring up their bags. They're out in the hall. [*Starts upstairs with* CORA.] I've given you girls Clarence's room, but he didn't know about it until this morning and he hasn't moved out yet. [VINNIE *and* CORA *disappear upstairs.*]

[MARY *follows more slowly and on the second step stops and looks back.* CLARENCE *has gone into the hall with his back toward* MARY *and stares morosely in the direction of their luggage.*]

CLARENCE: John, get their old bags.

[JOHN *disappears toward the front door. The voices of* VINNIE *and* CORA *have trailed off into the upper reaches of the house.* CLARENCE *turns to scowl in their direction and finds himself looking full into the face of* MARY.]

MARY: Cora didn't tell me about you. I never met a Yale man before. [*She gives him a devastating smile and with an audible whinny of girlish excitement she runs upstairs.* CLARENCE *stares after her a few seconds, then turns toward the audience with a look of* "What happened to me just then?" *Suddenly, however, his face breaks into a smile which indicates that, whatever has happened, he likes it.*]

[*Curtain*]

SCENE 2

The same day. Tea time.

VINNIE *and the* RECTOR *are having tea.* THE REVEREND DR. LLOYD *is a plump, bustling man, very good-hearted and pleasant.* VINNIE *and* DR. LLOYD *have one strong point in common: their devotion to the Church and its rituals.* VINNIE'S *devotion comes from her natural piety;* DR. LLOYD'S *is a little more professional.*

AT RISE—DR. LLOYD *is seated with a cup of tea.* VINNIE *is also seated and* WHITNEY *is standing next to her, stiffly erect in the manner of a boy reciting.* HARLAN *is seated next to his mother, watching* WHITNEY'S *performance.*

WHITNEY [*reciting*]: "—to worship Him, to give Him thanks; to put my whole trust in Him, to call upon Him—" [*He hesitates.*]

VINNIE [*prompting*]: "—to honor—"

WHITNEY: "—to honor His Holy Name and His word and to serve Him truly all the days of my life."

DR. LLOYD: "What is thy duty toward thy neighbor?"

WHITNEY: Whew! [*He pulls himself together and makes a brave start.*] "My duty toward my neighbor is to love him as myself, and to do to all men as I would they should do unto me; to love, honor, and succor my father and my mother; to honor and obey—"

VINNIE: "—civil authorities."

WHITNEY: "—civil authorities. To—to—to—"

VINNIE [*to* DR. LLOYD]: He really knows it.

WHITNEY: I know most of the others.

DR. LLOYD: Well, he's done very well for so young a boy. I'm sure if he applies himself between now and Sunday I could hear him again—with the others.

VINNIE: There, Whitney, you'll have to study very hard if you want Dr. Lloyd to send your name in to Bishop Potter next Sunday. I must confess to you, Dr. Lloyd, it's really my fault. Instead of hearing Whitney say his catechism this morning I let him play baseball.

WHITNEY: We won, too; 35 to 27.

DR. LLOYD: That's splendid, my child. I'm glad your side won. But winning over your catechism is a richer and fuller victory.

WHITNEY: Can I go now?

VINNIE: Yes, darling. Thank Dr. Lloyd for hearing you and run along.

WHITNEY: Thank you, Dr. Lloyd.

DR. LLOYD: Not at all, my little man.

[WHITNEY *starts out, turns back, takes a piece of cake and runs out.*]

VINNIE: Little Harlan is very apt at learning things by heart.

HARLAN [*scrambling to his feet*]: I can spell Constantinople. Want to hear me? [DR. LLOYD *smiles his assent.*] C-o-ennaconny — annaconny — sissaconny — tan-tan-tee — and a nople and a pople and a Constantinople!

DR. LLOYD: Very well done, my child.

VINNIE [*handing him a cake from the tea-tray*]: That's nice, darling. This is what you get for saying it so well.

[HARLAN *quickly looks at the cake and back to* DR. LLOYD.]

HARLAN: Want me to say it again for you?

VINNIE: No, darling. One cake is enough. You run along and play with Whitney.

HARLAN: I can spell "huckleberry pie."

VINNIE: Run along, dear.

[HARLAN *goes out, skipping in rhythm to his recitation.*]

HARLAN: H-a-huckle — b-a-buckle — h-a-huckle-high. H-a-huckle — b-a-buckle — huckleberry pie!

DR. LLOYD [*amused*]: You and Mr. Day must be very proud of your children. [VINNIE *beams.*] I was hoping I'd find Mr. Day at home this afternoon.

VINNIE [*evasively*]: Well, he's usually home from the office by this time.

DR. LLOYD: Perhaps he's gone for a gallop in the park—it's such a fine day. He's very fond of horseback riding, I believe.

VINNIE: Oh, yes.

DR. LLOYD: Tell me—has he ever been thrown from a horse?

VINNIE: Oh, no! No horse would throw Mr. Day.

DR. LLOYD: I've wondered. I thought he might have had an accident. I noticed he never kneels in church.

VINNIE: Oh, that's no accident! But I don't want you to think he doesn't pray. He does. Why, sometimes you can hear him pray all over the house. But he never kneels.

DR. LLOYD: Never kneels! Dear me! I was hoping to have the opportunity to tell you and Mr. Day about our plans for the new edifice.

VINNIE: I'm so glad we're going to have a new church.

DR. LLOYD: I'm happy to announce that we're now ready to proceed. The only thing left to do is raise the money.

VINNIE: No one should hesitate about contributing to that. [*The front door slams.*]

DR. LLOYD: Perhaps that's Mr. Day now.

VINNIE: Oh, no, I hardly think so. [FATHER *appears in the* archway.] Why, it is!

FATHER: Oh, damn! I forgot.

VINNIE: Clare, you're just in time. Dr. Lloyd's here for tea.

FATHER: I'll be right in. [*He disappears the other side of the archway.*]

VINNIE: I'll send for some fresh tea. [*She goes to the bell-pull and rings for the maid.*]

DR. LLOYD: Now we can tell Mr. Day about our plans for the new edifice.

VINNIE [*knowing her man*]: After he's had his tea.

[FATHER *comes back into the room.* DR. LLOYD *rises.*]

FATHER: How are you, Dr. Lloyd?

[CLARENCE *comes down the stairs and eagerly looks around for* MARY.]

CLARENCE: Oh, it was Father.

DR. LLOYD: Very well, thank you. [*They shake hands.*]

CLARENCE [*to Vinnie*]: They're not back yet?

VINNIE: No! Clarence, no!

[CLARENCE *turns, disappointed, and goes back upstairs.*]

DR. LLOYD: It's a great pleasure to have a visit with you, Mr. Day. Except for a fleeting glimpse on the Sabbath, I don't see much of you.

[FATHER *grunts and sits down.* DELIA, *a new maid, enters.*]

DELIA: Yes, ma'am.

VINNIE: Some fresh tea and a cup for Mr. Day. [DELIA *exits and* VINNIE *hurries down to the tea table to start the conversation.*] Well, Clare, did you have a busy day at the office?

FATHER: Damn busy.

VINNIE: Clare!

FATHER: Very busy day. Tired out.

VINNIE: I've ordered some fresh tea. [*To* DR. LLOYD.] Poor

Clare, he must work very hard. He always comes home tired. Although how a man can get tired just sitting at his desk all day, I don't know. I suppose Wall Street is just as much a mystery to you as it is to me, Dr. Lloyd.

DR. LLOYD: No, no, it's all very clear to me. My mind often goes to the business man. The picture I'm most fond of is when I envision him at the close of the day's work. There he sits—this hard-headed man of affairs—surrounded by the ledgers that he has been studying closely and harshly for hours. I see him pausing in his toil—and by chance he raises his eyes and looks out of the window at the light in God's sky and it comes over him that money and ledgers are dross. [FATHER *stares at* DR. LLOYD *with some amazement.*] He realizes that all those figures of profit and loss are without importance or consequence—vanity and dust. And I see this troubled man bow his head and with streaming eyes resolve to devote his life to far higher things.

FATHER: Well, I'll be damned!

[*At this moment* DELIA *returns with the fresh tea for* FATHER.]

VINNIE: Here's your tea, Clare.

[FATHER *notices the new maid.*]

FATHER: Who's this?

VINNIE [*quietly*]: The new maid.

FATHER: Where's the one we had this morning?

VINNIE: Never mind, Clare.

FATHER: The one we had this morning was prettier. [DELIA, *with a slight resentment, exits.* FATHER *attacks the tea and cakes with relish.*] Vinnie, these cakes are *good.*

DR. LLOYD: Delicious!

VINNIE: Dr. Lloyd wants to tell us about the plans for the new edifice.

FATHER: The new what?

VINNIE: The new church—Clare, you knew we were planning to build a new church.

DR. LLOYD: Of course, we're going to have to raise a large sum of money.

FATHER [*alive to the danger*]: Well, personally I'm against the church hop-skipping-and-jumping all over the town. And it so happens that during the last year I've suffered heavy losses in the market—damned heavy losses—

VINNIE: Clare!

FATHER: —so any contribution I make will have to be a small one.

VINNIE: But, Clare, for so worthy a cause!

FATHER: —and if your Finance Committee thinks it's too small they can blame the rascals that are running the New Haven Railroad!

DR. LLOYD: The amount everyone is to subscribe has already been decided.

FATHER [*bristling*]: Who decided it?

DR. LLOYD: After considerable thought we've found a formula which we believe is fair and equitable. It apportions the burden lightly on those least able to carry it and justly on those whose shoulders we know are stronger. We've voted that our supporting members should each contribute a sum equal to the cost of their pews.

[FATHER's *jaw drops.*]

FATHER: I paid five thousand dollars for my pew!

VINNIE: Yes, Clare. That makes our contribution five thousand dollars.

FATHER: That's robbery! Do you know what that pew is worth today? Three thousand dollars. That's what the last one sold for. I've taken a dead loss of two thousand dollars on that pew already. Frank Baggs sold me that pew when the market was at its peak. He knew when to get out. [*He turns to* VINNIE.] And I'm warning you now that if the market ever goes up I'm going to unload that pew.

VINNIE: Clarence Day! How can you speak of the Lord's temple as though it were something to be bought and sold on Wall Street!

FATHER: Vinnie, this is a matter of dollars and cents, and that's something you don't know anything about!

VINNIE: Your talking of religion in the terms of dollars and cents seems to me pretty close to blasphemy.

DR. LLOYD [*soothingly*]: Now, Mrs. Day, your husband is a business man and he has a practical approach toward this problem. We've had to be practical about it too—we have all the facts and figures.

FATHER: Oh, really! What's the new piece of property going to cost you?

DR. LLOYD: I think the figure I've heard mentioned is eighty-five thousand dollars—or was it a hundred and eighty-five thousand dollars?

FATHER: What's the property worth where we are now?

DR. LLOYD: Well, there's quite a difference of opinion about that.

FATHER: How much do you have to raise to build the new church?

DR. LLOYD: Now, I've seen those figures—let me see—I know it depends somewhat upon the amount of the mortgage.

FATHER: Mortgage, eh? What are the terms of the amortization?

DR. LLOYD: Amortization? That's not a word I'm familiar with.

FATHER: It all seems pretty vague and unsound to me. I certainly wouldn't let any customer of mine invest on what I've heard.

[*The doorbell rings.*]

DR. LLOYD: We've given it a great deal of thought. I don't see how you can call it vague.

[DELIA *passes along the hall toward the front door.*]

FATHER: Dr. Lloyd, you preach that some day we'll all have to answer to God.

DR. LLOYD: We shall indeed!

FATHER: Well, I hope God doesn't ask you any questions with figures in them.

[CORA's *voice is heard in the hall, thanking* DELIA. VINNIE *goes to the arch just in time to meet* CORA *and* MARY *as they*

enter, heavily laden with packages, which they put down.
FATHER *and* DR. LLOYD *rise.*]

CORA: Oh, Vinnie, what a day! We've been to every shop in
town and— [*She sees* FATHER.] Cousin Clare!

FATHER [*cordially*]: Cora, what are you doing in New York?

CORA: We're just passing through on our way to Springfield.

FATHER: We?

[CLARENCE *comes downstairs into the room with eyes only
for* MARY.]

VINNIE: Oh, Dr. Lloyd, this is my favorite cousin, Miss
Cartwright, and her friend, Mary Skinner. [*They exchange
mutual how-do-you-do's.*]

DR. LLOYD: This seems to be a family reunion. I'll just run
along.

FATHER [*promptly*]: Goodbye, Dr. Lloyd.

DR. LLOYD: Goodbye, Miss Cartwright. Goodbye, Miss—
er—

VINNIE: Clarence, you haven't said how-do-you-do to Dr.
Lloyd.

CLARENCE: Goodbye, Dr. Lloyd.

VINNIE [*to* DR. LLOYD]: I'll go to the door with you. [DR.
LLOYD *and* VINNIE *go out, talking.*]

FATHER: Cora, you're as welcome as the flowers in May!
Have some tea with us. [*To* DELIA.] Bring some fresh tea—and
some more of those cakes.

CORA: Oh, we've had tea! We were so tired shopping we
had tea downtown.

[*With a gesture* FATHER *countermands his order to* DELIA,
who removes the tea table and exits.]

MARY: At the Fifth Avenue Hotel.

FATHER: At the Fifth Avenue Hotel, eh? Who'd you say
this pretty little girl was?

CORA: She's Ed Skinner's daughter. Well, Mary, at last
you've met Mr. Day. I've told Mary so much about you,
Cousin Clare, that she's just been dying to meet you.

FATHER: Well, sit down! Sit down! Even if you have had

tea you can stop and visit for a while. As a matter of fact, why don't you both stay to dinner?

[VINNIE *enters just in time to hear this and cuts in quickly.*]

VINNIE: That's all arranged, Clare. Cora and Mary are going to have dinner with us.

FATHER: That's fine! That's fine!

CORA: Cousin Clare, I don't know how to thank you and Vinnie for your hospitality.

MARY: Yes, Mr. Day.

FATHER: Well, you'll just have to take pot luck.

CORA: No, I mean—

[VINNIE *speaks quickly to postpone the revelation that* FATHER *has house guests.*]

VINNIE: Clare, did you know the girls are going to visit Aunt Judith in Springfield for a whole month?

FATHER: That's fine. How long are you going to be in New York, Cora?

CORA: All week.

FATHER: Splendid. We'll hope to see something of you, eh, Vinnie?

[CORA *looks bewildered and is about to speak.*]

VINNIE: Did you find anything you wanted in the shops?

CORA: Just everything.

VINNIE: I want to see what you got.

CORA: I just can't wait to show you. [*She goes coyly to* FATHER.] But I'm afraid some of the packages can't be opened in front of Cousin Clare.

FATHER: Shall I leave the room? [*Laughs at his own joke.*]

CORA: Clarence, do you mind taking the packages up to our room—or should I say your room? [*To* FATHER.] Wasn't it nice of Clarence to give up his room to us for a whole week?

FATHER [*with a sudden drop in temperature*]: Vinnie!

VINNIE: Come on, Cora, I just can't wait to see what's in those packages.

[CORA, MARY, *and* VINNIE *start out.* CLARENCE *is gathering up the packages.*]

FATHER [*ominously*]: Vinnie, I wish to speak to you before you go upstairs.

VINNIE: I'll be down in just a minute, Clare.

FATHER: I wish to speak to you now!

[*The girls have disappeared upstairs.*]

VINNIE: I'll be up in just a minute, Cora.

[*We hear a faint "All right" from upstairs.*]

FATHER [*his voice is low but stern*]: Are those two women encamped in this house?

VINNIE: Now, Clare!

FATHER [*much louder*]: Answer me, Vinnie!

VINNIE: Just a minute—control yourself, Clare. [VINNIE, *sensing the coming storm, hurries to the sliding doors.* CLARENCE *has reached the hall with his packages and he, too, has recognized the danger signal and as* VINNIE *closes one door he closes the other, leaving himself out in the hall and* FATHER *and* VINNIE *facing each other in the room.*|

VINNIE [*persuasively*]: Now, Clare, you know you've always liked Cora.

FATHER [*exploding*]: What has that got to do with her planking herself down in my house and bringing hordes of strangers with her?

VINNIE [*reproachfully*]: How can you call that sweet little girl a horde of strangers?

FATHER: Why don't they go to a hotel? New York is full of hotels built for the express purpose of housing such nuisances.

VINNIE: Clare! Two girls alone in a hotel! Who knows what might happen to them?

FATHER: All right. Then put 'em on the next train. If they want to roam—the damned gypsies—lend 'em a hand! Keep 'em roaming!

VINNIE: What have we got a home for if we can't show a little hospitality?

FATHER: I didn't buy this home to show hospitality—I bought it for my own comfort!

VINNIE: Well, how much are they going to interfere with your comfort living in that little room of Clarence's?

FATHER: The trouble is, damn it, they don't live there. They live in the bathroom! Every time I want to take my bath it's full of giggling females—washing their hair. From the time they take, you'd think it was the Seven Sutherland Sisters. I tell you, I won't have it! Send 'em to a hotel. I'll pay the bill gladly, but get them out of here!

[CLARENCE *puts his head through the sliding door.*]

CLARENCE: Father, I'm afraid they can hear you upstairs.

FATHER: Then keep those doors closed!

VINNIE [*with decision*]: Clarence, you open those doors— open them all the way!

[CLARENCE *does so.*]

VINNIE [*to* FATHER, *lowering her voice, but maintaining her spirit*]: Now, Clare, you behave yourself! [FATHER *glares at her angrily.*] They're here and they're going to stay here.

FATHER: That's enough, Vinnie! I want no more of this argument. [*He goes to his chair by the window, muttering.*] Damnation!

CLARENCE [*to* VINNIE]: Mother, Cousin Cora's waiting for you.

FATHER: What I don't understand is why this swarm of locusts always descends on us without any warning. [*He sits down.* VINNIE *looks at him; then, convinced of her victory, she goes upstairs.*] Damn! Damnation! Damn! [*He follows her upstairs with his eyes; he remembers he is very fond of her.*] Vinnie! Dear Vinnie! [*He remembers he is very angry at her.*] Damn!

CLARENCE: Father, can't I go along with the rest of you to Delmonico's tonight?

FATHER: What's that? Delmonico's?

CLARENCE: You're taking Mother, Cora, and Mary to Delmonico's for dinner.

FATHER [*exploding*]: Oh, God! [*At this sound from* FATHER, VINNIE *comes flying downstairs again.*] I won't have it. I won't have it. [FATHER *stamps angrily across the room.*]

VINNIE [*on the way down*]: Clarence, the doors!

FATHER: I won't stand it, by God! I won't stand it!

[VINNIE *and* CLARENCE *hurriedly close the sliding doors again.*]

VINNIE: Clare! What's the matter now?

FATHER [*with the calm of anger that has turned to ice*]: Do I understand that I can't have dinner in my own home?

VINNIE: It'll do us both good to get out of this house. You need a little change. It'll make you feel better.

FATHER: I have a home to have dinner in. Any time I can't have dinner at home this house is for sale!

VINNIE: Well, you can't have dinner here tonight because it isn't ordered.

FATHER: Let me tell you I'm ready to sell this place this very minute if I can't live here in peace. And we can all go and sit under a palm tree and live on breadfruit and pickles.

VINNIE: But, Clare, Cora and Mary want to see something of New York.

FATHER: Oh, that's it! Well, that's no affair of mine! I am not a guide to Chinatown and the Bowery. [*Drawing himself up, he stalks out, throwing open the sliding doors. As he reaches the foot of the stairs,* MARY *comes tripping down.*]

MARY: I love your house, Mr. Day. I could just live here forever. [FATHER *utters a bark of disgust and continues on upstairs.* MARY *comes into the room a little wide-eyed.*] Cora's waiting for you, Mrs. Day.

VINNIE: Oh, yes, I'll run right up. [*She goes upstairs.*]

CLARENCE: I'm glad you like our house.

MARY: Oh, yes, I like it very much. I like green.

CLARENCE: I like green myself. [*She looks up at his red hair.*]

MARY: Red's my favorite color.

[*Embarrassed,* CLARENCE *suddenly hears himself talking about something he has never thought about.*]

CLARENCE: It's an interesting thing about colors. Red's a nice color in a house, too; but outside, too much red would be bad. I mean, for instance, if all the trees and the grass were red. Outside, green is the best color.

MARY [*impressed*]: That's right! I've never thought of it

that way—but when you do think of it, it's quite a thought! I'll bet you'll make your mark at Yale.

CLARENCE [*pleased, but modest*]: Oh!

[*The outer door is heard to slam.*]

MARY: My mother wants me to go to college. Do you believe in girls going to college?

CLARENCE: I guess it's all right if they want to waste that much time—before they get married, I mean.

[JOHN *comes in, bringing* The Youth's Companion.]

JOHN: Oh, hello! Look! A new *Youth's Companion!*

[*They say "Hello" to him.*]

CLARENCE [*from a mature height*]: John enjoys *The Youth's Companion.* [JOHN *sits right down and starts to read.* CLARENCE *is worried by this.*] John! [JOHN *looks at him non-plussed.* CLARENCE *glances toward* MARY. JOHN *remembers his manners and stands.* CLARENCE *speaks formally to* MARY.] Won't you sit down?

MARY: Oh, thank you! [*She sits.* JOHN *sits down again quickly and dives back into* The Youth's Companion. CLARENCE *sits beside* MARY.]

CLARENCE: As I was saying—I think it's all right for a girl to go to college if she goes to a girls' college.

MARY: Well, Mother wants me to go to Ohio Wesleyan—because it's Methodist. [*Then almost as a confession.*] You see, we're Methodists.

CLARENCE: Oh, that's too bad! I don't mean it's too bad that you're a Methodist. Anybody's got a right to be anything they want. But what I mean is—we're Episcopalians.

MARY: Yes, I know. I've known ever since I saw your minister—and his collar. [*She looks pretty sad for a minute and then her face brightens.*] Oh, I just remembered—my father was an Episcopalian. He was baptized an Episcopalian. He was an Episcopalian right up to the time he married my mother. *She* was the Methodist. [MARY's *tone would have surprised her mother—and even* MARY, *if she had been listening.*]

CLARENCE: I'll bet your father's a nice man.

MARY: Yes, he is. He owns the livery stable.

CLARENCE: He does? Well, then you must like horses.

MARY: Oh, I love horses! [*They are happily united again in their common love of horses.*]

CLARENCE: They're my favorite animal. Father and I both think there's nothing like a horse!

[FATHER *comes down the stairs and into the room. The children all stand.*]

MARY: Oh, Mr. Day, I'm having such a lovely time here!

FATHER: Clarence is keeping you entertained, eh?

MARY: Oh, yes, sir. We've been talking about everything— colors and horses and religion.

FATHER: Oh! [*To* JOHN.] Has the evening paper come yet?

JOHN: No, sir.

FATHER: What are you reading?

JOHN: *The Youth's Companion,* sir.

[WHITNEY *and* HARLAN *enter from the hall,* WHITNEY *carrying a small box.*]

WHITNEY: Look what we've got!

FATHER: What is it?

WHITNEY: Tiddle-dy-winks. We put our money together and bought it.

FATHER: That's a nice game. Do you know how to play it?

WHITNEY: I've played it lots of times.

HARLAN: Show me how to play it.

FATHER: Here, I'll show you. [*Opens the box and arranges the glass and disks.*]

MARY [*hopefully to* CLARENCE]: Are you going out to dinner with us tonight?

CLARENCE [*looking at* FATHER]: I don't know yet—but it's beginning to look as though I might.

FATHER: It's easy, Harlan. You press down like this and snap the little fellow into the glass. Now watch me— [*He snaps it and it goes off the table.*] The table isn't quite large enough. You boys better play it on the floor.

WHITNEY: Come on, Harlan, I'll take the reds, and you take the yellows

FATHER: John, have you practiced your piano today?

JOHN: I was going to practice this evening.

FATHER: Better do it now. Music is a delight in the home.

[JOHN *exits, passing* CORA *and* VINNIE *as they enter, coming downstairs.*]

VINNIE: Clare, what do you think Cora just told me? She and Clyde are going to be married this fall!

FATHER: Oh, you finally landed him, eh? [*Everybody laughs.*] Well, he's a very lucky man. Cora, being married is the only way to live.

CORA: If we can be half as happy as you and Cousin Vinnie—

VINNIE [*who has gone to the children*]: Boys, shouldn't you be playing that on the table?

WHITNEY: The table isn't big enough. Father told us to play on the floor.

VINNIE: My soul and body! Look at your hands! Delia will have your supper ready in a few minutes. Go wash your hands right away and come back and show Mother they're clean.

[*The boys pick up the tiddle-dy-winks and depart reluctantly. From the next room we hear* JOHN *playing "The Happy Farmer."*]

FATHER [*sitting down on the sofa with* MARY]: Vinnie, this young lady looks about the same age you were when I came out to Pleasantville to rescue you.

VINNIE: Rescue me! You came out there to talk me into marrying you.

FATHER: It worked out just the same. I saved you from spending the rest of your life in that one-horse town.

VINNIE: Cora, the other day I came across a tin-type of Clare taken in Pleasantville. I want to show it to you. You'll see who needed rescuing. [*She goes to the table and starts to rummage around in its drawer.*]

FATHER: There isn't time for that, Vinnie. If we're going to Delmonico's for dinner hadn't we all better be getting ready? It's after six now.

CORA: Gracious! I'll have to start. If I'm going to dine in

public with a prominent citizen like you, Cousin Clare—I'll have to look my best. [*She goes to the arch.*]

MARY: I've changed already.

CORA: Yes, I know, but I'm afraid I'll have to ask you to come along and hook me up, Mary.

MARY: Of course.

CORA: It won't take a minute and then you can come right back.

[FATHER *rises.* MARY *crosses in front of* FATHER *and starts toward the hall, then turns and looks back at him.*]

MARY: Mr. Day, were you always an Episcopalian?

FATHER: What?

MARY: Were you always an Episcopalian?

FATHER: I've always gone to the Episcopal church, yes.

MARY: But you weren't baptized a Methodist or anything, were you? You were baptized an Episcopalian?

FATHER: Come to think of it, I don't believe I was ever baptized at all.

MARY: Oh!

VINNIE: Clare, that's not very funny, joking about a subject like that.

FATHER: I'm not joking—I remember now—I never was baptized.

VINNIE: Clare, that's ridiculous, everyone's baptized.

FATHER [*sitting down complacently*]: Well, I'm not.

VINNIE: Why, no one would keep a little baby from being baptized.

FATHER: You know Father and Mother—free-thinkers, both of them—believed their children should decide those things for themselves.

VINNIE: But, Clare—

FATHER: I remember when I was ten or twelve years old, Mother said I ought to give some thought to it. I suppose I thought about it, but I never got around to having it done to me.

[*The shock to* VINNIE *is as great as if* FATHER *had calmly announced himself guilty of murder. She walks to* FATHER *staring at him in horror.* CORA *and* MARY, *sensing the coming battle, withdraw to the neutral shelter of the hall.*]

VINNIE: Clare, do you know what you're saying?

FATHER: I'm saying I've never been baptized.

VINNIE [*in a sudden panic*]: Then something has to be done about it right away.

FATHER [*not the least concerned*]: Now, Vinnie, don't get excited over nothing.

VINNIE: Nothing! [*Then as only a woman can ask such a question:*] Clare, why haven't you ever told me?

FATHER: What difference does it make?

VINNIE [*the panic returning*]: I've never heard of anyone who wasn't baptized. Even the savages in darkest Africa—

FATHER: It's all right for savages and children. But if an oversight was made in my case it's too late to correct it now.

VINNIE: But if you're not baptized you're not a Christian!

FATHER [*rising in wrath*]: Why, confound it, of course I'm a Christian! A damn good Christian, too. [FATHER's *voice tells* CLARENCE *a major engagement has begun. He hurriedly springs to the sliding doors and closes them, removing himself,* MARY, *and* CORA *from the scene of action.*] A lot better Christian than those psalm-singing donkeys in church!

VINNIE: You can't be if you won't be baptized.

FATHER: I won't be baptized and I will be a Christian! I beg to inform you I'll be a Christian in my own way.

VINNIE: Clare, don't you want to meet us all in Heaven?

FATHER: Of course! And I'm going to!

VINNIE: But you can't go to Heaven if you're not baptized!

FATHER: That's a lot of folderol!

VINNIE: Clarence Day, don't you blaspheme like that! You're coming to church with me before you go to the office in the morning and be baptized then and there!

FATHER: Vinnie, don't be ridiculous! If you think I'm going to stand there and have some minister splash water on me at my age, you're mistaken!

VINNIE: But, Clare—

FATHER: That's enough of this, Vinnie. I'm hungry. [*Draws himself up and starts for the door. He does not realize that he and* VINNIE *are now engaged in a battle to the death.*] I'm dressing for dinner. [*Throws open the doors, revealing* WHITNEY *and* HARLAN, *who obviously have been eavesdropping and have heard the awful revelation of* FATHER'S *paganism.* FATHER *stalks past them upstairs. The two boys come down into the room staring at their mother, who has been standing, too shocked at* FATHER'S *callous impiety to speak or move.*]

WHITNEY: Mother, if Father hasn't been baptized he hasn't any name. In the sight of the Church he hasn't any name.

VINNIE: That's right! [*To herself.*] Maybe we're not even married!

[*This awful thought takes possession of* VINNIE. *Her eyes turn slowly toward the children and she suddenly realizes their doubtful status. Her hand goes to her mouth to cover a quick gasp of horror as the curtain falls.*]

[*Curtain*]

ACT TWO

The same.
The following Sunday. After church.
The stage is empty as the curtain rises. VINNIE *comes into the archway from the street door, dressed in her Sunday best, carrying her prayer book, hymnal, and a cold indignation. As soon as she is in the room,* FATHER *passes across the hall in his Sunday cutaway and silk hat, carrying gloves and cane.* VINNIE *looks over her shoulder at him as he disappears.* CORA, WHITNEY, *and* HARLAN *come into the room,* CORA *glancing after* FATHER *and then toward* VINNIE. *All three walk as though the sound of a footfall might cause an explosion, and speak in subdued tones.*

HARLAN: Cousin Cora, will you play a game of tiddle-dy-winks with me before you go?

CORA: I'm going to be busy packing until it's time to leave.

WHITNEY: We can't play games on Sunday.

[*We hear the door close and* JOHN *enters and looks into the room apprehensively.*]

CORA: John, where are Clarence and Mary?

JOHN: They dropped behind—'way behind! [*He goes upstairs.* WHITNEY *takes* HARLAN'S *hat from him and starts toward the arch.*]

VINNIE: Whitney, don't hang up your hat. I want you to go over to Sherry's for the ice-cream for dinner. Tell Mr. Sherry strawberry—if he has it. And take Harlan with you.

WHITNEY: All right, Mother. [*He and* HARLAN, *trained in the good manners of the period, bow and exit.*]

CORA: Oh, Vinnie, I hate to leave. We've had such a lovely week.

VINNIE [*voice quivers in a tone of scandalized apology*]:

Cora, what must you think of Clare, making such a scene on his way out of church today?

CORA: Cousin Clare probably thinks that you put the rector up to preaching that sermon.

VINNIE [*tone changes from apology to self-defense with overtones of guilt*]: Well, I had to go to see Dr. Lloyd to find out whether we were really married. The sermon on baptism was his own idea. If Clare just hadn't *shouted* so—now the whole congregation knows he's never been baptized! But he's going to be, Cora—you mark my words—he's going to be! I just couldn't go to Heaven without Clare. Why, I get lonesome for him when I go to Ohio.

[FATHER *enters holding his watch. He's also holding his temper. He speaks quietly.*]

FATHER: Vinnie, I went to the dining-room and the table isn't set for dinner yet.

VINNIE: We're having dinner late today.

FATHER: Why can't I have my meals on time?

VINNIE: The girls' train leaves at one-thirty. Their cab's coming at one o'clock.

FATHER: Cab? The horse cars go right past our door.

VINNIE: They have those heavy bags.

FATHER: Clarence and John could have gone along to carry their bags. Cabs are just a waste of money. Why didn't we have an early dinner?

VINNIE: There wasn't time for an early dinner and church, too.

FATHER: As far as I'm concerned this would have been a good day to miss church.

VINNIE [*spiritedly*]: I wish we had!

FATHER [*flaring*]: I'll bet you put him up to preaching that sermon!

VINNIE: I've never been so mortified in all my life! You stamping up the aisle roaring your head off at the top of your voice!

FATHER: That Lloyd needn't preach at me as though I

were some damn criminal! I wanted him to know it, and as far as I'm concerned the whole congregation can know it, too!

VINNIE: They certainly know it now!

FATHER: That suits me!

VINNIE [*pleading*]: Clare, you don't seem to understand what the church is for.

FATHER [*laying down a new Commandment*]: Vinnie, if there's one place the church should leave alone, it's a man's soul!

VINNIE: Clare, dear, don't you believe what it says in the Bible?

FATHER: A man has to use his common sense about the Bible, Vinnie, if he has any. For instance, you'd be in a pretty fix if I gave all my money to the poor.

VINNIE: Well, that's just silly!

FATHER: Speaking of money—where are this month's bills?

VINNIE: Clare, it isn't fair to go over the household accounts while you're hungry.

FATHER: Where are those bills, Vinnie?

VINNIE: They're downstairs on your desk. [FATHER *exits almost eagerly. Figures are something he understands better than he does women.*] Of all times! [*To* CORA.] It's awfully hard on a woman to love a man like Clare so much.

CORA: Yes, men can be aggravating. Clyde gets me so provoked! We kept company for six years, but the minute he proposed—the moment I said "Yes"—he began to take me for granted.

VINNIE: You have to expect that, Cora. I don t believe Clare has come right out and told me he loves me since we've been married. Of course I know he does, because I keep reminding him of it. You have to keep reminding them, Cora.

[*The door slams.*]

CORA: That must be Mary and Clarence. [*There's a moment's pause. The two women look toward the hall—then at each other with a knowing sort of smile.* CORA *rises, goes up to the arch, peeks out—then faces front and innocently asks:*] Is that you, Mary?

MARY [*dashing in*]: Yes!

[CLARENCE *crosses the arch to hang up his hat.*]

CORA: We have to change our clothes and finish our packing. [*Goes upstairs.*]

[CLARENCE *returns as* MARY *starts up the stairs.*]

MARY [*to* CLARENCE]: It won't take me long.

CLARENCE: Can I help you pack?

VINNIE [*shocked*]: Clarence!

[MARY *runs upstairs.* CLARENCE *drifts into the living-room, somewhat abashed.* VINNIE *collects her hat and gloves, starts out, stops to look at* CLARENCE, *then comes down to him.*] Clarence, why didn't you kneel in church today?

CLARENCE: What, Mother?

VINNIE: Why didn't you kneel in church today?

CLARENCE [*troubled*]: I just couldn't.

VINNIE: Has it anything to do with Mary? I know she's a Methodist.

CLARENCE: Oh, no, Mother! Methodists kneel. Mary told me. They don't get up and down so much, but they stay down longer.

VINNIE: If it's because your father doesn't kneel—you must remember he wasn't brought up to kneel in church. But you were—you always have—and, Clarence, you want to, don't you?

CLARENCE: Oh, yes! I wanted to today! I started to—you saw me start—but I just couldn't.

VINNIE: Is that suit of your father's too tight for you?

CLARENCE: No, it's not too *tight*. It fits fine. But it *is* the suit. Very peculiar things have happened to me since I started to wear it. I haven't been myself since I put it on.

VINNIE: In what way, Clarence? How do you mean?

[CLARENCE *pauses, then blurts out his problem.*]

CLARENCE: Mother, I can't seem to make these clothes do anything Father wouldn't do!

VINNIE: That's nonsense, Clarence—and not to kneel in church is a sacrilege.

CLARENCF: But making Father's trousers kneel seemed more of a sacrilege.

VINNIE: Clarence!

CLARENCE: No! Remember the first time I wore this? It was at Dora Wakefield's party for Mary. Do you know what happened? We were playing musical chairs and Dora Wakefield sat down suddenly right in my lap. I jumped up so fast she almost got hurt.

VINNIE: But it was all perfectly innocent.

CLARENCE: It wasn't that Dora was sitting on my lap—she was sitting on Father's trousers. Mother, I've got to have a suit of my own. [CLARENCE's *metaphysical problem is one that* VINNIE *can't cope with at this particular minute.*]

VINNIE: My soul and body! Clarence, you have a talk with your father about it. I'm sure if you approach him the right way—you know—tactfully—he'll see—

[MARY *comes downstairs and hesitates at the arch.*]

MARY: Oh, excuse me.

VINNIE: Gracious! Have you finished your packing?

MARY: Practically. I never put my comb and brush in until I'm ready to close my bag.

VINNIE: I must see Margaret about your box lunch for the train. I'll leave you two together. Remember, it's Sunday. [*She goes downstairs.*]

CLARFNCE: I was hoping we could have a few minutes together before you left.

MARY [*not to admit her eagerness*]: Cora had so much to do I wanted to get out of her way.

CLARENCE: Well, didn't you want to see me?

MARY [*self-consciously*]: I did want to tell you how much I've enjoyed our friendship.

CLARENCE: You're going to write me when you get to Springfield, aren't you?

MARY: Of course, if you write me first.

CLARENCE: But you'll have something to write about—your

trip—and Aunt Judith—and how things are in Springfield. You write me as soon as you get there.

MARY: Maybe I'll be too busy. Maybe I won't have time. [*She sits on the sofa.*]

CLARENCE [*with the authority of* FATHER'S *trousers*]: You find the time! Let's not have any nonsense about that! You'll write me first—and you'll do it right away, the first day! [*Sits beside her.*]

MARY: How do you know I'll take orders from you?

CLARENCE: I'll show you. [*He takes a quick glance toward the hall.*] Give me your hand!

MARY: Why should I?

CLARENCE: Give me your hand, confound it!

[MARY *gives it to him.*]

MARY: What do you want with my hand?

CLARENCE: I just wanted it. [*Holding her hand, he melts a little and smiles at her. She melts, too. Their hands, clasped together, are resting on* CLARENCE'S *knee and they relax happily.*] What are you thinking about?

MARY: I was just thinking.

CLARENCE: About what?

MARY: Well, when we were talking about writing each other I was hoping you'd write me first because that would mean you liked me.

CLARENCE [*with the logic of the male*]: What's writing first got to do with my liking you?

MARY: Oh, you *do* like me?

CLARENCE: Of course I do. I like you better than any girl I ever met.

MARY [*with the logic of the female*]: But you don't like me enough to write first?

CLARENCE: I don't see how one thing's got anything to do with the other.

MARY: But a girl can't write first—because she's a *girl.*

CLARENCE: That doesn't make sense. If a girl has something to write about and a fellow hasn't, there's no reason why she shouldn't write first.

MARY [*starting a flanking movement*]: You know, the first few days I was here you'd do anything for me and then you changed. You used to be a lot of fun—and then all of a sudden you turned into an old sober-sides.

CLARENCE: When did I?

MARY: The first time I noticed it was when we walked home from Dora Wakefield's party. My, you were on your dignity! You've been that way ever since. You even dress like an old sober-sides. [CLARENCE'S *face changes as* FATHER'S *pants rise to haunt him. Then he notices that their clasped hands are resting on these very pants, and he lifts them off. Agony obviously is setting in.* MARY *sees the expression on his face.*] What's the matter?

CLARENCE: I just happened to remember something.

MARY: What? [CLARENCE *doesn't answer, but his face does.*] Oh, I know. This is the last time we'll be together. [*She puts her hand on his shoulder. He draws away.*]

CLARENCE: Mary, please!

MARY: But, Clarence! We'll see each other in a month. And we'll be writing each other, too. I hope we will. [*She gets up.*] Oh, Clarence, please write me first, because it will show me how much you like me. Please! I'll show you how much I like you! [*She throws herself on his lap and buries her head on his shoulders.* CLARENCE *stiffens in agony.*]

CLARENCE [*hoarsely*]: Get up! Get up! [*She pulls back her head and looks at him, then springs from his lap and runs away, covering her face and sobbing.* CLARENCE *goes to her.*] Don't do that, Mary! Please don't do that!

MARY: Now you'll think I'm just a bold and forward girl.

CLARENCE: Oh, no!

MARY: Yes, you will—you'll think I'm bold!

CLARENCE: Oh, no—it's not that.

MARY [*hopefully*]: Was it because it's Sunday?

CLARENCE [*in despair*]: No, it would be the same any day— [*He is about to explain, but* MARY *flares.*]

MARY: Oh, it's just because you didn't want me sitting on your lap.

CLARENCE: It was nice of you to do it.

MARY: It was nice of me! So you told me to get up! You just couldn't bear to have me sit there. Well, you needn't write me first. You needn't write me any letters at all, because I'll tear them up without opening them! [FATHER *enters the archway, a sheath of bills in his hand and his account book under his arm.*] I guess I know now you don't like me! I never want to see you again. I— I— [*She breaks and starts to run toward the stairs. At the sight of* FATHER *she stops, but only for a gasp, then continues on upstairs, unable to control her sobs.* CLARENCE, *who has been standing in unhappy indecision, turns to follow her, but stops short at the sight of* FATHER, *who is standing in the arch looking at him with some amazement.* FATHER *looks from* CLARENCE *toward the vanished* MARY, *then back to* CLARENCE.]

FATHER: Clarence, that young girl is crying—she's in tears. What's the meaning of this?

CLARENCE: I'm sorry, Father, it's all my fault.

FATHER: Nonsense! What's that girl trying to do to you?

CLARENCE: What? No, she wasn't—it was—I—how long have you been here?

FATHER: Well, whatever the quarrel was about, Clarence, I'm glad you held your own. Where's your mother?

CLARENCE [*desperately*]: I have to have a new suit of clothes —you've *got* to give me the money for it.

[FATHER's *account book reaches the table with a sharp bang as he stares at* CLARENCE *in astonishment.*]

FATHER: Young man, do you realize you're addressing your father?

[CLARENCE *wilts miserably and sinks into a chair.*]

CLARENCE: I'm sorry, Father—I apologize—but you don't know how important this is to me. [CLARENCE's *tone of misery gives* FATHER *pause.*]

FATHER: A suit of clothes is so—? Now, why should a—? [*Something dawns on* FATHER *and he looks up in the direction in which* MARY *has disappeared, then looks back at*

CLARENCE.] Has your need for a suit of clothes anything to do with that young lady?

CLARENCE: Yes, Father.

FATHER: Why, Clarence! [*Suddenly realizes that women have come into* CLARENCE'S *emotional life and there comes a yearning to protect this inexperienced and defenseless member of his own sex.*] This comes as quite a shock to me.

CLARENCE: What does, Father?

FATHER: Your being so grown up! Still, I might have known that if you're going to college this fall—yes, you're at an age when you'll be meeting girls. Clarence, there are things about women that I think you ought to know! [*He goes up and closes the doors, then comes down and sits beside* CLARENCE, *hesitating for a moment before he speaks.*] Yes, I think it's better for you to hear this from me than to have to learn it for yourself. Clarence, women aren't the angels that you think they are! Well, now—first, let me explain this to you. You see, Clarence, we men have to run this world and it's not an easy job. It takes work, and it takes thinking. A man has to be sure of his facts and figures. He has to reason things out. Now, you take a woman—a woman thinks—no I'm wrong right there—a woman doesn't think at all! She gets stirred up! And she gets stirred up over the damnedest things! Now, I love my wife just as much as any man, but that doesn't mean I should stand for a lot of folderol! By God! I won't stand for it. [*Looks around toward the spot where he had his last clash with* VINNIE.]

CLARENCE: Stand for what, Father?

FATHER [*to himself*]: That's the one thing I will not submit myself to. [*Has ceased explaining women to* CLARENCE *and is now explaining himself.*] Clarence, if a man thinks a certain thing is the wrong thing to do he shouldn't do it. If he thinks a thing is right he should do it. Now that has nothing to do with whether he loves his wife or not.

CLARENCE: Who says it has, Father?

FATHER: They do!

CLARENCE: Who, sir?

FATHER: Women! They get stirred up and then they try to get you stirred up, too. If you can keep reason and logic in the argument, a man can hold his own, of course. But if they can *switch* you—pretty soon the argument's about whether you love them or not. I swear I don't know how they do it! Don't you let 'em, Clarence! Don't you let 'em!

CLARENCE: I see what you mean so far, Father. If you don't watch yourself, love can make you do a lot of things you don't want to do.

FATHER: Exactly!

CLARENCE: But if you do watch out and know just how to handle women—

FATHER: Then you'll be all right. All a man has to do is be firm. You know how sometimes I have to be firm with your mother. Just now about this month's household accounts—

CLARENCE: Yes, but what can you do when they cry?

FATHER [*he gives this a moment's thought.*]: Well, that's quite a question. You just have to make them understand that what you're doing is for their good.

CLARENCE: I see.

FATHER [*rising*]: Now, Clarence, you know all about women. [*Goes to the table and sits down in front of his account book, opening it.* CLARENCE *rises and looks at him.*]

CLARENCE: But, Father—

FATHER: Yes, Clarence.

CLARENCE: I thought you were going to tell me about—

FATHER: About what?

CLARENCE: About women.

[FATHER *realizes with some shock that* CLARENCE *expected him to be more specific.*]

FATHER: Clarence, there are some things gentlemen don't discuss! I've told you all you need to know. The thing for you to remember is—be firm! [CLARENCE *turns away. There is a knock at the sliding doors.*] Yes, come in. [MARY *opens the doors.*]

MARY: Excuse me! [MARY *enters.* FATHER *turns his atten-*

tion to the household accounts. MARY *goes to the couch and picks up her handkerchief and continues around the couch.* CLARENCE *crosses to meet her above the couch, determined to be firm.* MARY *passes him without a glance.* CLARENCE *wilts, then again assuming firmness, turns up into the arch in an attempt to quail* MARY *with a look.* MARY *marches upstairs ignoring him.* CLARENCE *turns back into the room defeated. He looks down at his clothes unhappily, then decides to be firm with his father. He straightens up and steps toward him. At this moment* FATHER, *staring at a bill, emits his cry of rage.*]

FATHER: Oh, God!

[CLARENCE *retreats.* FATHER *rises and holds the bill in question between thumb and forefinger as though it were too repulsive to touch.* VINNIE *comes rushing down the stairs.*]

VINNIE: What's the matter, Clare? What's wrong?

FATHER: I will *not* send this person a check!

[VINNIE *looks at it.*]

VINNIE: Why, Clare, that's the only hat I've bought since March and it was reduced from forty dollars.

FATHER: I don't question your buying the hat or what you paid for it, but the person from whom you bought it—this Mademoiselle Mimi—isn't fit to be in the hat business or any other.

VINNIE: I never went there before, but it's a very nice place and I don't see why you object to it.

FATHER [*exasperated*]: I object to it because this confounded person doesn't put her name on her bills! Mimi what? Mimi O'Brien? Mimi Jones? Mimi Weinstein?

VINNIE: How do I know? It's just Mimi.

FATHER: It isn't just Mimi. She must have some other name, damn it! Now, I wouldn't make out a check payable to Charley or to Jimmy, and I won't make out a check payable to Mimi. Find out what her last name is and I'll pay her the money.

VINNIE: All right. All right. [*She starts out.*]

FATHER: Just a minute, Vinnie, that isn't all.

VINNIE: But Cora will be leaving any minute, Clare, and it isn't polite for me—

FATHER: Never mind Cora. Sit down. [CLARENCE *goes into the hall, looks upstairs, wanders up and down the hall restlessly.* VINNIE *reluctantly sits down opposite* FATHER *at the table.*] Vinnie, you know I like to live well, and I want my family to live well. But this house must be run on a business basis. I must know how much money I'm spending and what for. For instance, if you recall, two weeks ago I gave you six dollars to buy a new coffee pot—

VINNIE: Yes, because you broke the old one. You threw it right on the floor.

FATHER: I'm not talking about that. I'm simply endeavoring—

VINNIE: But it was so silly to break that nice coffee pot, Clare, and there was nothing the matter with the coffee that morning. It was made just the same as always.

FATHER: It was not! It was made in a damned barbaric manner!

VINNIE: I couldn't get another imported one. That little shop has stopped selling them. They said the tariff wouldn't let them. And that's your fault, Clare, because you're always voting to raise the tariff.

FATHER: The tariff protects America against cheap foreign labor. [*He sounds as though he is quoting.*] Now I find that—

VINNIE: The tariff does nothing but put up the prices and that's hard on everybody, especially the farmer. [*She sounds as though she is quoting back.*]

FATHER [*annoyed*]: I wish to God you wouldn't talk about matters you don't know a damn thing about!

VINNIE: I do too know about them. Miss Gulick says every intelligent woman should have some opinion—

FATHER: Who, may I ask, is Miss Gulick?

VINNIE: Why, she's that current-events woman I told you about and the tickets are a dollar every Tuesday.

FATHER: Do you mean to tell me that a pack of idle-minded females pay a dollar apiece to hear another female gabble about the events of the day? Listen to me if you want to know anything about the events of the day!

VINNIE: But you get so excited, Clare, and besides, Miss Gulick says that our President, whom you're always belittling, prays to God for guidance and—

FATHER [*having had enough of Miss Gulick*]: Vinnie, what happened to that six dollars?

VINNIE: What six dollars?

FATHER: I gave you six dollars to buy a new coffee pot and I find that you apparently got one at Lewis & Conger's and charged it. Here's their bill: "One coffee pot—five dollars."

VINNIE: So you owe me a dollar and you can hand it right over. [*She holds out her hand for it.*]

FATHER: I'll do nothing of the kind! What did you do with that six dollars?

VINNIE: Why, Clare, I can't tell you now, dear. Why didn't you ask me at the time?

FATHER: Oh, my God!

VINNIE: Wait a moment! I spent four dollars and a half for that new umbrella I told you I wanted and you said I didn't need, but I did, very much.

[FATHER *takes his pencil and writes in the account book.*]

FATHER: Now we're getting somewhere. One umbrella—four dollars and a half.

VINNIE: And that must have been the week I paid Mrs. Tobin for two extra days' washing.

FATHER [*entering the item*]: Mrs. Tobin.

VINNIE: So that was two dollars more.

FATHER: Two dollars.

VINNIE: That makes six dollars and fifty cents. And that's another fifty cents you owe me.

FATHER: I don't owe you anything. [*Stung by* VINNIE's *tactics into a determination to pin her butterfly mind down.*] What you owe me is an explanation of where my money's gone! We're going over this account book item by item. [*Starts to sort the bills for the purposes of cross-examination, but the butterfly takes wing again.*]

VINNIE: I do the very best I can to keep down expenses. And you know yourself that Cousin Phoebe spends twice as much as we do.

FATHER: Damn Cousin Phoebe!—I don't wish to be told how she throws her money around.

VINNIE: Oh, Clare, how can you? And I thought you were so fond of Cousin Phoebe.

FATHER: All right, I am fond of Cousin Phoebe, but I can get along without hearing so much about her.

VINNIE: You talk about your own relatives enough.

FATHER [*hurt*]: That's not fair, Vinnie. When I talk about my relatives I criticize them.

VINNIE: If I can't even speak of Cousin Phoebe—

FATHER: You can speak of her all you want to—but I won't have Cousin Phoebe or anyone else dictating to me how to run my house. Now this month's total—

VINNIE [*righteously*]: I didn't say a word about her dictating, Clare—she isn't that kind!

FATHER [*dazed*]: I don't know what you said, now. You never stick to the point. I endeavor to show you how to run this house on a business basis and you wind up by jibbering and jabbering about everything under the sun. If you'll just explain to me—

[*Finally cornered,* VINNIE *realizes the time has come for tears. Quietly she turns them on.*]

VINNIE: I don't know what you expect of me. I tire myself out chasing up and down those stairs all day long—trying to look after your comfort—to bring up our children—to do the mending and the marketing and as if that isn't enough, you want me to be an expert bookkeeper, too.

FATHER [*touched where* VINNIE *has hoped to touch him*]: Vinnie, I want to be reasonable; but can't you understand?—I'm doing all this for your own good. [VINNIE *rises with a moan.* FATHER *sighs with resignation.*] I suppose I'll have to go ahead just paying the bills and hoping I've got money enough in the bank to meet them. But it's all very discouraging.

VINNIE: I'll try to do better, Clare.

[FATHER *looks up into her tearful face and melts.*]

FATHER: That's all I'm asking. [*She goes to him and puts her arm around his shoulder.*] I'll go down and make out the checks and sign them. [VINNIE *doesn't seem entirely consoled, so he attempts a lighter note to cheer her up.*] Oh, Vinnie, maybe I haven't any right to sign those checks, since in the sight of the Lord I haven't any name at all. Do you suppose the bank will feel that way about it too—or do you think they'll take a chance? [*He should not have said this.*]

VINNIE: That's right! Clare, to make those checks good you'll have to be baptized right away.

FATHER [*retreating angrily*]: Vinnie, the bank doesn't care whether I've been baptized or not!

VINNIE: Well, I care! And no matter what Dr. Lloyd says, I'm not sure we're really married.

FATHER: Damn it, Vinnie, we have four children! If we're not married now we never will be!

VINNIE: Oh, Clare, don't you see how serious this is? You've got to do something about it.

FATHER: Well, just now I've got to do something about these damn bills you've run up. [*Sternly.*] I'm going down-stairs.

VINNIE: Not before you give me that dollar and a half!

FATHER: What dollar and a half?

VINNIE: The dollar and a half you owe me!

FATHER [*thoroughly enraged*]: I don't owe you any dollar and a half! I gave you money to buy a coffee pot for me and somehow it turned into an umbrella for you.

VINNIE: Clarence Day, what kind of a man are you? Quibbling about a dollar and a half when your immortal soul is in danger! And what's more—

FATHER: All right. All right. All right. [*He takes the dollar and a half from his change purse and gives it to her.*]

VINNIE [*smiling*]: Thank you, Clare. [VINNIE *turns and leaves the room. Her progress upstairs is a one-woman march of triumph.*]

[FATHER *puts his purse back, gathers up his papers and his dignity, and starts out.* CLARENCE *waylays him in the arch.*]

CLARENCE: Father—you never did tell me—can I have a new suit of clothes?

FATHER: No, Clarence! I'm sorry, but I have to be firm with you, too! [*He stalks off.* JOHN *comes down the stairs carrying a traveling bag, which he takes out toward the front door. He returns empty-handed and starts up the stairs again.*]

CLARENCE: John, come here a minute.

JOHN [*coming into the room*]: What do you want?

CLARENCE: John, have you got any money you could lend me?

JOHN: With this week's allowance, I'll have about three dollars.

CLARENCE: That's no good. I've got to have enough to buy a new suit of clothes.

JOHN: Why don't you earn some money? That's what I'm going to do. I'm going to buy a bicycle—one of those new low kind, with both wheels the same size—you know, a safety.

CLARENCE: How are you going to earn that much money?

JOHN: I've got a job practically. Look, I found this ad in the paper. [*He hands* CLARENCE *a clipping from his pocket.*]

CLARENCE [*reading*]: "Wanted, an energetic young man to handle household necessity that sells on sight. Liberal commissions. Apply 312 West Fourteenth Street, Tuesday from eight to twelve." Listen, John, let me have that job.

JOHN: Why should I give you my job? They're hard to get.

CLARENCE: But I've got to have a new suit of clothes.

JOHN: Maybe I could get a job for both of us. [*The doorbell rings.*] I'll tell you what I'll do, I'll ask the man.

FATHER [*hurrying to the foot of the stairs*]: Vinnie! Cora! The cab's here. Hurry up! [*Goes through the arch toward the front door.*]

CLARENCE: John, we've both got to get down there early Tuesday—the first thing.

JOHN: Oh, no you don't—I'm going alone. But I'll put in a good word with the boss about you.

FATHER [*off*]: They'll be right out. Vinnie! Cora! [*He comes back to the foot of the stairs and calls up.*] Are you coming? The cab's waiting!

VINNIE [*from upstairs*]: We heard you, Clare. We'll be down in a minute.

[FATHER *comes into the room.*]

FATHER: John, go upstairs and hurry them down.

[JOHN *goes upstairs.* FATHER *crosses to the window and looks out, then consults his watch.*]

FATHFR: What's the matter with those women? Don't they know cabs cost money? Clarence, go see what's causing this infernal delay!

[CLARENCE *goes out to the hall.*]

CLARFNCE: Here they come, Father.

[MARY *comes sedately downstairs. She passes* CLARENCE *without a glance and goes to* FATHER.]

MARY: Goodbye, Mr. Day. I can't tell you how much I appreciate your hospitality.

FATHER: Not at all! Not at all!

[VINNIE *and* CORA *appear at top of stairs and come down.* JOHN *follows with the bags and takes them out.*]

CORA: Goodbye, Clarence. [*She starts into the room.*]

FATHER: Cora, we can say goodbye to you on the sidewalk.

VINNIE: There's no hurry. Their train doesn't go until one-thirty.

FATHER: Cabs cost money. If they have any waiting to do they ought to do it at the Grand Central Depot. They've got a waiting-room there just *for* that.

VINNIE [*to* MARY]: If there's one thing Mr. Day can't stand it's to keep a cab waiting.

CORA: It's been so nice seeing you again, Clarence. [*She kisses him.*]

[MARGARET *enters with a box of lunch.*]

MARGARET: Here's the lunch.

FATHER: All right. All right. Give it to me. Let's get started.

[MARGARET *gives it to him and exits.*]

CORA: Where's John?

FATHER: He's outside. Come on. [*Leads the way.* CORA *and* VINNIE *follow.* MARY *starts.*]

CLARENCE: Mary, aren't you going even to shake hands with me?

MARY: I don't think I'd better. You may remember that when I get too close to you you feel contaminated. [*Starts out.* CLARENCE *follows her.*]

CLARENCE: Mary! [*She stops in the arch. He goes to her.*] You're going to write me, aren't you?

MARY: Are you going to write first?

CLARENCE [*resolutely*]: No, Mary. There are times when a man has to be firm.

[JOHN *enters.*]

JOHN: Mary, Mother says you'd better hurry out before Father starts yelling. It's Sunday.

MARY: Goodbye, John. I'm very happy to have made *your* acquaintance. [*She walks out. We hear the door close.* JOHN *goes out.* CLARENCE *takes a step toward the door, stops, suffers a moment, then turns to the writing desk, takes paper and pen and ink to the table, and sits down to write a letter.*]

CLARENCE [*writing*]: Dear Mary—

[*Curtain*]

SCENE 2

The same.

Two days later. The breakfast table.

HARLAN *and* WHITNEY *are at the table, ready to start breakfast.* CLARENCE *is near the window reading the paper. The places of* JOHN *and* VINNIE *and* FATHER *are empty.* NORA, *a new maid, is serving the fruit and cereal.* NORA *is heavily built and along toward middle age. The doorbell rings and we hear the postman's whistle.* CLARENCE *drops the paper and looks out the window toward the door.* NORA *starts toward the arch.*

CLARENCE: Never mind, Nora. It's the postman. I'll go. [*He runs out through the arch.*]

WHITNEY [*to* NORA]: You forgot the sugar. It goes here between me and Father.

[CLARENCE *comes back with three or four letters which he sorts eagerly. Then his face falls in utter dejection.* FATHER *comes down the stairs.*]

FATHER: Good morning, boys! John late? [*He shouts.*] John! John! Hurry down to your breakfast.

CLARENCE: John had his breakfast early, Father, and went out to see about something.

FATHER: See about what?

CLARENCE: John and I thought we'd work this summer and earn some money.

FATHER: Good! Sit down boys. [*Goes to his chair.*]

CLARENCE: We saw an ad in the paper and John went down to see about it.

FATHER: Why didn't you go, too?

CLARENCE: I was expecting an answer to a letter I wrote, but it didn't come. Here's the mail. [*He seems depressed.*]

FATHER [*sitting*]: What kind of work is this you're planning to do?

CLARENCE: Sort of salesman, the ad said.

FATHER: Um-hum. Well, work never hurt anybody. It's good for them. But if you're going to work, work hard. King Solomon had the right idea about work. "Whatever thy hand findeth to do," Solomon said, "do thy damnedest!" Where's your mother?

NORA: If you please, sir, Mrs. Day doesn't want any breakfast. She isn't feeling well, so she went back upstairs to lie down again.

FATHER [*uneasily*]: Now, why does your mother do that to me? She knows it just upsets my day when she doesn't come down to breakfast. Clarence, go tell your mother I'll be up to see her before I start for the office.

CLARENCE: Yes, sir. [*He goes upstairs.*]

HARLAN: What's the matter with Mother?

FATHER: There's nothing the matter with your mother. Perfectly healthy woman. She gets an ache or a twinge and instead of being firm about it, she just gives in to it. [*The postman whistles. Then the doorbell rings.* NORA *answers it.*] Boys, after breakfast you find out what your mother wants you to do today. Whitney, you take care of Harlan.

[NORA *comes back with a special-delivery letter.*]

NORA: It's a special delivery.

[*She hands it to* FATHER, *who tears it open at once.* CLARENCE *comes rushing down the stairs.*]

CLARENCE: Was that the postman again?

WHITNEY: It was a special delivery.

CLARENCE: Yes? Where is it?

WHITNEY: It was for Father.

CLARENCE [*again disappointed*]: Oh— [*He sits at the table.*]

[FATHER *has opened the letter and is reading it. Bewildered, he turns it over and looks at the signature.*]

FATHER: I don't understand this at all. Here's a letter from some woman I never even heard of. [FATHER *tackles the letter again.* CLARENCE *sees the envelope, picks it up, looks at the postmark, worried.*]

CLARENCE: Father!

FATHER: Oh, God!

CLARENCE: What is it, Father?

FATHER: This is the damnedest nonsense I ever read! As far as I can make out this woman claims that she sat on my lap and I didn't like it. [CLARENCE *begins to turn red.* FATHER *goes on reading a little further and then holds the letter over in front of* CLARENCE.] Can you make out what that word is? [CLARENCE *begins feverishly to read as much as possible, but* FATHER *cuts in.*] No, that word right there. [*He points.*]

CLARENCE: It looks like—"curiosity."

[FATHER *withdraws the letter,* CLARENCE'S *eyes following it hungrily.*]

FATHER [*reads*]: "I only opened your letter as a matter of curiosity." [*Breaks off reading aloud as he turns the page.*]

CLARENCE: Yes? Go on.

FATHER: Why, this gets worse and worse! It just turns into a lot of sentimental lovey-dovey mush. [*Crushes the letter, stalks across the room, and throws it into the fireplace,* CLARENCE *watching him with dismay.*] Is this someone's idea of a practical joke? Why must I be the butt—

[VINNIE *comes hurrying down the stairs. Her hair is down in two braids over her shoulder. She is wearing a lacy combing jacket over her corset cover, and a striped petticoat.*]

VINNIE: What's the matter, Clare? What's wrong?

FATHER [*going to her*]: Nothing wrong—just a damn fool letter. How are you, Vinnie?

VINNIE [*weakly*]: I don't feel well. I thought you needed me, but if you don't I'll go back to bed.

FATHER: No, now that you're here, sit down with us. [*He moves out her chair.*] Get some food in your stomach. Do you good.

VINNIE [*protesting*]: I don't feel like eating anything, Clare.

[NORA *enters with a tray of bacon and eggs, stops at the serving table.*]

FATHER [*heartily*]: That's all the more reason why you should eat. Build up your strength! [*He forces* VINNIE *into her chair and turns to speak to* NORA, *who has her back to him.*] Here— [*Then to* CLARENCE.] What's this one's name?

CLARENCE: Nora.

FATHER: Nora! Give Mrs. Day some of the bacon and eggs.

VINNIE: No, Clare! [NORA, *however, has gone to* VINNIE'S *side with the platter.*] No, take it away, Nora. I don't even want to smell it.

[*The maid retreats, and serves* FATHER; *then* CLARENCE; *then serves coffee and exits.*]

FATHER: Vinnie, it's just weak to give in to an ailment. Any disease can be cured by firmness. What you need is strength of character.

VINNIE: I don't know why you object to my complaining a little. I notice when you have a headache you yell and groan and swear enough.

FATHER: Of course I yell! That's to prove to the headache that I'm stronger than it is. I can usually swear it right out of my system.

VINNIE: This isn't a headache. I think I've caught some kind of a germ. There's a lot of sickness around. Several of my friends have had to send for the doctor. I may have the same thing.

FATHER: I'll bet this is all your imagination, Vinnie. You hear of a lot of other people having some disease and then you get scared and think you have it yourself. So you go to bed and send for the doctor. The doctor—all poppycock!

VINNIE: I didn't say anything about my sending for the doctor.

FATHER: I should hope not. Doctors think they know a damn lot, but they don't.

VINNIE: But Clare, dear, when people are seriously ill you have to do something.

FATHER: Certainly you have to do something! Cheer 'em up—that's the way to cure 'em!

VINNIE [*with slight irony*]: How would you go about cheering them up?

FATHER: I? I'd tell 'em—bah! [VINNIE, *out of exasperation and weakness, begins to cry.* FATHER *looks at her amazed.*] What have I done now?

VINNIE: Oh, Clare—hush up! [*She moves from the table to the sofa, where she tries to control her crying.* HARLAN *slides out of his chair and runs over to her.*] Harlan dear, keep away from Mother. You might catch what she's got. Whitney, if you've finished your breakfast—

WHITNEY [*rising*]: Yes, Mother.

VINNIE: I promised Mrs. Whitehead to send over Margaret's recipe for floating-island pudding. Margaret has it all written out. And take Harlan with you.

WHITNEY: All right, Mother. I hope you feel better.

[WHITNEY *and* HARLAN *exit.* FATHER *goes over and sits beside* VINNIE *on the sofa.*]

FATHER: Vinnie. [*Contritely.*] I didn't mean to upset you.

I was just trying to help. [*He pats her hand.*] When you take to your bed I have a damned lonely time around here. So when I see you getting it into your head that you're sick, I want to do something about it. [*He continues to pat her hand vigorously with what he thinks is reassurance.*] Just because some of your friends have given in to this is no reason why you should imagine you're sick, Vinnie.

VINNIE [*snatching her hand away*]: Oh, stop, Clare!—get out of this house and go to your office!

[FATHER *is a little bewildered and somewhat indignant at this rebuff to his tenderness. He gets up and goes out into the hall, comes back with his hat and stick, and marches out of the house, slamming the door.* VINNIE *rises and starts toward the stairs.*]

CLARENCE: I'm sorry you're not feeling well, Mother.

VINNIE: Oh, I'll be all right, Clarence. Remember last fall I had a touch of this and I was all right the next morning.

CLARENCE: Are you sure you don't want the doctor?

VINNIE: Oh, no. I really don't need him—and besides doctors worry your father. I don't want him to be upset.

CLARENCE: Is there anything I can do for you?

VINNIE: Ask Margaret to send me up a cup of tea. I'll try to drink it. I'm going back to bed.

CLARENCE: Do you mind if John and I go out today or will you need us?

VINNIE: You run right along. I just want to be left alone. [*She exits up the stairs.* CLARENCE *starts for the fireplace eager to retrieve Mary's letter.* NORA *enters. He stops.*]

CLARENCE: Oh!—Nora—will you take a cup of tea up to Mrs. Day in her room?

NORA: Yes, sir. [*Exits.*]

[CLARENCE *hurries around the table, gets the crumpled letter, and starts to read it feverishly. He reads quickly to the end, then draws a deep, happy breath. The door slams. He puts the letter in his pocket.* JOHN *enters, carrying two heavy packages.*]

CLARENCE: Did you get the job?

JOHN: Yes, for both of us. Look, I've got it with me.

CLARENCE: What is it?

JOHN: Medicine.

CLARENCE [*dismayed*]: Medicine! You took a job for us to go out and sell medicine!

JOHN: But it's wonderful medicine. [*Gets a bottle out of the package and reads from the label.*] "Bartlett's Beneficent Balm—A Boon to Mankind." Look what it cures! [*He hands the bottle to* CLARENCE.]

CLARENCE [*reading*]: "A sovereign cure for colds, coughs, catarrh, asthma, quinsy, and sore throat; poor digestion, summer complaint, colic, dyspepsia, heartburn, and shortness of breath; lumbago, rheumatism, heart disease, giddiness, and women's complaints; nervous prostration, St. Vitus' dance, jaundice, and la grippe; proud flesh, pink eye, seasickness, and pimples." [*As* CLARENCE *has read off the list he has become more and more impressed.*]

JOHN: See?

CLARENCE: Say, that sounds all right!

JOHN: It's made "from a secret formula known only to Dr. Bartlett."

CLARENCE: He must be quite a doctor!

JOHN [*enthusiastically*]: It sells for a dollar a bottle and we get twenty-five cents commission on every bottle.

CLARENCE: Well, where does he want us to sell it?

JOHN: He's given us the territory of all Manhattan Island.

CLARENCE: That's bully! Anybody that's sick at all ought to need a bottle of this. Let's start by calling on friends of Father and Mother.

JOHN: That's a good idea. But wait a minute. Suppose they ask us if we use it at our house?

CLARENCE [*a little worried*]: Oh, yes. It would be better if we could say we did.

JOHN: But we can't because we haven't had it here long enough.

[NORA *enters with a tray with a cup of tea. She goes to the table and puts the sugar bowl and cream pitcher on it.*]

CLARENCE: Is that the tea for Mrs. Day?

NORA: Yes.

[*The suspicion of a good idea dawns on* CLARENCE.]

CLARENCE: I'll take it up to her. You needn't bother.

NORA: Thank you. Take it up right away while it's hot.
[*She exits.* CLARENCE *watches her out.*]

CLARENCE [*eying* JOHN]: Mother wasn't feeling well this morning.

JOHN: What was the matter with her?

CLARENCE: I don't know—she was just complaining.

JOHN [*getting the idea immediately and consulting the bottle*]: Well, it says here it's good for women's complaints.

[*They look at each other.* CLARENCE *opens the bottle and smells its contents.* JOHN *leans over and takes a sniff, too. Then he nods to* CLARENCE, *who quickly reaches for a spoon and measures out a teaspoonful, which he puts into the tea.* JOHN, *wanting to be sure* MOTHER *has enough to cure her, pours still more into the tea from the bottle as the curtain falls.*]

[THE CURTAIN *remains down for a few seconds to denote a lapse of three hours.*]

[*When the curtain rises again, the breakfast things have been cleared and the room is in order.* HARLAN *is kneeling on* FATHER'S *chair looking out the window as if watching for someone.* MARGARET *comes down from upstairs.*]

MARGARET: Has your father come yet?

HARLAN: Not yet.

[NORA *enters from downstairs with a steaming tea-kettle and a towel and meets* MARGARET *in the hall.*]

MARGARET: Hurry that upstairs. The doctor's waiting for it. I've got to go out.

NORA: Where are you going?

MARGARET: I have to go and get the minister.

[NORA *goes upstairs.*]

HARLAN: There's a cab coming up the street.

MARGARET: Well, I hope it's him, poor man—but a cab doesn't sound like your father. [*She hurries downstairs.*]

[HARLAN *sees something through the window, then rushes to the stairwell and shouts down to* MARGARET.]

HARLAN: Yes, it's Father. Whitney got him all right. [*Runs back to the window. The front door slams and* FATHER *crosses the arch and hurries upstairs.* WHITNEY *comes into the room.*] What took you so long?

WHITNEY: Long? I wasn't long. I went right down on the elevated and got Father right away and we came all the way back in a *cab.*

HARLAN: I thought you were never coming.

WHITNEY: Well, the horse didn't go very fast at first. The cabby whipped him and swore at him and still he wouldn't gallop. Then Father spoke to the horse personally—How is Mother?

HARLAN: I don't know. The doctor's up there now.

WHITNEY: Well, she'd better be good and sick or Father may be mad at me for getting him up here—'specially in a cab.

[FATHER *comes down the stairs muttering to himself.*]

FATHER [*indignantly*]: Well, huh!—It seems to me I ought to be shown a little consideration. I guess I've got some feelings, too!

WHITNEY [*hopefully*]: Mother's awfully sick, isn't she?

FATHER: How do I know? I wasn't allowed to stay in the same room with her.

WHITNEY: Did the doctor put you out?

FATHER: No, it was your mother, damn it! [*He goes out and hangs up his hat and stick, then returns.* FATHER *may be annoyed, but he is also worried.*] You boys keep quiet around here today.

WHITNEY: She must be pretty sick.

FATHER: She must be, Whitney! I don't know! Nobody ever tells me anything in this house. Not a damn thing!

[DR. HUMPHREYS *comes down the stairs. He's the family-doctor type of the period, with just enough whiskers to make him impressive. He carries his satchel.*]

DR. HUMPHREYS: Mrs. Day is quieter now.

FATHER: How sick is she? What's the matter with her?

DR. HUMPHREYS: She's a pretty sick woman, Mr. Day. I had given her a sedative just before you came—and after you left the room I had to give her another. Have you a telephone?

FATHER: A telephone! No—I don't believe in them. Why?

DR. HUMPHREYS: Well, it would only have saved me a few steps. I'll be back in ten minutes. [*He turns to go.*]

FATHER: Wait a minute—I think I'm entitled to know what's the matter with my wife.

[DR. HUMPHREYS *turns back.*]

DR. HUMPHREYS: What did Mrs. Day have for breakfast this morning?

FATHER: She didn't eat anything—not a thing.

DR. HUMPHREYS: Are you sure?

FATHER: I tried to get her to eat something, but she wouldn't.

DR. HUMPHREYS [*almost to himself*]: I can't understand it.

FATHER: Understand what?

DR. HUMPHREYS: These violent attacks of nausea. It's almost as though she were poisoned.

FATHER: Poisoned!

DR. HUMPHREYS: I'll try not to be gone more than ten or fifteen minutes. [*He exits.*]

FATHER [*trying to reassure himself*]: Damn doctors! They never know what's the matter with anybody. Well, he'd better get your mother well, and damn soon or he'll hear from me.

WHITNEY: Mother's going to get well, isn't she?

[FATHER *looks at* WHITNEY *sharply as though he is a little angry at anyone even raising the question.*]

FATHER: Of course she's going to get well!

HARLAN [*running to* FATHER]: I hope she gets well soon. When Mamma stays in bed it's lonesome.

FATHER: Yes, it is, Harlan. It's lonesome. [*He looks around the room and finds it pretty empty.*] What were you boys supposed to do today?

WHITNEY: I was to learn the rest of my catechism.

FATHER: Well, if that's what your mother wanted you to do, you'd better do it.

WHITNEY: I know it—I think.

FATHER: You'd better be sure.

WHITNEY: I can't be sure unless somebody hears me. Will you hear me?

FATHER [*with sudden willingness to be useful*]: All right. I'll hear you, Whitney.

[WHITNEY *goes to the mantel and gets* VINNIE'S *prayer book.* FATHER *sits on the sofa.* HARLAN *climbs up beside him.*]

HARLAN: If Mamma's still sick will you read to me tonight?

FATHER: Of course I'll read to you.

[WHITNEY *opens the prayer book and hands it to* FATHER.]

WHITNEY: Here it is, Father. Just the end of it. Mother knows I know the rest. Look, start here. [*He points.*]

FATHER: All right. [*Reading.*] "How many parts are there in a Sacrament?"

WHITNEY [*reciting*]: "Two; the outward visible sign, and the inward spiritual grace."

[FATHER *nods in approval.*]

FATHER: "What is the outward visible sign or form in Baptism?"

WHITNEY: "Water; wherein the person is baptized, in the name of the Father, and of the Son, and of the Holy Ghost.' You haven't been baptized, Father, have you?

FATHER [*ignoring it*]: "What is the inward and spiritual grace?"

WHITNEY: If you don't have to be baptized, why do I have to be confirmed?

FATHER [*ignoring this even more*]: "What is the inward and spiritual grace?"

WHITNEY: "A death unto sin, and a new birth unto right-eousness; for being by nature born in sin, and the children of wrath, we are hereby made the children of grace." Is that why you get mad so much, Father—because you're a child of wrath?

FATHER: Whitney, mind your manners! You're not sup-posed to ask questions of your elders! "What is required of persons to be baptized?"

WHITNEY: "Repentance, whereby—whereby—" [*He pauses.*]

FATHER [*quickly shutting the book and handing it to* WHITNEY]: You don't know it well enough, Whitney. You'd better study it some more.

WHITNEY: Now?

FATHER [*softening*]: No, you don't have to do it now. Let's see, now, what can we do?

WHITNEY: Well, I was working with my tool chest out in the back yard. [*Edges toward the arch.*]

FATHER: Better not do any hammering with your mother sick upstairs. You'd better stay here.

WHITNEY: I wasn't hammering—I was doing wood-carving.

FATHER: Well, Harlan—how about you? Shall we play some tiddle-dy-winks?

HARLAN [*edging toward* WHITNEY]: I was helping Whitney.

FATHER: Oh—all right. [*The boys go out.* FATHER *goes to the stairwell.*] Boys, don't do any shouting. We all have to be very quiet around here. [*He stands in the hall and looks up toward* VINNIE, *worried. Then he tiptoes across the room and stares gloomily out of the window. Then he tiptoes back into the hall and goes to the rail of the basement stairs, and calls quietly.*] Margaret! [*There is no answer and he raises his voice a little.*] Margaret! [*There is still no answer and he lets loose.*] Margaret! Why don't you answer when you hear me calling?

[*At this moment* MARGARET, *hat on, appears in the arch from the right, having come through the front door.*]

MARGARET: Sh—sh—

[FATHER *turns quickly and sees* MARGARET.]

FATHER: Oh, there you are!

MARGARET [*reprovingly*]: We must all be quiet, Mr. Day— Mrs. Day is very sick.

FATHER [*testily*]: I know she's sick. That's what I wanted you for. You go up and wait outside her door in case she needs anything. [MARGARET *starts upstairs.*] And what were you doing out of the house, anyway?

MARGARET: I was sent for the minister.

FATHER [*startled*]: The minister!

MARGARET: Yes, he'll be right in. He's paying off the cab.

[MARGARET *continues upstairs. The door slams.* THE REVEREND DR. LLOYD *appears in the archway and meets* FATHER *in the hall.*]

DR. LLOYD: I was deeply shocked to hear of Mrs. Day's illness. I hope I can be of some service. Will you take me up to her?

FATHER [*with a trace of hostility*]: She's resting now. She can't be disturbed.

DR. LLOYD: But I've been summoned.

FATHER: The doctor will be back in a few minutes and we'll see what he has to say about it. You'd better come in and wait.

DR. LLOYD: Thank you. [*Comes into the room.* FATHER *follows him reluctantly.*] Mrs. Day has been a tower of strength in the parish. Everyone liked her so much. Yes, she was a fine woman.

FATHER: I wish to God you wouldn't talk about Mrs. Day as if she were dead.

[NORA *comes down the stairs and looks into the room.*]

NORA: Is the doctor back yet?

FATHER: No. Does she need him?

NORA: She's kinda' restless. She's talking in her sleep and twisting and turning. [*She goes downstairs.* FATHER *looks up toward* VINNIE'S *room, worried, then looks angrily toward the front door.*]

FATHER: That doctor said he'd be right back. [*He goes to the window.*]

MARGARET [*coming downstairs*]: Here comes the doctor. I was watching for him out the window. [*She goes to the front door. A moment later* DR. HUMPHREYS *enters.*]

FATHER: Well, doctor—seems to me that was a pretty long ten minutes.

DR. HUMPHREYS [*indignantly*]: See here, Mr. Day, if I'm to be responsible for Mrs. Day's health, I must be allowed to handle this case in my own way.

FATHER: Well, you can't handle it if you're out of the house.

DR. HUMPHREYS [*flaring*]: I left this house because— [DR. SOMERS, *an imposing medical figure, enters and stops at* DR. HUMPHREY'S *side.*] This is Dr. Somers.

DR. SOMERS: How do you do?

DR. HUMPHREYS: I felt that Mrs. Day's condition warranted my getting Dr. Somers here as soon as possible for consultation. I hope that meets with your approval.

FATHER [*a little awed*]: Why, yes, of course. Anything that can be done.

DR. HUMPHREYS: Upstairs, doctor! [*The two doctors go upstairs.* FATHER *turns back into the room, obviously shaken.*]

DR. LLOYD: Mrs. Day is in good hands now, Mr. Day. There's nothing you and I can do at the moment to help.

[*After a moment's consideration* FATHER *decides there is something that can be done to help. He goes to* DR. LLOYD. FATHER *indicates the seat in front of the table to* DR. LLOYD *and they both sit.*]

FATHER: Dr. Lloyd, there's something that's troubling Mrs. Day's mind. I think you know what I refer to.

DR. LLOYD: Yes—you mean the fact that you've never been baptized.

FATHER: I gathered you knew about it from your sermon last Sunday. [*Looks at him a second with indignant memory.*] But let's not get angry. I think something had better be done about it.

DR. LLOYD: Yes, Mr. Day.

FATHER: When the doctors get through up there I want you to talk to Mrs. Day. I want you to tell her something.

DR. LLOYD [*eagerly*]: Yes, I'll be glad to.

FATHER: You're just the man to do it! She shouldn't be upset about this—I want you to tell her that my being baptized would just be a lot of damn nonsense.

[*This isn't what* DR. LLOYD *has expected and it is hardly his idea of how to help* MRS. DAY.]

DR. LLOYD: But, Mr. Day!

FATHER: No, she'd take your word on a thing like that— and we've got to do everything we can to help her now.

DR. LLOYD [*rising*]: But baptism is one of the sacraments of the Church—

FATHER [*rising*]: You're her minister and you're supposed to bring her comfort and peace of mind.

DR. LLOYD: But the solution is so simple. It would take only your consent to be baptized.

FATHER: That's out of the question! And I'm surprised that a grown man like you should suggest such a thing.

DR. LLOYD: If you're really concerned about Mrs. Day's peace of mind, don't you think—

FATHER: Now see here—if you're just going to keep her stirred up about this, I'm not going to let you see her at all. [*He turns away.* DR. LLOYD *follows him.*]

DR. LLOYD: Now, Mr. Day, as you said, we must do everything we can— [*The doctors come downstairs.* FATHER *sees them.*]

FATHER: Well, doctor, how is she? What have you decided?

DR. HUMPHREYS: We's just left Mrs. Day. Is there a room we could use for our consultation?

FATHER: Of course. [MARGARET *starts downstairs.*] Margaret, you go back upstairs! I don't want Mrs. Day left alone!

MARGARET: I have to do something for the doctor. I'll go back upstairs as soon as I get it started.

FATHER: Well, hurry. And, Margaret, show these gentlemen downstairs to the billiard room.

MARGARET: Yes, sir. This way, doctor—downstairs. [*Exits, followed by* DR. SOMERS. FATHER *delays* DR. HUMPHREYS.]

FATHER: Dr. Humphreys, you know now, don't you—this isn't serious, is it?

DR. HUMPHREYS: After we've had our consultation we'll talk to you, Mr. Day.

FATHER: But surely you must—

DR. HUMPHREYS: Just rest assured that Dr. Somers will do everything that is humanly possible.

FATHER: Why, you don't mean—

DR. HUMPHREYS: We'll try not to be long. [*Exits.* FATHER *turns and looks at* DR. LLOYD. *He is obviously frightened.*]

FATHER: This Dr. Somers—I've heard his name often—he's very well thought of, isn't he?

DR. LLOYD: Oh, yes indeed.

FATHER: If Vinnie's really—if anyone could help her, he could—don't you think?

DR. LLOYD: A very fine physician. But there's a greater Help, ever present in the hour of need. Let us turn to Him in prayer. Let us kneel and pray. [FATHER *looks at him, straightens, then walks to the other side of the room.*] Let us kneel and pray. [FATHER *finally bows his head.* DR. LLOYD *looks at him and, not kneeling himself, raises his head and speaks simply in prayer.*] Oh, Lord, look down from Heaven —behold, visit, and relieve this Thy servant who is grieved with sickness, and extend to her Thy accustomed goodness. We know she has sinned against Thee in thought, word, and deed. Have mercy on her, O Lord, have mercy on this miserable sinner. Forgive her—

FATHER: She's not a miserable sinner and you know it! [*Then* FATHER *speaks directly to the Deity.*] Oh God! You know Vinnie's not a miserable sinner. She's a damn fine woman! She shouldn't be made to suffer. It's got to stop, I tell You, it's got to stop!

[VINNIE *appears on the stairway in her nightgown.*]

VINNIE: What's the matter, Clare? What's wrong?

FATHER [*not hearing her*]: Have mercy, I say, have mercy, damn it!

VINNIE: What's the matter, Clare? What's wrong?

[FATHER *turns, sees* VINNIE, *and rushes to her.*]

FATHER: Vinnie, what are you doing down here? You shouldn't be out of bed. You get right back upstairs. [*He now has his arms around her.*]

VINNIE: Oh, Clare, I heard you call. Do you need me?

FATHER [*deeply moved*]: Vinnie—I know now how much I need you. Get well, Vinnie. I'll be baptized. I promise. I'll be baptized.

VINNIE: You will? Oh, Clare!

FATHER: I'll do anything. We'll go to Europe, just we two

—you won't have to worry about the children or the house-hold accounts— [VINNIE *faints against* FATHER's *shoulder.*] Vinnie! [*He stoops to lift her.*]

DR. LLOYD: I'll get the doctor. But don't worry, Mr. Day —she'll be all right now. [FATHER *lifts* VINNIE *up in his arms.*] Bless you for what you've done, Mr. Day.

FATHER: What did I do?

DR. LLOYD: You promised to be baptized!

FATHER [*aghast*]: I did? [*With horror* FATHER *realizes he has been betrayed—and by himself.*] OH, GOD!

[*Curtain*]

ACT THREE

The same.
A month later. Mid-afternoon.
VINNIE *is seated on the sofa embroidering petit point.* MAR-
GARET *enters, as usual uncomfortable at being upstairs.*

MARGARET: You wanted to speak to me, ma'am?

VINNIE: Yes, Margaret, about tomorrow morning's breakfast—we must plan it very carefully.

MARGARET [*puzzled*]: Mr. Day hasn't complained to me
about his breakfasts lately. As a matter of fact, I've been
blessing my luck!

VINNIE: Oh, no, it's not that. But tomorrow morning I'd
like something for his breakfast that would surprise him.

MARGARET [*doubtfully*]: Surprising Mr. Day is always a
bit of a risk, ma'am. My motto with him has always been
"Let well enough alone."

VINNIE: But if we think of something he especially likes,
Margaret—what would you say to kippers?

MARGARET: Well, I've served him kippers, but I don't
recall his ever saying he liked them.

VINNIE: He's never said he didn't like them, has he?

MARGARET: They've never got a stamp on the floor out of
him one way or the other.

VINNIE: If Mr. Day doesn't say he doesn't like a thing you
can assume that he does. Let's take a chance on kippers,
Margaret.

MARGARET: Very well, ma'am. [*She starts out.*]

VINNIE [*innocently*]: And, Margaret, you'd better have
enough breakfast for two extra places.

MARGARET [*knowingly*]: Oh—so that's it! We're going **to** have company again.

VINNIE: Yes, my cousin, Miss Cartwright, and her friend are coming back from Springfield. I'm afraid they'll get here just about breakfast time.

MARGARET: Well, in that case I'd better make some of my Sunday morning hot biscuits, too.

VINNIE: Yes. We *know* Mr. Day likes those.

MARGARET: I've been getting him to church with them for the last fifteen years. [*The door slams.* MARGARET *goes to the arch and looks.*] Oh, it's Mr. Clarence, ma'am. [*Goes off downstairs and* CLARENCE *enters with a large package.*]

CLARENCE: Here it is, Mother. [*He puts it on the table.*]

VINNIE: Oh, it was still in the store! They hadn't sold it! I'm so thrilled. Didn't you admire it, Clarence? [*She hurries over to the table.*]

CLARENCE: Well, it's unusual.

VINNIE [*unwrapping the package*]: You know, I saw this down there the day before I got sick. I was walking through the bric-a-brac section and it caught my eye. I was so tempted to buy it! And all the time I lay ill, I just couldn't get it out of my head. I can't understand how it could stay in the store all this time without somebody snatching it up. [*She takes it out of the box. It is a large china pug dog.*] Isn't that the darlingest thing you ever saw! It does need a ribbon, though. I've got the very thing somewhere. Oh, yes, I know. [*Goes to the side table and gets a red ribbon out of the drawer.*]

CLARENCE: Isn't John home yet?

VINNIE: I haven't seen him. Why?

CLARENCE: Well, you know we've been working, and John went down to collect our money.

VINNIE: That's fine. [*She ties the ribon around the dog's neck.*] Oh, Clarence, I have a secret for just the two of us; who do you think is coming to visit us tomorrow?—Cousin Cora and Mary.

CLARENCE: Yes, I know.

VINNIE: How did you know?

CLARENCE: I happened to get a letter.

[JOHN *enters, carrying two packages of medicine.*]

VINNIE: John, did you ever see anything so sweet?

JOHN: What is it?

VINNIE: It's a pug dog. Your father would never let me have a real one, but he can't object to one made of china. This ribbon needs pressing. I'll take it down and have Margaret do it right away. [*Exits with the beribboned pug dog.*]

CLARENCE: What did you bring home more medicine for? [*Then, with sudden fright.*] Dr. Bartlett paid us off, didn't he?

JOHN: Oh, yes!

CLARENCE [*heaving a great sigh of relief*]: You had me scared for a minute. When I went down to McCreery's to get that pug dog for Mother, I ordered the daisiest suit you ever saw. Dr. Bartlett owed us sixteen dollars apiece, and the suit was only fifteen. Wasn't that lucky? Come on, give me my money.

JOHN: Clarence, Dr. Bartlett paid us off in medicine.

CLARENCE: You let him pay us off with that old Benificent Balm!

JOHN: Well, he thanked us, too, for our services to mankind.

CLARENCE [*in agony*]: But my suit!

JOHN: You'll just have to wait for your suit.

CLARENCE: I can't wait! I've got to have it tomorrow—and besides they're making the alterations. I've got to pay for it this afternoon! Fifteen dollars!

JOHN [*helpfully*]: Why don't you offer them fifteen bottles of medicine?

[CLARENCE *gives it a little desperate thought.*]

CLARENCE: They wouldn't take it. McCreery's don't sell medicine.

[JOHN *is by the window and looks out.*]

JOHN: That's too bad. Here comes Father.

CLARENCE: I'll have to brace him for that fifteen dollars. I hate to do it, but I've got to—that's all—I've got to.

JOHN: I'm not going to be here when you do. I'd better hide this somewhere, anyway. [*Takes the packages and hurries upstairs. The door slams.* FATHER *enters and looks into the room*]:

CLARENCE: Good afternoon, sir.

FATHER: How's your mother, Clarence? Where is she?

CLARENCE: She's all right. She's downstairs with Margaret. Oh, Father—

[FATHER *goes off down the hall and we hear him calling downstairs.*]

FATHER: Vinnie! Vinnie! I'm home. [*Comes back into the room, carrying his newspaper.*]

CLARENCE: Father, Mother will be well enough to go to go to church with us next Sunday.

FATHER: That's fine, Clarence. That's fine.

CLARENCE: Father, have you noticed that I haven't been kneeling down in church lately?

FATHER: Clarence, don't let your mother catch you at it.

CLARENCE: Then I've got to have a new suit of clothes right away!

FATHER [*after a puzzled look*]: Clarence, you're not even making sense!

CLARENCE: But a fellow doesn't feel right in cut-down clothes—especially your clothes. That's why I can't kneel down in church—I can't do anything in them you wouldn't do.

FATHER: Well, that's a damn good thing! If my old clothes make you behave yourself I don't think you ought to wear anything else.

CLARENCE [*desperately*]: Oh, no! You're you and I'm me! I want to be myself! Besides, you're older and there are things I've got to do that I wouldn't do at your age.

FATHER: Clarence, you should never do anything I wouldn't do.

CLARENCE: Oh, yes,—look, for instance: Suppose I should want to kneel down in front of a girl?

FATHER: Why in Heaven's name should you want to do a thing like that?

CLARENCE: Well, I've got to get married sometime. I've got to propose to a girl *sometime*.

FATHER [*exasperated*]: Before you're married, you'll be earning your own clothes, I hope. Don't get the idea into your head I'm going to support you and a wife, too. Besides, at your age, Clarence—

CLARENCE [*hastily*]: Oh, I'm not going to be married right away, but for fifteen dollars I can get a good suit of clothes.

FATHER [*bewildered and irritated*]: Clarence! [*He stares at him. At this second,* VINNIE *comes through the arch.*] Why, you're beginning to talk as crazy as your mother. [*He sees her.*] Oh, hello, Vinnie. How're you feeling today?

VINNIE: I'm fine, Clare. [*They kiss.*] You don't have to hurry home from the office every day like this.

[CLARENCE *throws himself in the chair by the window, sick with diasppointment.*]

FATHER: Business the way it is, no use going to the office at all.

VINNIE: But you haven't been to your club for weeks.

FATHER: Can't stand the damn place. You do look better, Vinnie. What did you do today? [*Drops on the sofa.* VINNIE *stands behind the sofa. Her chatter does not succeed in diverting* FATHER *from his newspaper.*]

VINNIE: I took a long walk and dropped in to call on old Mrs. Whitehead.

FATHER: Well, that's fine.

VINNIE: And, Clare, it was the most fortunate thing that ever happened. I've got wonderful news for you! Who do you think was there? Mr. Morley!

FATHER [*not placing him*]: Morley?

VINNIE: You remember—that nice young minister who substituted for Dr. Lloyd one Sunday?

FATHER: Oh, yes! Bright young fellow, preached a good sensible sermon.

VINNIE: It was the only time I ever saw you put five dollars in the plate!

FATHFR: Ought to be more ministers like him. I could get along with that young man without any trouble at all.

VINNIE: Well, Clare, his parish is in Audubon—you know, 'way up above Harlem.

FATHER: Is that so?

VINNIE: Isn't that wonderful? Nobody knows you up there. You'll be perfectly safe!

FATHER: Safe? Vinnie, what the devil are you talking about?

VINNIE: I've been all over everything with Mr. Morley and he's agreed to baptize you.

FATHER: Oh, he has—the young whippersnapper! Damn nice of him!

VINNIE: We can go up there any morning, Clare—we don't even have to make an appointment.

FATHER: Vinnie, you're just making a lot of plans for nothing. Who said I was going to be baptized at all?

VINNIE [*aghast*]: Why, Clare! *You* did!

FATHER: Now, Vinnie!—

VINNIE: You gave me your promise—your Sacred Promise. You stood right on that spot and said: "I'll be baptized. I promise—I'll be baptized."

FATHER: What if I did?

VINNIE [*amazed, she comes down and faces him*]: Aren't you a man of your word?

FATHER [*rising*]: Vinnie, that was under entirely different circumstances. We all thought you were dying, so naturally I said that to make you feel better. As a matter of fact, the doctor told me that's what cured you. So it seems to me pretty ungrateful of you to press this matter any further.

VINNIE: Clarence Day, you gave me your Sacred Promise!

FATHER [*getting annoyed*]: Vinnie, you were sick when I said that. Now you're well again.

[MARGARET *enters with the pug dog, which now has the freshly pressed ribbon tied around its neck. She puts it on the table.*]

MARGARET: Is that all right, Mrs. Day?

VINNIE [*dismissingly*]: That's fine, Margaret, thank you. [MARGARET *exits*]. My being well has nothing to do with it. You gave me your word! You gave the Lord your word. If you had seen how eager Mr. Morley was to bring you into the fold. [FATHER, *trying to escape, has been moving toward the arch when suddenly the pug dog catches his eye and he stares at it fascinated.*] And you're going to march yourself up to his church some morning before you go to the office and be christened. If you think for one minute that I'm going to—

FATHER: What in the name of Heaven is that?

VINNIE: If you think I'm going to let you add the sin of breaking your Solemn and Sacred Promise—

FATHER: I demand to know what that repulsive object is!

VINNIE [*exasperated in her turn*]: It's perfectly plain what it is—it's a pug dog!

FATHER: What's it doing in this house?

VINNIE [*defiantly*]: I wanted it and I bought it.

FATHER: You spent good money for that?

VINNIE: Clare, we're not talking about that! We're talking about you. Don't try to change the subject!

FATHER: How much did you pay for that atrocity?

VINNIE: I don't know. I sent Clarence down for it. Listen to me, Clare—

FATHER: Clarence, what did you pay for that?

CLARENCE: I didn't pay anything. I charged it.

FATHER [*looking at* VINNIE]: Charged it! I might have known. [*To* CLARENCE.] How much was it?

CLARENCE: Fifteen dollars.

FATHER: Fifteen dollars for that eyesore?

VINNIE [*to the rescue of the pug dog*]: Don't you call that lovely work of art an eyesore! That will look beautiful sitting on a red cushion by the fireplace in the parlor.

FATHER: If that sits in the parlor, I won't! Furthermore, I don't even want it in the same house with me. Get it out of here! [*He starts for the stairs.*]

VINNIE: You're just using that for an excuse. You're not going to get out of this room until you set a date for your baptism.

[FATHER *turns at the foot of the stairs.*]

FATHER: I'll tell you one thing! I'll never be baptized while that hideous monstrosity is in this house. [*He stalks upstairs.*]

VINNIE [*calling after him*]: All right! [*She goes to the pug dog.*] All right! It goes back this afternoon and he's christened first thing in the morning.

CLARENCE: But, Mother—

VINNIE: Clarence, you heard him say that he'd be baptized as soon as I got this pug dog out of the house. You hurry right back to McCreery's with it—and be sure they credit us with fifteen dollars.

[*The fifteen dollars rings a bell in* CLARENCE's *mind.*]

CLARENCE: Oh, say, Mother, while I was at McCreery's, I happened to see a suit I would like very much and the suit was only fifteen dollars.

VINNIE [*regretfully*]: Well, Clarence, I think your suit will have to wait until after I get your father christened.

CLARENCE [*hopefully*]: No. I meant that since the suit cost just the same as the pug dog, if I exchanged the pug dog for the suit—

VINNIE: Why, yes! Then your suit wouldn't cost Father anything! Why, how bright of you, Clarence, to think of that!

CLARENCE [*quickly*]: I'd better start right away before McCreery's closes. [*They have collected the box, wrapper, and tissue paper.*]

VINNIE: Yes. Let's see. If we're going to take your father all the way up to Audubon—Clarence, you stop at Ryerson & Brown's on your way back and tell them to have a cab here at eight o'clock tomorrow morning.

CLARENCE: Mother, a cab! Do you think you ought to do that?

VINNIE: Well, we can't walk to Audubon.

CLARENCE [*warningly*]: But you know what a cab does to Father!

VINNIE: This is an important occasion.

CLARENCE [*with a shrug*]: All right! A brougham or a Victoria?

VINNIE: Get one of their best cabs—that kind they use at funerals.

CLARENCE: Those cost two dollars an hour! And if Father gets mad—

VINNIE: Well, if your father starts to argue in the morning, you remember—

CLARENCE [*remembering his suit*]: Oh, he agreed to it! We both heard him!

[VINNIE *has removed the ribbon and is about to put the pug dog back in the box.*]

VINNIE [*regretfully*]: I did have my heart set on this. [*An idea comes to her.*] Still—if they didn't sell him in all that time, he might be safe there for a few more weeks. [*She gives the dog a reassuring pat and puts him in the box. She begins to sing "Sweet Marie" happily.* FATHER *comes down the stairs.* CLARENCE *takes his hat and the box and goes happily and quickly out.* FATHER *watches him.*] I hope you notice that Clarence is returning the pug dog.

FATHER: That's a sign you're getting your faculties back. [VINNIE *is singing quietly to herself in a satisfied way.*] Good to hear you singing again, Vinnie. [*Suddenly remembering something.*] Oh!—on my way uptown I stopped in at Tiffany's and bought you a little something. Thought you might like it. [*He takes out of his pocket a small ring-box and holds it out to her. She takes it.*]

VINNIE: Oh, Clare. [*She opens it eagerly.*] What a beautiful ring! [*She takes the ring out, puts it on her finger, and admires it.*]

FATHER: Glad if it pleases you. [*He settles down to his newspaper on the sofa.*]

VINNIE: I don't know how to thank you. [*She kisses him.*]

FATHER: It's thanks enough for me to have you up and

around again. When you're sick, Vinnie, this house is like a tomb. There's no excitement.

VINNIE [*sitting beside him*]: Clare, this is the loveliest ring you ever bought me. Now that I have this, you needn't buy me any more rings.

FATHER: Well, if you don't want any more.

VINNIE: What I'd really like now is a nice diamond necklace.

FATHER [*alarmed*]: Vinnie, do you know how much a diamond necklace costs?

VINNIE: I know, Clare, but don't you see?—your giving me this ring shows that I mean a little something to you. Now, a diamond necklace—

FATHER: Good God, if you don't know by this time how I feel about you! We've been married for twenty years and I've loved you every minute of it.

VINNIE: What did you say? [*Her eyes well with tears at* FATHER'S *definite statement of his love.*]

FATHER: I said we'd been married twenty years and I've loved you every minute of it. But if I have to buy out jewelry stores to prove it—if I haven't shown it to you in my words and actions, I might as well— [*He turns and sees* VINNIE *dabbing her eyes and speaks with resignation.*] What have I done now?

VINNIE: It's all right, Clare—I'm just so happy.

FATHER: Happy!

VINNIE: You said you loved me! And this beautiful ring—that's something else I didn't expect. Oh, Clare, I love surprises. [*She nestles against him.*]

FATHER: That's another thing I can't understand about you, Vinnie. Now, *I* like to know what to expect. Then I'm prepared to meet it.

VINNIE [*putting her head on his shoulder*]: Yes, I know. But, Clare, life would be pretty dull if we always knew what was coming.

FATHER: Well, it's certainly not dull around here. In this house you never know what's going to hit you tomorrow.

VINNIE [*to herself*]: Tomorrow! [*She starts to sing,* FATHER *listening to her happily.*]

"Every daisy in the dell,
Knows my secret, knows it well,
And yet I dare not tell,
Sweet Marie!"

[*Curtain*]

SCENE 2

The same.
The next morning. Breakfast. All the family except JOHN *and* VINNIE *are at the table and in good spirits.*

JOHN [*entering*]: Mother says she'll be right down. [*He sits at the table.*]

[MAGGIE, *the new maid, enters with a plate of hot biscuits and serves* FATHER. *As* FATHER *takes a biscuit, he glances up at her and shows some little surprise.*]

FATHER: Who are you? What's your name?

MAGGIE: Margaret, sir.

FATHER: Can't be Margaret. We've got one Margaret in the house.

MAGGIE: At home they call me Maggie, sir.

FATHER [*genially*]: All right, Maggie. [MAGGIE *continues serving the biscuits.*] Boys, if her name's Margaret, that's a good sign. Maybe she'll stay awhile. You know, boys, your mother used to be just the same about cooks as she is about maids. Never could keep them for some reason. Well, one day about fifteen years ago—yes, it was right after you were born, John—my, you were a homely baby. [*They all laugh at* JOHN's *expense.*] I came home that night all tired out and what did I find?—no dinner, because the cook had left. Well, I decided I'd had just about enough of that, so I just marched over to the employment agency on Sixth Avenue and said to the woman in charge: "Where do you keep the cooks?" She tried to hold me up with a lot of red-tape folderol, but I just walked into the room where the girls were waiting, looked 'em over, saw Margaret, pointed at her, and said: "I'll take that one." I walked her home, she cooked dinner that night, and she's been cooking for us ever since. Damn good cook, too. [*He stamps on the floor three times.*]

[VINNIE *comes down the stairs dressed in white. Somehow she almost has the appearance of a bride going to her wedding.*]

VINNIE: Good morning, Clare. Good morning, boys.

[*The boys and* FATHER *rise.* VINNIE *takes her bonnet and gloves and lays them on the chair below the fireplace.* FATHER *goes to* VINNIE'S *chair and holds it out for her, glancing at her holiday appearance.* VINNIE *sits.*]

FATHER: Sit down, boys. [*As* FATHER *returns to his own chair, he notices that all of the boys are dressed in their Sunday best.*] Everyone's dressed up this morning. What's on the program for this fine day?

[VINNIE, *who always postpones crises in the hope some miracle will aid her, postpones this one.*]

VINNIE: Well, this afternoon May Lewis's mother is giving a party for everyone in May's dancing class. Harlan's going to that.

HARLAN: I don't want to go, Mamma.

VINNIE: Why, Harlan, don't you want to go to a party and get ice cream and cake?

HARLAN: May Lewis always tries to kiss me.

[*This is greeted with family laughter.*]

FATHER [*genially*]: When you get a little older, you won't object to girls wanting to kiss you, will he, Clarence?

[MARGARET *comes hurrying in.*]

MARGARET: What's wanting?

FATHER: Margaret, these kippers are good. [MARGARET *makes her usual deprecatory gesture toward him.*] Haven't had kippers for a long time. I'm glad you remembered I like them.

MARGARET: Yes, sir.

[MARGARET *and* VINNIE *exchange knowing looks.* MARGARET *goes out happy.*]

FATHER: What's got into Margaret this morning? Hot biscuits, too!

VINNIE: She knows you're fond of them. [*The doorbell rings.* MAGGIE *goes to answer it.* VINNIE *stirs nervously in her chair.*] Who can that be? It can't be the mail man because he's been here.

FATHER [*with sly humor*]: Clarence has been getting a good many special deliveries lately. Is that business deal going through, Clarence?

[*The family has a laugh at* CLARENCE. MAGGIE *comes back into the arch with a suit box.*]

MAGGIE: This is for you, Mr. Day. Where shall I put it?

CLARENCE [*hastily*]: Oh, that's for me, I think. Take it upstairs, Maggie.

FATHER: Wait a minute, Maggie, bring it here. Let's see it.

[CLARENCE *takes the box from* MAGGIE, *who exits. He holds it toward his father.*]

CLARENCE: See, it's for me, Father—Clarence Day, Jr.

FATHER: Let me look. Why, that's from McCreery's and it's marked "Charge." What is it?

VINNIE: It's all right, Clare. It's nothing for you to worry about.

FATHER: Well, at least I think I should know what's being charged to me. What is it?

VINNIE: Now, Clare, stop your fussing. It's a new suit of clothes for Clarence and it's not costing you a penny.

FATHER: It's marked "Charge fifteen dollars"—it's costing me fifteen dollars. And I told Clarence—

VINNIE: Clare, can't you take my word it isn't costing you a penny?

FATHER: I'd like to have you explain why it isn't.

VINNIE [*triumphantly*]: Because Clarence took the pug dog back and got the suit instead.

FATHER: Of course, and they'll charge me fifteen dollars for the suit.

VINNIE: Nonsense, Clare. We gave them the pug dog for the suit. Don't you see?

FATHER: Then they'll charge me fifteen dollars for the pug dog.

VINNIE: But, Clare, they can't! We haven't got the pug dog. We sent that back.

FATHER [*bewildered, but not convinced*]: Now wait a minute, Vinnie. There's something wrong with your reasoning.

VINNIE: I'm surprised, Clare, and you're supposed to be so good at figures. Why, it's perfectly clear to me.

FATHER: Vinnie! They're going to charge me for one thing or the other.

VINNIE: Don't you let them!

[FATHER *gets up and throws his napkin on the table.*]

FATHER: Well, McCreery's aren't giving away suits and they aren't giving away pug dogs. [*He walks over to the window in his irritation.*] Can't you get it through your— [*Looking out the window.*] Oh, God!

VINNIE: What is it, Clare? What's wrong?

FATHER: Don't anybody answer the door.

VINNIE: Who is it? Who's coming?

FATHER: Those damn women are back!

WHITNEY: What women?

FATHER: Cora and that little idiot. [CLARENCE *dashes madly up the stairs clutching the box containing his new suit.*] They're moving in on us again, bag and baggage! [*The doorbell rings.*] Don't let them in!

VINNIE: Clarence Day, as if we could turn our own relatives away!

FATHER: Tell them to get back in that cab and drive right on to Ohio. If they're extravagant enough to take cabs when horse cars run right by our door—

[MAGGIE *crosses the hall to answer the doorbell.*]

VINNIE: Now, Clare—you be quiet and behave yourself.

They're here and there's nothing you can do about it. [*She starts toward the hall.*]

FATHER [*shouting after her*]: Well, why do they always pounce on us without warning?—the damn gypsies!

VINNIE [*from the arch*]: Shhh!—Clare! [*Then in her best welcoming tone.*] Cora! Mary! It's so nice to have you back again.

CORA: How are you, Vinnie? We've been so worried about you.

VINNIE: Oh, I'm fine now!

[CORA *and* MARY *and* VINNIE *enter and* CORA *sweeps right down into the room.*]

CORA: Hello, Harlan! Whitney! Well, Cousin Clare. Here we are again! [*Kisses* FATHER *on the cheek. He draws back sternly.* MARY *looks quickly around the room for* CLARENCE, *then greets and is greeted by the other boys.*] And John! Where's Clarence?

MARY: Yes, where is Clarence?

VINNIE: John, go find Clarence and tell him that Cora and Mary are here.

JOHN: Yes, Mother. [*Goes upstairs.*]

VINNIE: You got here just in time to have breakfast with us.

CORA: We had breakfast at the depot.

VINNIE: Well, as a matter of fact, we'd just finished.

FATHER [*with cold dignity*]: *I* haven't finished my breakfast!

VINNIE: Well, then sit down, Clare. [*To* CORA *and* MARY.] Margaret gave us kippers this morning and Clare's so fond of kippers. Why don't we all sit down? [*Indicates the empty places and the girls sit.* FATHER *resumes his chair and breakfast in stony silence.* MAGGIE *has come into the room to await orders.*] Maggie, clear those things away. [*She indicates the dishes in front of the girls, and* MAGGIE *removes them.* FATHER *takes a letter from his stack of morning mail and opens it.*] Clare, don't let your kippers get cold. [*To* CORA.] Now—tell us all about Springfield.

CORA: We had a wonderful month—but tell us about you, Cousin Vinnie. You must have had a terrible time.

VINNIE: Yes, I was pretty sick, but I'm all right again now.

CORA: What was it?

VINNIE: Well, the doctors don't know exactly, but they did say this—that they'd never seen anything like it before, whatever it was.

CORA: You certainly look well enough now. Doesn't she, Clare?

[*Whatever is in the letter* FATHER *has been reading comes to him as a shock.*]

FATHER: Oh, God!

VINNIE: What's the matter, Clare? What's wrong?

FATHER: John! John!

[JOHN *is seen halfway up the stairs with the girls' bags. He comes running down the stairs, going to* FATHER.]

JOHN: Yes, Father?

FATHER: Have you been going around this town selling medicine?

JOHN [*a little frightened*]: Yes, Father.

FATHER: Dog medicine?

JOHN [*indignantly*]: No, Father, not dog medicine!

FATHER: It must have been dog medicine!

JOHN: It wasn't dog medicine, Father—

FATHER: This letter from Mrs. Sprague says you sold her a bottle of this medicine and that her little boy gave some of it to their dog and it killed him! Now she wants ten dollars from me for a new dog.

JOHN: Well, he shouldn't have given it to a dog. It's for humans! Why, it's Bartlett's Beneficent Balm—"Made from a secret formula"!

FATHER: Have you been going around among our friends and neighbors selling some damned Dr. Munyon patent nostrum?

JOHN: But it's good medicine, Father. I can prove it by Mother.

FATHER: Vinnie, what do you know about this?

VINNIE: Nothing, Clare, but I'm sure that John—

JOHN: No, I mean that day Mother—

FATHER: That's enough! You're going to every house where you sold a bottle of that concoction and buy it all back.

JOHN [*dismayed*]: But it's a dollar a bottle!

FATHER: I don't care how much it is. How many bottles did you sell?

JOHN: A hundred and twenty-eight.

FATHER [*roaring*]: A hundred and twenty-eight!

VINNIE: Clare, I always told you John would make a good business man.

FATHER [*calmly*]: Young man, I'll give you the money to buy it back—a hundred and twenty-eight dollars. And ten more for Mrs. Sprague. That's a hundred and thirty-eight dollars. But it's coming out of your allowance! That means you'll not get another penny until that hundred and thirty-eight dollars is all paid up.

[JOHN *starts toward the hall, counting on his fingers, then turns and addresses his father in dismay.*]

JOHN: I'll be twenty-one years old!

[FATHER *glares at him.* JOHN *turns and goes on up the stairs, with the bags.*]

VINNIE [*persuasively*]: Clare, you know you've always encouraged the boys to earn their own money.

FATHER: Vinnie, I'll handle this. [*There is a pause. He buries himself in his newspaper.*]

CORA [*breaking through the constraint*]: Of course, Aunt Judith sent her love to all of you—

VINNIE: I haven't seen Judith for years. You'd think living so close to Springfield—maybe I could run up there before the summer's over.

CORA: Oh, she'll be leaving for Pleasantville any day now Grandpa Ebbetts has been failing very fast and that's why I have to hurry back.

VINNIE: Hurry back? Well, you and Mary can stay with us a few days at least.

CORA: No, I hate to break the news to you, Vinnie, but we can't even stay overnight. We're leaving on the five o'clock train this afternoon.

VINNIE [*disappointed*]: Oh, what a pity!

[FATHER *lowers the paper.*]

FATHER [*heartily*]: Well, Cora, it certainly is good to see you again. [*To* MARY.] Young lady, I think you've been enjoying yourself—you look prettier than ever.

[MARY *laughs and blushes.*]

WHITNEY: I'll bet Clarence will think so.

[*The doorbell rings.* MAGGIE *crosses to answer it.*]

FATHER: That can't be another special delivery for Clarence. [*To* MARY, *slyly.*] While you were in Springfield our postman was kept pretty busy. Sure you girls don't want any breakfast?

MARY: No, thank you. [*Rises and goes to the arch and stands looking upstairs, watching for* CLARENCE.]

CORA: Oh, no, thank you, Cousin Clare, we've had our breakfast.

FATHER: At least you ought to have a cup of coffee with us. Vinnie, you might have thought to order some coffee for the girls.

CORA: No, no, thank you, Cousin Clare.

[MAGGIE *appears again in the arch.*]

MAGGIE: It's the cab, ma'am. [*Exits.*]

FATHER: The cab! What cab?

VINNIE: The cab that's to take us to Audubon.

FATHER: Who's going to Audubon?

VINNIE: We all are. Cora, the most wonderful thing has happened!

CORA: What, Cousin Vinnie?

VINNIE [*happily*]: Clare's going to be baptized this morning.

FATHER [*not believing his ears*]: Vinnie—what are you saying?

VINNIE [*with determination*]: I'm saying you're going to be baptized this morning!

FATHER: I am not going to be baptized this morning or any other morning!

VINNIE: You promised yesterday that as soon as I sent that pug dog back you'd be baptized.

FATHER: I promised no such thing!

VINNIE: You certainly did!

FATHER: I never said anything remotely like that!

VINNIE: Clarence was right here and heard it. You ask him!

FATHER: Clarence be damned! I know what I said! I don't remember exactly, but it wasn't that!

VINNIE: Well, I remember. That's why I ordered the cab!

FATHER [*suddenly remembering*]: The cab! Oh, my God, that cab! [*He rises and glares out the window at the cab, then turns back and speaks peremptorily.*] Vinnie! You send that right back!

VINNIE: I'll do nothing of the kind. I'm going to see that you get to Heaven.

FATHER: I can't go to Heaven in a cab!

VINNIE: Well, you can start in a cab! I'm not sure whether they'll ever let you into Heaven or not, but I know they won't unless you're baptized.

FATHER: They can't keep me out of Heaven on a technicality.

VINNIE: Clare, stop quibbling! You might as well face it—you've got to make your peace with God.

FATHER: I never had any trouble with God until you stirred Him up!

[MARY *is tired of waiting for* CLARENCE *and chooses this moment to interrupt.*]

MARY: Mrs. Day?

[VINNIE *answers her quickly, as if expecting* MARY *to supply her with an added argument.*]

VINNIE: Yes, Mary?

MARY: Where do you suppose Clarence is?

FATHER: You keep out of this, young lady! If it hadn't been for you, no one would have known whether I was baptized or not. [MARY *breaks into tears.*] Damn! Damnation!

VINNIE: Harlan! Whitney! Get your Sunday hats. [*Calls upstairs.*] John! Clarence!

[HARLAN *and* WHITNEY *start out, but stop as* FATHER *speaks.*]

FATHER [*blazing with new fire*]: Vinnie, are you mad? Was it your plan that my own children should witness this indignity?

VINNIE: Why, Clare, they'll be proud of you!

FATHER: I suppose Harlan is to be my godfather! [*With determination.*] Vinnie, it's no use. I can't go through with this thing and I won't. That's final.

VINNIE: Why, Clare dear, if you feel that way about it—

FATHER: I do!

VINNIE: —the children don't have to go.

[JOHN *enters.*]

JOHN: Yes, Mother?

[FATHER *sees* JOHN *and an avenue of escape opens up.*]

FATHER: Oh, John! Vinnie, I can't do anything like that this morning. I've got to take John down to the office and give him the money to buy back that medicine. [*To* JOHN] When I think of you going around this town selling dog medicine!—

JOHN [*insistently*]: It wasn't dog medicine, Father.

FATHER: John, we're starting downtown this minute!

VINNIE: You're doing no such thing! You gave me your Sacred Promise that day I almost died—

JOHN: Yes, and she would have died if we hadn't given her some of that medicine. That proves it's good medicine!

FATHER [*aghast*]: You gave your mother some of that dog medicine!

VINNIE: Oh, no, John, you didn't! [*Sinks weakly into the chair below the fireplace.*]

JOHN: Yes, we did, Mother. We put some in your tea that morning.

FATHER: You did what? Without her knowing it? Do you realize you might have killed your mother? You did kill Mrs. Sprague's dog. [*After a solemn pause.*] John, you've done a serious thing. I'll have to give considerable thought as to how you're going to be punished for this.

VINNIE: But, Clare—

FATHER: No, Vinnie. When I think of that day—with the house full of doctors—why, Cora, we even sent for the minister. Why, we might have lost you! [*He goes to* VINNIE, *really moved, and puts his hand on her shoulder.*] It's all right now, Vinnie, thank God. You're well again. But what I went through that afternoon—the way I felt—I'll never forget it.

VINNIE: Don't talk that way, Clare. You've forgotten it already.

FATHER: What do you mean?

VINNIE: That was the day you gave me your Sacred Promise.

FATHER: But I wouldn't have promised if I hadn't thought you were dying—and you wouldn't have almost died if John hadn't given you that medicine. Don't you see? The whole thing's illegal!

VINNIE: Suppose I had died! It wouldn't make any difference to you. You don't care whether we meet in Heaven or not—you don't care whether you ever see me and the children again.

[*She almost succeeds in crying.* HARLAN *and* WHITNEY *go to her in sympathy, putting their arms around her.*]

FATHER [*distressed*]: Now, Vinnie, you're not being fair to me.

VINNIE: It's all right, Clare. If you don't love us enough there's nothing we can do about it.

[*Hurt,* FATHER *walks away to the other side of the room.*]

FATHER: That's got nothing to do with it! I love my family as much as any man. There's nothing within reason I wouldn't do for you, and you know it! All these years I've struggled and worked just to prove——[*He has reached the window and looks out.*] There's that damn cab! Vinnie, you're not well enough to go all the way up to Audubon.

VINNIE [*perkily*]: I'm well enough if we ride.

FATHER: But that trip would take all morning. And those cabs cost a dollar an hour.

VINNIE [*with smug complacence*]: That's one of their best cabs. That costs two dollars an hour.

[FATHER *stares at her a second, horrified—then explodes.*]

FATHER: Then why aren't you ready? Get your hat on! Damn! Damnation! Amen! [*Exits for his hat and stick.* VINNIE *is stunned for a moment by this sudden surrender, then hastily puts on her bonnet.*]

WHITNEY: Let's watch them start! Come on, Cousin Cora, let's watch them start!

CORA: I wouldn't miss it!

[WHITNEY, HARLAN, *and* CORA *hurry out.* VINNIE *starts, but* JOHN *stops her in the arch.*]

JOHN [*contritely*]: Mother, I didn't mean to almost kill you.

VINNIE: Now, don't you worry about what your father said. [*Tenderly.*] It's all right, dear. [*She kisses him.*] It worked out fine! [*She exits.* JOHN *looks upstairs, then at* MARY, *who has gone to the window.*]

JOHN: Mary! Here comes Clarence! [JOHN *exits.* MARY *sits in* FATHER'S *chair.* CLARENCE *comes down the stairs in his new suit. He goes into the room and right to* MARY. *Without saying a word he kneels in front of her. They both are starry-eyed.*]

[FATHER, *with hat and stick, comes into the arch on his way out. He sees* CLARENCE *kneeling at* MARY'S *feet.*]

FATHER: Oh, God!

[CLARENCE *springs up in embarrassment.* VINNIE *re-enters hurriedly.*]

VINNIE: What's the matter? What's wrong?

CLARENCE: Nothing's wrong, Mother—[*Then, for want of something to say.*] Going to the office, Father?

FATHER: No! I'm going to be baptized, damn it!

[*He slams his hat on angrily and stalks out.* VINNIE *gives a triumphant nod and follows him. The curtain starts down, and as it falls,* CLARENCE *again kneels at* MARY'S *feet.*]

[*Curtain*]

HOWARD LINDSAY AND RUSSEL CROUSE

Howard Lindsay was born on March 29, 1899, in Waterford, New York. He went to Harvard University and afterward attended the American Academy of Dramatic Arts. He began acting in 1909, but his first big success came in *Dulcy* in 1920. He began playwriting in 1933 by adapting Edward Hope's story as a play, *She Loves Me Not.* In 1935, he launched himself (with Damon Runyon) as a producer, the two bringing out *A Slight Case of Murder.* He also produced musicals and plays with Russel Crouse.

Russel Crouse was born on February 20, 1893, in Findlay, Ohio, and was educated in Toledo. He became a newspaper writer, working in Cincinnati, Kansas City, and then in New York as a reporter and columnist. He was also press agent for the Theatre Guild for five years. In 1930 he published his book, *Mr. Currier and Mr. Ives,* and the same year began writing for the stage with *The Gang's All Here.* In 1933, he collaborated with Corey Ford in *Hold Your Horses.*

Messrs. Lindsay and Crouse began writing together in 1934 when they wrote the "book" for the musical, *Anything Goes.* Their association was something of an accident but has proved most successful. Their other musicals were *Red Hot and Blue* (1936) and *Hooray for What* (1937), and together they produced *Arsenic and Old Lace* (1941) and *The Hasty Heart* (1944).

Their first play was *Life with Father,* which they also produced and in which Lindsay acted in the title role. This was an immediate success, as it had been in its original form—Clarence Day's reminiscent story of his father. The play has had the longest run in American theatrical history, wearing out several casts, and has recently made a hit all over again as a motion picture.

Since *Life with Father,* Lindsay and Crouse have written *State of the Union,* which won the Pulitzer Prize in 1946. This is a telling drama of the American scene, showing the clash between political ambition and one man's conscience.

Their plays and the dates of their first productions:
Life with Father, November 8, 1939.
Strip for Action, September 30, 1942.
State of the Union, November 14, 1945.

CRITICAL COMMENTS

LIFE WITH FATHER

"Life With Father," (Empire Theater) is a delightful affair and well calculated to please equally those who do and those who do not know the various reminiscences by Clarence Day upon which it is founded. Russel Crouse and Howard Lindsay, who put it together, have done something considerably more difficult than merely to select and give continuity—they have almost miraculously preserved a flavor which might have been expected to defy translation into another form.

Father was a fine flower of Victorian manhood, and in those days virility didn't mean what D. H. Lawrence means by the word. Manliness was something whose outward expressions were big cigars and high blood pressure, a hearty contempt for women's notions and the sure conviction (wrong, of course, since some things are eternal) that *pater familias* was master in his own house. It was also likely to mean, as it certainly did in the case of the elder Day, an egocentric view of the universe so naive that the Master was never able to understand why everyone else should not be as anxious for him to have his own way as he was himself.

Considered merely as a case history, Father was an obtuse bully; but Father was loved by his wife and remembered with enormous affection by the son who celebrated both his rages and all those final decisions which mother so quietly revised. The triumph of the play, like the triumph of the sketches upon which it is based, lies in the fact that it makes the paradox understandable, not by explaining it in any rational terms, but by communicating something which portraiture can communicate and case histories cannot. Merely to say that Father meant well would be to add insult to injury; but Father did mean well, and we forgive him as a living person what we could not possibly forgive him as an abstraction. Something is perhaps explained by the fact that in that household which lived in perpetual crisis there were rages and the joy of battle but no rancor and no cruelty, something more perhaps by the fact that Father protected the family against God as well as against anyone else who threatened it, and would no more permit the minister to pray for mother as "a miserable sinner" when God knew as well as everybody else that she was a good woman than he would consent to the assumption that "a mere technicality" like his own failure to get himself baptized would keep him out of heaven. But no catalogue of details will really explain the mystery. The family formed a *Gestalt* which meant something other than the sum of its parts, and it is the *Gestalt* which the play captures.

[Joseph Wood Krutch, "When Men Were Men," in *The Nation*, 149 (Nov. 18, 1939), p. 560. Reprinted by permission.]

LIFE WITH FATHER

In a scholarly book on "Masters of Dramatic Comedy," by Henry Ten Eyck Perry. I have just stumbled on this profound definition quoted from some other source: "The greatest comedy is rooted, not in the social order, but in the supreme human paradox that man, who lays claim to an immortal spirit, is nevertheless confined in a body and must rely upon the exercise of five imperfect senses for his perception of order, truth and beauty in his earthly pilgrimage." We do not have to promote "Life With Father" into the category of illustrious comedy in order to see that a similar inequality of balance extends to the plot of this play. Although Father is indisputably the master of his home, he is defeated on nearly every issue. Things will not fall into place according to plan. The new maid does not serve perfectly the first time she pokes her nose into the house. Clarence cannot wait until Autumn for a new suit. The doctors cannot bring mother back to health on their first visit. Visiting relatives cannot be kept out of the house. Taxes cannot be kept from rising.

There is no malice or cunning involved in Father's successive defeats. His wife and boys respect him and return his warm, though laconic, affection, and would doubtless resent any suggestion that he does not boss the home. But the ways of the world will not conform to the logical plan that Father carries around in his head, and this natural paradox redeems "Life With Father" from routine laugh-making and gives it distinction as a piece of genuine comedy writing. Things that are simple are sometimes more discerning than they have any intention of being.

[Brooks Atkinson, "Speak Up, Father," in the *New York Times* (Nov. 19, 1939), X, 1:1. Reprinted by permission.]